William Randolph Hearst
The Early Years, 1863–1910

Orrin Peck, *William Randolph Hearst*, 1894

William Randolph Hearst

The Early Years, 1863–1910

Ben Procter

New York   Oxford
OXFORD UNIVERSITY PRESS
1998

Oxford University Press

Oxford   New York
Athens   Auckland   Bangkok   Bogotá   Bombay
Buenos Aires   Calcutta   Cape Town   Dar es Salaam
Delhi   Florence   Hong Kong   Istanbul   Karachi
Kuala Lumpur   Madras   Madrid   Melbourne
Mexico City   Nairobi   Paris   Singapore
Taipei   Tokyo   Toronto   Warsaw

associated companies in
Berlin   Ibadan

Copyright © 1998 by Ben Procter

Published by Oxford University Press
198 Madison Avenue, New York, New York 10016

Oxford is a registered trademark of Oxford University Press

Library of Congress Cataloging-in-Publication Data
Procter, Ben
William Randolph Hearst, the early years,
1863–1910 / Ben Procter
p.   cm. Includes Index
ISBN 1-19-511277-6
1. Hearst, William Randolph, 1863–1951.
2. Publishers and publishing—United States—Biography.
3. Newspaper publishing—United States—History—19th century.
4. Newspaper publishing—United States—History—20th century.
I. Title
Z473.H4P76 1998   070.5'092
[b]—DC21   97-24574

1 3 5 7 9 8 6 4 2
Printed in the United States of America
on acid-free paper

To my wife, Phoebe,
and my son, Ben

Contents

Preface

In the fall of 1966 I noticed in the American Historical Association Bulletin that the Bancroft Library (at Cal-Berkeley) had received several hundred letters and other manuscript materials concerning William Randolph Hearst—and that more were expected from the family. Although W. A. Swanberg had written *Citizen Hearst* in 1961, I decided that this new information might warrant an updated biography. Within the next few months I had an opportunity to discuss this possibility with Professor Robert E. Burke of the University of Washington, who in 1950 had been the Purchasing Director for the Bancroft in England. He doused my excitement for this project by stating that papers from the Hearst warehouse in New York City had been trickling in yearly to the Bancroft, but not in sufficient quantity—or quality—for me to anticipate a biography. Thus the matter rested for the time being.

But as Burke knows, I am like an "ole dog" with a bone. I chew around on it—sometimes hungrily, other times by habit—until I decide to let go of it or continue to gnaw. In the case of Hearst the gnawing prevailed. Every six months or so I noticed more Hearst acquisitions by the Bancroft; and each time Burke received a call. His answer was still the same—not enough quantity or quality in the manuscript collection. In the summer of 1976, however, I decided to check for myself and, after spending a week at the Bancroft, I excitedly called Burke, stating that considerable amounts of information in the Hearst papers of the past fifteen years conflicted with Swanberg's book and that a new assessment of Hearst now might be in order. Burke still urged me to postpone the project, but for the first time he was not negative. As a consequence, during a sabbatical in 1981, I committed myself to this enterprise.

And now after sixteen years of "living" with Hearst, I feel, at times, that I should have been committed to an institution with padded walls surrounded by verdant fields, where I could sniff the daisies. I should have known better. My Ph.D. dissertation was a biography of John H. Reagan of Texas, who lived from 1818 to 1906—eighty-eight years. I pledged during that ordeal that I would never again write a biography, except on someone like William Barrett Travis who was only twenty-seven at the time of his death at the Alamo. Now I have embarked on Hearst who lived from 1863 to 1951—the eighty-eight-year syndrome again. Since this work takes him only to 1910, a second volume will soon be in progress. Obviously I must have masochistic tendencies or a death wish—or both.

Despite such protestations, I still find that William Randolph Hearst excites me. And why? He affected the lives of the American people and the policies of presidential administrations. His journalistic efforts created a climate that erupted into the Spanish-American War. And while American historians still debate whether he was responsible for the crusade for "Cuba Libre," Hearst had no doubts. Day after day in 1898 he proclaimed across the masthead of his New York newspapers "The Journal's War." His crusades for Progressive causes from 1896–1910, a fifteen-year period of his life that other biographers have, to a certain extent, overlooked, also influenced the course of American domestic and foreign policies, as well as the day-to-day politics of New York state.

Hearst built a journalistic empire by 1910 that encompassed eight newspapers (and two magazines) in five of the largest cities in the United States with an estimated readership of almost three million people. Equally important, he was an active player in the game of politics; other participants could not afford to ignore or overlook him. Hearst also affected the course of American newspapers, whether for good or evil. Some of what he printed through the Hearst formula of distributing information was purposely slanted or completely fictionalized and sometimes "right on the money." In all, his papers were wonderfully exciting and good reading, challenging and innovative and entertaining. Yet, if for no other reason for this study, I have found Hearst to be an intriguing, fascinating personality with sizable frailties, but also with tremendous talent and ability, sometimes bordering on genius. Few individuals in American history—with the exception of certain Presidents—have affected or helped shape the course of this nation's history over a fifty-year period, either favorably or wrongly, more than William Randolph Hearst.

Often in this study I became a detective, attempting to separate myth from history while seeking to discover the "real" Hearst who, in fact, was not averse to distorting actual occurrences or fictionalizing certain events of his life. I therefore decided that the only way to "get inside the mind and character of Hearst" was to investigate his journalistic creations thoroughly. Hence, I took voluminous notes on the San Francisco Examiner, reading every issue from 1881 to 1895, and April to September, 1906. The same was true of the New York Morning Journal (which eventually became the New York American) from September, 1895, through 1909, balancing the Hearst newspapers with such competitors as the *New York World* (1896–1900), *New York Times* (1898–1909), and *New York Tribune* (1898, 1900, 1904–1909). As a consequence, I spent a tremendous amount of time reading microfilm. I also practiced on-the-scene, investigative research techniques used by such scholars as Francis Parkman and Herbert Eugene Bolton.

Two examples, out of literally hundreds, demonstrate my concern for historical accuracy. At the beginning of my research I discovered that Hearst invented part of his family lineage and history, that George and Phoebe Apperson Hearst, the parents of WRH, were not married in Stedville, Missouri. After visiting the area, I realized that no such place existed, but I did find their marriage certificate that named Steelville, Missouri. Again in the summer of 1989 I visited the site of La Hacienda del Pozo de Verona, which had been the impressive Hearst estate, where Phoebe often resided until her death in 1919. Swanberg, in *Citizen Hearst*, stated that it was at Pleasanton, just across the bay from San Francisco; actually, it is thirty miles south of San Francisco on the eastern slope of the Coastal Range Mountains.

As an historian, I have also had the advantage of colleagues whose expertise has greatly enhanced this biography through their studies and works on such related subjects having to do with ancestry, Western mining, the Spanish-American War, New York City politics, and national personalities as Bryan, Hughes, Taft, and Theodore Roosevelt. As one of many examples, George Hearst, in his memoirs, stated that the Hearsts were Lowland "Scotch" Presbyterians. In questioning this statement, I called upon Grady McWhiney, a history colleague at Texas Christian University who had studied "name analysis" extensively; one-and-a-half hours later he produced seven scholarly works, which revealed that the Hearsts were originally of English or Anglo-Irish descent, most likely from Lancashire or Yorkshire in northwestern England, but possibly from Ulster or Connaught in Ireland. The present-day Hearsts had accepted George Hearst's statement at face value as had previous biographers. Such research by other scholars over the past thirty-five years has also helped enlighten this biographer's understanding of events in which Hearst was interested or became involved. Librarians and archivists, whose specific knowledge of their manuscript and resource materials is at times awesome, have also been instumental in uncovering information for me. As a result, much of the data in this work is different from other Hearst biographies.

Acknowledgments

I owe a tremendous debt of gratitude to any number of people who helped this biography become a reality. Let me be specific. The starting point has to be the personnel at the Bancroft Library, especially the late director James D. Hart, Curator of Western Americana Bonnie Hardwick, Estelle Rebec, Richard Ogar, Franz Enciso, David Farrell, and Anthony Bliss. The staff members of the Harry Ransom Humanities Research Center at the University of Texas at Austin were also extremely helpful, with Head Librarian Richard Oram and Ken Cravens deserving particular mention. And Dr. Martin Ridge of the Huntington Library, Judith Ann Schiff and Nicole Bouche (formerly at the Bancroft) of the Yale University Archives, Henry Rowen of the Rare Books Collection at Columbia, Archivist David Levesque of the Ohstram Library at St. Paul's, Archivist Metta Hake at the San Simeon Library, Ralph Gregory and Mrs. Mabel Reed of the Phoebe Apperson Hearst Historical Society of St. Clair, Missouri, and Dr. David Wigdor at the Manuscript Collection of the Library of Congress as well as the staffs at Harvard University Archives, Newberry Library, New York City Library, California State Library at Sacramento, Library of Congress manuscript and newspaper collections, and the TCU Library deserve special recognition and my thanks.

A number of individuals at Texas Christian University encouraged and abetted me, making life easier and bearable: Interlibrary Loan specialist Joyce Martindale, who suffered with me in hunting out books and newspapers and magazines from distant archives and libraries, and Sandy Peoples in Circulation, who kept me up-to-date on the numerous books checked out in my possession; Dr. Larry Adams, an associate vice chancellor for Academic Affairs, who aided my research by urging me to seek grants from the TCU Research Fund; Dr. Spencer Tucker, friend and colleague, who helped me acquire several necessary sabbaticals; Vice Chancellor of Academic Affairs Bill Koehler who approved of my research and encouraged me to complete "the task"; and Dean of Arts and Sciences Michael McCracken, who claimed to be my "inspiration" or "conscience" by continually greeting me with the question, "Is the Hearst manuscript completed yet?"

Special thanks go to certain members of the Hearst family: two sons of Hearst, the late William Randolph Hearst, Jr. and Randolph Apperson Hearst, and grandson John Randolph "Bunky" Hearst, who granted me interviews; grandson William Randolph Hearst III, who helped and encouraged; and Mr. and Mrs. Jack Cooke, who granted me access to Wyntoon and directed me to the site of La Hacienda del Pozo de Verona.

I have been especially pleased to work with Sheldon Meyer, valued friend and long-time editor at Oxford University Press who continually encouraged me to complete this work, then provided constructive comments and trenchant insights. I have also enjoyed a happy association with Helen Mules, production editor at Oxford, who helped improve the Hearst manuscript while guiding me past the perils of deadlines.

I am also grateful and beholden to a number of individuals who encouraged and abetted me in this project. Melinda and Estil Vance of Fort Worth, Rick Roberts of Corpus Christi, and Mrs. Peggy Hoyt and son Dirk of Houston afforded sanctuaries away from Fort Worth. Drs. Roger Tuller, Mark Barringer, and Mark Beasley, three former grad students, read chapters of this work and made pertinent comments. Frank Carroll of the Newspaper Division of the Library of Congress was of tremendous assistance in providing me with necessary microfilm reels; without his professional guidance, I would still be researching and writing. Dr. Bob Burke, professor emeritus at the University of Washington, who first introduced me to the magnitude of the Hearst collections, was a constant catalyst and valued friend. Two professors at Harvard University, the late Frederick Merk, who directed me toward biography and Western History, and Oscar Handlin, professor emeritus, who first introduced me to historical writing, such as the application of topic sentence, active voice, transition, and word choice, I am forever indebted. And to long-time colleagues and dear friends, such as Dr. Walter Ehrlich of the University of Missouri at St. Louis who helped me in acquiring necessary historical data in the Meramec Valley, and Dr. John Pratt, emeritus at SUNY-Stonybrook and Dr. David Trask, one of the foremost authorities on the Spanish-American War, I am eternally grateful for their close scrutiny of my manuscript and their scholarly advice. And to Dr. Richard Lowitt of the University of Oklahoma, who "comforted me when I was afflicted and afflicted me when I was comfortable," I will always be grateful and appreciative.

But, most of all, I am indebted to wife, Phoebe, and son, Ben, who at first offered pertinent comments about my Hearst manuscript and then became valuable research assistants. To them, I dedicate this book.

William Randolph Hearst
The Early Years, 1863–1910

1 | The Romantic Legend of the Hearsts

O n April 13, 1919, Phoebe Apperson Hearst died quietly at La Hacienda del Pozo de Verona, her luxurious estate on the east side of the mountains at Pleasanton, thirty miles south of San Francisco. Although well known for her philanthropies to education—kindergarten programs, libraries, girls' training schools, and the University of California at Berkeley—she also contributed generously to orphanages, havens for unwed mothers, and hospitals, mainly in California but in other areas of the United States as well. In addition, she was the wife of the late George Hearst, an extremely wealthy miner and businessman who had been a U.S. senator from California. But more than anything else, she was the mother of newspaper mogul William Randolph Hearst.[1]

After appropriate encomiums and profuse eulogies, Phoebe Hearst was laid to rest, and to a certain extent so were her wishes. To her only son she bequeathed most of her fortune, in excess of $25 million, and to relatives and close friends amounts ranging anywhere from $1,000 to $50,000. But her niece and confidante, Ann Flint, would not, as Phoebe had wished, receive Wyntoon Castle, her summer home on the McCloud River in northern California (Siskiyou County). Nor would Adele Brooks, her designated official biographer, write her obituary or publish a prepared manuscript. Hearst would dismiss the author, instructing her to "turn over to him" all notes and manuscript materials concerning his mother. Then nine years later he commissioned Winifred Black Bonfils, the original "sob sister," whose pen name was "Annie Laurie," to write his mother's biography. After twelve days and fifty-four thousand words, she completed her assignment, and Hearst published *The Life and Personality of Phoebe Apperson Hearst*.[2]

❧ ❧ ❧

The romanticized legend of the Hearsts thus began. In 1928, with journalist John K. Winkler's *W. R. Hearst: An American Phenomenon*, and in 1936, with Mrs. Fremont Older's equally favorable *William Randolph Hearst: American*, the legend became deeply ingrained and solidified as fact. As a result, Hearst was able to fashion and re-create his own ancestry, especially in regard to his mother and father. It went something like this. In 1850 thirty-year-old George Hearst, a poor, struggling, but ambitious farmer in Franklin County, Missouri, journeyed to the California goldfields and, after incredible hardships—contracting cholera, sleeping at times in mud with rain pelting down upon him, and having only "a five-franc piece" between him and bankruptcy—"he wanted to die." But he recovered from all such adversities and, upon enduring ten years of rugged prospecting in the Sierra Nevadas, "struck it rich" as a one-sixth owner of the Ophir mine, which was part of the fabulous Comstock Lode. In 1860 he returned to Franklin County to comfort his dying mother as well as settle family business affairs. During the next two years he met Phebe Elizabeth Apperson,* a pretty, vivacious schoolteacher "whom he had carried on his shoulder" when she was just "a child." Although bearded and rough-hewn, somewhat unlettered, and more than twice her age, he dazzled her with stories of California, of adventure and romance in the Far West; he was "different from all other men she knew." And even though unaware of his wealth and despite initial protestations at first from her parents, who were "the richest . . . in the county" and descended from a "long line" of Virginia and South Carolina landowners, the "inexperienced" Phebe announced her marriage plans. After elaborate wedding preparations—"people didn't step around the corner to the nearest Justice of the Peace & get married in those days, not people of the Apperson standing"—George and Phebe Hearst were joyously united at Stedville, Missouri (which was, and is, a nonexistent town in the state), then departed for California, where the next year their only son, William Randolph Hearst, was born.[3]

❧   ❧   ❧

So much for legends! More than sixty-five years and seven biographers later, here, according to extant data, is the story of William Randolph Hearst.

Late in the spring of 1803 Americans were jubilant, optimistic, ever aggressive about their future. With one stroke of the pen, President Thomas

---

* In 1899, Mrs. Hearst decided to change the spelling of her name, Phebe, to the classical spelling—Phoebe.

Jefferson doubled the size of the United States by purchasing the Louisiana Territory from Napoleon. Now, a foreign power and the Mississippi River were no longer barriers to settlement; now, virgin lands beckoned pioneer farmers westward. Quickly into the newly created Territory of Orleans the migration began, so much so that by 1812 Congress granted statehood to Louisiana. Farther to the north, and not quite as accessible, the land called Missouri, where Americans Daniel Boone and Moses Austin had earlier decided to take up residence, proved to be almost as inviting. Since the Northwest Ordinance of 1787 prohibited the transportation of slaves north of the Ohio River, Southerners sought other lands with a climate and environment conducive to their farming and herding practices. So within six years, from 1804 to 1810, Missouri doubled in population—10,000 to 20,845 people—with Americans swarming over the countryside, building their double-log cabins, clearing the land for planting, cultivating crops for harvest.[4]

Into the grassy valleys and forested hills of the Meramec River, approximately fifty miles to the south and west of St. Louis, William G. Hearst, together with his parents and brother Joseph, migrated in 1808, following the American frontier patterns practiced by his ancestors for more than a century. Of English or Anglo-Irish descent, most likely from Lancashire or Yorkshire in northwestern England, but possibly from Ulster or Connaught in Ireland, the Hearsts or Hursts later confused the issue even more by saying that they were Lowland "Scotch" Presbyterians.[5] They first settled in Isle of Wight County, Virginia, late in the seventeenth century, where a John Hearst (whose surname means "wood" or "thicket") died in 1727. One of his sons, also named John, moved to Abbeville, South Carolina, in 1766, where he and his kin, including another George Hearst, raised large crops of corn and children while investing in slaves and livestock and land. Then in 1808 William G., who was the fifth son of George, pushed forward into Missouri.[6]

Settling on the Meramec in Franklin County across from the mouth of Indian Creek, the Hearsts survived on the Missouri frontier but did not prosper. Together with other Americans, they scattered in rather isolated farms, eking out a living from corn and wheat while trying at times to supplement their meager income by lead mining. But with Shawnee Indians ever threatening during those first years, with the climate hot and humid in the summer and penetratingly cold in the winter, they merely existed; and even after the marriage in 1817 of William G. Hearst to Elizabeth Collins, whose family was among the first pioneers in the area, conditions did not improve significantly. In fact, the Hearsts and Collinses left for

Spanish Texas soon thereafter in hope of securing their elusive fortunes.[7]

After two years of deprivation and sickness on the Texas frontier, this small group of Americans decided that, in comparison, conditions in Missouri were far better than in Texas. So they retraced their steps and, through determination and work, steadily enhanced their lives. William Hearst immediately purchased his old homestead from the U.S. government, then enlarged his holdings through inheritance (his father, George, died in 1822) and by buying out his brother's half share. To cultivate these lands as well as others acquired, estimated by written deposition at 703 to 843 acres, he bought nineteen slaves and hired a number of whites, easily outdistancing all others as the largest and wealthiest landowner in Franklin County. Hearst also engaged in copper and lead mining. As a result of his standing in the community he assumed a number of civic responsibilities. In 1828 he was appointed as one of three school-land commissioners for "Merrimac" Township as well as an overseer of the first road district; then in 1832 he served on a commission that selected the seat of government for neighboring Jefferson County.[8]

In all this time William and Elizabeth Hearst reared three children—George, Martha, and Jacob—but the only one of historical significance was their elder son. Born on September 3, 1820, George Hearst had what he later termed "a wild sort of childhood." He had "to work very hard," he recalled, at first doing chores required of a young boy—chopping wood, gathering eggs, watching after the family geese, chickens, and livestock; then, in his teens, struggling with the unyielding earth, plowing and planting and harvesting. Consequently young George had little time for school, and throughout his life he demonstrated his lack of formal training, his deficiencies in education, almost to the point of illiteracy. As late as 1882, after being nominated for governor at the California Democratic Convention at San Jose, and in answering criticisms about educational inadequacies, he retorted: "My opponents say that I haven't the book learning that they possess. They say I can't spell. They say I spell bird, b-u-r-d. If b-u-r-d doesn't spell bird, what in hell does it spell?"

Yet Hearst had certain intuitive traits that benefited him tremendously throughout his life. For instance, in arithmetic class he "never did a sum in the way the rule stated. I would always figure it out in my own way." And, when engaged in mining, he was a natural. He had an instinctive knowledge about geological formations, a mineralogist whose methods were "altogether practical." Reportedly he so impressed the neighboring Indians that they called him "Boy-That-Earth-Talked-To." Even more remarkable, he would visit mining sites or out-of-the-way locations and, years later, "see them," he candidly asserted, "just as vividly today in my mind as then." [9]

In November, 1844, upon the death of his father, George Hearst was forced to assume much greater responsibilities; he was especially unhappy and insecure concerning such duties because, at age twenty-four, he believed that people "over thirty years old" knew much more than "anybody else." Although in 1848 his mother would marry Judge Joseph Funk, the postmaster at Traveler's Repose (now St. Clair), thereby freeing him from some obligations, Hearst still had to manage the family estate of more than eight hundred acres. He thus paid all past debts (except for $300 to $500); cared for his sister, Martha, and crippled brother, Jacob (who died in 1846); and tended to numerous daily tasks. He also operated mineral lands, which were generally known as the "Hearst Copper Mines," and with James N. Inge invested in a general store at nearby Virginia Mines. But seemingly he had to farm continually. To him such work was drudgery without much compensation. It left him little time to pursue his natural bent for prospecting and mining in the surrounding areas. [10]

As a result, when gold was discovered near Sutter's millrace in California in 1848 and hence the subsequent mad rush of the Forty-Niners, George Hearst was also caught up in this national hysteria. For almost a year he withstood all irresponsible impulses, but with the urging and approval of his family and after Dr. William N. Patton, his personal physician and close friend, agreed "to handle his affairs," Hearst left for the "promised land" on May 12, 1850.

What a horrible ordeal the journey was! For five months he endured appalling hardships, quite similar to those others had experienced in traveling overland to California. At Fort Laramie in eastern Wyoming he contracted cholera, or so he believed, but dispelled the "first symptoms," he stated, by drinking brandy and taking "some pills which a man in St. Louis gave me." Joining a small wagon train of pioneers, he trudged laboriously over the Oregon Trail, from the rolling prairies alongside the North Platte River and in the Wyoming Basin through the rugged uplands of South Pass and thence over the California Trail to the barren, alkali wastes of Utah and Nevada. In the Humbolt region of dreadful sands and shadows, of cactus and tumbleweed and desert sage, he succumbed to a strength-sapping fever, but recovered in time to scale the steep slopes of the forested Sierra Nevadas and find his way to Hangtown (Placerville) on the western side of the mountains. And not too soon! He was in a weakened condition and had "just a five-franc piece left." [11]

Hearst soon discovered, however, that California was not a land of gold just for the taking, at least not for a majority of migrants. At Grass Valley in the foothills of the Sierras, he practiced survival for nine years, hopeful of finding a huge bonanza. At nearby Nevada City he opened a general store with Hamlet Davis, who later became the town's first mayor. At every opportunity Hearst would placer mine, his tools for success being a pick and shovel, a wash pan, and endless optimism. Because of severe weather and lack of supplies in the fall and winter of 1853–54, he came out of the mountains and proceeded southwestward to Sacramento City, where he became involved in wholesale merchandizing and real estate. But the tantalizing lure of mining always drew him back to the Sierras. In the meantime, after having to sell one claim because of undercapitalization, he agreed to run a quartz mill in the Grass Valley–Nevada City area to accumulate funds so necessary for large mining ventures. And even after learning in February, 1858, that his sister, Martha, had died (in 1854) and that his mother was gravely ill, he refused to leave because, as he wrote his stepfather, Judge Funk, "to return home without money is out of the question." [12]

But in 1859 Hearst seemed to make all the right moves and, even better, his luck improved. He obtained a share in a local mine called the Lecompton and was confident of acquiring considerable profits. Then, in July, Grass Valley assayer Melville Atwood excitedly revealed to him "in strictest confidence" a startling secret. Prospectors from across the mountains in the Washoe (the Virginia City area of Nevada), where gold had been discovered at the Comstock earlier in the year, had brought him some "blue stuff" to be assayed. "The ore is almost pure silver," Atwood gushed, "with a heavy percentage of gold. It's too incredibly rich to be possible. It's worth $3,000 a ton." And, what was even more incredible, the Washoe miners did not realize the "blue stuff's" value; they were "throwing it away." [13]

Despite his dislike for what he considered to be a godforsaken region of crags and rocks, of torrid heat and desert vegetation, Hearst left immediately for the Washoe, with Atwood proclaiming: "You're bound to become rich." Within four days he arrived in Virginia City and thus began to build a fortune. He contracted to buy for $7,000 a one-sixth interest in the Ophir mine (which had a huge vein of the "blue stuff") before returning to Nevada City. Still undercapitalized, he obtained the necessary financing by selling his share of the Lecompton mine and by borrowing $1,000 from a local businessman. Then back across the mountains he went and, together with his partners, furiously mined thirty-eight tons of "selected ore," which they packed by mule to San Francisco before the winter snows set in. And the results! Hearst and his partners were $91,000 richer and a madness for the "ore of the Ophir" began.[14]

The Ophir was not without problems, however—flooding by underground water, cave-ins, and several Piute Indian massacres near Virginia City in the spring of 1860, which threatened to scare away precious manpower as well as deplete supplies. But within a year, after such difficulties had been resolved, Hearst was ready to return home to Franklin County. He felt good about his fortune, his estimated worth in the vicinity of $200,000 after having made another lucrative investment, which cost him only $450, in the Gould and Curry mining properties. Remembering vividly his previous hardships, he was not about to go the overland route to Missouri. Instead, he sailed from San Francisco on August 1, 1860, via the Isthmus of Panama to New York City, thence by train to St. Louis, arriving in St. Clair on September 1 after a ten-year absence.[15]

For the next two years George Hearst involved himself in family responsibilities and local activities. He immediately learned that his rather sizable estate had been mismanaged and that several former associates had judgments against his properties or, in some instances, had already taken them over. He therefore responded by instituting legal proceedings, which would continue until 1876. He was also deeply concerned about his mother, helplessly watching life ebb from her body until death on April 1, 1861. And being a former slaveholder and ardent Southerner, he became caught up in the 1860 presidential election and the subsequent disruption of American democracy, so much so that, while visiting St. Louis in the summer of 1861, he was arrested—and briefly jailed—for "opinions" Union authorities "deemed seditious."[16]

Soon after his mother's death, Hearst became interested in Phebe Elizabeth Apperson. As far as her parents, Drusilla Whitmire and Randolph Walker Apperson, were concerned, she was far too good for him. Born on December 3, 1842, Phebe Apperson had ancestry that, if not exceptional, was surely commendable. One grandfather, George Frederick Whitmire, had arrived at Philadelphia in 1858 from Stuttgart, Germany. He then proceeded to Newberry County, South Carolina, where the Whitmires were "comfortable" economically until a "general exodus" occurred between 1800 and 1810, first to Ohio and then in 1820 to Missouri. Her other grandfather, John Apperson, was a medical doctor in Washington County, Virginia, and had surrounded his family in "relative elegance" before moving to Franklin County in 1829. Even though the Whitmires and Appersons did not attain either the economic or political successes of the Hearsts, they prided themselves in being better educated—George's mother, Elizabeth, signed her name with an "X"—and considered themselves culturally superior.

And in 1861 eighteen-year-old Phebe was the epitome of their union. Lithe and petite at five feet and under a hundred pounds, with dark-brown, curly hair, blue-gray eyes, and creamy skin, she may have been poor—in 1847 her father hired out to George Hearst over a two-day period for two dollars—but she had youth and education and gentility going for her. From early childhood she had exhibited an insatiable desire for knowledge, a fervent passion for a "more complete understanding of the world," indeed an intense longing to experience the existence that her books described. By sheer force of will and fierce determination, she became precise in English grammar and somewhat fluent in French. In fact, at age sixteen, she had enough formal education, and nerve, to accept a three-month teaching assignment at the Reedville School, some forty miles away from St. Clair, where she was both successful and popular.[17]

While young Phebe was demure and soft-spoken, at times reticent and lacking confidence, although demonstrating good breeding both in dress and manner, George Hearst was, by contrast, quite a shock. A man large and rugged in appearance, twenty-two years her senior, his clothes often rumpled and shirtfront sometimes stained with tobacco juice, Hearst emphasized practicality over education, business and money over culture and refinement. He had no social graces or pretensions, and he wanted none—"hog and hominy," accompanied by a glass of bourbon, were good enough for him. After all, he was a prospector who had not only survived rowdy mining camps such as Hangtown and Grass Valley and Virginia City but also had, by his own cunning and ability, "struck it rich." He was a self-made man—and obviously proud of it—boisterously loud, at times vulgar and crude, but assured of his opinions and comfortable with his prejudices. Although not handsome, he exuded a virility that some considered appealing, his high forehead and deep-set eyes and prominent nose framed by dark hair and a shaggy beard.[18]

Yet George Hearst and Phebe Elizabeth Apperson shared certain character traits, and therein lay their bond of understanding, the glue for marital union. Both were willful and headstrong to the point of having "it my own way or not at all." Both were tough-minded; neither could be intimidated nor swayed by sentimentality. Both knew what they wanted out of life and, in their own way, strove to attain it. Desperately wishing to escape the provinciality of the Meramec Valley as well as the cultural and intellectual vacuum of her present existence, Phebe recognized the wealthy Hearst as a means of unshackling her hopes for a better life, as a passport to the exotic world of her dreams. In turn, George wanted Phebe for a wife, with all that she could bring to such a marriage.[19]

So the two struck a deal. On June 14, 1862, they journeyed to Steelville (not Stedville), Missouri, where in the judge's chambers of the Crawford County Courthouse they drew up the following prenuptial agreement:

> This marriage contract made & entered into this 14th day of June, 1862 between, George Hearst of the one part & Phebe E. Eperson [sic] of the other part both of the County of Franklin & State of Missouri "to wit." The parties to this instrument in consideration of the covenants & stipulation hereinafter mentiones promises & agrees to intermarry with each other within a reasonable and convenient time after the execution hereof. 2. The said George Hearst in consideration of said future marriage hereby for himself conveys assigns & sits over unto the said Phebe E. Eperson Fifty Shares of stock in the Goaldine & Curry Gold and Silver Mining Company of Virginia City Nevada Territory U.S. out of this interest which said Hearst had in said Mining Company to be held for & during the natural life of said Phebe E. Eperson and at her death revert to the said George Hearst his heirs or legal representatives.
>
> [Signed] George Hearst
[Signed] P. E. Apperson

Although the contract had numerous spelling errors, the two signed the agreement. Then the next day, June 15, 1862, without any fanfare or elaborate preparations, "W. P. Renick, Minister" married nineteen-year-old Phebe Apperson and forty-one-year-old George Hearst.[20]

During the next few months the newlyweds were difficult to trace. No question about it, however, George Hearst was going to leave Missouri and return to California. But how? Because of his "seditious" language the previous year in support of the Confederate States of America, travel clearance to New York City was questionable, that is, until Dr. Silas Reed, a former neighbor and close friend of the couple, who was attached to the military hospital at St. Louis, intervened in their behalf. They therefore departed late in September for New York City, where on October 11 they boarded the steamer *Ocean Queen*. Ten days later they reached Panama, quickly crossed the Isthmus by train, took passage on the steamer *Sonora* that evening, and were once again on their way. While the Pacific leg of this trip remained relatively calm and uneventful, Phebe—already pregnant—was frequently ill, but received both kindness and attention from Mrs. David M. Peck, who was also traveling to San Francisco with her husband and two-year-old son Orrin.[21]

Upon arrival on November 6, George and Phebe once again left no trail. Although most Hearst biographers categorically concur that the couple went immediately to the Lick House before transferring to the Stevenson House at "California and Montgomery streets," San Francisco newspapers did not record their existence at either place, as was customary. They may well have gone immediately to the residence-office of Dr. Vincent Gilcich and, as suggested by researcher Vonnie Eastham, stayed there for an indefinite time. But regardless of the mystery about Phebe's pregnancy, the birth of a son did occur. And for posterity the couple established the date as April 29, 1863, and named their offspring after his paternal and maternal grandfathers, William Randolph Hearst.[22]

2 | The Rebel from California

෯

In 1863 Phebe Hearst was a young bride and new mother who, over the past year, had experienced an extended honeymoon to San Francisco via New York City and Panama. Yet, once in California, life was far from idyllic for her, at least at first. Although previous biographers have written that George Hearst ensconced her at San Francisco in "a handsome brick dwelling on fashionable Rincon Hill" and then showered her with silks and laces and jewels, such was not the case. Early in June, 1863, fewer than six weeks after her son's birth, she accompanied her husband, George, to Nevada City, enduring a 160-mile stagecoach ride over dusty roads and rugged terrain. Upon arrival, conditions did not improve appreciably. The weather was insufferable, the temperature rising to more than one hundred degrees during June and July, the town fathers continually dousing the planked streets and sidewalks with water to prevent the possibility of fire. Even though housed at the National Exchange Hotel, which was easily the best accommodation in town, and having a personal maid to help with young Willie (as they called him), Phebe was alone much of the time, far from family and friends. And what did she do to occupy her time? The answer was dismally rhetorical. George was away for extended periods, overseeing his business interests across the mountains in Virginia City. So in this remote mining community on the side of a forested slope, she felt completely isolated, unable to cultivate, much less replenish, her cultural and intellectual needs.[1]

෯ ෯ ෯

Phebe Hearst would soon change these circumstances, however. By the end of July she took young Willie back to civilization, as represented by the Russ House in San Francisco, before purportedly moving into a "brick dwelling on fashionable Rincon Hill." [2] She was also determined to have her parents nearby, especially her father, with whom she was particularly close. As a consequence, in October, 1863, Randolph Apperson disposed of his holdings in Franklin County for $300, then proceeded with his wife along the St. Louis–New York City–Isthmus of Panama route that the Hearsts had journeyed the previous year. In December the Appersons arrived in San Francisco and, with Phebe's help, bought a pear-orchard ranch near the old mission town of Santa Clara, some forty miles away. And since George was thoroughly immersed in moneymaking—mining ventures as well as San Francisco real estate with William M. Lent—Phebe needed a reliable nurse to tend Willie while she was pursuing her dreams of self-fulfillment. That someone turned out to be Eliza Pike, an Irish governess who came to be known as Willie's "second mother." [3]

Yet Willie Hearst was by no means neglected. As an only child and grandson, he did not have to compete with anyone for the affections of doting parents and grandparents. A frequent visitor at the Apperson ranch, he was "happy as a lark," noticing not just the cows and horses, Phebe fondly wrote, but also "every bird & flower." Consequently he received all kinds of gifts, often in the form of pets, his favorite being a sad-eyed Newfoundland dog named Prince. [4]

In her own way the ever-watchful, sometimes hovering, Eliza Pike added to this ambiance of overindulgence. One day she met Phebe "at the door," obviously "greatly excited," biographer Mrs. Fremont Older recounted. "Madam, I love the baby like my own flesh and blood, and couldn't sleep at nights for thinkin' he might die—There is always maysles and dipthayria, and scarlet fayver," Eliza announced in her delightful Irish brogue.

"Eliza! Eliza, what's the matter?" Phebe fearfully exclaimed. "Did you let the baby fall?"

"The baby is all right, madam, but he might have died. So I took him down to my own church to-day. Blissed, dear, good Fayther baptized him."

"But Eliza," Phoebe protested, "I am a Presbyterian."

"No matter, madam, the baby is a Christian!" [5]

Willie responded accordingly to this euphoric environment, enrapturing those about him with his precociousness and affectionate nature. Listen to an adoring mother record her son's progress to Eliza Pike. On July 2, 1865: "Willie keeps well & fat though he grows tall . . . is brown as a berry & so active and mischievous . . . he is a very good boy. You have no idea how much he talks . . . he seems to understand everything . . . likes his books so much, can tell all about Cocky Locky & Henny Penny. Knows more of Mother Goose than ever . . . knows several words in french . . . he is so cunning." A year later, on September 18, 1866: "Willie is sound asleep. I wish you could see him. He is a great comfort to me. He talks to me sometimes when we are alone like an old man. He understands so much . . . loves me as big as the house and sky." On November 18: "I scarcely ever leave Willie with anyone now. He can't bear to stay when I go down town . . . His being with me so constantly has made him perfectly devoted to me. He is a real little calf about me. He never wants anyone else to do anything for him, and I think I love him better than ever before. Some days I do very little but amuse him. He knows several of his letters and will soon learn them all. He is very wise & sweet." On December 9: "He has improved very much. . . . He was very put out when his Papa came home because he could not sleep with me. I talked to him & told him when his Papa went away, he could sleep with me." On February 20, 1867: "Willie waked me up in the night to tell me he loved me, bless his little heart." On March 29: "Last week I had some pictures of him taken . . . He looks like a little, old judge. I do wish you could hear him talk. You would laugh yourself almost sick. He takes particular pains to correct his papa, & if he thinks I am teased about anything he will say, 'now you shan't talk so to my Mama.' He is a great comfort to me." Again on June 27: "He is a splendid little boy . . . I don't know how I could do without him. He knows all his letters perfectly. Will soon learn to spell. He likes his book. I have not made him feel it was tiresome or a task to learn, but make it interesting & funny." And again on September 15: "You would be astonished to hear him spell & pronounce words of three letters. Can count [to] one hundred, & knows what country, state & city he lives in, also who discovered America, & about the world being round." [6]

Nor was George Hearst much different in attitude, only in style and approach. "Billy Buster," as he sometimes called him, was a source of paternal pride, "the greatest boy in the world." But since Phebe could not, under any circumstances, inflict corporal punishment on her child, George became the disciplinarian. Yet only once, after Willie had orchestrated an April Fool's prank by staging a fake fire in the room of a neighbor's home, complete with half a dozen Bengal lights, which "flare up in red fire and have at a distance every semblance of a considerable conflagration," did George react physically. While Phoebe was greatly relieved "to find her darling boy alive," George grabbed his son "by the scruff of the neck" and asked solicitously:

"Were you very warm in that room while the fire was going on, Willie?"

"No, Papa, I wasn't warm at all."

"'Well,' said Papa, laying Willie across his knee, bottomside up, 'you're going to be warmed now, son, where it will do you the most good.'"

Yet Willie was not "warmed" much on this occasion or, for that matter, ever again. So discipline was out, and gifts were in. One day, for instance, "Billy Buster" asked his father to "treat" him and his playmates at a local ice-cream parlor. The boys wondered: "Would Willie get 'two bits' or 'four bits?' Neither, George Hearst gave . . . twenty dollars" and was, to the boys, "the grandest man in San Francisco." [7]

No wonder that Willie developed an obvious narcissism, a deep self-love. No wonder that, as one biographer put it, he felt "that other people existed mainly to gratify his own whims and desires." And in 1866, when his father moved the family into a double French chalet on Chestnut Street, with balconies overlooking a beautiful garden and then eastward the sparkling glitter of San Francisco Bay, and when his parents installed a playhouse, filling it with toys as well as a Punch and Judy show, "the first owned by a boy in San Francisco," young Willie never questioned the premise of self-indulgence, of "the world was his oyster." [8]

But unknown to Willie, the Hearst household was not in happy accord. Phebe and George really had little in common except love for their son. Otherwise, their ambitions, their interests, indeed their cultures were poles apart. George Hearst, focusing on money and what it could buy, never cared for social amenities. In the mining camps of the Far West and the rough-and-tumble world of business he was well liked and, even more gratifying, respected. He had a penchant for finding gold and silver, his word "absolutely sacred, no matter if millions were involved." In 1865, without any appreciable effort on his part, he was elected as a Democrat to the California State Assembly. Because of his pro-Southern leanings and his vote against ratifying the Thirteenth Amendment (prohibiting slavery and involuntary servitude), he quickly lost favor with his San Francisco constituency. But no matter! He was "hooked" on politics. To create a favorable image for public office, he was determined to make the necessary personal sacrifices. As a result, Phebe, who had endured his vulgarities in manners and speech, who had suffered more than once his embarrassing interruption of a dinner party by his walking "barefooted past the awe-struck diners . . . without saying a word," and who had borne the mental anguish of "another woman," was able to reach an accommodation with George along the same lines as their marriage contract. Instead of an armed truce, which seemed to reflect their continuing relationship, she proposed a modus vivendi. In return for the picture of a wholesome family life and a devoted wife who would lavishly, and with propriety, entertain his political friends—so necessary for a public figure—she would have unlimited funds to pursue her own endeavors, specifically educational improvement, social refinement, involvement in worthy charities, travel abroad, and the personal supervision of her only son. It was a fair exchange. And to their credit both participants, strong-willed, tough-minded, and ambitious, carried out these arrangements admirably, seldom showing moments of pique or revealing any unhappiness with each other, but settling rather comfortably into their prescribed roles.[9]

The two soon exhibited this new detente effectively. Late in the 1860s George Hearst informed Phebe that his luck had soured, that he was on the verge of bankruptcy. Revenue from the Ophir mine was drastically down; several investments had "backfired"; and he had lost heavily at cards. With his cash reserves almost depleted, George set forth to prospect the desert and mountain reaches of California, Nevada, Utah, and Wyoming, to regain his Midas touch. In turn, Phebe rented the Chestnut Street chalet, dismissed their servants, and sold their horses and carriages as well as some of her jewels. She and Willie then went to live at her parents' ranch near Santa Clara. In fact, so desperate were their financial straits that in the 1870 Census George Hearst listed a personal estate of only $600.[10]

But not for long! Before the end of 1870 George Hearst had begun to recoup his fortune; he was once again "on a financial roll," one that would continue throughout his life. Besides making a real-estate deal, that netted $100,000, and several small mining strikes, he formed an unbeatable partnership with a swarthy, soft-spoken Christian Turk named James Ben Ali Haggin and with Lloyd Tevis, "a beefy, full-blooded Scot, with thistles and heather in his throat." The three of them together would make mining history. In 1872, after Hearst sold his stock in the Ophir to Ben Holiday of the Overland Stagecoach lines, Hearst, Haggin, and Tevis bought the Ontario mine of Utah, which thereafter produced prodigious amounts of silver. Within five years (June, 1877) they bought another mining operation for $70,000—the fabulous Homestake of Lead, South Dakota, which yielded $715 million in gold from 1878 to 1962. And in 1880–81 they became full partners for $30,000 with a gregarious and likable Irishman, Marcus Daly, in the Anaconda mine at Butte, Montana, soon to be recognized as the greatest copper find in the United States.[11]

Young Willie Hearst would, of course, be the direct beneficiary of such parental accord and financial successes. Yet the year 1868 was not a good one for him. In May, while the Chestnut Street chalet was being rented,

Phebe decided to visit relatives in Missouri and "show off" her young son. What a mistake! She soon remembered the urgent reasons for leaving the area in the first place. Her birthplace was a dismal revelation, especially during the summer months, even though Willie enjoyed riding horses and visiting his cousins. After five weeks of ever-present fever and debilitating dysentery and blistering heat, Phebe wrote that she was "completely worn out & sick" from the trip. "I wish I was at home," she lamented. "This is miserable country." Her return to San Francisco via New York City and Panama on December 1 was even more traumatic. Willie, thin and drawn, contracted typhoid fever near Acapulco, and for nine days en route she did everything "just to keep life in him." [12]

Once back in San Francisco, however, Willie recuperated quickly, his spirits raised considerably by a deluge of Christmas gifts and, in March, 1869, a return to the Chestnut Street home and playhouse. Bright and inquisitive, he was anything but average mentally. Not many four- or five-year-olds would consider lessons by a solicitous mother, who began teaching him "as soon as he could walk," to be "play." Not many would ask their grandfather "innumerable questions" about threshers and reapers at the ranch, then "come to the house and build" them, in miniature, with remarkable accuracy. Nor, for that matter, would many at that age begin to understand the power of money—and use it to their advantage. For instance, after Willie attended kindergarten under the tutelage of a cultured Englishwoman named K. Mullins, the Hearsts, especially George, decided that their son should "have the benefit of a democratic public school education" by attending North Cosmopolitan Grammar School. Within a short time the neatly dressed, well-scrubbed Willie became "teacher's pet" and sat "near her desk." Well aware of his unpopularity with other students, he dissuaded Phebe from sending the family carriage to collect him after school, while pleading in vain "to have patches sewn all over my trousers so I'll look like the other boys." But "in the dangerous, primitive world of children," as one author so aptly characterized it, young Willie was facing far worse punishment: an old-fashioned country licking by the school gang. So he invited the leader, the class "tough," to his Chestnut Street home and "fed him jelly, ice cream, and cake." The judicious use of money solved the problem; Willie was one of the gang. [13]

Acceptance gave breadth to Willie's intellect and personality. At home, with an attentive, schoolteacher mother, he memorized the French alphabet and asked "for everything on the table, vegetables, fruits, meats, fishes . . . in French." An adept tease and mimic, he also amused Phebe by "learning Chinese from our [house]boy" and then imitating the servant's actions and expressions. More and more he enjoyed "reading interesting books," studying geography, accompanying his mother to Woodward's Gardens on Mission Street to observe hundreds of reproductions by "great masters." How proud Phebe was of her "innocent child," how determined "to keep him so as long as I can." [14]

At the same time Willie Hearst was, as he later admitted, "an ordinary American brat." When forced by his mother to attend Lunt's Dancing Academy in San Francisco, he led his friends—Orrin Peck, Eugene Lent, and Fred Moody—in a rock assault on the entrance and, as a "young barbarian," rejoiced in being excluded from instruction. Periodically, small animals seemed to find their way into his pockets and were set loose at an appropriate time. And on another occasion, during one of his mother's receptions for a prominent group of ladies, he temporarily disrupted proceedings by placing a mechanical mouse in their midst. Consequently they became a "little apprehensive" whenever "Willie entered the room." For all such misconduct Willie went unpunished, Phebe seemingly oblivious to her son's capers, mentioning only in her letters that "he is such a big boy." [15]

By the end of 1872, while George Hearst roamed the West to compile his fortune, Phebe decided, with her husband's encouragement, to fulfill her dreams—a twenty-month trip to Europe with Willie. But first came sixty days of intensive preparation. Orderly and systematic in approach to problems and goal-oriented in her cultural development, Phebe was not about to leave anything to chance. She planned to cross the country by train, visiting friends and relatives whenever possible before leaving from New York City for a year's tour of the Continent. To anticipate her every whim or change of plans, she hired a travel agency; but in the main she arranged for day-to-day travel and accommodations. At the same time she leased for a year the Chestnut Street chalet overlooking the bay, sold certain household items as well as some of Willie's pets, and stored everything else at "Pa's" ranch near Santa Clara. She also, in precision-like manner, organized each day before departure: continuing six French lessons a week until she could "speak it quite well," studying German with Willie and tutoring him with "all his lessons," then reading voraciously about the places they would visit. At night she indefatigably maintained a crowded social schedule—civic functions, dinner parties at home, and the theater.

Yet Phebe was ever cognizant of Willie, of his welfare and interests. For his continuing education abroad she hired Thomas Barry, a young Harvard graduate with a heavy concentration in the classics, as a tutor. Then, just prior to departure, she invited all of his ten-year-old companions for a farewell party, complete with ice cream, cake, and fireworks. So successful was this celebration—"Willie loved fireworks"—that he begged for "another and another." Of course, his wishes were granted, thus extending the "fun" for ten days. In fact, playmate Fred Moody fondly recalled, "the neighborhood was really dead after Willie Hearst went away."[16]

On March 18, 1873, the first leg of the grand tour began innocently enough. After six days mother and son reached Franklin County, via St Louis, and once again became appreciative of San Francisco, especially with "much sickness in the country." Willie developed a loathing for bacon, which was a staple diet of his Missouri relatives. Soon, however, they happily escaped to Bloomington, Illinois, visiting with Willie's beloved former nurse Eliza Pike for a few days before traveling by train to Boston by way of Chicago and upper New York. During a brief stay with Clara (Reed) Anthony, who was Phebe's childhood companion during the Franklin County days, Willie and the Anthony children had "a splendid time playing in the parks" or investigating "much of" the historic city, while the two mothers attended luncheon parties and evening concerts. Then on April 18 the Hearsts were once more on their way, going by train to New York City and, the next day, sailing on the White Star Line steamer *Adriatic*, their destination Ireland.[17]

After a pleasant, uneventful voyage, mother and son arrived in Dublin on May 2, and thereafter Willie Hearst—as revealed in Phebe's amazingly detailed letters—displayed a remarkable awareness of the world, an inquisitiveness and maturity bordering not just on precociousness but even genius. In fact, this twenty-month European tour contributed to the development of his character, to certain contradictive actions and habits, to shaping, as one contemporary observed, "the whole course" of his "future." At age ten he was surprisingly cognizant of poverty and injustice as well as the power of money when used judiciously; he had an extraordinary ability, when interested, to comprehend technical accomplishments; and he expanded his knowledge of history, geography, art, architecture, and languages, yet often reverted to juvenile mischief and puerile pranks of outrageous proportions.[18]

For seven weeks the Hearsts "discovered" the British Isles. In Dublin they delighted in visiting Parliament and other government buildings, then going to Queen's Court, where Willie was "greatly amused" by the judges and lawyers in their "funny grey wigs and strange black gowns." For several days they enjoyed the Irish countryside, the magnificent castles, and the ancient churches, before Willie became painfully aware of how "terribly poor" the peasants were, even to the point of "wanting to give away all his money and clothes." Nor did he especially like Ireland, "because the men are so bad to the women and horses." [19]

After a brief sojourn to Belfast, Phebe and Willie sailed to Scotland, arriving early enough on the morning of May 12 "to enjoy the scenery up the Clyde." With Phebe as guide in Glasgow and Edinburgh, Willie received continuing historical lessons for over a week. "Getting along very well alone," they enjoyed touring parts of both cities, the public buildings, the churches, and "great cathedral," so much so that "Willie wanted to remain longer." They also "saw the crown jewels and the regalia of Scotland," the prison room of Mary, Queen of Scots, "the window from which she lowered her child and sent him away," and the armory of a castle where a dirk of the famous Scottish freebooter Rob Roy was on display. Willie was so fascinated that he immediately read a book on the period and wanted a Highland costume. Then onward they went to the National Gallery; to several museums; to statues of Sir Walter Scott and Robert Burns; to St. Giles, where John Knox preached and the house where he lived. And all the time Phebe expounded on the history and literature and art of Scotland to a receptive and attentive Willie. [20]

By May 23 the Hearsts arrived in London, but Willie, prior to leaving Edinburgh, contracted whooping cough, thus disrupting their plans. The ever-cautious Phebe, although keeping to a hectic tour and social schedule, "was almost sick" with worry over Willie. After ten days at the exclusive St. James Hotel she rented an apartment uptown, partly to economize but also to provide more room for him. As always, however, her major concerns had to do with Willie. To lessen the boredom of confinement, she furnished him with a constant supply of books as well as "a magic lantern for evening amusement." Whenever weather permitted, she took him to Hyde Park to watch "elegantly dressed ladies and *swell* Englishmen," in all their finery, ride by. On one "bright day" they went to the Zoological Garden, where Willie saw a lumbering rhinoceros and huge hippopotamus, then thrilled to riding "an immense elephant."

But as soon as his health returned early in June, Phebe revived the tour in full, taking Willie "everywhere it was possible to do so." At Westminister Abbey they observed, besides the "grand tomb" of Queen Elizabeth and those of many eminent men, the magnificent architecture and the excellent quality of numerous statues. "Willie was greatly impressed," Phebe noted, and "will remember much of what he has seen." At the Tower of London they delighted in the pomp and ceremony of history, as guides, known as "wardens," dressed "in the times of Henry the 8th and Queen

Elizabeth with buckled shoes [and] pants fastened at the knees," expounded upon past events. Within the same area they passed by the Bell Tower and Traitors Gate and the Bloody Tower, where Richard III had Prince Edward V and the Duke of York put to death and where all the royal jewels were housed—the crown of Queen Victoria, the Sceptre Sword of State, and other bejeweled and ermine-bordered and silk-lined regalia. From there they toured Hampton Court, the home of "many kings and queens," which was "about twelve miles from the city." Tirelessly and enthusiastically Phebe and Willie examined "some magnificent old carved furniture" of past monarchs, studied approximately two thousand paintings, and scrutinized tapestries "of exquisite richness and beauty of design." On other days they visited art galleries, museums, and botanical gardens. Then, just before leaving England, they attended a band concert and, to Willie's delight, a magnificent fireworks display at the Crystal Palace, before journeying to Windsor Castle, "twenty-one miles from the city." After a thorough investigation of the state rooms, sculptures, paintings, tapestries, and furniture over a two-day period, Phebe wrote prophetically, "Willie would have liked to live there." [21]

Late on June 25 the Hearsts left London by train, then boarded "a very ordinary steamer" for Belgium. The next morning they arrived in Antwerp, where Phebe continued Willie's education. In churches and museums they viewed remarkable works of art, the best of Rubens, Van Dyck, and other great masters, "who were natives of the city." Willie was inspired; he surprised Phebe by taking up drawing and, temporarily, deciding to be a painter. [22]

By July 1 they traveled to Holland—Amsterdam, Rotterdam, and The Hague—with the ubiquitous Phebe functioning well as travel agent, tour guide, and educational director. For most of July and all of August they toured Germany and, despite a dislike for the "cooking" and a limited diet, really enjoyed their German experience. On a leisurely trip up the Rhine, they explored lofty castles from which feudal lords and barons had once ruled, thus prompting Willie to read *Legends of the Rhine*. [23]

During a brief interlude in mid-July, however, the tour became burdensome because, after four months, Willie had tired of his mother's overscheduling and longed for a companion of comparable age. Phebe soon resolved these problems. At Hanover she bought a number of "little tin soldiers" so that her son, in the guise of Napoleon, could "amuse" himself "for hours fighting the battle of Waterloo." She also interested him in helping her figure the confusing rates of exchange between German and Austrian money. And she scheduled events that would stimulate his curiosity.

At the Royal Palace of Herrenhausen, "about 1 1/2 miles out of town," they visited the stables—since Willie loved animals—and admired "the white and cream-colored horses of the breed which for two centuries have drawn the Kings and Queens of England." Then Phebe remarked: "I . . . *wickedly* wished for a p[ai]r. Willie wanted four." At an old castle "called Lowenberg," which for a time was the "residence of Napoleon III," she allowed Willie, "who was quite excited," to roam "through the grand apartments," to marvel at a "great fountain 190 ft. high," and to climb a huge thirty-one-foot copper statue of Hercules and stand "in the hollow of the club which rests in his arms."

In Berlin early in August they explored the King's Palace, "principally built by Frederick the Great's father." After admiring the superb apartments, the beautifully inlaid floors, the gorgeous furniture, rare works of art, paintings, and bronzes, Phebe proudly noted that "Willie was very much interested. He has a mania for antiquities . . . studying and prying into everything." But by August 8 at Dresden, Phebe completely satisfied Willie by finding "a good boarding place" with a local family named Schonfelder. For the first time since March he had other children to play with. He also enjoyed having to speak German at every meal, so much so that he took lessons daily to improve. Yet what really fascinated him were comic picture books called *Bilder Bucher*, which he read and collected by the hundreds—and which twenty-two years later would be the source of the famous comic strip "Katzenjammer Kids."[24]

Although Willie wanted to remain at Dresden indefinitely, Phebe was not about to alter the grand tour plans. On August 23 they were on their way again—and for the next three months their schedule was routinely predictable. During three weeks in Vienna they assiduously investigated an international exhibition, visited the Austrian royal palace, and attended operas and band concerts. By mid-September they were en route to Switzerland by way of Munich, at which time Willie became highly frustrated. At "a very elegant building . . . containing the finest statuary and frescoes I have yet seen," Phebe recorded, Willie was barred from entering because of a "no one under 17" rule. He tried every possible ploy to circumvent what he considered to be an insulting regulation, even offering the guard a bribe. Eventually, however, by being "very good natured," he was allowed to "look into three rooms."[25]

In Switzerland, Phebe relaxed somewhat and granted Willie more time to indulge himself. For most of the next two months they lived in Geneva with a French-speaking family, which allowed Willie once again a chance to improve his language capabilities. He played with children his own age, thrilled to fishing on Lake Lucerne (catching seventeen "keepers" with new gear, he proudly wrote his father), and extended his endeavors as a collector. To an already sizable number of comic books, he added stamps, coins, beer steins, wood carvings, watches, and clocks, the cost being of little importance as long as the product was good. Continually he and his mother marveled at the beauty of the Swiss countryside, being able to see for thirty miles at one high location.[26]

In mid-November they proceeded to Italy for six months, their adaptability to living out of a suitcase becoming increasingly apparent. Anticipating a lengthy stay, Phebe restructured their schedules. While at Florence, Willie attended to studies for three to four hours each weekday morning. Besides easily absorbing history and geography, which both surprised and delighted tutor Thomas Barry, he received instruction in English and mathematics (concerning which, Phebe noted, "he was somewhat backward"). For specific subjects such as French, German, and drawing, however, Phebe hired special tutors two to four times a week to augment Willie's regular lessons. Then in the afternoon she and Willie explored museums, palaces, churches, and historical places. And in the evening they attended the opera, spent time with acquaintances, or toured the parks and suburbs.[27]

In Rome, however, after arriving on January 27, 1874, Phebe switched their tour adventures to the morning hours and, because of so much to see, limited Willie's studies to two or three hours in the afternoon. What a tourist's delight Rome turned out to be! During the first week a three-day carnival excited Willie and "tired" his mother. Hundreds of participants dressed in "strange," "handsome," or "very amusing" costumes paraded the streets, before a fireworks display capped off the events of the last evening. Then their extensive exploration began—St. Peter's four times, the Vatican six. On one of these occasions, February 7, Phebe proudly announced that they "were presented to the Pope" who "came to Willie . . . placed his hand on his head and blessed him." Of course, the Colosseum and Forum as well as numerous galleries with sculptures and paintings were also "musts."[28]

But during the six months in Italy Phebe began to notice in Willie certain marked changes. "He is picture crazy," she wrote to George. "I do not mean to say he has any special talent, and would not wish him to be an artist (unless a *great* one) but he frequently surprises me in expressions concerning the best pictures." Equally apparent were his expensive tastes. While in Venice for several days he was so impressed with the great paintings, "rare marbles," and Venetian glass that Phebe had difficulty convincing him that "we could not buy all we saw." His intellectual growth and powers of concentration were also unusual, if not remarkable. Besides preparing for lessons each weekday, he read, on the average, five books a month to "feed" his interests. And his imaginative, curious, often unconventional side was perhaps most evident when, upon seeing an altar light in Rome (which had burned, a guide pointed out, for a thousand years), he tried in vain to think of some way to extinguish it, to do what no one else had ever accomplished.[29]

Because Willie was sick for a month, Phebe delayed their departure to Paris until April 19, 1874. But upon arrival the next day Willie would, by his actions, alter the tour; in fact, this segment of the trip could easily have been titled "Willie Hearst's Assault on Paris." Mrs. William M. Lent and her son Eugene (Genie), who were San Francisco neighbors and close friends, were awaiting them. While the mothers decided to "take in" Paris together, tutor Thomas Barry was placed in charge of their sons. On any number of occasions he led the boys on historical expeditions, trying to follow in the "footsteps" of Napoleon and Charlemagne, while discussing their lives and ambitions and accomplishments. And even though Willie embraced the two great French leaders as his lifelong heroes—especially Charlemagne—he eventually wearied of this structured supervision and sought relief. With an enthusiastic accomplice and follower in the person of Genie Lent, he thus became the prototype of *Peck's Bad Boy*. On one of his first days in Paris he bent his mother's hairpins into hooks and led an expedition to catch goldfish, which were in the Tuileries fountains across the street from their "modest" boardinghouse; a French gendarme unceremoniously dragged them by the ears to an embarrassed Phebe.

Although "grounded"—confined to the boardinghouse—Willie was not at all discouraged; the two would play "cowboys and Indians." But they had no wild animals, that is, until they espied the "beautiful, purry Persian cat" of a Madame Pincee, who owned the establishment. After Genie tied a tight string around its tail, Hearst later recounted, "the cat was then the wildest animal Paris had seen in many a day," streaking like "blue lightning, only touching the side walls and the ceiling and going right through the Louis Quinze brick-a-brac cabinets." When Madame Pincee and her staff finally corralled her precious pet and discovered the reason for its actions, the boys were remanded to their rooms.

Another mistake! By the next day, after Genie brought out one of his toys, a "graceful" sailboat, Willie excited their imaginations by suggesting "a fire at sea." Into a washbasin the boys launched the small craft, saturated it with alcohol, and set it ablaze. "Magnifique!" Willie exclaimed. So why not a grander exploit—"a fire on land"—one "épateur tout Paris" (to scandal all of Paris)? They therefore accumulated large amounts of straw that, when dampened, "would not burn, but . . . smudge," bought flashing red lights from a nearby store, and then began their escapade. As smoke filled the hallways and an alarm was turned in, "Genie, in calling for help," Hearst again noted, "managed to dislodge one of the green shutters of the back window, which fell through the glass roof of the kitchen beneath and put Mme. Pincee's chef in the hospital for three weeks." After brass-helmeted firefighters arrived and flooded the room as well as drowning out some guests below, the Hearsts and Lents paid all costs and were requested to leave. Although meticulous in detailing events of this twenty-month tour, Phebe curiously never mentioned one word of these escapades.[30]

In their new location at the elegant Hôtel d'Albe on the Champs Élysées, the mothers held tight rein over their two sons for almost three months, that is, until Willie and his imagination once again erupted. In the large drawing-room suite occupied by both families, its walls of paneled damask, its ceiling of plastered "graceful nymphs and chubby cupidons disporting in the clouds," Willie decided to experiment with a toy chassepot, a miniature type of breech-loading rifle he had bought. While resting the butt on the floor, he drove a ramrod "down the barrel to hammer the charge home." A resounding explosion, which embedded the ramrod a foot or two into the plastered ceiling, "filled" Willie "with dismay." The hotel concierge, angrily spouting all manner of unkind phrases, tried to dislodge the ramrod, Hearst recalled, and brought "the whole dodgasted plaster ceiling . . . down on him, pretty little cupids, voluptuous nymphs, clouds and everything." The mothers were once more embarrassed, forced to pay for damages, and then leave—again no mention of this episode in Phebe's letters.[31]

The remaining months of the grand tour went smoothly. For the rest of the summer Phebe and Willie revisited England, enjoying such historic sites as Stratford-on-Avon and Oxford University, which she had previously been unable to schedule. Then in September they briefly returned to Paris before sailing on October 10 from Liverpool on the Cunard Line steamer *Cuba* and, after a rough voyage, docked at New York City on October 23, 1874. Phebe, although weary and homesick, felt "obliged" to remain several days until their "loot" was safely through customs before booking passage by train to San Francisco. Early in November, 1874, they arrived home, their glorious adventure of twenty months over.[32]

After such a lengthy absence, adjustments were necessary, but not easy, for the Hearsts. Because the Panic of 1873 had caused severe economic hardship in the United States and because the Ontario mine was not producing as much silver as anticipated, George Hearst was hard pressed for money once again, especially after Phebe's costly European tour. He therefore continued to prospect throughout the West in 1874 and 1875, even though in poor health for much of the time. To economize, he and Phebe decided to sell their beautiful Chestnut Street home and reside at a "refined" boardinghouse in San Francisco, which was operated by old friends, the Winns. In the meantime Phebe had to find places to store all of her new acquisitions—porcelains, sculptures, paintings, tapestries, and books. Eventually, on August 1, 1875, she rented a "furnished house" at Sutter and Jones, while planning to build a "home to suit us" by the next year. But more importantly, Phebe attended to her Willie. During the next several years she enrolled him intermittently at Lincoln and Washington grammar schools, while allowing him the freedom and expanse of his grandfather's Santa Clara ranch in the summertime and on vacations.[33]

Late in the summer of 1876, however, Phebe decided to expand Willie's horizons once again, this time with a trip to the eastern part of the United States. Willie was delighted; he was escaping formal education for the rest of the year. With Phebe in her favorite role as tour guide and director, they visited the Centennial Exposition and accompanying celebrations in Philadelphia. Although slowed by huge crowds—"yesterday . . . 257,000 people. It was dreadful," Phebe wrote on September 30—they both thrilled to the numerous exhibitions that highlighted the modern technology and industrial advancement of the United States, indeed which forecast, through new inventions, a modern society benefiting all Americans.

In mid-October they proceeded to New York City. Arriving in the midst of the intense 1876 presidential campaign between Democrat Samuel J. Tilden of New York and Republican Rutherford B. Hayes of Ohio, they watched the hoopla and extravaganza of late nineteenth-century American politics—uniformed marching bands, scores of American flags, torchlight parades, and immense crowds responding to campaign oratory. To Willie, such spectacles were greater than "those imaginary dramas in Europe; better than Dickens' foggy London with its grim Tower; better than Fontainebleau of the magnificent Louis and Napoleon; better than even St. Denis where Charlemagne was crowned; better than the gay Carnival of Rome; the Forum; or the Colosseum." And then for the pièce de résistance, Phebe took Willie to a reception at the Tilden home in Gramercy Park (after all, George Hearst was a big contributor to the

Democratic Party). Willie thereafter elevated the Democratic nominee to his "hero list" along with Charlemagne and Napoleon, naming his dog "Governor Tilden." [34]

After visiting Clara Anthony in Boston and Eliza Pike in Bloomington, Illinois, Phebe and Willie returned by train to San Francisco on December 28, 1876. Although deciding to rent the second floor of a "nice house" on California Street near Powell because of the "good price," she seldom had to worry about finances ever again; George Hearst's talent for obtaining excellent bargains in mining and real estate became legendary. In addition to developing the lucrative Ontario, Homestake, and Anaconda properties, he had bought the 40,000-acre Piedra Blanca Ranch in 1865 for approximately sixty cents an acre and would continue to add huge parcels of land in San Luis Obispo and Monterey counties (275,000 acres in all), which abutted the Bay of San Simeon. Through his close friendship with Mexican dictator Porfirio Díaz he acquired early in the 1880s the one-million-acre Babicora Ranch in Chihuahua for forty cents an acre as well as 1,000 square miles in the Mexican states of Yucatán, Campeche, and Vera Cruz. He also invested in northern California timberlands, a ranch in New Mexico (with James Ben Ali Haggin and A. E. Head), and "large acreage" in Arizona and Texas. [35]

Such enormous financial windfalls, coupled with a doting mother who had sequestered her son from a number of childhood experiences, significantly affected Willie Hearst as a teenager, producing an unevenness in his intellectual and social pursuits, a certain imbalance of maturity, in some ways an unusual combination of positive strengths and glaring weaknesses. Thrust into, and having to cope with, an adult world, he was already an avid collector (rare tomes and comic books, coins, and stamps) as well as a budding connoisseur of paintings and sculpture and furniture. Well read in both history and literature, he had a particular penchant for the wit of William Makepeace Thackeray, the pageantry of Sir Walter Scott, and especially the writing style of Charles Dickens—its "variety, humor, and understanding." He also "delighted" in, and would always be enthralled with, the theater and its participants, never forgetting the performances of Edwin Booth as Hamlet, Adelaide Neilson as Juliet, and Clara Morris as Camille. At times, center stage would tempt him as well. Adept at mimicry, he would go to the theater and, positioning himself with "chin on chest," watch "every motion" of minstrel comedian Billy Emerson, "absorbing the nuances of his dialect, registering each word, tone and note, like a recording machine," then entertain friends with his own minstrel show or stage play. [36]

Willie became accustomed to the pleasures of wealth. With such friends as Gene Lent and Orrin Peck, he frequently dined in the courtyard of San Francisco's luxurious Palace Hotel before attending a play. Whenever possible, he accompanied his father—sometimes with several school companions—to the San Simeon ranch and temporarily lived the life of a *vaquero*, riding over rugged terrain of the California Coastal Range, tossing a *riata*, strumming a guitar, singing ditties in Spanish and English. And in 1878, when Phebe bought a massive white stucco mansion of Spanish design on Taylor Street, he persuaded her to outfit one of the large stables as a theater. Then late in 1878 he went with Phebe on another European tour, which to a certain extent was a maternal going-away present before having to enroll in an eastern prep school for the fall semester.[37]

Even with Phebe overscheduling in an attempt to see everything, this 1878–79 trip was less frenetic and, in many ways, quite different for young Will Hearst (his parents and friends began dropping the "ie" in Willie). Because of nagging illnesses Phebe understandably was less energetic; she allowed tutor Thomas Barry to arrange accommodations for travel, lodging, and entertainment as well as to accompany, or shepherd, Will on daily excursions. As a result of her 1873–74 European experiences she decided to change their tour schedule, proceeding first to Rome and Florence during the winter and spring, next to Barcelona in May, and to Paris, Amsterdam, Antwerp, and London in the summer months. In turn, sixteen-year-old Will, although still fascinated by, and eager to see, the historical places and art treasurers of Europe, enlarged his scope of interests. While continuing to study geography, history, Greek, Latin, mathematics, and algebra daily for three to four hours (each morning except Sunday and from eight o'clock to nine o'clock in the evenings), he scheduled afternoon workouts at the gymnasium—he took fencing lessons in Paris—and, whenever possible, attended the theater or opera in the evening. In Paris, however, he sometimes avoided the companionship of his old school chum Gene Lent (who arrived in June), tutor Thomas Barry, and even his mother "to see," Barry recorded on June 13, "petite mademoiselle again—third time!" But even more unusual about the tour, while Phebe went to Germany "to take the cure" for her ailments, Will sailed on the Cunard Line steamer *Scythia* from Liverpool on August 15, accompanied only by Thomas Barry. They arrived in New York City on August 26, just in time for Will to enroll at St. Paul's Episcopal School in Concord, New Hampshire.[38]

To Will Hearst, St. Paul's was a definite shock: the area remote; the climate cold and bleak; the housing, as was customary at eastern prep schools, Spartan. From the very beginning in September, 1879, he was un-happy. "Everything is so dull," he wrote his mother. "I am just homesick all the time." Even rooming with Will Tevis, the son of his father's San Fran-cisco mining partner, did not help. Desperately he pleaded with Phebe to return from Germany by November, to help him escape, much like his hero Napoleon, from exile. "If you will get well, you shall never have any-thing to make you sick again, if I can help it," he promised. "I often think how bad I have been and how many unkind words I have said, and I am sure that when you come back I will be good and never be so bad again."

No wonder he suffered. For a California teenager who was accustomed to freedom of movement and an unlimited supply of cash, the beautifully landscaped St. Paul's, where 250 students were trained to play cricket in-stead of baseball on "a carefully groomed English lawn such as one might see at Harrow or Rugby or Eton," was worse than any prison. Hearst could "only go into town once a month," he lamented, "and only have four dollars a month to spend." And in lieu of a doting mother, a Dr. Coit, the school's headmaster, whom Hearst regarded as "an old hypocrite," became his surrogate parent for a year.[39]

Nor did Hearst register any improvement in his situation during the fall of 1879. Besides studying nine hours a day, "and even then can hardly keep up with the form," he had to attend each day and three times on Sun-day compulsory church services—"camp meetings," he cynically called them. Oh, how Hearst hated St. Paul's. "I believe that every old minister in this country comes here to practice on us, and shove off old sermons that no one else will listen to," he complained to Phebe. "Last Sunday we had a German ... [who] talked 'shus' like Gus Williams. Nearly half the boys in school got ... [on] report for laughing." And the Sunday before that "we had a minister who kept forgetting his place," repeating over and over again his text, "Oh foolish Galatians who has bewitched you." Only head-master Coit preached "pretty well," even though, Hearst added, he "hollers too much."[40]

Hearst, sometimes successfully but more often futilely, employed ways to endure the dismal school year of 1879–80. Because of the harsh climate, which reportedly reached "twenty-five degrees below zero," he "took box-ing for exercise" in the gymnasium and, when possible, played baseball, usually on Saturday, even being elected captain on one of several school baseball teams. Hearst also devised a "special fish and potato fast on Fri-day," which hopefully would keep him alert, he sarcastically wrote, for his "sacred studies."

But usually thoughts of escape, in some form, occupied his mind. At first he hoped that Phebe would come to Concord and stay the winter; and while such did not occur, she did arrive in time to whisk him off to New York City and Boston for the Christmas holidays. In desperation he thereafter resorted to sending telegrams to a Mr. Hughes, an uncle of boyhood friend Orrin Peck, who lived in New York City, frantically beseeching: "For God's sake, please ask me to New York." But other than numerous letters from his mother and a subscription to the London *Times*, which Hearst greatly enjoyed, what really bolstered his spirits was that by the summer of 1880 he would be returning home to California.[41]

Young Will, knowing that both Phebe and George Hearst were determined to send him to Harvard University, reluctantly returned to St. Paul's for another year of rigorous preparation. But not for long! Although several biographers stated that Hearst was summarily dismissed during the year for infractions of institutional rules and "for the good of the school," such suppositions were incorrect. Hearst persuaded his mother to rescue him from another frozen "penitential term," promising faithfully to study with private tutors in readiness for application to Harvard. Phebe and headmaster Coit mutually agreed to a suitable withdrawal.[42]

Will Hearst reveled in his release from eastern incarceration. In San Francisco again, he responded well to familiar and happy surroundings, enjoying this period of grace before his next exile. Since acceptance at Harvard in the fall of 1882 was a prerequisite to escaping parental indignation and wrath, he worked with a private tutor on a regular schedule. At the same time he observed somewhat disapprovingly—but with a certain detachment—his father pursue a political career. As early as 1880 George Hearst, to ingratiate himself with California Democrats, had bought the *San Francisco Examiner* and had turned it into a blatant advertisement for the state party as well as a political organ to advance himself. In May, 1881, he also helped organize the Manhattan Club, which constituted the "high-toned elements of the party" and which opposed Chris Buckley, "the blind boss of San Francisco." George Hearst was thus maneuvering to run for governor of California in 1882.[43]

But Will Hearst had much greater concerns; he had fallen in love with Sybil Sanderson, the daughter of a state supreme court judge. Early in the summer of 1882 the two had first met at the scenic Hotel Del Monte overlooking the bay at Monterey. After an intense, all-consuming romance, they became engaged. But Mama Sanderson, who considered Sybil to be a talented singer and prettier than actress Adelaide Neilson, was not about to allow her gifted daughter to marry a tall, blond-haired, somewhat thin and gangly teenager, no matter what his pedigree—and apparently Phebe agreed, at least by all subsequent actions. Late in the summer Sybil was on her way to attend a conservatory in Paris, while young Will, disconsolate but resigned to the situation, traveled to Cambridge to enroll at Harvard.[44]

During his freshman year Will Hearst adjusted rather well to Harvard life; at least in his letters he revealed none of the sarcasm and venom evidenced at St. Paul's. Possibly the fact that Phebe accompanied him to Cambridge and decided to remodel a rather plain apartment in Matthews Hall with her own distinct taste, building library shelves in the walls and buying beautiful mahogany tables "equipped with Harvard-red smoking sets," may have had something to do with his attitude. Surely the prescribed course load for a freshman was not a surprise—Latin, Greek, German, chemistry, algebra, and "every Monday a lecture on Greek & Roman writers and their works." Nor was it too difficult to pass at a "70%" (gentleman's C) level, Will wrote his father, unless the student wished to attain "very high marks." And, to resolve any homesickness, Phebe took him to New York City for the Christmas holidays, extended to him an unlimited expense account—he spent $454 one weekend in Manhattan—and urged him to visit close family friend Mrs. Clara Anthony in nearby Boston. But, whatever the reasons, Hearst termed his first-year performance as "very satisfactory." Besides having Gene Lent as a classmate and cementing a lifelong friendship with Californian Jack Follansbee, Hearst happily announced to Phebe the first reports of his spring examinations: "Classical Lecture 74%, German 93%, Max. Math 84%." [45]

Yet during his sophomore year at Harvard (1883–84), Hearst did not fare too well, his morale suffering one setback after another. Without a doubt he missed Jack Follansbee (who had left Harvard in June because of financial difficulties) and, except for E. L. "Phinney" Thayer and Gene Lent, he questioned any "college friendships lasting for life." For much of the winter and spring he seemed to be "run down" physically, to be afflicted continually with some illness—intermittent colds, a lingering case of "pink eye," tonsillitis, and a sore throat. In May, Hearst summarized his condition much more candidly to Phebe. "I always have a cold. All winter my nose has been vibrating between the two conditions of constipation and diarrhea in a manner awful to behold." Nor could he do anything to dislodge it. "I have coaxed it with acconite [sic] and belladonna. I have tortured it with iron and quinine. I have asphixiated it with concentrated essence of ammonia; in fact," he asserted, "I have almost prostrated myself but the cold, thank you, is feeling very well. It won't vacate. It won't be evicted, and it won't pay rent. It's worse than an Irish tenant."

Hearst thus became negative about almost everything. His baseball team won regularly but was "decidedly amateur and ought to satisfy our esteemed President whose aversion to Professionals is well known"; his new accommodations were "much larger," but the landlady, a Mrs. Buckland, tormented him, "showing everybody my rooms and introducing them to the distressed occupant"; and the climate was horrendous, raining and snowing with "no intention" of being "pleasant" and "agreeable." How homesick Hearst became, longing for, he dejectedly wrote, not only the warming sun of California but the "towering mountains, the majestic pines, the grand impressive scenery of the 'Far West.'"

The culmination of this terrible year occurred on April 29, 1884, which "marked" twenty-one years, he thanked his mother, that "W. R. Hearst, statesman and patriot, first breathed the air of liberty." Instead of celebrating uproariously, as befitted the occasion, he labored to complete a half-finished "150-page thesis on the public land system of the U.S." which "Prof. [J. Lawrence] Laughlin" had "said in class" would be due "by next Thursday." As a consequence, Hearst performed badly in his spring studies, failing to take an exam in political economy and being "deficient," the Harvard registrar informed him in July, "to the extent of 2 1/5 courses." [46]

After a recuperative and gratifying summer in California, however, Hearst returned to Harvard late in September, 1884, rejuvenated in health, revived in spirit, and determined to graduate. A wily and seasoned veteran of academic wars after two years, he now knew how to survive rigorous classroom demands with a minimum of effort, while focusing on extracurricular activities. Or as one classmate put it, "he had enormous power of application for a brief period, and he was capable of learning enough of a textbook in a night to pass an examination." He therefore "dropped" Greek and Latin, even discontinuing German. For a brief time he sat in on a philosophy class, that is, until the professor "got up one day and began to talk about the as it wereness of the sometimes," Hearst wrote his mother, "and I lit out." Consequently he took courses for which he had a real affinity and genuine understanding—enjoying natural history (geology) under Nathanial Thayer, who had, besides "original humor," an "entertaining interpretation"; English under Le Baron Russell Briggs and Barrett Wendell, who made literature "enthralling"; and the history of fine arts under the distinguished Charles Eliot Norton, who "really gave a history of the world." Overall, in each semester at Harvard, Hearst took six courses, including political economy (again), history, and chemistry. "No Wonder," he announced to Phebe, "that I'm getting prematurely bald. But we'll pass that." [47]

By his junior year at Harvard, Hearst had also achieved some recognition as well as a certain notoriety. A tall, somewhat loose-jointed, blond youth, with hair parted down the middle and a thin wisp of a mustache, he liked sports, although not especially athletic, having been elected vice president of the college baseball association. Still painfully shy, partly because of his thin, high-pitched voice, he tried to compensate for, if not overcome, this obvious shortcoming in a number of ways. He wore expensive, outlandish, plaid clothing (of the Piccadilly Square variety), and "screaming" scarves or neckties that demanded attention. He also sported "large cigars," although considered "bad form in the Yard," classmate George Santayana recalled, and drank beer with friends, without relish or success, until taking a pledge of "total abstinence" late in November, 1884. As in the past, he became a leader of his peers, seemingly without much concentrated effort. Gifted at mimicry, at ease in strumming a banjo or guitar, able to do a subtle soft shoe or sing songs "both comic and weepy"—when on stage he portrayed someone else and forgot himself—Hearst attracted people to him by exciting their imaginations. Who else at Harvard prepared delicious Welsh rarebit and steaming baked potatoes at midnight suppers? Who else staged all-night poker parties, assaulted performers at the Howard Athenaeum with custard pies, and blatantly "stretched" or broke college rules to the consternation of a disapproving administration and faculty? Who else liked to startle unsuspecting fellow students in his room with a pet alligator that, because of its ability to consume liberal amounts of wine, was named "Champagne Charlie"? And who else had the effrontery and gall to spirit a jackass into one of his professor's rooms with an attached card that read: "Now there are two of you"? [48]

Hearst further enhanced his collegiate stature by displaying a strong business sense. In February, 1884, he was persuaded by Gene Lent to become a co-business manager of the financially troubled Harvard humor magazine, appropriately named the *Lampoon*. He immediately hounded Cambridge merchants for advertisements, beginning with "his own tailor and haberdasher." In fact, he applied his father's money so liberally in buying porcelains and other merchandise—before asking for magazine support—that the "Lampy" expanded its next issue from four to six pages in advertisements. He then wrote letters to Harvard alumni, requesting subscriptions (at $3 a year), and instructed the "Lampy" staff to continue these effective salesmanship tactics. By the fall of 1884 Hearst had enlarged the subscription list from 300 to 450 (an additional revenue of $450), while increasing advertisements from $400 to $900, thus "leaving

$650 clear profit after the debt is paid," he wrote his mother. Then euphorically—and prophetically—he concluded: "Show this to Papa, and tell him just to wait until Gene and I get hold of the old *Examiner* and we'll boom her in the same way—she needs it." [49]

Yet, among his colleagues, Hearst received mixed reviews. Although Gene Lent, Francis Lester Hawks "Cosy" Noble, cartoonist Fred Briggs, and E. L. "Phinney" Thayer were appreciative and congratulatory, some classmates were disapprovingly skeptical of his motives. For example, with the surplus funds of the "Lampy," he regaled the staff with a number of meals and provided them with individual keys to a large room or "Sanctum" that was "carpeted, warmed by a stove, and supplied with wooden arm-chairs and long tables by which all the illustrated comic papers in the world were displayed." But George Santayana, together with several others, disdainfully rejected "Hearst's munificence" as an attempt to buy their friendship, although he acknowledged years later that "Hearst alone took a responsible view of the situation . . . [while] the rest of us cultivated a philosophic disbelief in Space and Time." [50]

During the fall of 1884 Hearst became more and more involved in Harvard life. "I am getting so conceited," he wrote Phebe, "that I almost hope for a third marshalship of the ['86] class." He was already a member of four societies and then was elected (by invitation) to the prestigious Hasty Pudding Club. As a result, he took part in one of its stage productions, a musical comedy titled *Joan of Arc, or the Old Maid of New Orleans*, playing the role of Pretzel, the German valet, so well that he received several encores each performance. [51]

A further result of all such activities, however, was a desperate need for additional funds. Frantically he wrote, then telegraphed, his parents to increase his "already liberal" $150 monthly allowance, to subsidize his more involved lifestyle and expensive tastes. Besides $100 for club dues, he faced further assessments of $197 "in addition to the London News and Graphic, a bill from the hat store and some campaign expenses." He was therefore "destitute," he wrote Phebe, "in spite of the $200" and another $100 already received. As a consequence, his parents soon sent an additional $500. [52]

But what really brought Hearst a high profile during the fall semester were his political activities, which shocked and at times even traumatized staid, tradition-bound Harvard. In the hotly contested, bitterly fought presidential campaign of 1884 he, like his father in California, became inoculated with politics, ardently supporting Democrat Grover Cleveland of New York over Republican James G. Blaine of Maine. Will Hearst therefore helped organize forty members of the Harvard student body for the Democrats and, with an extremely generous application of his father's money, produced political extravaganzas that the Cambridge populace and Harvard faculty had never before experienced firsthand—brass bands, torchlight parades, flags and banners, wagonloads of beer for thirsty supporters who were entertained with partisan speakers and fireworks displays.

During several October nights these rowdy, ear-splitting productions continued, trying the level of tolerance, indeed the patience, of the academic community. Exuberantly Hearst described such exciting events to his parents: "Night before last was a unique night in Cambridge. The oldest inhabitants can remember nothing like [it] and must get up and make room for the fortunate individual who was present [at] a Hearst's flag raising. Oh it was grand." But the rally was just beginning, with an enthusiastic procession of people listening to an animated orator who "finished his speech by proposing three cheers for Grover." As the evening progressed with "more speeches, more music and more fireworks," Hearst happily reported, "a gentleman in the crowd mounted the rostrum and said that it gave him great pleasure to note the interest taken in Cleveland's election by the young men as well as the old, that here was an example where Papa Hearst in one end of the continent and sonny Hearst at the other were both working in the same great cause. He then proposed three cheers for Father and Son and I was quite overcome," Hearst concluded, "and ran away and hid so that I wouldn't have to make a speech."

On election night (November 4) and for the next few days, Hearst was very active. With Cleveland's narrow win, he not only financed a raucous night of parades and speeches and fireworks but also afflicted Harvard Yard with a bevy of roosters that awakened the inhabitants early the next morning, symbolically crowing for the first Democrat in the White House in twenty-four years. Outside his room Hearst triumphantly flew an American flag "with Victory painted in large letters on a strip of canvas at the bottom." [53]

These activities did not go unnoticed. Nor was the Harvard faculty inclined to tolerate such conduct, especially for a student such as Hearst, who was already on academic probation. On February 3, 1885, they reviewed his case and, for the time being, agreed that he should be "continued until the end of the [school] year." But on March 31, eight weeks later, with Hearst demonstrating no change in attitude, no improvement in class attendance or grades—he accompanied his parents to Washington, D.C., to celebrate President Cleveland's inauguration on March 4, performed in the Hasty Pudding Club play both in New York City and Boston, and supported the Harvard baseball team in out-of-town games—the faculty "rusticated" him. In other words, they voted that his "probation be closed at the end of the year," the "choleric" dean of the college unceremoniously informed him.[54]

Hearst did not take "rustication" well. While Phebe wrote President Charles W. Eliot of Harvard to intervene in her son's behalf, Hearst negated her efforts by reacting badly. To each of his professors' residences he sent a chamber pot, which was a euphemism describing a "vessel for urine," that was "adorned [on the bottom] with the recipient's name and photograph." He then wrote Phebe not "to attempt the disagre[e]able and impossible task of conciliating the faculty," because "I have just practically upset the pepper in the plate." Nor did he "propose to eat any more crow" or "serve any to the rest of the family," he bitterly announced, for "I assured the gentlemen of the Faculty of Harvard College that I didn't regret so much having lost my degree as having given them an opportunity to refuse it to me."[55]

Although outwardly an unreconstructed rebel from California, both unrepentant and unapologetic, Hearst still hoped to graduate with the '86 class. Together with Phebe's strenuous efforts to reverse his "rustication," he petitioned the Harvard faculty on September 30, 1885, to give him "special examinations for the purpose of rejoining" his class—but to no avail. Again on May 4, 1886, after hiring tutors and studying intensely, he asked "to be allowed to present himself for examinations in eight courses in order to become a candidate for a degree," and again was refused.[56]

So at age twenty-two William Randolph Hearst was at loose ends, without purpose and direction. Soon, however, he would decide upon another avenue for his energies, a new field of endeavor, much to the consternation and horror of his parents.

3 | The Newspaperman

❦

San Francisco in the 1880s was the "queen of the Pacific," the golden gate through which the hardy Argonauts of 1849 had funneled en route to the goldfields at Sutter's Fort and the American River. Already the ninth-largest city in the United States and recognized as the most important trading center west of Chicago—increasing in population from 34,780 in 1850 to almost 234,000 in 1880—San Francisco was "envied" by most Californians, historian R. Hal Williams observed, but "admired" by only a few. Like most cities of the post-Civil War era, it had a plethora of problems that needed to be solved. While city leaders in the 1870s had wisely expanded the school system, doubled the size of law enforcement, created public parks, provided electric fire and police alarms for emergencies, and, most importantly, established a street railway system (including a cable car route), the city government, as established in the 1850s, was resistant to change. And why? It was boss-riddled, with corruption and graft seemingly a fixed way of life. Because of its size and wealth, San Francisco dominated state politics for the benefit of its citizens and to the detriment of the rural areas. Hence a system of favors, of "spoils" for the victors, was a natural progression, of which Chris Buckley, "the blind boss of San Francisco," was the embodiment in the 1880s.[1]

But more than any other American city, San Francisco was one of glaring contrasts. Since disproportionate numbers of the population were male, in the main transients and "unmarried members of a growing labor pool," and since the populace was approximately 40 percent foreign-born, the economic and cultural life fluctuated—between gentility or sophistication by the urban rich, and violence, aggressiveness, and at times lack of inhibitions by the frontier poor. The disparities of wealth were obvious and omnipresent: rich, powerful businessmen versus ambitious labor leaders, who continually recruited for their unions because of an ever-expanding job market; the "splendid isolation" of Nob Hill, the grandiose hotels and impressive business establishments of the downtown areas as compared to shacks and slum buildings in Chinatown and the Barbary Coast; exclusive French restaurants and "discreet," high-class pleasure salons in contrast to cheap dining rooms and wide-open bawdy houses; and theaters, museums, libraries, and learned societies on the one hand, with dance halls and 2,000 saloons (one for every 117 residents) on the other.[2]

During the forty-year span after 1849 in which Americans had become a dominating force, San Franciscans had developed a uniquely colorful heritage and history. Because of the tremendous wealth generated by the miners, a legacy of mob violence, of unmitigated outlawry, and of extralegal organizations had emerged. Still within the memory of many inhabitants were the vigilance committees of 1851 and 1856; even more vivid were the riots of 1877, when the Irish demagogue Dennis Kearney had railed against the Chinese, inciting huge mobs to violence by shouting, while dangling a noose in his hands, that "a little judicious hanging right here and now would be the best course to pursue"; and in 1879 equally shocking and even more scandalous, the publisher of the *Morning Call*, Charles De Young (together with his brother), had shot at and wounded the overly amorous city mayor, Baptist minister Isaac Kalloch; in retaliation, De Young was murdered six months later by Kalloch's son. And roaming the streets during most of this time was the pathetic, semi-tragic, sometimes ludicrous figure of Joshua Norton who, in a demented condition for twenty years after going bankrupt in 1859, had proclaimed himself Norton I, Emperor of the United States and Protector of Mexico. No wonder that Robert Louis Stevenson asked in 1880: "In what city would a harmless madman . . . have been so fostered and encouraged?" No wonder that Rudyard Kipling noted in 1889 that "San Francisco is a mad city—inhabited for the most part by perfectly insane people." No wonder that William Randolph Hearst would so often be homesick for the land by the bay, be enchanted, indeed lured to return by the siren's song, and thus begin his life's work.[3]

In the summer of 1885, however, Hearst had no direction in his life, only a nebulous future, that is, unless "Mama" could minimize, if not rectify, his past mistakes. Consequently, he worked on the premise that no one could withstand Phebe's considerable persuasive powers or endure her formidable opposition—not even the "choleric" Harvard dean. But in that assumption Hearst was wrong. After a brief respite in California, he returned to the East in the fall, commuting between Washington, D.C., and New York City while studying a schedule of courses each day with a tutor. At the same time "Mama," together with intermediator Dr. J. P. Oliver of Cambridge, tried to negotiate a deal with Harvard College. With President Eliot they had no difficulty, agreeing to "secure a competent tutor and prepare for the final examination next June." As an alternative proposal Hearst would register at Johns Hopkins University for a year and then graduate with the Harvard class of '87. But all such plans, President Eliot cautioned them, must have the consent of the Harvard faculty. The major hurdle, therefore, was the dean of the college, whom Hearst, himself, must face and seek forgiveness. At a meeting in October between the two, Hearst's humiliation was final—and complete. "Will . . . was obligated to wait until that stern individual was ready to look up and then speak to him," Phebe informed her husband. "The Dean then said, '*You here again?* I thought the letter I sent to San Francisco would keep you there.'" Nor was any inkling of conciliation or rapprochement apparent; the dean would not give "any encouragement," obviously intent upon getting "rid of him." And at the next faculty meeting in February, 1886, he did.[4]

Despite such a humbling experience, Hearst was by no means dispirited. During the fall and winter of 1885–86 he continued his studies intermittently but, to Phebe's distress, devoted an increasing amount of time to less demanding pursuits. Since his father kept him liberally supplied with cash, as much as $250 a month, despite Phebe's protests to the contrary, he frequently attended dinners and plays in New York City with Harvard classmates. He also escorted a number of young ladies to the theater in Washington, his mother noted somewhat disconsolately, specifically a beautiful young actress named Eleanor Calhoun, a Californian from Tulare County who claimed to be a descendant of John C. Calhoun of South Carolina. Yet Washington, of all cities, held a special fascination for Hearst—the sessions of Congress where issues were debated and laws affecting the American people were enacted, the newly dedicated and awe-inspiring Washington Monument, and the presence of tradition and history at practically every corner. His father's desire to become an active participant in national politics also piqued his ambition and stimulated his dreams; indeed, the lure of public office tantalized Hearst throughout his life. He urged his father to buy "a suitable residence" in Washington for the Hearsts (both father and son) and thus house "the future leaders of the Democratic party"—a U.S. senator and a congressman from California. Nor should his father worry about having to hunt for an appropriate abode, young Will wrote enthusiastically. He had found an appropriate "house . . . (106 x 106 ft.)," which included "*furniture*, the stable, and the lot on which the stable stands . . . for the disgusting small sum of $159,000." Hearst also suggested a finder's fee of 3 percent "to your affectionate son," and then asked: "Shall we draw on Wells & Fargo for the amount or will you send the money by mail?" [5]

In the spring of 1886, with "rustication" by Harvard a reality, Hearst decided to pursue a new field of endeavor; he went to New York City and hired on as a reporter for Joseph Pulitzer's *New York World*. Since his days on the Harvard *Lampoon* all aspects of journalism, especially advertising techniques, had fascinated him. Whenever possible, Hearst had familiarized himself with the newspaper business, from basic plant mechanics to new inventions and time-saving improvements. In the spring of 1884, after obtaining an introduction to Charles H. Taylor, the distinguished proprietor of the *Boston Globe*, he was allowed to haunt both its editorial and press rooms as well as all areas of the plant, his interest focusing as much on the latest methods of photoengraving as on the *Globe*'s new high-speed presses. [6]

As his interest in journalism grew, Hearst developed an all-consuming ambition to be a newspaperman—from which he would never waver or falter. Since George Hearst had bought the *San Francisco Examiner* in October, 1880, specifically as a propaganda organ to further his own career in Democratic politics, Hearst began comparing the *Examiner* with other West Coast journals as well as the *New York Post*, *New York Tribune*, and especially the *New York World*, which he considered to be "the best newspaper" in the country. He was appalled at his findings and therefore sent letters periodically to his father that not only damned *Examiner* policies but were also rife with constructive criticism. As early as January 4, 1885, while still at Harvard, he suggested that his father hire as editor of the *Examiner* the experienced, albeit high-priced Ballard Smith, formerly of the *New York Herald*. Again later in the year he sent the *Examiner* editor a letter that castigated the "illustrations, if you may call them such," he informed his father, "which have lately disfigured the paper." Without a doubt they were "the crowning absurdity of illustrated journalism," bearing "an unquestionable resemblance to the Cuticura Soap advertisement." And again in January, 1886, he wrote his father that, in comparing the illustrations of the *New York World* with those of the *Examiner*, he found the pictures to be an "insult to our readers" and "of repulsive deformity." In fact, the accompanying article represented, he caustically asserted, an "imbecility so detestable that it would render the death of the writer justifiable homicide." [7]

In the fall of 1885, however, the twenty-two-year-old Hearst demonstrated in a remarkable letter to his father an unusual depth of understanding about newspapers as well as an extraordinary insight concerning
journalism of the future. Equally important, he revealed a confidence in
his own abilities, outlining his ideas and ambitions, which were the culmination of his newspaper experiences during the past two years. In part, the
letter read:

Dear Father:

    ... I have begun to have a strange fondness for our little paper—a ten-
derness like unto that which a mother feels for a puny or deformed offspring, and I should hate to see it die now after it had battled so long and so
nobly for existence; in fact, to tell the truth, I am possessed of the weakness
which at some time or other of their lives pervades most men. I am con-
vinced that I could run a newspaper successfully.

    Now if you should make over to me the *Examiner*—with enough money
to carry out my schemes—I'll tell you what I would do. In the first place I
would change the general appearance of the paper and make seven wide
columns where we now have nine narrow ones, then I would have the type
spaced more, and these two changes would give the pages a much cleaner
and neater appearance. Secondly, it would be well to make the paper as far
as possible original, to clip only when absolutely necessary and to imitate
only some such leading journal as the New York World which is undoubtedly the best paper of that class to which the *Examiner* belongs—that class
which appeals to the people and which depends for its success upon enterprise, energy and a certain startling originality and not upon the wisdom
of its political opinions or the lofty style of its editorials. And to accomplish this we must have—as the *World* has—active, intelligent and energetic young men; we must have men who come out west in the hopeful
buoyancy of youth for the purpose of making their fortunes and not a
worthless scum that has been carried there by the eddies of repeated failures. Thirdly, we must advertise the paper from Oregon to New Mexico
and must also increase our number of advertisements if we have to lower
our rates to do it, thus we can put on the first page that our circulation is
such and advertisements so and so and constantly increasing. And now
having spoken of the three great essential points let us turn to details. The
illustrations are a detail, though a very important one. Illustrations embellish a page; illustrations attract the eye and stimulate the imagination of
the lower classes and materially aid the comprehension of an unaccus-
tomed reader and thus are of particular importance to that class of people
which the *Examiner* claims to address. Such illustrations, however, as have
heretofore appeared in the paper, nauseate rather than stimulate the
imagination and certainly do anything but embellish a paper. Another de-

tail of questionable importance is that we actually or apparently establish some connection between ourselves and the New York World, and obtain a certain prestige in bearing some relation to that paper. We might contract to have important private telegrams forwarded or something of that sort, but understand that the principal advantage we are to derive is from the attention such a connection would excite and from the advertisement we could make of it. Whether the World would consent to such an arrangement for any reasonable sum is very doubtful, for its *net profit* is over one thousand dollars a day and no doubt it would consider the *Examiner* as beneath its notice. Just think, over one thousand dollars a day and four years ago it belonged to Jay Gould and was losing money rapidly.

And now to close with a suggestion of great consequence, namely, that all these changes be made not by degrees but at once so that the improvement will be very marked and noticeable and will attract universal attention and comment....

Well, good-by. I have given up all hope of having you write to me.... By the way, I heard you had bought 2,000 acres of land the other day and I hope some of it was in the land adjoining our ranch that I begged you to buy in my last letter.

> Your affectionate son,
> W. R. Hearst[8]

As a reporter for Pulitzer's *World* in 1886, Hearst solidified his convictions concerning reforms for the *Examiner* as well as intensifying his ambitions to institute them personally. And why? Through example, the *World* was a constant catalyst, a daily reminder of what he thought future journalism ought to be. As Hearst biographer W. A. Swanberg so aptly put it: "If a man can be in love with a newspaper, Hearst was downright passionate about the *World*." During the day Hearst continually "picked the brain" of Ballard Smith, now an editor for the *World*, whose brilliance awed him to the point of reverence. Oftentimes in the evening at his residence at the Hoffman House (usually at the hotel bar) Hearst discussed the many different aspects of journalism with Samuel S. Chamberlain, a "fashion plate" complete with monocle in the eye and gardenia in his lapel, whose experiences on a number of newspapers both intrigued and fascinated him. And often at night he spread the pages of the *World* about his room—a habit that he continued throughout his life—in an attempt to dissect the different features of the day's edition. And such an examination further confirmed his ideas for overhauling the *Examiner*.

Here was what Hearst increasingly realized. In this new journalism, the *World* catered to the immigrant, the workingman, the semiliterate, who had swelled the population of New York City to almost 3 million. Headlines were therefore of utmost importance for an urban newspaper; they must be concise, direct, informative—and definitely "bold" and large in type. As one immigrant put it, the headlines "are easy to understand, and you know all the news." Sketches, both profuse and descriptive, were a necessary companion to any story, which must be told in a simple, direct way; in other words, the sentence structure must be "uncomplicated" and the vocabulary "simple." Equally important, reporters must focus on stories of interest: the ageless success formula of love and sex, tragedy and pathos, crime and violence. But above all else, Hearst realized that the *World* was entertaining, with stories having to do with sensationalism as well as local concerns. This formula, overall, meant increased circulation for the *World*—15,770 copies on May 6, 1883, to 153,213 copies on May 10, 1885—hence, a rush by businessmen to place advertisements before such a wide audience.[9]

George Hearst, who believed that "newspapers aren't a business . . . they are deficits," became extremely concerned about his son; he hoped to substitute a more substantial, and definitely a more lucrative, occupation for this journalistic fascination. But none of his suggestions and ideas, no matter how grandiose, appealed to young Will. On a trip to Mexico he had him invite as guests two of his closest friends, Gene Lent and Jack Follansbee. After they had lived for weeks like "Spanish grandees" at the one-million-acre Babicora ranch in Chihuahua—"on four plateaus separated by mountain ranges"—George Hearst promised to deed it over immediately, provided that Will would accept management responsibilities; the answer was a resounding "no." He could not do that "business better than anybody else." George Hearst then offered him the beautiful 275,000-acre San Simeon ranch north of San Luis Obispo; next the productively rich Anaconda copper mines in Montana; and finally the pièce de résistance, the fabulous Homestake gold mine in South Dakota. All proffers received the same response: "You are very kind but I'd rather have the *Examiner*."[10]

Ever so gradually in 1886 Will Hearst strove to attain his dream. For a number of months, while working for the *World*, he continued to observe and investigate firsthand all aspects of its operations. Whenever possible he sounded out experienced newsmen such as Sam Chamberlain, posing questions to which they could apply their journalistic knowledge. But most of all he sought the services of the *World*'s new editor, his hero Ballard Smith, who more than once received the full Hearst persuasion treatment to desert the *World* for the *Examiner*. In fact, young Will proposed a

$7,000 salary, which his father objected to as outrageously high. He thus, in a somewhat admonishing tone, replied: "You must reconcile yourself to paying the salary or give up the *Examiner*. It has been conclusively proven that poor wages and mediocre talent will not do, and the only thing that remains to be tried is first-class talent and corresponding wages." He then suggested that they "guarantee" to Smith "a certain interest in the paper in case ... of a glittering success." Yet in this struggle, wherein George Hearst resisted temporarily the expensive innovativeness of his son and Phebe Hearst hoped to persuade young Will to follow a more respectable profession, possibly becoming an American diplomat, one idea emerged that terrified both parents. Ballard Smith, upon refusing Hearst's final persuasive offers, suggested: "Don't hire any of these high-priced New York editors. Be your own editor. In my opinion, you are qualified right now to edit a newspaper." [11]

In the meantime, political events in California were also working in his favor. In March, 1886, after U.S. Republican senator John F. Miller died, George Hearst received the ad interim appointment from Democratic governor George Stoneman; then in January, 1887, Hearst was elected by the California legislature to a full six-year term. So the *Examiner*, which for almost seven years had been a costly propaganda tool for George Hearst on behalf of himself as well as California Democrats, took on added significance, a fact that Will Hearst fully realized. Late in 1886 he visited the *Globe-Democrat* in St. Louis to interview H. H. Small as a possible business manager for the *Examiner*. But what impressed him most after a tour of the plant, he wrote his father, was "the magnificent press which . . . prints and pastes—Pastes, mind you, four or six or eight or *ten* or twelve pages and is one of the finest if not the finest machine in the country." Again late in January or early February, 1887, he wrote: "I am anxious to begin work on the *Examiner*. I have all my pipes laid, and it only remains to turn on the gas." Then, in discussing what results would take place due to his management, he confidently predicted: "In a year we will have increased at least ten thousand in circulation. In two years we will be paying. And in five years we will be the biggest paper on the Pacific slope. We won't be paying for two years because up to that time I propose turning back into the improvement of the paper every cent that comes in." [12]

George Hearst readily admitted that he "did not understand his son." But he did know one fact for certain: he could not resist the demands of young Will—money, property, and least of all a dream. "There's one thing sure about my boy Bill," he once observed. "I've been watching him, and I notice that when he wants cake, he wants cake; and he wants it now. And I notice that after a while he gets his cake." That was exactly what happened. After being informed by his accountant that, with his son as editor, the *Examiner* would probably cost him $100,000 a year, he exclaimed: "Hell! That ain't no money." So on March 4, 1887, a notice on page 2 of the *Examiner* read: W. R. Hearst . . . Proprietor.[13]

Such a transfer of power and direction attracted little attention in the San Francisco journalistic community at first. After all, Will Hearst was a millionaire's son, a supposed dilettante who had a new toy to play with, a young man who needed something to do with his time. His past record at various schools, of wasteful expenditures and outlandish pranks, of hedonistic impulses and self-indulgence, surely did not inspire confidence. Nor, for that matter, did his appearance and demeanor. Within two months of being twenty-four, Hearst was of size at six feet, one inch, yet not powerfully built—noticeably slender but not all arms and legs. Although easily recognizable by his flamboyant cravats and expensive, sometimes excessive attire, he was not impressive in appearance, with blond, brownish hair (parted in the middle), pale skin, and blue-grayish eyes that were unfathomable and "curiously close together." A straight, strong nose, fringed by a well-trimmed mustache, which partially obscured thin lips, dominated a face that was not handsome, yet at the same time not unappealing. But most striking about Hearst was his speaking ability, or lack thereof, his voice that of a high tenor and his delivery being a cross between Harry Truman and Truman Capote—at times a slight lisp was apparent.[14]

But those who did not take Hearst seriously would soon realize their mistake, as the *Examiner* changed, according to the reader's perspective, either gradually or radically. As early as February 20, 1887, when he was already on the job, the front-page makeup began to take on a new face. One-half-inch black headlines, usually three or four in eight columns (instead of nine), appeared where previously one-fourth-inch headlines had been the standard. By March 8 these attention-getters increased to every column and were up and down the page instead of only at the top. Above the masthead in the upper left-hand corner—and within two weeks also in the upper right-hand corner—and bordered in black, a comment or statement extolled the paper (and its leadership) to readers. For instance, it stated on March 5, "The *Examiner* has startled the community with its *New York Herald* cablegrams and fairly taken the bull by the horns—*Jewish Progress*"; on March 6, "The remarkable enterprise displayed by the *San Francisco Examiner* places it at once in the lead of all Pacific Coast Journals. There is evidently a master hand at the helm—*Dixon* (Cal.) *Tribune*"; and on March 7, "The Examiner was compelled to print an extra edition [Sunday's paper] of 5000 copies." Whereas under the old management several columns of advertisements had sometimes occupied the right side of page one, news stories from around the world, each one significantly recognized as "[special to the Examiner]," were now prominently displayed. And whereas the Examiner had been a blatant advertisement for the Democratic Party and its previous proprietor, such propaganda was noticeably absent. In fact, the name of Senator George Hearst did not appear in print until May 3, 1887—and then on page three.[15]

Equally significant was the overall philosophy and direction of the Examiner. Hearst, at least for the moment, did not object to being thought of as the Joseph Pulitzer of West Coast journalism. He was determined to cater to the masses, to make his paper a family attraction, to create public concern as well as local pride in what was occurring in San Francisco and California. As a consequence, increased circulation would attract more business advertisements, which he considered essential to the existence of "a first-class paper." Hearst specifically became concerned about auction advertisements that Surveyor General R. P. Hammond and Collector of the Port John S. Hager were diverting to rival papers. "I want you to use your political influence . . . [with President Grover Cleveland] and help me for a while," he candidly wrote his father in March, 1887. "We are bound to succeed but whether we succeed in one year or in five depends largely upon the work of all of us." Although never recording whether his father was successful, Hearst did begin publishing a full page of auction sales on April 1. In anticipation of such expansion, he announced on March 10 that the daily edition would be enlarged from six to eight pages and the Sunday paper from twelve to sixteen. Yet to emphasize the importance of reading the Examiner, of using its pages for advertisements, he followed the philosophy that everyone wanted to be associated with a winner. On March 11, in half-page advertisements, he publicized the Examiner as the "MONARCH OF THE DAILIES! THE LARGEST, BRIGHTEST AND BEST NEWSPAPER ON THE PACIFIC COAST," which had "Thousands of New Readers! Eight Pages Every Day! Over 3,000 Pictures Each Year!"[16]

To back up such claims Hearst surrounded himself with the best staff that friendship and money could buy. From his Lampoon days at Harvard he brought in Gene Lent (financial and social), Fred Briggs (cartoonist), and E. L. "Phinney" Thayer, who later won literary fame for his poem "Casey at the Bat." They were subsequently joined by Francis Lester Hawks "Cosy" Noble, who became Sunday editor. Then Hearst, after shocking managing editor E. B. Henderson into retirement with his "radical" ideas, recruited his old drinking companion Sam Chamberlain from New York City and furnished him unlimited funds to hire a "crackerjack reportorial staff." [17]

So late in the 1880s, from newsrooms across the United States, talented but underpaid warriors of the press became attracted to this new California Valhalla, where a young Odin showered them with presents for "scoops" in investigative reporting, rewarded their versatility and good writing with bonuses or salary increases, and encouraged their enterprise and imagination to follow Hearst's ultimate credo: "Get results." What a fantastic corps of individuals the *Examiner* assembled! Scottish-born, acid-tongued Arthur McEwen, ably assisted by Mark Twain's nephew Sam Moffett, became the major editorial writers; and Joe Ward, aided by the competent A. M. "Andy" Lawrence, agreed to be city editor. Prominent investigative reporters, whom Hearst fondly nicknamed the "*Examiner* detective corps," were such incisive, insightful journalists as Edward H. Hamilton, Frederick Lawrence, William N. Hart, and Charles Michelson as well as Henry D. "Petey" Bigelow and Edward Morphy, "both flagrantly unreliable in their habits but able writers, hence pardonable." Running the sports department, which Hearst enthusiastically promoted, was "Big Bill" Naughton, who was assisted by turf expert Charles Travathan and two talented baseball writers, Jake Dressler and Charles Dryden. The art department, under Charles Tebbs, included Homer Davenport, Jimmy Swinnerton, T. A. "Tad" Dorgan, Haydon Jones, Harrison Fisher, Theo Hamp, Harold Carter, and "Bud" Fisher. The business office personnel were especially efficient, headed by Charles Palmer and William F. "Bogey" Bogart, and eventually Edward W. Townsend, the trusted private secretary to Senator George Hearst. And as a final complement to this well-paid and star-studded cast, Ambrose Bierce, "widely admired—and even more widely feared" because of his brilliant satire and caustic wit—was compelled (by an economic offer he could not refuse) to join the *Examiner* staff. He agreed to write a Sunday column called "Prattle," which would "not be edited" by anyone and would appear regularly on the editorial page beginning on March 17, 1887. [18]

Possibly the best example of Bierce's style was the description of his first encounter with Hearst. Upon hearing "a gentle tapping" at his apartment door, the asthmatic Bierce, who was a master of invective and sarcasm and denigration, answered, only to find, he wrote, "a young man, the youngest young man, it seems to me, that I had ever confronted. His appearance, his attitude, his entire personality suggested extreme diffidence."

The dyspeptic Bierce, with customary politeness and usual cordiality, said: "Well?"

> To which the young man replied "in a voice like the fragrance of violets made audible: 'I am from the *San Francisco Examiner*' . . . and backed away a little."
>
> "Oh," Bierce exclaimed, "you come from Mr. Hearst?"
>
> "Then that unearthly child lifted his blue eyes and cooed, 'I am Mr. Hearst.'" [19]

Late in March, with the nucleus of *Examiner* personnel in place, the psychological warfare against competitors, the all-out assault to attract subscribers and gain new advertisements began in earnest. San Franciscans, indeed Californians, had never seen anything like it. Besides solid news coverage on the national and international levels, the *Examiner* dealt with individual frailties, sex and crime, economic failures, as well as human-interest stories and strange or mysterious happenings to San Franciscans. Headlines constantly focused on, indeed overworked such adjectives or nouns as "fatal," "tragic," "crime," "victim," "suicide," "slain," "accidental"; stories regularly appeared concerning women—divorce, infidelity, love, hardship, depravity, misadventure. [20]

But the *Examiner* was more than a litany of human suffering. Hearst expanded sports coverage from two to five and six columns, then placed horse racing, baseball games, boxing, even yachting on page one. He also emphasized community achievements and leadership, supplying biographical sketches and pictures on area nurses, firefighters, labor leaders, and exceptional students. He ran serial stories—Jules Verne's "The Clipper of the Clouds" and "North and South," Julian Hawthorne's "The Great Bank Robbery," and H. Rider Haggard's "Allan Quatermain." And in the Sunday edition (usually on page twelve or fourteen) he published the words and music of stage-play songs ("'The Toboggan Slide' as sung in Edward Haggard's New Play *McNooney's Visit*"). Yet what Hearst encouraged, in fact demanded, of his men was that the news never be boring, never be dull or hackneyed—and that meant not only imaginative, skilled writing but also an emphasis on the "scoop," with accompanying illustrations or cartoons. Possibly the goateed Scotsman Arthur McEwen put it best. "Any issue the front page of which failed to elicit a 'Gee Whiz!' from its readers was a failure, whereas the second page ought to bring forth a 'Holy Moses!' and the third an astounded 'God Almighty!'" [21]

Hearst, although claiming a "great scoop" on March 28 that gave the results of an international yacht race, did not fire his first major salvo at the San Francisco populace until six days later. After learning that the seaside luxury Hotel Del Monte in Monterey had burned during the night of April 1, he immediately hired a special train from the Southern Pacific and emptied the *Examiner* offices to cover the disaster. As a result, on Sunday, April 3, the *Examiner's* front page was alive with such headlines as "HUNGRY FRANTIC FLAMES. They Leap Madly Upon the Splendid Pleasure Palace by the Bay of Monterey!" With three eye-catching sketches from "on the Spot by Our Special Artist" prominently displayed, one reporter described in detail what had happened, while others recounted the "personal experiences" of a number of guests, the heroism of a man who saved "his daughter and her child," and the possibility of arson by "dissatisfied workmen." Yet, no matter what the topic, the ever-present theme was the extraordinary service provided by the *Examiner* in publishing three editions demanded by its news-hungry subscribers and "the efforts [and expense] put forth . . . to give . . . faithful and vivid pictures," which were obviously the correct responses of a "great paper." [22]

For the next three months this display of constant braggadocio, of imaginative investigation and reporting, of psychological warfare against opposition journals continued. San Franciscans never knew what would appear next. But they were ever expectant, ever informed and entertained—and seldom disappointed. Specific themes seemed to take precedence. For instance, personal interviews with prominent personages required both pictures and space. Actress Lily Langtry talked at length with an *Examiner* reporter about buying a home in California, about her "faithful" little Chinese lad named Moe, and her opinion concerning "certain other English actors"; Queen Kapiolani of Hawaii allowed an *Examiner* newsman to accompany her royal party during daylong festivities in San Francisco; and actress Sarah Bernhardt became practically a captive after Hearst sent a "special correspondent 374 miles into the Nevada desert [Virginia City] to meet her." As a guest of the *Examiner*, she "visited points of interest in San Francisco, including Chinatown at night."[23]

Concern for civic improvement and individual betterment received considerably more coverage. Almost immediately the *Examiner* campaigned against, and helped defeat, a new city charter that "would entrench the local bosses in power." Better-paved streets, a more efficient sewer system, well-built schools, and competent teaching were constant demands. Yet Hearst looked past obvious public concerns. At his direction, one *Examiner* reporter got himself admitted to the House of Inebriates, which "received monthly municipal aid." After two frightful weeks in residence he wrote an exposé revealing conditions that should "not be permitted to exist in any portion of the civilized world." Still another staff

member investigated the Home of the Adult Blind, where the superintendent had "installed himself and family" in a "handsome residence" and
"where he ... [opened] champaign [sic] for his friends"—all at the taxpay-
ers' expense. The *Examiner* thus demanded an immediate investigation by
the grand jury.[24]

The staff concentrated the news even more on crime and police venal-
ity. And in these areas Hearst had a field day, since graft and corruption
seemed to be a way of life in San Francisco. In May, 1887, several *Examiner*
reporters uncovered a monstrous plot in which a "band of murderers" in
the city was "killing men to collect insurance." Again in June another story
revealed that the Police Insurance Fund had been "plundered," thus rob-
bing widows of much-needed subsistence. Still again in June a staff reporter discovered that police had promised "a favor to a complaining
witness" in lieu of dropping charges against a fellow officer. And who was
to blame for such blatant wrongdoing? To the *Examiner* the answer was
obvious—"Law-Breakers in Public Office," naming specifically "the three
police commissioners—Deford, Tobin, and Hammond—as well as the
Police Clerk ... [Alfred] Clarke." In fact, editorial after editorial acidly demanded a grand-jury investigation which would validate all charges and
revelations.[25]

But more than anything else, the *Examiner* was fresh in its approach,
creative in its methods, imaginative in its proposals—and willing to spend
money, regardless of the amount, to satisfy its growing constituency. For
the "detection and conviction of any person" who stole the *Examiner* from a
subscriber's residence, Hearst offered a $50 reward. And for those who
wished to read their "favorite newspaper" at breakfast on Sunday morning, he contracted three, then four, special trains to speed out of San Francisco at an early hour to all parts of the state.[26]

Whatever the strides of the *Examiner*, whatever the progress, Hearst
was responsible. He was the glue that held his "madhouse" of journalists
together, the catalyst that spurred them to uncover startling, at times dramatic happenings. "So full of ideas that they tumbled over each other," he
seemed always to be at hand, checking editorials, making suggestions concerning sketches and cartoons, sending his "talented and erratic young
men" into all parts of the city to obtain "scoops." He was the focal point of
staff camaraderie and esprit de corps, "a mad boss," George P. West recounted, "who flung away money, lived like a ruler of the late Empire at his
house above the water at Sausalito, and cheered them on ... [to make]
newspaper history."[27]

Yet Hearst never revealed to staff members another side of his character, the one of doubts and worries, of fears and frustrations; he reserved those only for his parents. Although to the outside world he philosophized that "nothing that is live and vigorous is tranquil," those first months on the *Examiner* undermined such reasoning considerably. "I don't suppose I will live more than two or three weeks if this strain keeps up," he confided to his mother late in the spring of 1887. "I don't get to bed until two o'clock and I wake up at seven in the morning and can't get to sleep again, for I must see the paper and compare it to the [*San Francisco*] *Chronicle*. If we are the best I can turn over and go to sleep with quiet satisfaction but if the *Chronicle* happens to scoop us, that lets me out of all sleep for the day." And then he candidly admitted: "The newspaper business is no fun and I had no idea quite how hard a job I was undertaking when I entered upon the editorial management of the *Examiner*." At about the same time he wrote his father that "right now is a crisis in the history of our paper. If we hesitate a moment or fall back a step we are lost and can never hope to make anything out of the *Examiner* while it remains in our hands." He therefore asked his father for help—"to get" Senator Leland Stanford and other influential Californians "interested in the progress of the paper" and "to make friends with . . . powerful eastern newspapermen," even the "nasty, unscrupulous, damned" *New York World*, "because the Jew [Pulitzer] who owns it . . . is too powerful for us to insult."

Late in the fall of 1887, when circulation had almost doubled, Hearst wrote his father that "I positively will go crazy about this paper unless I get some help." He thus urged the senator, in a rare outburst of profanity, to apply pressure on "McAtee, Baldwin and Hammond and Tevis and Fisher [who] withdrew ads and went over to the *Chronicle*. As these sons of bitches are principally indebted to you for whatever they have, I think this is the goddamdest low down business I ever heard of. I don't apologize for the swear words for I think the circumstances excuse them." In fact, Hearst was so concerned that he reverted completely from his old ways, refusing a $1,000 Christmas gift. "Money is so tight and Stump [the business accountant] is borrowing so much that I guess I won't take it," he stated, concluding that "using your influence for the paper" will be "all the Xmas I want." [28]

Because of his father's political and financial support, Hearst was free to pursue his quest for circulation and advertisements, to enhance this new kind of journalism on the West Coast. During the "dog days of summer" in 1887, with headlines at a premium, the *Examiner* seemed at times to lose momentum, as accounts of baseball games and other sports occupied almost half the front-page columns. Yet, with regularity, the staff provided San Franciscans with interesting exposés. Beginning on July 20, *Examiner* journalists investigated Folsom Prison, which was "worse than the Bastil[l]e." For two weeks they interviewed prison personnel and inmates, who painted a sickening picture of inhumane existence—unsavory living conditions, bland and at times unpalatable food, the brutality of prisoners and guards, and the ultimate punishment: a pit called the "Black Hole," where incorrigibles were dropped into the nothingness of solitary confinement. Then during the next three months the "*Examiner* detective corps" bested the police in a number of cases, finding a thirteen-year-old girl who had been missing for four days, solving two murders, one in which a man had been wrongfully convicted, and unearthing information that a former city councilman, together with a female accomplice, had lured young girls into posing nude for photographs, which would "destroy their souls." [29]

At the same time the *Examiner* took firm stands on certain local and national issues. During the fall of 1887 and the winter of 1888, editorial after editorial railed against police corruption, epitomized by Police Clerk Alfred Clarke; on December 19 he was finally pressured to resign. In both January and February, 1888, editorial lamentations concerning "educational failure" demanded more money for school facilities and higher teacher salaries. And intermittently the *Examiner* criticized Congress for high tariff acts, which hurt both farmers and laborers; demanded stricter legislation on Chinese immigration; and supported a "strong defense," especially in regard to the building of a new American navy and better harbor defenses at San Francisco. [30]

More significantly, however, the *Examiner* reflected the imaginative processes of Hearst's mind as well as a genius in sales techniques. For *Examiner* subscribers wishing to celebrate July 4, Hearst prominently displayed on page one a coupon ticket to clip out that entitled them to a free picnic and a boat ride around San Francisco Bay. For "bright school children" he formulated a newspaper quiz that they should bring to the *Examiner* office in the "afternoon between three and six o'clock"; those who answered correctly received a "Scholar's Companion . . . a strong, neatly finished, seven-inch box . . . containing a six-inch rule, a lead-pencil, slate-pencil and pen holder." For businessmen and individuals who could not afford a large outlay in a newspaper, Hearst initiated the "Small Ad"—inexpensive one, two, or three lines—and then dramatically opened six new *Examiner* offices for their convenience. And for Californians who proudly reveled in their name and wished further recognition for their state, he lobbied the Democratic Party to bring its national convention to San Francisco in the summer of 1888. Despite considerable expense (an estimated $80,000), Hearst and part of the *Examiner* staff moved to Washington, D.C., in February to win this campaign and on two consecutive days published 10,000 copies of the newly created *Washington Examiner*. Although unsuccessful in this undertaking, he achieved a tremendous amount of public goodwill for the *Examiner*.[31]

On March 4, 1888, the *Examiner*, although established as early as 1865, celebrated its first birthday, the length of time that Hearst had been in charge. What changes a year had wrought! While critics have argued that the *Examiner* circulation had "almost quadrupled, rising from 8,000 to 30,000" in the six years prior to his takeover (1881–87) and that his journalism was "borrowed," demonstrating "no evidence" of "any originality at all"—the *New York Times* (in the Boss Tweed investigations during the 1860s) and Pulitzer's *World* had already used the exposé effectively and "E. W. Scripps [had] established the first newspaper chain in 1875"—Hearst's rivals in the San Francisco area, the *Chronicle* and *Call* and *Bulletin*, were hard-pressed to agree. For a year Hearst had assaulted them with his ideas, his unusual tactics and procedures as well as a new breed of reporter, all seemingly without regard to cost. And whether or not his journalism was "borrowed," it surely was revolutionary to West Coast newspapers, forcing them to imitate in order to compete. Almost daily Hearst bombarded them with statistics, exulting in the rapid growth of the *Examiner* and thus blatantly expounding that no other newspaper was meeting the needs of its constituency. During this first year under Hearst, the *Examiner* almost "doubled in circulation," the daily edition expanding from 26,475 to 49,790 and the Sunday paper from 26,000 to 57,000. Accordingly, the "Want Ads" had grown dramatically, averaging 625 per day for a 25 percent increase from the previous year, all of which reinforced, the *Examiner* proudly claimed, its chosen appellation "Monarch of the Dailies."[32]

Hearst thus continued his formula of success during the next two years, concentrating on themes of public concern while discarding projects of questionable interest. Even more fully than the previous twelve months, the *Examiner* became a family newspaper, one that reflected the immediate interests and the daily anxieties of San Franciscans. First and foremost the *Examiner* was pro-Californian and pro-American, hence often xenophobic, especially regarding the Chinese, but also the Germans (after a U.S. naval confrontation at Samoa in January, 1889), and at times the French and English. But the "yellow peril" was omnipresent. In San Francisco the Chinese multiplied, the *Examiner* noted, at "an alarming rate."

The negative aspects of their culture and lifestyle were constantly denounced—opium dens, prostitution, payoffs to police, unwillingness to
speak English and participate in local affairs. But, more importantly, the
Chinese worked longer hours for less pay, thereby depriving Americans of
a livelihood in the factories and businesses in San Francisco as well as the
California vineyards and farms. So in January, 1889, the *Examiner* proposed a "labor train" that would bring "white labor" to the state, but after a
month, because of little public reaction, Hearst discarded this idea as un-
feasible. Late in February, 1889, he thus decided to open an *Examiner* un-
employment office as a "service"—and "no fee charged"—to "white male
and female" applicants of the city. It was an immediate success, the *Examiner* triumphantly claiming "175 positions filled" by the end of the first
week (March 3), 1,406 on March 31, and 4,753 on July 1. Unquestionably,
the *Examiner* was identifying with American workers.[33]

At the same time Hearst was determined to establish the reputation of
the *Examiner* as an organization whose objectives and goals served the
community, yet without the appearance of financial self-gain. Daily, in column after column, Hearst initiated two-line attention-getters such as
"ARE you looking for a house? See the 'Houses to Let' in the EXAMINER."
Or "YOUR 'Want' ad in SUNDAY'S EXAMINER will be seen by the most
people." Or "YOUR Little ad will be seen among the 1,000 'Want' ads in
SUNDAY'S EXAMINER." Or "WHEN looking for an investment, see the
real estate bargains in the EXAMINER."

Hearst also continued to instruct the "*Examiner* Detective Corps" to expose human frailties in city government and urban life. Hence, stories appeared with increasing frequency about conditions affecting the paper's
constituency in a negative way—the wretched life of women factory
workers, the disgraceful lack of money for public schools and teacher salaries and city parks, the need for a fully paid fire department because of
abominable safety standards in local theaters, schools, and churches, effective security regulations for local cable cars, and the outrageous overcharging of customers by the gas company (amounting to $70,000).[34]

But more than anything else, the *Examiner* was an interesting, indeed an
exciting newspaper. Or, as one historian observed, "in the vernacular of
any era it was fun to read" because no one, least of all Hearst's competitors,
knew what next to expect. The creativity and imagination—and
money—of Hearst made it happen. While still emphasizing national and
international news as well as sports on the front pages, the *Examiner* continued to concentrate on women's issues, shocking scandals, and human
tragedy. It proceeded to run such popular stories in serial form (usually

two a month) as Julian Hawthorne's "The Fatal Letter," Robert Louis Stevenson's "The Outlaws of Tunstall Forest," and H. Rider Haggard's "Cleopatra."

At the same time, reporters wrote exposés that were always informative and oftentimes amusing. What reader could keep from smiling about an *Examiner* newsman's report—and frantic plight—of being an inmate in the state insane asylum for a week, of a tortuous day-by-day account in the disciplined life of a Salvation Army volunteer, of the "shame" in being "snubbed" by parishioners (the reporter was disguised "in rags") at an affluent city church? Then, for a change of pace, one of the "*Examiner* Detective Corps" purportedly interviewed a notorious train robber, known as "Black Bart," in the primitive fastness of his mountain hideaway; another discovered a "missing man" for whom the police had been searching for ten days. And still another, upon investigating a local physician's claim of inventing "an elixir of life," discovered that several elderly men had received a youthful "injection" and that the secret ingredients had been partially extracted from dogs and lambs.[35]

Hearst, however, seemed inherently to understand the public mood as well as certain basic character traits of Americans: their competitive nature, their compulsion to enter contests, their desire to be a winner—and, if possible, render as true the old cliché "gain something for nothing." He therefore involved the *Examiner* in gamesmanship, in the psychology of attaining awards through participation. So Hearst increasingly applied his money to promotions. For instance, he offered a year's subscription of the *Examiner* for the outlandishly low price of $1.50, the huge Sunday edition for $2.00, and a weekly edition for $1.50. Then during April, 1888, he challenged *Examiner* readers to "guess" the total number of "Want" ads in the paper for the month, with the winner awarded $50 and the runner-up $25. Late in October he initiated a costly presidential polling survey in San Francisco, predicting that President Grover Cleveland would win over Republican rival Benjamin Harrison by as much as 7 percent. Then on election night (November 6) Hearst hosted a huge party in front of the *Examiner*, posting the vote results in large print on a giant canvas hanging from the building. And throughout December he offered "free books for children" to anyone placing an ad in the *Examiner*.[36]

As a result, on March 4, 1889, after two years at the helm, Hearst had reshaped and reinvigorated a dying paper. The *Examiner* boasted that daily circulation for the year had increased from 49,790 to 55,029 and the Sunday average from 57,000 to 62,240. The "Want" ads had again risen by more than 20 percent, the average now exceeding 800 per day. And although the *Examiner* was still not making a profit—from August, 1887, to August, 1888, Hearst had personally spent $47,939 and had "drawn for the *Examiner*" as much as $184,513—he was driving the *Call* toward bankruptcy and was forcing the *Chronicle* to emulate many of his ideas and activities.[37]

Yet Hearst was already mounting a more vigorous assault against his rivals. Even though admitting to his father that "the *Chronicle* is fighting tremendously hard, and ... does not hesitate to adopt any idea we bring out," he was confident of success. Despite Phebe's constant pleadings to put young Will on an economic leash, George Hearst became caught up in the dream of his son—and "backed" every endeavor of the *Examiner* with a seemingly endless flow of cash. Hence, young Will Hearst, oftentimes working at the *Examiner* well past midnight, established himself as the leader of this new breed of West Coast journalists, who commanded his "knights of the newsroom" to uncover evil and corruption within their city while serving as defenders of the poor and the disinherited.[38]

Hearst wasted little time in mounting his new offensive, sparing no cost. On March 10, 1889, he hired Tom Nast, formerly of *Harper's Weekly* and the foremost political cartoonist in the United States; and, thereafter, at least two or three times a week, a Nast rendition appeared, usually on the front page of the *Examiner*. In May and for two weeks in June, Hearst offered "a month's trip to Paris" to "the brightest boy or girl" in the San Francisco school system. After an intense competition, which the *Examiner* prominently displayed, a senior high student named May Ayers became the celebrated winner. Then in August he engaged readers in a "whodunit" mystery called "Written In Red" or "The Conspiracy in the North Case." The *Examiner* offered $100 for the "person nearest the solution of the authors"; on the last day of competition (September 15), the staff selected 3 winners out of 3,126 entries. And also in August, Hearst offered 3 "premium" books (eventually distributing 2,500) and prizes worth $25,000, including a ten-acre tract of land worth $1,500 and a $1,500 "thoroughbred, yearling filly"—of course, only to *Examiner* weekly subscribers.[39]

But even more impressive events were in store for San Franciscans. Since May, Hearst had been anticipating the acquisition of two new high-speed presses, appropriately named "Monarch" (of the Dailies) and "Jumbo," which printed as many as "twenty-four pages at a time." At last, on October 20, 1889, he was able to use them, publishing a Sunday edition of forty pages, with larger type, in seven columns instead of eight, and with a multitude of illustrations. The *Examiner* thus ran "99 Columns of

Ads" in an astounding one-day Sunday circulation of "over 100,000 copies." To add to this crescendo of journalistic endeavors, Hearst intrigued readers by initiating on October 29 a "Weather Probabilities Forecast" (at the top of page 1). Early in November, he captured their imagination even more by bringing "a monster grizzly" to the city zoo for "all to see." Hearst decided to distribute free tickets which, not too surprisingly, were attainable from the *Examiner's* upper left and right corners of the front page, so that San Franciscans, and especially the children, could witness firsthand, through the community service of a "concerned" newspaper, one of California's vanishing animals. For more than a week vast crowds were "fascinated" by the huge bear, which was named "Monarch." Then, just prior to Thanksgiving and the holiday season, Hearst opened his father's purse strings once again, offering valuable gifts—gold watches, gold bracelets, violins, bronze mantel figures as well as "handsome books"—to all children who sold at least three *Examiner* subscriptions.[40]

And during the fall, in rounding out his year-long campaign of innovation and creativity and salesmanship, Hearst hired Winifred Black —when women were "a novelty in the newspaper world"—as a reporter. Talented and able, she would become famous as the "first sob sister" of American journalism under the pen name of "Annie Laurie." Although previously a chorus girl with a touring theatrical group, she soon impressed colleagues with her imaginative talent and investigative abilities. For instance, late in October, she applied one of the "*Examiner* Detective Corps" ploys to test complaints that the city was not caring for its poor and "stricken." Disguised in the rags of a "street person," she collapsed on Market Street, one of the crowded thoroughfares. After a seemingly "interminable" length of time in which a crowd had gathered, a policeman with "a bourbon breath" finally appeared and ironically attempted to discern if she were drunk. After a jolting ride to the City Receiving Hospital in a police wagon, she suffered insults and "pawing" from "vulgar interns," was given hot water and mustard as an emetic, then unceremoniously discharged. As a result of her exposé on the hospital's lack of concern for the poor, a "shake-up" occurred and the attending physician was discharged.[41]

To cap the *Examiner's* year of accomplishment, Hearst decided on one last extravaganza, a final coup de grâce to the *Call* and *Chronicle*. On December 29, 1889, he published a "mammoth" Sunday edition of forty-four pages, whose 75,000 copies were sold out by 10:00 A.M. In keeping with the philosophy that the American public loves a winner, the *Examiner* bragged about its new circulation records—weekly, 64,500; Sunday, 62,623; daily, 55,680. And even though the *Examiner* was not as yet self-sustaining, the time was fast approaching. Hearst, in fewer than three years, had implemented his policies and was realizing his dream; the *Examiner* had indeed become the "Monarch of the Dailies." And as the new leader of West Coast journalism, he was readying himself for new challenges, for larger arenas of combat, for even more significant fields of endeavor.[42]

4 | "Monarch of the Dailies"

&

Excitement, anticipation, experimentation, the steady drumbeat of an organization on the rise! Such ideas, such emotions and expressions permeated the *Examiner* offices at the beginning of 1890—and for good reason. Already a staff of talented professionals, well trained in "sniffing out" the news and gifted in writing attention-getting stories, had passed the circulation of one city rival, the *Call*, and had drawn even with the previously dominant *Chronicle*. Compensatory recognition in the form of large salaries and generous bonuses was equally satisfying, thereby encouraging excellence and heightening morale. But most important a youthful employer, a kindred spirit who at times seemed to personify "a mad bull in a China shop," labored with them oftentimes past midnight, stimulating their imagination with his creativity. They thus sought daring assignments, even concocted outlandish schemes, because their leader required, indeed demanded, only two work standards, ability and loyalty, requisites that they abundantly displayed.[1]

Hearst, although sensing these feelings of exhilaration, of hope and optimism, realized that the *Examiner* was not yet self-sustaining, that the past three years of accomplishment could go for naught unless he pressed "for the kill" against his city rivals. As a consequence, he employed any inventive means, any technique or experiment, to attract new readers. And, as some of his colleagues recorded, the *Examiner* reflected his thinking and ingenuity, his confidence and daring. In many ways Hearst seemed to hold the "pulse" of San Franciscans; whatever he considered fascinating and entertaining seemed to please *Examiner* readers. Journalist Lincoln Steffens characterized it this way: "All Hearst papers" bore the "imprint of one common personality—William Randolph Hearst."[2]

And what was the Hearst "personality"? It was surely complex, often enigmatic, at times a bundle of contradictions; and, without question, his interests were unusual and multifaceted. More specifically, Hearst bordered on "genius," impressing the *Examiner* staff continually with a vivid imagination as well as an artistic temperament. Cartoonist Thomas Nast appreciated his concern and welcomed any suggestion; George E. Pancoast, who became his personal secretary and later invented a color press photography, argued that Hearst knew much more about the subject; in fact, no one seemed to have a greater knowledge or keener interest concerning presses and printing. Some observers characterized his intense concentration and penchant for work as "fanatical"—and, when applied to journalistic endeavors or one of his hobbies, it was.[3]

Hearst reveled in these first years on the *Examiner*. What great fun, what excitement, what challenges! He could play out his fantasies on a grandiose scale. Having never been denied anything by either parent, he operated on a "pleasure principle"—immediate satisfaction. And that meant experimenting with any idea that intrigued him and probing any new methods of journalism that created flare or provocation, all with the paramount intent of increasing circulation—and, of course, winning out over all competitors. Hence, the *Examiner* newsroom became a Hearst laboratory, "a happy and extravagant world" in which staff members, "drunk with life in a city that never existed before or since," were encouraged to stretch their imaginations and "make newspaper history."[4]

These talented, somewhat erratic men and women who composed the *Examiner* staff exulted in their leader, his optimism and ability, his attitude and eccentricities. Hearst, at age twenty-six, had not changed much over the past few years. Still slender, with a thin golden mustache and brownish-blond hair parted down the middle, he continued to wear expensive clothes and outlandish cravats. His voice, while possibly not sounding like "crushed violets made audible," was surely high-pitched and reedy. And, at times, he appeared, as staffer Florence Finch Kelly remembered, "boyish and slightly diffident in manner and still a bit under the influence of the impish high spirits of youth."[5]

Yet no one mistook this persona as a sign of weakness and vulnerability, not even Ambrose Bierce. Hearst was never "one of the boys," even though he cavorted with them at times in the pressroom or on one of his "invitational" outings. Everyone, except for a few longtime associates or friends, addressed him as "Mr. Hearst," never "Willie" or "Bill." Nor did he encourage familiarity. His mere formality of presence and obvious shyness, his brainpower and culture, set him apart. Colleagues marveled at his "tremendous vocabulary," his background in history and literature (Dickens and Shakespeare were his favorite authors), his awesome knowledge of art and the antiquities. And few could match his industry. "He was the hardest working person I ever knew," attorney John Francis Neyland recollected. In fact, cartoonist Jimmy Swinnerton laughingly remarked that "he killed off two or three secretaries working for him." Hence, Hearst found himself shut off from much of the world—and often alone.[6]

Yet Hearst had no one to blame but himself; he chose this way of life—and he wanted no other. Without question he was a nonconformist, unimpressed with social mores and caring not what others thought. He blatantly shocked San Franciscans by his association with Tessie Powers, the pretty barmaid he had "maintained" at Harvard after the departure of Jack Follansbee; Hearst now supported "the Harvard widow" (or "Dirty Drawers," as some mockingly referred to her) at his hillside home in the small fishing village of Sausalito across the bay from San Francisco. Much like his father, with whom he increasingly identified and sought approval, Hearst despised formal dinners, preferred a simple diet to French and Italian cuisines, and loathed parties, except those initiated by himself. Thus, not too surprisingly, he never sought the limelight, preferring to associate with the *Examiner* staff rather than those of his economic and social stature.[7]

Hearst, "without the loss of personal dignity," maintained a close camaraderie with the *Examiner* staff, a "supervised" display with little ceremony and no "high-hat" responses in the work place. He liked nothing better than to listen to or better yet, tell a good story, especially when able to forget his shyness and apply humor as well as effective mimicry, a talent he had polished so well as a boy. The staff also came to appreciate his eccentricities and methods of doing business. Sometimes, just prior to announcing a decision, he drummed his fingers nervously on a desk or table, but more often he appeared at the office door of Sam Chamberlain, then did an energetic "jig" or dance step before making a suggestion. When someone needed to discuss matters of importance, whether business or personal, Hearst became a devout listener, "never allowing his eyes off you" while patiently hearing the conversation.

Nor were such actions fabricated and insincere. He continually demonstrated a concerned responsibility for the *Examiner* staffers, at times elevating salaries of those in financial difficulties or, without their knowledge, paying off a debt. And whenever in the mood for relaxation, especially after a long workweek or a "scoop" over the opposition papers, Hearst invited staff members to celebrate with him by setting off firecrackers or flying kites. On more than one occasion he took them on balloon rides over the city (Hearst loved flying) or provided an afternoon and evening of sailing around the bay in his expensive yacht *Aquila*.

But the pièce de résistance, the ultimate reward, was a weekend invitation to San Simeon, his father's 275,000-acre ranch approximately 200 miles south of San Francisco, where Hearst was totally at peace with himself. On the rugged, arid mountains overlooking the Pacific at San Simeon Bay the visitors erected tents and built campfires, then went on horseback rides or fished for trout or hunted deer and quail with their host. And Hearst, who genuinely enjoyed cooking and was good at it, provided his guests a meal of venison with "special sauce" and, when possible, his favorite Harvard concoction of Welch rarebit.[8]

Hearst was an "easy boss" to work for. Although described by some as "puritanical" (he quit smoking while at Harvard and seldom drank more than a glass of wine), he placed few restrictions on the *Examiner* editors and reporters; he was, as biographer W. A. Swanberg noted, "remarkably indulgent with his prodigals." In the journalistic world of evening deadlines and pressure-filled "scoops," sobriety was often a stranger. Sam Chamberlain, who had helped Hearst fashion *Examiner* policies from their days in New York, was at times "in his cups," so much so that, when Hearst was on one of his periodic European trips, an *Examiner* editor cabled: "Chamberlain drunk again. May I dismiss him?" To which Hearst immediately replied: "If he is sober one day in thirty that is all I require." Arthur McEwen, the tall, goateed Scot, a brilliant editorial crusader with a cynical flair for justice, would often disappear after a long period of abstinence; in turn, his brother-in-law Charles Michelson, who was a young staffer, led a "rescue squad" through every saloon in the city to find him; again, on another occasion, Hearst searched for McEwen throughout the <u>Examiner</u> offices, eventually finding "him stretched comatose under the half-closed rolltop of his desk"—yet no dismissal. And still again, one reporter, who incurred a "disagreeable" assignment, "plead intoxication" and asked for a furlough. Several days later, "perfectly sober," he encountered Hearst, then lamely explained that "he had honestly intended to get drunk, but lacked the price." Ambrose Bierce, in utter disbelief, related: "Mr. Hearst gave him enough money to reestablish his character for veracity and passed on."[9]

Hearst, although fostering competition and, at times, rivalry among *Examiner* employees by crediting their works with bylines or giving generous bonuses, never wanted staffers to go elsewhere because of possible dissension or, for that matter, to be "fired," even if such action was warranted. "He kept a real sympathy for the submerged man and woman," journalist

Will Irwin observed, "a real feeling of his own mission to plead their cause." He also believed in his own intuitive judgment in choosing personnel, without reference to background checks and monetary demands. Even though Allen Kelly, as city editor, became disillusioned with certain *Examiner* policies and practices, Hearst willingly assigned him as a feature writer with "a sort of roving commission." After young printer George Pancoast became furious with copy editor Ike Allen for changing his written word and retaliated by displaying a sarcastically humorous but impudent poster, Hearst asked: "Who's the comedian?" Then, upon being introduced to Pancoast, he inquired: "Do you take shorthand?" "No," Pancoast replied, "but I can write longhand if you don't talk too fast." The response had just the right touch of humor; thus began a friendship and close working relationship that lasted a lifetime.[10]

But the most outrageous, yet clearly most illuminating episode showing Hearst's desire to maintain a loyal staff as well as displaying his enigmatic whims revolved around reporter Alfonso "Blinker" Murphy, a holdover from the George Hearst era. One night Assistant City Editor Jake Dressler, furious about the continual delinquency of Murphy, bellowed out in a deep bass voice across the *Examiner* offices: "You're fired!" Murphy instantly retorted in his distinct Irish brogue: "That's all ver-ry well, but you cannot fire me."

"The hell I can't!" Dressler yelled. Then as the two glared at each other, with all the staff watching, Murphy pivoted toward the luxurious "antique-furnished" office of the "boss," with Dressler in hot pursuit. Hearst, in shirtsleeves, looked up from his desk and asked them to tell him the problem. After each animatedly gave his own version of the quarrel, Hearst inquired somewhat hesitantly: "Mr. Murphy, it has always been my understanding that it was the right of the city editor to discharge a man if he felt it necessary. I don't know that we can make an exception. What reason do you have for suggesting we make one?"

"Mr. Hearst, I have a very good reason," Murphy instantly replied. "The reason is that I refuse to be fired."

Hearst sat silently for seemingly an interminable minute, momentarily stunned by the answer, then to his editor, "lifting his hands in resignation," smilingly commented: "Under the circumstances, Mr. Dressler, I don't see what we can do about this." Both participants and staffers soon enjoyed the humor of the situation—and the Hearst mystique continued to grow.[11]

Hearst created this enigmatic aura, this almost inexplicable persona, by inserting his ideas into the *Examiner* pages, by nourishing and developing his inner self through journalistic endeavors. Without a doubt, he was a promoter, a showman, in some ways a carnival huckster selling the wares of the *Examiner* to the public. But he was also an innovator, an "overgrown adolescent," as one observer put it, who experimented with different schemes, such as games and puzzles and contests, thereby foisting upon *Examiner* readers what he thought to be interesting and enjoyable and exciting. His imagination seemed to be inexhaustible, his ideas so many, biographer John Winkler admiringly noted, "that they tumbled over each other." And whether merely adapting previously tried programs or devising new schemes was irrelevant; Hearst revolutionized West Coast journalism and eventually that of the nation.[12]

What other newspaper intrigued its readers like the *Examiner?* What other journal was more entertaining? Hearst, always in his quest for increased circulation, continued his courtship of San Franciscans—businessmen, professionals, union laborers, teachers and students, city employees, and especially women. The editorial page was unusually fascinating, with constant demands on the local level for better roads, sewage disposal, schools, hospitals, fire and police protection; on the national front for low tariffs, an eight-hour workday, immigration restriction (especially the Chinese), the Australian (secret) ballot, direct election of senators, a strong navy, and a monetary system including the coinage of silver—all of which appealed to a majority of San Franciscans. Hearst, however, was determined to concern his readers to the point that the *Examiner* became an integral part of their lives. Hence, at Thanksgiving and Christmas he involved San Franciscans with local charities; at the behest of the *Examiner*, citizens donated money or toys or food and clothing to the orphaned and destitute—and, each day, Hearst encouraged such benevolence with still another innovation, that of printing the names of contributors, together with the amount given. He instituted such "firsts" in the daily *Examiner* as "Answers to Various Inquiries" (Letters to the Editor), "Of Interest to Women," a day for "Swaps and Sales" at the *Examiner* offices, and weather reports accompanied by area maps.

The Sunday *Examiner* was a greater crowd pleaser. Hearst continued his policy of numerous and impressive illustrations (sometimes a full page in size) as well as equally effective cartoons. He devoted three to four pages to the particular interests of women, such as Paris and New York fashions, home furnishings, cooking tips, and the latest area tidbits in a feature titled "Pandora's Gossip." Patrons of the arts learned about local stage shows and performers in "The Players' Column," enjoyed seeing the words and lyrics of a popular tune, and read the latest stories, sometimes in serial form, by such recognized (or soon-to-be-famous) authors as Jules Verne, H. Rider Haggard, Rudyard Kipling, Robert Louis Stevenson, A. Conan Doyle, Alexander Dumas, Gertrude Atherton, Ambrose Bierce, Bret Harte, and Mark Twain. Sports enthusiasts also received ample consideration with several pages devoted daily to baseball, football, racing, yachting, archery, or boxing (especially since heavyweight champion James J. "Gentleman Jim" Corbett was a "local boy"). And, for all, the *Examiner* provided exciting entertainment week after week in the form of puzzles and contests, in which prizes ranging from $20 to $10,000 tantalized Californians. At the same time, Hearst seemed determined to upgrade his audience intellectually and artistically by offering "for free" outstanding fiction and nonfiction works as well as prints of world-famous paintings. In fact, one historian mused that Hearst, in his role as proprietor of the *Examiner*, furnished every home in San Francisco with attractively covered walls and a considerable library.[13]

Hearst, while charming and delighting *Examiner* readers, surely mystified his cohorts, as he would throughout his life. For contemporaries and chroniclers alike he was an enigma, indeed, a continual "bundle of contradictions." While terribly shy and diffident, he was aggressive, even pugnacious, against competitors, funneling money into a project without regard to cost. Here was a man who disliked formal parties and crowds, yet was a mimic and showman with *Examiner* staffers and a blatant, at times obnoxious huckster through the pages of his newspaper. Although a workaholic and perfectionist, he was also impulsive in decision-making. And, through example, Hearst demonstrated intense loyalty and personal fidelity to his staff and associates, yet, ironically, while admired by many, had few close friends.[14]

In 1890, however, Hearst needed to increase circulation and thereby solve his financial problems. He therefore continued his journalistic onslaught against opposition newspapers; it was devastating. On January 1 he issued a forty-four-page edition of the *Examiner*, a mind-boggling, costly publication, the size of which stunned the *Call* and the *Chronicle*, and which impressed the readers, so much so that Hearst had to print more than ninety thousand copies. Three days later he scooped the competition by directing a life-saving operation at Point Bonita off Golden Gate, where five fishermen were perilously marooned on a "jagged rock." *Examiner* reporter Henry R. Haxton voluntarily "leaped into the boiling sea" and, with the help of former editor but now staff member Allen Kelly, saved one of the five stranded men from the "treacherous" waters. Consequently, the *Examiner* devoted a full front page, together with graphic illustrations, to this "heroic" rescue. Nor was Hearst reticent in pointing out to his readers that competing morning papers reported the "men still storm-bound on the rock." Again, late in January, Hearst sent help, as well as the "Sunday edition," to "blockaded" towns along the flooded Sacramento River, noting that the *Examiner* placed service to its customers above all else. And again, on February 1, 1890, he delivered supplies—without concern for cost—to a train snowbound in the Sierras for fourteen days, along with Allen Kelly and Winifred Black, to pique reader interest in passenger survival and to demonstrate once again that civic virtue was one of the paper's mainstays.[15]

But with the arrival of spring, Hearst decided that the *Examiner* news-room, which was appropriately referred to as "the madhouse," was not living up to its reputation, that he needed to inject a greater curiosity and feverish excitement into the paper's columns and recapture what Arthur McEwen referred to as "the gee-whiz emotion." So on April 6, even though financial "watchdog" Irwin Stump lamented that the Hearst family was spending $1 million a year, with much of it going to the *Examiner*—and therefore urging retrenchment—Hearst stunned San Franciscans by publishing a mammoth edition of fifty pages that announced a "contest of brains" known as "The *Examiner's* Census Competition." He offered an astounding $75,000 worth of prizes in the form of thoroughbreds, livestock, furniture, household articles, carriages, mining machinery, agriculture implements, and acreage, with the top two awards being a filly named "The Princess" ($7,500) and the "*Examiner* Premium Cottage" in San Francisco ($7,000). And what were the rules for entry? Californians must buy a year's subscription ($7.80) to the daily *Examiner* between April 1 and June 30; then, to win a prize, they must guess the closest population estimate for one of nineteen selected West Coast cities and states plus that of the United States in the forthcoming 1890 Census. To enlist subscribers Hearst sent staffers, at considerable expense, on an "*Examiner* Special Train," which visited towns and cities in the Sacramento and San Joaquin valleys during the next two months.[16]

But Hearst was by no means finished with his promotions, with his campaign to "snowball" circulation. During the first week of March, 1890, a staffer had written a rather innocent article titled "What is the Ideal Wife?" in which a number of men displayed a prevalent male bias. Women readers immediately voiced their displeasure, inundating the *Examiner* with letters; for weeks thereafter Hearst encouraged this resulting furor by setting aside ample newspaper space. He also coaxed local residents to participate daily in an opinion poll concerning the location of the proposed federal post office by supplying a blank-form ballot. During this continuum of new ideas he encouraged businessmen and merchants to place "Want Ads" in the *Examiner* by initiating a "free messenger service" at fourteen downtown locations. And, in keeping with his emphasis on education (but always with circulation in mind), Hearst offered a leather-bound *Webster's Unabridged Dictionary* for $4 with a year's subscription to the weekly *Examiner* and $10 with the daily *Examiner*. Since its price alone was between $11 and $12, he reasoned to subscribers: "It costs less by the pound than tenderloin steak—if necessary starve the body one day and feed the mind." Then on May 21, 1890, Hearst culminated his spring of "madness" and innovation, which surely alarmed economic "watchdog" Irwin Stump even more. At the corner of Market and Third, he purchased—for $650,000—"a suitable site" for a projected twelve-story *Examiner* building.[17]

But Hearst was not about to allow the *Call* and the *Chronicle* a respite; with his ideas swirling about the *Examiner* offices unchecked and unabated, he continued the quest for circulation. On July 2 he offered the ten-volume *Americanized Encyclopedia Britannica*, with ninety-six colored maps, to readers for the ridiculously low price of $5, but which had to include a year's subscription of the daily *Examiner*; this proposal became so popular with readers that it lasted more than two years to October, 1892. Then on July 25, within six weeks after announcing the winners of the $75,000 Census competition, he initiated a new contest, this one aimed at circulation expansion outside the San Francisco area. Anyone purchasing a year's subscription ($1.50) to the weekly *Examiner* prior to November 14, 1890 (the cutoff date would later be extended to December 1), was eligible for $50,000 in awards, which included blooded stock, furniture, and farm implements, but mainly acreage in Washington, Oregon, and California. For instance, the first two prizes—determined by a lottery drawing—were "ten acres of orange land in Thermalito [California], with cottage and barn" ($3,500) and "six lots in Olympia, Washington" ($3,000). Hearst, a continual crusader for an elevated culture, also included a gift for every new subscriber—the choice of a reprinted masterpiece in modern art (Makoffsky's *Russian Wedding Feast*, Rosa Bonheur's *Scottish Raid*, Millet's *Angelus*, or Meissonier's *Friedland 1807*).[18]

Yet *Examiner* readers had even more to look forward to, for Hearst continued his onslaught of gimmicks and games, enhanced by a seemingly endless supply of money. On three separate occasions from August to November, 1890, he offered a cookbook or photograph "for free" to anyone placing an ad in the *Examiner*. On October 2 he set a prize of $20 to anyone guessing the "nearest" number of ads in the October 5 Sunday *Examiner*. But the idea that stirred the most interest revolved around an organization known as the Order of the Native Sons of the Golden West. Since this group was, befittingly, holding its annual meeting at San Francisco in September to celebrate California's fortieth-year "admission day" into the Union, Hearst proposed a contest where "an open ballot"—of course, provided at convenient locations by the *Examiner*—would decide who was the "most popular Native Son." Hearst, himself, helped design for the winner "a magnificent badge" of gold with diamonds (costing $1,500). Four weeks and 560,153 votes later, the *Examiner* announced the results in full.[19]

But the holiday season of 1890 was still ahead—hence, another journalistic innovation, although somewhat by accident. Late in November, "Annie Laurie" wrote two sympathetic stories, titled "The Orphans' Santa Claus," that depicted the grim plight of orphaned children in San Francisco and their bleak outlook for Christmas. She then asked "who would be the first to contribute to the Santa Claus fund." The response was overwhelming. So Hearst decided to devote front-page coverage in the *Examiner*; but, more importantly, he encouraged "giving" by listing daily the names of the donors plus the amounts of their donations—a technique that he, as well as future charitable fund-raisers, found to be both popular and successful. Then, just prior to Christmas, the *Examiner* sponsored a baseball game and a grand matinee, the proceeds of which would go into the "*Examiner's* Fund" on behalf of five thousand orphans.[20]

As a result of this year-long campaign the *Examiner* surpassed the *Chronicle*, its closest rival, both in circulation and advertisements. Hearst was ecstatic. Despite huge outlays of cash, the *Examiner* was, at last, self-sufficient and on the way to becoming extremely profitable. Continuing to apply proven techniques would bring about even greater successes, creating a snowball effect. Nor was he alone in this belief. On December 28, 1890, Hearst proudly noted that the *New York World*, the journal he most admired and had tried to emulate, announced that "the *Examiner* takes the FOURTH place in the whole world as an advertising medium." Circulation was also astounding, especially for a city of 300,000. By March, 1893, the daily edition averaged 65,045 copies per day; the Sunday, 76,725; and the weekly, 76,000. Sixteen months later, by the end of July, 1894, the daily had increased to 77,430; the Sunday to 91,230; and the weekly to 80,250.[21]

Early in 1891, with financial worries subsiding and the *Examiner* staff working well together, Hearst was able to relax somewhat, to spend more time with Tessie Powers at his Sausalito home overlooking San Francisco

Bay. But not for long! In Washington on January 22, seventy-year-old George Hearst became seriously ill, a general deterioration caused by kidney failure diagnosed as Bright's disease. Despite receiving the best medical care, he died peacefully during the evening of February 28, with Phebe and Will at his bedside.[22]

George Hearst, unlettered and at times crude in manners and speech, was genuinely well liked and appreciated. Because of his mining instincts and knowledge of land, he had built a financial base that neither his wife nor his son could exhaust. After all, what man could have acquired the "luck" or skill in one lifetime to invest substantially in four of the greatest mining properties in U.S. history—the Comstock Lode in Nevada (gold and silver), the Ontario Mine in Utah (silver), Anaconda in Montana (copper), and the Homestake in South Dakota (gold)? And what man could have anticipated the fabulous possibilities of the 275,000-acre San Simeon Ranch or could have negotiated with a foreign government to buy the one-million-acre Babicora Ranch in northern Mexico? Despite such wealth, George Hearst remained unassuming and unpretentious, a man who had the capacity for warmth and a talent for friendship. With his wife, Phebe, he had reached a comfortable, indeed pleasurable arrangement; and she had brought everything to the marriage he had anticipated: the beautiful and accomplished wife of a U.S. senator. His relationship with "Willie" had also matured into one of affection and appreciation. He surely admired his son's management of the *Examiner* and, despite costing him $750,000 in 1890, he continued unflagging financial support, with but one exception: early in the fall he rejected a request for $50,000.[23] In turn, young Will returned his father's love, even to the point of emulation. More and more after 1887 he became a "Papa's boy," to such an extent that George Hearst supposedly, on his deathbed, "exhorted his son to lead a serious life" and give up his affair with Tessie Powers.[24]

Will Hearst, however, had never taken instruction well, unless it was for his own benefit; and soon it was. When his father's will left everything to Phebe, a mere $18 million (a deceptive figure, since land prices as well as production at the Homestake and Anaconda mines soon increased dramatically), he was reportedly quite upset, even though writing his mother that "Father never did a better thing than when he made the will he did." But he soon realized that "Mama" controlled much of his financial future; that, despite her willful ways, he genuinely loved her; and that, equally important, she had seldom refused him anything.[25]

But Hearst, too, was quite willful. What had his parents ever denied him? Hence, soon after Phebe left on a European tour, he also decided to travel extensively, leaving the *Examiner* under the capable direction of Sam Chamberlain and Charles Palmer. Accompanied by "that woman"—as Phebe distressingly referred to Tessie Powers—and good friend and private secretary George Pancoast, he revisited England, Scotland, and Wales before crossing the English Channel to France and Switzerland. At every turn he and Pancoast enthusiastically photographed their surroundings, whether castles or monuments or battlefields or, as one biographer humorously commented, "celebrities and strange animals." During the summers of 1892 and 1893 he and his two constant companions again returned to Europe, enjoying themselves immensely. As a consequence in 1893, Hearst decided to "invade" Egypt, whereupon he embarked upon "a photographic orgy," returning home with thirty-two hundred negatives of the Nile and pyramids and natural surroundings.[26]

During these annual summer treks, which were sometimes extended several months, Hearst was at his economic worst, subject both to whim and caprice. And Pancoast, his boon companion, "a nighthawk, available at all hours and ever ready to tackle anything new and exciting," served only to escalate and intensify such self-indulgence. For instance, Hearst, while touring Italy in 1892, visited a courtyard in Verona with "long iron balconies" overhead. In the center rested an old circular stone wellhead. "Look at that well," he enthusiastically exclaimed to Pancoast, whereupon he bought the whole setting (five to six tons), which was shipped to California and installed in the garden of "El Rancho del Oso" near Pleasanton; Phebe would appropriately rename her favorite habitat "La Hacienda del Pozo de la Verona." Again in 1893, while in Paris, Hearst became quite ill—termed a "slight bilious attack." He therefore instructed Pancoast to return home without him and Tessie, but to take pictures of the Irish countryside while en route. After a long and arduous trip, Pancoast arrived in San Francisco, only to find this cablegram: "Going to Egypt. Would you like to go? Please suit your own convenience entirely." Of course, this request was a thinly veiled "order." Hence, Pancoast wearily returned to Paris, but no Hearst. After ten days of anxious waiting, he received this message from the quaint resort town of Chamonix in the French Alps: "Come here at once. Bring two thousand dollars." After considerable difficulty with local bankers he finally arrived with the prescribed amount, with Hearst happily greeting him: "Hello, George, beautiful views here. Hope you had a pleasant trip."[27]

The most familiar story of Hearst economic excesses and overindulgence, however, had to do with his trip to Egypt in 1893. While in Paris, Hearst and Pancoast ate some rich food at a local cafe, causing them con-

siderable indigestion. A few nights later they dined at an American restaurant, where Pancoast exulted in a meal of beans, codfish, and chowder.
The two, facing three months of Egyptian food along the Nile, "hatched" a
plan. After learning that the proprietor had obtained such "delicacies" in
"cans" from the United States, Hearst immediately drafted this message to
Ike Allen, the eastern representative of the *Examiner* in New York City:
"Rush dozen cans Boston beans dozen cans clam chowder two codfish Alexandria Egypt. Hearst."

The cablegram completely baffled Allen. After checking with several
individuals to see if they could decipher the intended meaning, he apolo-
getically wired Hearst: "What code are you using?" To which came the immediate reply: "No Code. Want beans chowder codfish."

Hence, Hearst "and company"—as always—"roughed it" in the Egyptian back country, photographing both the living and the dead or, as one
historian put it, "anything that moved." Not only did Hearst spend exorbi-
tant amounts of money on trunkloads of pictures but also on artifacts and
a collection of mummies.[28]

But such blatant conduct, such flouting of social mores and accepted
morality would soon end: "Mama" would see to that. She had earlier suffered emotional trauma with husband George over "another woman" and
emerged victorious, vitiating further indiscretions and thus saving their
marriage. In her role as family protector she had previously directed—or,
more appropriately, "interfered with"—Will's social life. In 1883 she had
ended his brief "summer romance" with Sybil Sanderson, whose family,
with her strong encouragement, "whisked" young Sybil to a music conservatory in Paris. Then late in 1885 Hearst fell desperately in love with Elea-
nor Calhoun, a talented actress two years his senior, whom Phebe termed
"the Devil fish." After an anguishing eighteen months, during which time,
she wrote, "Will [was] so ugly and cruel to me," Phebe persuaded this "de-
signing woman" to study for the stage in London.[29]

But as for Tessie Powers no amount of motherly persuasion, no crescendo of earnest entreating and fervent supplication could persuade him
from his present lifestyle; for "in questions of morality," one biographer
noted, "she and her son did not speak the same language." When news
reached her that Will intended to construct a new ranch house, supposedly for Tessie, she exclaimed within earshot of her fifteen-year-old niece
Anne Drusilla, "he is going too far." So she decided on a drastic course of
action to protect "her boy." Late in 1893 she secretly arrived in San Francisco at the new California Hotel on Bush Street, accompanied by her
niece. She effected a liaison with Tessie Powers, unbeknownst to Hearst,

and either by threat or money—or both—persuaded her to end the affair. Although truly devoted to Hearst, Tessie reportedly returned East with $150,000.[30]

Hearst was heartbroken, devastatingly distraught, and disconsolate by Tessie's abandonment, so much so that Phebe became concerned; she had not anticipated the aftereffects of her motherly interference. She therefore cabled close friend Orrin Peck, who was a resident artist in Munich, to help Will weather this extended melancholia; he arrived within a month. She then moved Will out of his Sausalito home into the luxurious, seven-story Palace Hotel, where she and Peck and niece Anne Drusilla Apperson carefully watched over him, ever cognizant of any undue swing in mood and temperament. In this campaign to rehabilitate her son during the winter of 1893–94, Phebe tried every means to uplift his spirits—playful antics by Orrin Peck, lighthearted parties, frequent dinners at the beautiful Palace Hotel dining room, followed by evenings at the theater. She also persuaded Will to sit for weeks, as Peck painted an excellent portrait of him in oils.[31]

Only one tonic, however, could lift Hearst out of the doldrums, could energize his spirit and refocus his life: the *Examiner*. And it did. Even during his winter of discontent he still supplied the staff with "brainwaves"—and as usual they came "tumbling out." Always aware of the news, he enjoyed the daily *Examiner*'s increased circulation of 4,333 copies during December, but it had not yet reached the 70,000 mark. Since the state fair had opened nearby at "Dream City" on December 11, 1893, he decided to publish a 70-page "Mid-Winter Fair Edition" on January 28, 1894; Californians bought 104,000 copies. The next day he offered a "$5,000 *Examiner* Gold Cup," together with two handsome silver trophies (for second and third places), which would "be awarded to the county making the best and most representative exhibit." Of course, the *Examiner* provided ballots in each edition as well as at several booths on the fairgrounds. In turn, the *Examiner* recorded the votes daily until, on July 8, with more than 2 million votes cast, the contest closed and the winners were announced.

On February 3, 1894, in quick succession, the *Examiner* offered an exquisite trophy "of pure silver" as a prize to the "best marksman" at a shooting festival. It also proffered to readers "The Edition de Luxe of Views of the World's Fair" for fifteen cents and one or two coupons printed within the *Examiner*. And it set "An *Examiner*'s day at the Fair" (February 23) for 23,000 San Francisco school children, who would receive transportation, food, and "everything but fireworks" free of charge. Then came the ultimate extravaganza. Hearst established another lottery of 9,000 prizes, to-taling $148,000, with the only requisite for entry being a subscription to the weekly *Examiner* ($1.50). Hearst, although still grieving for Tessie, was beginning to recover, especially with the daily circulation reaching the 70,000 mark on March 10, 1894.[32]

During those first years of the 1890s the *Examiner* maintained its success formula, changing ever so gradually. Hearst was determined that staffers receive credit for their work, that readers recognize their abilities. He therefore elevated them to celebrity status by promoting bylines. Acerbic Ambrose Bierce was a fixture with his Sunday column "Prattle," as was humorist Bill Nye with his lighthearted observations. By February, 1895, Alfonso "Blinker" Murphy (of "you-can't-fire-me" fame) also had a space on the Monday editorial page titled "Blinker at Sacramento" or wherever he was residing at the moment. And Henry "Petey" Bigelow achieved luminary status by obtaining interviews with notorious train robbers Chris Evans and John Sontag in their lofty Sierra retreat during September and October, 1892, even as California lawmen, frustrated and chagrined, were attempting unsuccessfully to discover their whereabouts. When the *Chronicle* and *Call* questioned the authenticity of the interviews, the *Examiner* produced sworn statements by Evans legitimizing the story—and "Petey" Bigelow became a household name.[33]

But the most renowned of all *Examiner* reporters was Winifred Black, who was better recognized by San Franciscans as "Annie Laurie." Readers delighted in her interviews and empathized with her stories. No task seemed too difficult, no assignment too outrageous. What woman of the 1890s would have had the temerity, the self-assuredness, to write about audience participation at a local prizefight, interview heavyweight champion James J. Corbett, or, for that matter, query members of the Stanford University football team prior to an important game? She wrote about women, from those prominently in the news to prostitutes in "dives" to the wives and daughters of men on strike. No one was beyond the reach of her pen, whether King Kalakaua I of the Sandwich Islands or Sister Gertrude among the lepers in Hawaii or Governor Edwin Markham of California or Standing Bear, chief of the Sioux. Whatever the subject she wrote with clarity and, what Hearst equally appreciated, a strain of sympathy for the underdog.[34]

The *Examiner* also changed somewhat in bulk and makeup as well as in content. In 1890 the daily edition had been eight-to-ten pages in capacity and the Sunday sixteen-to-twenty pages; by the fall of 1894 the daily averaged twelve-to-sixteen pages and the Sunday twenty-eight to thirty-six.

Of course, one reason for such expansion was the numerous "Want Ads" run by the *Examiner*, which, Hearst announced in the spring of 1895, were "equal to the other two dailies combined." But also important to such growth were new types of attention-getters. In 1892 the *Examiner* began creating "fac-similies" of letters, cablegrams, and telegrams (and on one occasion a will) from prominent personages, all of which occupied considerable space. By 1894 each edition, using emboldened headlines of almost an inch, liberally sprinkled effective cartoons and huge illustrations throughout the pages to support various stories (again more space). Two men quickly gained recognition among *Examiner* readers. Jimmy Swinnerton, who had joined the staff when only seventeen, began drawing a comic strip about the adventures of small bears; and Homer Davenport, a former brakeman for the Northern Pacific Railroad who then became "a nursemaid" to animals in a small circus, was allowed to develop his considerable talents as a political cartoonist. Still another change occurred in the fall of 1892. Hearst abandoned a nonpartisan stance for the *Examiner* and revealed his Democratic Party sympathies; in fact, early in November, 1892, he not only began publishing a complete slate of all nominees on the ballot, but also endorsed specific candidates on the national, state, and local levels, only a scattering of whom were Republicans or Independents.[35]

But one negative aspect of Hearst journalism, definitely a disturbing trend, began evolving. Whereas during the first three years investigative reporters had verified their facts and written stories tending toward objectivity, some of the "mad house" staffers noticed a change—what they considered to be news exploitation to increase circulation. Allen Kelly and his wife, Florence, were especially disillusioned, protesting that the *Examiner* was appealing to the "emotions, the lower phases of intelligence and the baser instincts of readers, and disguising this by playing up occasional intellectual interests of real value." In fact, Kelly asked for reassignment as city editor in 1891 because, seemingly, Hearst was deliberately trying "to color, misinterpret and even falsify current happenings." Such disenchantment continued among some staffers, especially when Hearst elevated several to "stardom." For instance, many observers questioned the veracity of "Petey" Bigelow, that he ever discovered the hideout of the notorious train robbers, Evans and Sontag, then interviewed them, while a posse of law officers was unsuccessfully in pursuit.[36]

An even more alarming direction for the *Examiner* and West Coast journalism revolved around Eddie Morphy, his questionable ethics, yet general acceptance. The humorous story of "The Last of the McGintys"—whether or not apocryphal—surely was indicative of future Hearst

newspaper policies. Morphy related it this way. One day Hearst dashed in
with another "brainwave," proposing to devote an entire page of the next
Sunday edition to "interesting" San Franciscans—seven in all or one per
column. He suggested two or three names, then allowed the reporter's discretion to choose the rest. A few days later Morphy had written all but
one; he could not "think of another colorful personality." So with Hearst
pressing him, he invented a "touching" story titled "The Last of the
McGintys" that depicted an orphan boy who solely supported two
younger brothers. A sympathetic outpouring of reader reaction was overwhelming—and Phebe Hearst added to the problem by sending Morphy
a heartfelt note with five twenty-dollar bills to purchase "food and clothing for the youngsters."

"I was in a dilemma. There were no McGintys," Morphy recalled. He
therefore told his predicament to the city editor, who suggested that they
"go over to the Mint [a neighboring saloon] to break one of those twenties,
and think things over." After lengthy deliberations during which they consumed most of one twenty—and joined by several colleagues—they arrived at "a solution." They quickly "rounded up five or six dirty, ragged kids
from the street," photographed and sketched them "in all their dirtiness,"
then dressed them in new clothes. In the next Sunday edition the pictured
contrast appeared, and as Morphy recollected, "it was great stuff," that is,
until a young reporter of the rival *News-Letter* uncovered the truth and
printed it.

"I made it my business," Morphy stated, to vanish when Mrs. Hearst
"was around." But one day she chanced upon him and said: "Oh, Mr. Morphy, how could you do such a thing?" While he was searching for an ade-
quate explanation, she continued, "Well, anyway, Mr. Morphy, that was a
wonderful story you wrote about the McGintys. It had me weeping for
several hours."[37]

Hearst, however, never shied away from criticism or blame; he willingly
accepted responsibility for *Examiner* policies. Amazingly, some cog within
him seemed to immunize, to insulate him from bitter censure and hurtful
personal attacks. After all, he headed a newspaper that was constantly
judgmental about the activities of public officials. Why should he be ex-
empt? The *Examiner*, although Democratic in sympathy, had successfully
waged bitter campaigns to oust local Democratic Party leaders "Blind
Boss" Chris Buckley and his successor Sam Rainey because of their blatant corruption. After May, 1893, *Examiner* editorials also scathingly attacked President Grover Cleveland, especially for his actions to alleviate a
severe depression (the Panic of 1893), for the administration's antisilver

policy, and for its failure to lower the tariff.[38]

But the worst of all public villains, Hearst believed, was the Southern Pacific Railroad (S.P.) and its leader, Collis P. Huntington. Hearst, like his father, fiercely resented the domination of this railroad over Californians. In 1892, through prominent coverage as well as editorials, the *Examiner* was highly critical of the S.P., so much so that company officials purchased $30,000 worth of advertising with an appended secret agreement stating that, "although the company would not be immune to criticism, the tone of it would be gentler." But Hearst could not countenance the railroad's practices of charging the public "all that the traffic will bear" and of arbitrarily granting certain corporations rebates and drawbacks, which the Interstate Commerce Act of 1887 had declared unlawful. The S.P., however, was guilty of far worse "crimes" against the people, Hearst believed; it had refused to pay millions of dollars in state taxes. Then during the summer of 1894, with severe depression curtailing revenue and adversely affecting income, Huntington pressed the U.S. Senate to pass a "funding bill" in his behalf. Hearst now had a cause, and the *Examiner*, through the political cartoons of Davenport and Swinnerton, was his cudgel. Day after day he railed against Huntington, the *Examiner* advocating government ownership through a petition drive that acquired almost two hundred thousand names in fewer than two months. Again, from the fall of 1894 through the spring of 1895, Hearst ardently pushed in the *Examiner* for "a People's Road," emanating from San Francisco and stretching throughout the San Joaquin Valley, that hopefully would link up with the Santa Fe Railroad and do financial harm to Huntington.[39]

Hearst also committed his staffers to a local cause that caused his "brainwaves" to work overtime. On November 25, 1894, "Annie Laurie" wrote a sympathetic piece about the terrible conditions at the Children's Hospital in San Francisco. The resident physician lamented to her that, due to lack of funds as well as available space, the staff could care for only seventy babies and other youngsters, although hundreds needed medical attention. To illustrate his point, the doctor told the heartwrenching story about a seven-year-old child named Jim, who was crippled and malnourished and dying. The mother begged the hospital to house and feed him during his last days, but to no avail. Crestfallen and disconsolate, she turned to her little boy and said: "Come, Jim, we will go back again. Nobody wants us." In conclusion, "Annie Laurie" asked this poignant question: "What is going to become of Little Jim?" And then she added: "Ought there not to be some place in San Francisco where a poor sick little boy can creep away and rest until peace comes to him?" Hearst thus began a campaign for the "Little Jim Fund," sparing no effort, no amount of money, for its success. Every day the *Examiner* prominently displayed the specific contributions of donors, pictured the sad plight of needy children with graphic illustrations, and promoted several theatrical benefits and children's fairs "to swell the funds." Then Hearst outdid himself. He determined that "women only" would produce the forty-page Christmas edition of the *Examiner*, titled "Empress of the Dailies," with the proceeds going to the "Little Jim Fund." As a result, San Franciscans bought 130,000 copies, which swelled contributions in January to more than $20,000.[40]

So by 1895, with the *Examiner* far outdistancing its rivals and achieving financial success, now just by sheer momentum, Hearst was ready for a new challenge—and he knew what it would be. As early as 1892 he had investigated the journalistic scene in New York City, comparing its overall circulation figures with the population. He thus decided that the demographics demonstrated a need for another newspaper, especially one with new vision and exciting ideas. First, he sent *Examiner* business manager Charles Palmer "on an exploratory trip east." Palmer discovered that the price tag for the fading *New York Times* was $1.25 million and the *Chicago Morning Record* $2 million—both far too expensive even for the Hearst pocketbook. He then approached "Mama" for a "loan," but she steadfastly rejected all pleas and overtures. Consequently, Hearst bided his time; however, soon thereafter, while crossing the bay to his Sausalito home, he displayed a map to close friend and confidant George Pancoast, circled with a pencil certain cities, and announced: "George, someday, a paper here and here and here." [41]

His patience was soon rewarded. Within three years his ambitions began to materialize. In 1895, Phebe Hearst sold her seven-sixteenths share of Anaconda Copper Mining Company to the Rothschilds of London for $7.5 million. She then completely capitulated to son Will, possibly because he had learned about her "meddling" with Tessie Powers. Regardless of the reason, he received the full share of the sale; the only restriction imposed by his mother was that Edward Hardy Clark, her business manager, would be the "controlling officer" in any new enterprises. But no matter! Hearst was now a multimillionaire and seldom, if ever, had he not gotten his way.[42]

Again the hunt for a newspaper was on. In July, 1895, while Hearst was enjoying another European tour, Palmer met him in Paris and received specific instructions to buy a New York daily. He soon reported that the *Times, Recorder,* and *Advertiser* were available, but the cost prohibitive. Palmer also mentioned the *Morning Journal*, but added that its reputation was the worst in New York—a "spicy sheet" called the "chambermaids' delight"—which Albert Pulitzer, whose brother Joseph owned the *World*, had sold to wealthy Cincinnati publisher John McLean in 1894. Palmer then dutifully pointed out that, within a year, the *Morning Journal* had dropped in daily circulation from 135,000 to 30,000 and that advertising was almost nil. Nothing more needed to be said. Hearst, who coined the expression "The impossible is only a little more difficult than the possible," instructed him to buy it. And Palmer did. After much business posturing and lengthy price haggling by both parties, McLean agreed to sell the *Morning Journal* for $180,000. On September 25, 1895, Hearst acquired formal title, and the Hearst invasion of New York began.[43]

5 | News War in New York

～

For William Randolph Hearst, no place in the world held a greater attraction than New York City in the fall of 1895. Here was the center of American business activity, the hub of high society in the United States, the mecca for millions of immigrants who desired to pursue the "American Dream," the siren's song for rural Americans who sought the excitement and glamor of a city on the move. On every corner, change was readily apparent. Skyscrapers, pointing majestically upward, followed the innovative principle set forth by architect Louis Sullivan that "form follows function." They increasingly dotted the horizon. Elevated trains, in a rumbling cacophony of grinding starts and stops, roared continuously throughout many areas of the metropolis, bringing hordes of people into the center of the city to work, and returning them home again at the end of the day. Electric lights illuminated the streets, enhancing urban night-life with glittering theaters and quality restaurants such as Delmonico's. Electric wiring for telephones was also increasingly evident. All these factors made New Yorkers realize that technology was changing their lives from year to year, if not from day to day.[1]

New York was a city of contrasts. With the population exploding in the 1890s from 1.5 million to almost 3.5 million, the gulf between rich and poor was ever widening. The posh hotels along lower Fifth Avenue and the magnificent graystone mansions of Mrs. William Astor, A. T. Stewart, J. P. Morgan, William C. Whitney, and the Vanderbilts opposite Central Park mirrored the vast wealth of American captains of industry, while nearby, along the East Side, the "rocky wastes" of Shantytown stretched for miles from 42nd to 110 streets, where, as one historian noted, "Irish squatters, goats, and pigs [were] living promiscuously together." In contrast to the "pillared citadels" of capital along Wall Street

were the festering slums of the Bowery, where wretched depravity signi-
fied the poverty and despair of the human spirit. And with immigrants
flooding in from southern and eastern Europe, people who neither understood nor appreciated Anglo-Saxon culture and its roots, New York became a city of ethnic exclusion rather than inclusion. One visitor
characterized such disparities, such contradictions, as "a lady in ball costume, with diamonds in her ears, and her toes out at her boots." [2]

Hearst was well aware of the contrasts and distinctions between New
York City and San Francisco, in attitude as well as outlook. New Yorkers
looked upon California as the hinterlands, as a faraway frontier struggling
to attain civilization. They considered San Francisco—with fewer than
500,000 people—provincial, lacking either in monetary and political
power or in intellectual acumen and social graces. For instance, New
Yorkers regarded President Grover Cleveland (of Buffalo) as local news,
trading with the Rothschilds of London a common occurrence, expensive
wedding outlays for one of Mrs. Astor's "Four Hundred" high society an
expected event. Nor did they consider the University of California or
newly established Stanford University comparable to, much less equaling,
such time-honored Ivy League schools as Harvard, Yale, Columbia, and
Princeton. And West Coast journalism, as represented by the *San Francisco Examiner* and its young upstart publisher and editor, could not compare with Pulitzer's *New York World*, James Gordon Bennett's *Herald*, and
Charles Dana's *Sun*. [3]

New York City was also somewhat intimidating to Hearst, at least for
a brief time. A student of history and ever conscious of the fabulous journalistic tradition of which he was trying to become a part, Hearst was
caught up in the significance of the moment. Soon after Charles Palmer
had informed him of the *Journal's* purchase late in August, 1895, whereupon he performed a characteristic jig of triumph followed by an enthusiastic heel-clicking, Hearst visited his new publishing plant. And there, on
Park Row in the triangular Printing House Square, he dreamed fanciful
thoughts of success and fame while imagining the actions and feelings of
the journalistic giants of yesteryear. As Mrs. Fremont Older recollected,
"the dingy sign and the low building [known as Horace Greeley's *Tribune*]
at the corner of Spruce Street and Park Row," that represented "the paper
that had become his" and where he would spend most of his waking
hours over the next five years, "seemed beautiful." What an impressive
history, what an awesome tradition, this plot of real estate encompassed!
Just opposite the Federal Building in Printing House Square was the
Syndicate Building, twenty stories high and one of the tallest structures

in the world. Equally, if not more impressive, was the gilt dome of Pulitzer's *World* Building, gleaming triumphantly as "a monument" to its owner. And at the opposite end of City Hall Park was the *Sun*, operated by the distinguished author and publisher Charles A. Dana. And even though James Gordon Bennett had moved his *Herald* uptown to Herald Square, Hearst still sensed his presence that afternoon, as well as that of Horace Greeley; for in the midst of all this history in Printing House Square arose a huge statue of Benjamin Franklin—the symbol of American journalism.[4]

But Hearst could not afford too much reverie or too many fanciful flights into the past; he had to exhume a moribund newspaper that reflected a history of failure similar to that of the pre-Hearst *Examiner*. Consequently he relied on the same style and proven formula of past successes. Of course, that meant obtaining the most talented and experienced staff in the American journalistic field, no matter what the means, no matter what the cost. And he did. Hearst immediately persuaded the "stars" of the *Examiner* to assist him in this "new adventure." Sam Chamberlain, debonair and cosmopolitan, a fashion plate in dress and manners, was delighted to return to New York as the *Morning Journal's* managing editor. The brilliant but sometimes erratic editorial writer Arthur McEwen also agreed to embark on this New York crusade that Hearst called "the big picture," as did reporters and close friends Frank "Cosy" Noble and Charles Michelson, photographic expert George Pancoast, artist Charles Tebbs, Winifred Black of "Annie Laurie" fame, political cartoonist Homer Davenport, acerbic columnist Ambrose Bierce (Sunday's "Prattle"), and business manager Charles Palmer.[5]

Even with this gifted nucleus, Hearst needed a more powerful arsenal of talented individuals to succeed in this all-out war for newspaper supremacy. With pockets seemingly full of cash, he encouraged defections from newsrooms across the country through high salaries and long-term contracts. Or as business manager Palmer wryly commented to a visitor: "Oh, we don't bother about money around here. Open any closet and you'll smell . . . [it] burning." Hence, humorist Bill Nye, who had previously worked for the *Examiner*, quickly agreed to terms. Hearst then "raked in" one of the most impressive staffs ever assembled: Stephen Crane, Julian Hawthorne, Edgar Saltus, Alfred Henry Lewis (whose pen name was "Dan Quinn"), humorist Mark Twain, editor-in-chief Willis J. Abbot, theatrical critic Alan Dale, editorial writer Julian Ralph, and foreign correspondents Richard Harding Davis, Henry W. Fisher, and Murat Halstead.[6]

From late September to early November, 1895, Hearst, while assembling a staff, also attended to the production of a newspaper. At best, the *Morning Journal* was a journalistic nightmare, an excellent example of lethargic writing and unimaginative organization. In eight pages of print for the daily—and twenty-four for Sunday—it treated subscribers to a dull rendition of the news, with little or no mention of national and foreign events, a few local stories poorly fashioned with vapid headlines and unlively, almost pointless illustrations, and a "blah" account of sports. Editorials, often in the form of gossip columns, reflected the overall fatigue of the publisher, as did its less than one page of advertisements.[7]

On November 7, 1895, Hearst changed the course of the *Journal* in his quest for journalistic supremacy. As with the *Examiner* in 1887, he imitated Pulitzer's *World* in page size, general appearance, and reader appeal. What a change in format from the previous edition! A huge illustration depicting the wedding of Consuelo Vanderbilt to the Duke of Marlborough occupied almost all of the front page. Features concerning women (again with eye-catching displays) were on page two, while at the top of page six for the first time appeared the name of the publisher, "W. R. Hearst." In turn, the editorial page addressed world, national, and local events, while in the left-hand column appeared the "official" weather forecast, together with informative tidbits on world issues or interesting commentary about local and state politics. And even though advertisements were noticeably few in number, Hearst expanded the *Journal* to twelve pages and reduced its cost to a penny. He then assailed the *World*, which cost two cents, with this masthead slogan: "You can't get more than all the news. You can't pay less than one cent."[8]

For the next three months Hearst continued his assault on the *World*, applying proven techniques to attract subscribers. Quickly aware of the citywide craze for cycling, he launched an "Age and Youth Contest" over a ten-day period in which the *Journal* offered bicycles, totaling "approximately $1,000," to the first ten readers who could identify the youthful pictures of eleven famous men such as Christopher Columbus and Grover Cleveland. At the same time, Homer Davenport became a household name with devastatingly effective political cartoons, and Winifred Black (for the moment discarding her Annie Laurie pseudonym) intrigued readers with interesting interviews and shocking exposés: the horrible conditions facing fellow New Yorkers in a crowded police court, a modern-day messiah (at Denver, Colorado) who cured the sick and the lame by "laying on hands," the "tribulations and sorrows of a young girl" who waited tables in a popular local restaurant, and the assisted apprehension of a "respectable" young female shoplifter who then explained that "she wanted to be caught." [9]

Because of the differences between New York and San Francisco, Hearst also focused on the problems and interests affecting the largest city in the United States. Increasingly, stories relating to crime, especially robbery and murder, occupied more newspaper space. Tenement fires, police corruption, and the political shenanigans of Tammany Hall Democratic chieftain Richard Croker and state Republican boss Thomas C. Platt (accompanied by eye-grabbing illustrations) received ample attention. Of course, articles designed to interest women—marriage, divorce, Paris fashions, problems in homemaking as well as jobs in the workplace—received prominent exposure. Sporting events were also featured, but with new emphases. Unlike San Franciscans, New Yorkers became seriously involved with bicycling, golf, billiards, the Yale-Princeton football game. And in regard to high society, the *Journal* reflected the fabulous activities of Mrs. Astor's peerless "Four Hundred" families. Weddings in area churches were grander; receptions at the Waldorf-Astoria more lavish; horse and dog shows at Madison Square Garden and nights at the opera more remarkable; plush mansions and extravagant parties at Newport, Rhode Island—later described by Thorstein Veblein as typical functions of the "Idle Rich"—more ostentatious and grandiose. [10]

Hearst was in his element in New York. He immediately took a bachelor apartment at the Hoffman House (known as a gathering place for Democrats), while joining the fashionably sedate Union and Metropolitan clubs. He also set a routine to his liking, one too rigorous for most men. But he was young; he thrived on hard work; and, as biographer John Winkler recollected, "newspaper life satisfied him." By habit and inclination a late riser, Hearst appeared at the *Journal* offices just after lunch and proceeded to oversee every aspect of the next edition—headlines, illustrations, selectivity and position of stories, and editorials. Usually by late afternoon he returned to the Hoffman House, changed into formal evening attire, then attended the latest Broadway stage play or musical, followed by "a lively supper" with George Pancoast or some other friend. Soon after midnight, as if by clockwork, he burst into the *Journal* pressrooms, "filled with scintillating ideas" and, despite feeble protests that the edition was already "put to bed," spread each page on his office floor and reshuffled stories and illustrations as well as oversaw every editorial. After each decision, while staff members watched with amusement, he performed his characteristic nervous jig of triumph, accompanied at times with heel-clicking and snapping of fingers. [11]

At the same time Hearst, as showman and promoter extraordinaire, did not forget proven techniques of success against competitors. Despite taunts from the *World* staff that "no one from the West lasts in New York," especially anyone associated with the "kid" from California who was spending his way into bankruptcy, Hearst continued his quest for newspaper dominance through greater circulation. While the *Journal* gave its readers a free copy of a popular song that "would cost 50 cents anywhere" and followed up this promotion by offering subscribers the high-priced *Journal Atlas-Almanac and Cyclopedia for 1896* for "only 25 cents," he blatantly hammered the *World* with self-indulgent advertising. Where else could New Yorkers receive such a bargain as the *Journal?* In February, 1896, Hearst enlarged the daily to fourteen and, at times, sixteen pages, all for the price of a penny. "Why spend two cents when one buys the Journal?" Hearst bragged repeatedly, not just on the *Journal's* masthead but also on billboards, elevated trains, streetcars, and wagons throughout the city. After all, he was providing New Yorkers—by means of a seemingly inexhaustible personal money supply—with news from all over the world as well as entertaining them with human-interest stories, impressively illustrated and intriguingly presented.[12]

But Hearst realized that several important ingredients for success in this journalistic war with the *World* had not, as yet, materialized, that certain pieces for victory had not fallen into place. More specifically, he needed talented, imaginative leaders in several key positions. Even though the *Journal* had increased its daily circulation from 30,000 to almost 130,000 in just three months (November–January), the Sunday edition was lagging far behind that of the *World*. To Hearst, the answer was obvious. Morrill Goddard was the brilliant young editor of the Sunday *World*, who had increased subscriptions from 266,000 in 1893 to more than 450,000 by the end of 1895. So the solution was even more apparent; acquire his services and at the same time cripple Pulitzer.[13]

Morrill Goddard, a native of Maine and a Dartmouth College graduate, was known in New York as the "infant marvel" of journalism and was justifiably recognized as the "greatest circulation go-getter on earth." Once Hearst determined to hire him, the outcome was never really in doubt. At the Hoffman House in January, 1896, the two agreed to meet. Hearst then laid out this proposal to Goddard: the editorship of the *Journal's* Sunday supplement, a substantial salary increase, and complete discretion to recruit part, or all, of the Sunday *World* staff. "Your proposition might interest me, Mr. Hearst," Goddard candidly replied, "but I don't want to change a certainty for an uncertainty. Frankly, I doubt if you will last three months in this town." In rebuttal, Hearst, "smiling faintly," reached into his vest pocket, pulled out a crumpled piece of paper, and tossed it across the table; it was a Wells, Fargo & Company draft for $35,000. "Take all or any part of that," Hearst calmly announced. "That ought to convince you I intend to remain in New York quite some time." Goddard accepted immediately.[14]

This scenario, however, had not yet run its course. Pulitzer ordered *World* business manager Solomon S. Carvalho to "lure" Goddard and his staff back with higher salaries. And for twenty-four hours the *World* recovered its Sunday complement, that is, until Hearst unleashed his checkbook once again and outbid everyone.[15]

Joseph Pulitzer, at age forty-eight, failing in health and almost blind, his nervous system so sensitive that the mere rattling of paper could cause him pain, was the foremost newspaper publisher in the world. Over the past several months he had seemed oblivious to, or had tried to ignore, the activities of this upstart Californian who was, he confidently announced, fiscally irresponsible—no one could produce a sixteen-page daily for a penny and survive financially. But gradually he was forced to consider the Hearst challenge. Weekly, if not hourly, the *Journal* was depleting the *World* of valuable staffers—first hiring humorist Bill Nye (with a 50 percent raise), then cartoonist T. E. Powers, drama critic Alan Dale, as well as the Sunday *World* staff, which included R. F. Outcault, an imaginative artist who had created a popular cartoon strip called "The Yellow Kid." As a consequence, the prevailing story on Park Row was that newsmen hoped to receive a business card with the enclosed statement: "Mr. Hearst would be pleased to have you call." Nor did Carvalho improve Pulitzer's disposition, constantly reminding him of the Hearst "danger," of the "first real menace you have had since you came to New York."[16]

With the wholesale theft of the Sunday *World* staff, Pulitzer was out of patience; he angrily declared all-out war against the *Journal*, as his loathing for Hearst escalated. Upon learning that renegotiations with Goddard had taken place in the offices of the *San Francisco Examiner*, which occupied the eleventh floor of the Pulitzer Building, he canceled the lease and ordered an immediate evacuation of the premises, stating that "I won't have my building used for purposes of seduction!" Then, in February, 1896, at the behest of such trusted advisers as Carvalho, he reduced the price of the daily *World* to a penny. And he decided to combat Hearst dollar for dollar in this war for newspaper supremacy and "smash the interloper once and for all."[17]

Hearst could not have been more delighted. He believed that Pulitzer was cracking under the pressure and had unwittingly begun playing a game dictated by Hearst rules. He therefore accelerated his policies of journalistic entertainment—crayon portraits and contest prizes for subscribers, huge illustrations, acerbic political cartoons, titillating topics ranging from "shooting Niagara Falls in a barrel" to the world's smallest baby to interviews with such notables as Lillian Russell. Of course, Hearst usually planned something memorable to promote his newspapers during holidays. Hence, the Easter Sunday *Journal* edition (costing only three pennies) was a sixty-page extravaganza, replete with appealing stories accompanied by handsome pictures or adroit sketches.[18]

Hearst, although working tirelessly to complete his master plan for journalistic supremacy, still needed talented executives in several key positions. Consequently, he once again undermined Pulitzer's image of invincibility by raiding his staff. In February, 1896, he hired *World* city editor Richard A. Farrelly, just one day prior to a banquet that Pulitzer had planned to honor him. It was canceled. But Hearst was still not satisfied. Solomon S. Carvalho, of Portuguese-Jewish ancestry, a swarthy, "satanic"-looking individual with a decided limp, who was first trained by Charles Dana of the *Sun*, was his next objective. Reputedly having an "encyclopedic knowledge of the publishing business," he had justifiably become invaluable to Pulitzer both as a business manager and a trusted adviser. Carvalho, however, had become disenchanted with his boss who, although eventually persuaded to cut the daily price to a penny, disregarded his further advice and increased advertisement rates. Carvalho thus rightly predicted that angry New York businessmen would desert to the *Journal.* So on April 1, 1896, Hearst enlisted another valued executive.[19]

Only one last piece of *Journal* leadership was now missing; yet Hearst was uncharacteristically patient, allowing events to play themselves out and work for him. Arthur Brisbane was the target. This native New Yorker, who at age twenty-three had become the managing editor of Dana's *Evening Sun*, had now progressed to the same position with the *Evening World*. But Brisbane was also a talented writer who believed that editorializing on the front page—especially with his own byline—would be a unique and exciting newspaper innovation. On several occasions, when Pulitzer was overseas during the summer of 1896, he applied this idea, only to receive a "furious" cablegram from his boss that read: "Stop that column at once. I don't want the *Evening World* to have an editorial policy. If you want good editorials, rewrite those in the morning *World*." Soon thereafter at the Café Martin, a disgruntled Brisbane happened upon

Hearst who, after exchanging greetings, said to him: "I wish you were with us. If you come over, you may name your own salary. Suppose we talk it over tomorrow?" The next day the two met at the Hoffman House and agreed on terms. By the fall of 1896 Hearst had his executive complement in place, again at the expense of Pulitzer and the *World*.[20]

From the very beginning of the Hearst takeover, the *Journal* pressroom, much like that of the *Examiner* after 1887, was a picture of disorganization, pandemonium with purpose, or, as one staffer recollected, a "lunatic asylum" run by a "mad" overseer. And Hearst loved every minute of it, even more than the days in San Francisco. Shirtsleeved and with blue pencil in hand, he reshuffled and edited the *Journal* pages on his office floor into the wee hours of the morning. His staffers, at times, played practical jokes on one another or "shot craps" on the floor while awaiting his decisions. Hearst contributed further to this controlled chaos by forming a special "Murder Squad" of reporters to seek out clues and help bring criminals to justice. In fact, if some story was breaking, Hearst, emulating his childhood heroes—Caesar, Charlemagne, and Napoleon—would personally lead the *Journal* legions to all parts of the city. As biographer John Winkler reported, "he would come leaping from his office, long legs covering the ground like a champion runner, eyes gleaming and a little wild, and jump into a hansom," as a "motley procession followed pell-mell . . . messenger boys, stray dogs, excited bystanders." And Hearst always added to the prevailing excitement, to this atmosphere of confusion, by encouraging ingenuity and creativeness. Hence, during the chaotic fall of 1896, on the advice of Pancoast, Hearst risked further financial losses by buying from R. Hoe & Co. a special press that printed "from four to sixteen pages in all colors." With the success of this gamble he then published an eight-page comic section so vivid and kaleidoscopic, the *Journal* boasted, that it made "the rainbow look like a lead pipe" and the *World's* "black and tan" comic supplement "wishy-washy" and a "desolate waste of black." [21]

With each passing day the *Journal* became a reflection of the Hearst mentality: his knowledge of the American character and mind-set, his innate sense of what would interest and intrigue and entertain the public. He focused on sports, on competition and winning, devoting two, three, at times four pages to such events. He continued to concentrate on women's interests; he initiated a "Rainy-day Costume Contest" wherein the top three choices would have their designs acknowledged as well as created "by the leading tailor of New York." In much the same vein Hearst initiated "The Mill of Silence" mystery, offering $3,000 to "women and girls who furnish[ed] the best solution." And, more and more, he realized the mass fascination for attractive women; consequently, the *Journal* continually featured illustrations of beautiful females, whether in Paris, New York high society, the Broadway stage, or the horse show at Madison Square Garden. Rather surprisingly at this time, Hearst also realized that Easterners, unlike Californians, were infatuated with court trials and juror selections, especially when involving a prominent individual or a grotesque crime. But even more important during the 1890s Hearst sensed that Americans, besides being absorbed in "the game of politics," were becoming extremely nationalistic—at times rabidly xenophobic—in attitude and thought, reveling in their growing industrial prowess and ever cognizant of their democratic institutions. He therefore advocated a "noble" cause for his countrymen: independence for Cubans, who were "underdogs" rebelling "heroically" against a "tyrannical" Spain.

So what were the results of such Hearst programs and promotions? The *Journal* was high entertainment, fascinating, at times lurid, and always "fun" reading. From February to August, 1896, the daily circulation increased from 103,014 to 310,000; the Sunday paper from 86,056 to 252,953; and *Das Morgen Journal*, a German-language edition that Hearst had unknowingly acquired in the original purchase, from approximately 3,000 to more than 40,000. Consequently, Hearst incessantly exclaimed to all New York: "You want the best reading possible . . . TRY THE JOURNAL." [22]

Despite mounting circulation and increased advertisements in the daily, despite Morrill Goddard successfully breathing new life into the Sunday *Journal* with sensational stories and lurid topics—often referred to as "crime and underwear" journalism—Hearst was rapidly depleting his cash reserves, as much as $2 million by the spring of 1896. And even though a concerned Phebe sent her financial manager, Edward Hardy Clark, to oversee expenditures at the *Journal*, for the purpose of frugality, "her Willie" completely intimidated him and continued his extravagance uninterrupted. So when winter weather enveloped the city, he distributed heavy sweaters to the cold and needy. When Pulitzer employed five bands of musicians for publicity, Hearst hired ten. Then, when Pulitzer decided to economize, Hearst spent more and more. Or as one staffer aptly observed, "some of us . . . day after day inhaled the fumes of his burning money." Yet, even so, Hearst was about to embark on an even more costly enterprise. [23]

In the summer of 1896, with the presidential elections at hand, the American political scene was in turmoil. At St. Louis in June, the Republicans selected William McKinley of Ohio as their standard-bearer. In their platform they secured the financial and industrial interests of the North and East by advocating a high protective tariff as well as coming out, somewhat equivocally, for the gold standard. Then they emphasized—at least to their way of thinking—the economic policies of the Cleveland administration (1893–97) that had failed to evict the United States from severe depression (the Panic of 1893) by adopting the campaign slogan "Vote for Bill McKinley, the advance agent of prosperity."

The Democrats, meeting at Chicago in July, chose thirty-six-year-old William Jennings Bryan of Nebraska, who was the antithesis of Republican policies, especially concerning "cheap money" in hard economic times. In particular, he favored the "free and unlimited coinage of silver," a platform plank that American farmers and laborers wholeheartedly endorsed. Thus the country, for the first time since the Civil War, split roughly along class and regional lines—the industrial and creditor North and East versus the agricultural and debtor South and West. Historians dubbed this classic campaign over the nation's monetary policies "The Battle of the Standards." [24]

Hearst was in a quandary over the presidential election. Although a Democrat since his college days at Harvard, he agonized over what stance the *Journal* should assume. Since the fall of 1890 he had "blistered" McKinley continually in the editorial columns of the *San Francisco Examiner*; yet he did not know the Democratic nominee, much less approve of his "silver" platform. Nor did a majority of New Yorkers appreciate Bryan. Wall Street was highly critical of his fiscal policies; big businessmen were fearful of his "radicalism" and outraged at his denunciation of them; and an important faction of the state Democratic Party, led by Senator David B. Hill, was increasingly opposed to his candidacy. Nor were publishers unaware of the prevailing sentiment; every New York newspaper of any size—except the *Journal*—was endorsing the Republicans or staying unobtrusively neutral. But *Journal* reporter Willis J. Abbot, who was sent to the Democratic National Convention at Chicago, where he was the first to interview Bryan immediately after his nomination, urged Hearst to endorse the nominee and thereby "make the *Journal* in one campaign the leading Democratic paper in the East." In fact, he and Bryan, in the candidate's "hotel bathroom," fashioned a "very comprehensive telegram to that effect." [25]

So Hearst had to make a decision—and he did. In a hastily called meeting of his major executives and editors, he laid out every aspect of this dilemma, then encouraged discussion. While Sam Chamberlain and Alfred Henry Lewis voiced either opposition to or dislike of Bryan, Business

Manager Charles Palmer was much more vehement. The Democratic stance for coinage of silver (at a ratio to gold of sixteen to one) was as abhorrent to him as it was to most New Yorkers, but more importantly, he argued, merchants and businessmen would withdraw advertisements to show their disfavor for the Democratic platform. The *Journal* could not afford such a financial drain, such a ruinous path toward bankruptcy. Then the goateed Scot Arthur McEwen, ever the proponent of lost causes, spoke on behalf of Bryan—and the issue was settled, because Hearst's "blue-grey eyes," Mrs. Fremont Older recorded, noticeably "brightened." Hearst thus announced: "Unlimber the guns; we are going to fight for Bryan."

After all, he, along with his father, had been lifelong Democrats. Except for the silver plank, he was surely in favor of, and had endorsed previously, any number of national party reforms for laborers and farmers. And despite Charles Palmer's dire fiscal predictions, he had never backed away from a fight, no matter who the opponent, no matter how costly the consequences. Hearst therefore asked McEwen to write an editorial endorsing Bryan. Then, almost as an afterthought, he turned to the obscure and almost unnoticed editor of the small German-language daily *Das Morgen Journal* and instructed him to follow this policy. "Sehr gut!" the editor enthusiastically replied. "We have already supported Herr Bryan since three days." [26]

With a cause to be won, Hearst immediately mobilized for an all-out assault. He appointed Willis Abbot as the nominal head of the *Journal* campaign, with only one limitation: "Say nothing about free silver." But within three weeks Hearst realized the absurdity of his request upon the campaign and yielded, Abbot noted, "with a sigh." That ended all ambivalence. Hearst quickly dispatched such creative writers as Julian Hawthorne, Alfred Henry Lewis, Henry George, and Arthur McEwen either to report firsthand on the Bryan campaign or to write editorials explaining all ramifications of his "silver" stance. For a ten-day period, Hearst also hired Bryan's close friend and supporter Senator Richard "Silver Dick" Bland of Missouri to accompany—and chronicle every action of—the candidate, thereby giving New Yorkers and other Easterners personal glimpses into his character and thinking. For the women, who had no vote but a certain undefined political influence, Winifred Black often interviewed Mrs. Bryan, who detailed the hardships of a national campaign as well as a personal view of "her man." [27]

The presidential campaign of 1896 was unlike any that Americans had witnessed since the Andrew Jackson era. During the difficult depression times of the 1890s, silver became known as "the poor man's friend," the symbol of cheap money and low interest rates for "the struggling masses" and "the laboring interests and toilers everywhere," as Bryan had so graphically described at the National Democratic Convention in Chicago. In turn, gold was characterized as the tool of Wall Street and big business, the personification of wealth and greed, the harbinger of oppression to the poor and downtrodden. But what intensified this "crusade" for silver even more was the youthfully energetic Bryan himself. While McKinley greeted delegation after delegation at his home in Canton, Ohio—political etiquette of the day frowned on intensive campaigning by presidential nominees—Bryan introduced "the whistle stop" tour into American politics. On two separate occasions he "invaded" New York, once in August and again late in September, speaking ten, fifteen, even twenty times a day to large, enthusiastic crowds. But he was more effective in the Midwest and West, thereby alerting Republicans to the possibility of defeat.[28]

The reactions to the Bryan campaign in New York, as well as in Republican ranks, were immediate—unadulterated fear and unapologetic hatred. "Big business, fearing for its privileges," historian Henry Steele Commager wrote, "acted as if the Hun were thundering at the gates" and used every means possible to win. Early in August, Republican campaign manager Marcus Alonzo Hanna of Ohio, McKinley's close friend and financial adviser, was having difficulty raising necessary funds to combat the Bryan phenomenon, that is, until railroad magnate James J. Hill accompanied him through "the high places of Wall Street." The Republican "war chest" immediately swelled to $12 million (and eventually to $16 million)—and Mark Hanna was in business. He had already mobilized fourteen hundred campaigners; he now "paid their expenses and sent them wherever their services were most needed." He also distributed more than one hundred million tracts of "educational literature" eulogizing McKinley, while characterizing Bryan as "a destructive radical" and "a danger to our institutions." And with hysteria rampant and rumors abounding—one predicting Eastern secession if the Democrats carried the election—churches were soon enlisted in this surging patter of calumny. One minister described Bryan as "a mouthing, slobbering demagogue whose patriotism was all in his jawbone," while another, from the pulpit, set aside time to "denounce the Chicago [Democratic] platform" because "that platform was made in Hell." [29]

Such scurrilous campaigning was not one-sided, however—at least not as long as Hearst was alive. While Bryan alone spoke for the cause of silver (the national Democratic Party was out of funds), Hearst waged total, unrestricted warfare in the *Journal*. He decided to strike directly at the disease rather than treat the symptoms; he therefore focused on Hanna instead of McKinley. And what better way than by ridicule and humiliation? For this mean-spirited task Hearst commissioned Homer Davenport, whose political cartoons soon won him worldwide acclaim and notoriety. Hanna was caricatured as a huge, potbellied creature, having hoglike features—squinty eyes, heavy jowls, and a down-turned mouth. His clothing pattern was that of dollar signs, his watch fob that of a skull, upon which was the caption "Labor." He was portrayed as the "Beast of Greed," a ruthless political boss who provided scads of money for votes, a conniving campaign manipulator who had McKinley, like a puppet, sitting on his knee and therefore "well in hand." [30]

Hearst seemed bent on winning, regardless of the methods. He awarded a special assignment to Alfred Henry Lewis, who proved to be an expert in character assassination as well as a purveyor of half-truths, if not outright lies. Early in 1896 Lewis wrote a vicious article—presumably derived from a personal interview—that depicted Hanna, according to biographer Herbert Croly, as a "fool and a braggart." As a consequence, Hanna contemplated a libel suit, but decided against it because Lewis and Hearst seemed intent on involving him in controversy and "were aiming at precisely that result." So Lewis, free from all journalistic constraints and ethical considerations, temporarily moved to Cleveland (Hanna's political and business headquarters), purportedly to provide firsthand, authentic stories of his past activities. Lewis then slanted actual events or contrived malicious accounts in which Hanna had "starved out" employees, had driven workers from "half-paid-for homes," and had heartlessly thwarted the efforts of striking miners. Lewis also implied that Hanna and his "syndicate" had a financial stranglehold on McKinley; they were carrying a $118,000 note incurred in the Panic of 1893. Hearst, despite such misrepresentations of Hanna, seemingly approved of and, at times, encouraged this particular brand of tabloid journalism. [31]

In this "crusade" for silver, Hearst abandoned any pretense of impartiality and objectivity. The *Journal* became a screaming advertisement for the Democratic Party. Bryan repeatedly received coverage on page one; reports about McKinley and Hanna were usually relegated to page eight or ten, the exceptions, of course, being the Davenport caricatures and the Lewis exposés. As the campaign intensified into October, 1896, Bryan occupied three to five pages of *Journal* space. Since the national Democratic Party was financially insolvent, Hearst decided to establish a "*Journal* Fund," allowing readers an opportunity to contribute to the Bryan campaign; as a further stimulus, he promised to match all donations dollar for dollar. Consequently, on October 13, Hearst closed out the fund with great fanfare by writing two $15,000 checks. Early in November, in one last attempt at victory, Hearst incessantly published accounts predicting a Democratic triumph, although recognizing that Republican money and organization were decidedly swinging a number of key states toward McKinley.[32]

Hearst, however, never forgot one of his fundamental maxims for success: that of publishing an intriguing and entertaining newspaper, which guaranteed a growing circulation. Always the showman and at times an innovator, he promoted a "Transcontinental Relay Race" from the *Examiner* building in San Francisco to the *Journal* offices in New York City. Participants on bicycles emulated the Pony Express of the 1860s by carrying messages a certain distance before handing them to another rider. Over a two-week period (August 24 to September 7) Hearst publicized each day's progress and, upon the arrival of the final biker, sponsored a huge *Journal-Examiner* parade—at considerable cost—that was capped off by "fireworks, music and a grand illumination" as well as the presentation of "splendid prizes" to local bicycle clubs and procession participants. Little more than a week later (September 20) the *Journal* also created quite a "stir" among New Yorkers by publishing drama critic Alan Dale's interview with beautiful Broadway actress Anna Held, who received him "attired in a 'nightie.'" Then, on September 28, with the R. Hoe & Co.'s black-and-white cylinder presses in place, Hearst initiated the *Evening Journal*, with the brilliant Arthur Brisbane as editor. And again on October 18, 1896, he published an eight-page Sunday supplement—all in colors—that featured such comic strips as "The Yellow Kid" and "McFadden's Row of Flats."[33]

These productions, these innovations, were expensive in the extreme; Hearst lost a minimum of $100,000 a month, totaling $2 million for the year—Business Manager Charles Palmer had sagely predicted huge revenue losses in advertisements with the *Journal*'s endorsement of Bryan. Yet Hearst, as always, remained oblivious to costs and expenditures, confident that the growing popularity of his newspapers would eventually resolve all financial matters. And again he was right. On November 3, 1896, the night of the presidential election, he choreographed another Hearst extravaganza. For "Greater New York and Jersey" the *Journal* filled the sky with three "monster" balloons, equipped with "colored electric lights" that flashed bulletins of the election results—red for Bryan and green for McKinley. At the *Journal* building, where thousands of onlookers gathered, Hearst entertained the excited crowd with several bands and "moving picture machines showing wonderful views." Hence, on November 4, although McKinley defeated Bryan convincingly in the electoral college, the *Journal* registered an astounding circulation record by selling 1,506,634 copies of the morning, evening, and German editions. Hearst, as the publisher of the most prominent Democratic newspaper in the United States, had easily outdistanced Pulitzer and the *World*.[34]

So Hearst, with Bryan publicly acknowledging his gratitude to the *Journal*, found some solace in defeat—but not completely. He may have performed a job well done, but the crusade had not been won. Yet Cuba and an ongoing rebellion against Spain offered another chance.[35]

6 | Yellow Journalism

❧

As the United States progressed toward the twentieth century, a new spirit seemed to arise throughout the land, one of new identity, of confident optimism, at times of bellicose chauvinism. In 1893, historian Frederick Jackson Turner announced that Americans were uniquely different from all other peoples of the world. Through their efforts in conquering each succeeding American frontier from the Atlantic to the Pacific over the past three centuries, they had formulated democratic institutions and fashioned a way of life far superior to that of their European counterparts. They should therefore be justly proud of their history and traditions and accomplishments—and they were. Through the discovery and exploitation of such fabulous natural resources as oil and gas, coal and iron ore, gold and silver, the United States had become the foremost industrial power in the world, surpassing both England and Germany. Five transcontinental railroads, their iron tentacles inextricably linking together the agrarian and urban areas of the nation, had created new markets and numerous jobs for a population nearing seventy-five million. And American ingenuity, as evidenced by the genius of Thomas Alva Edison and Alexander Graham Bell, seemed to illustrate the manifold blessings of a free society as well as the obvious advantages of a democratic system of government.

Many Americans in the 1890s also exuded a certain restless energy, an increasing appetite for challenge, together with a need to extend their growing pride of nationalism. And why? Possibly, young men had listened too longingly to romantic stories by Civil War veterans, who were enamored with the valor and heroism of individuals in battle, while overlooking the bloody slaughter of soldiers and the anguishing misery of defeat. Or, perhaps, with the Plains Indians of the West and Southwest subdued by the mid-1880s, Americans sought other foes to conquer, other enemies of their energized republic to subdue. Or, since such nations as England, France, Germany, and Japan were vigorously engaged in a new imperialism—a building of empires in Africa, China, and the South Seas—some Americans desired to counter such activities by spreading their own brand of Judeo-Christian beliefs as well as their extraordinary democratic institutions to far-off lands. But whatever the reasons this spirit of patriotic expansion, of confidence in and superiority of American values, was there, whether in the stirring strains of John Philip Sousa's "Stars and Stripes Forever" or in the statements of U.S. naval captain Alfred Thayer Mahan, the intellectual philosopher of this growing imperialism, who wrote: "Whether they will or no, Americans must now begin to look outward." [1]

William Randolph Hearst also seemed intuitively to sense this growth of nationalism, this pride in positive achievement and self-accomplishment. During almost a decade in the newspaper business he had seldom been wrong in his assessment of the American people's strengths and foibles, of their wishes and desires. By "taking his own pulse," a reflection of what he considered interesting or dull, outlandish or commonplace, tasteful or improper, Hearst instinctively mirrored this restlessness in a changing society, the frustrations for world recognition within a growing nation. All such pent-up emotions would thus emerge, then burst forth, in what Hearst orchestrated as an American "crusade" for Cuban independence against "Spanish tyranny."

Hearst was, and has been, an enigma to contemporaries and historians alike, especially in regard to the Spanish-American War. Biographer John Winkler alluded to Hearst's "congenital aversion to injustice and oppression of the weak," but critics have cynically rejected this explanation. Journalists Oliver Carleson and Ernest Bates explained his motivation as "solely for . . . private profit"; several others agreed by pointing to the titanic struggle between Pulitzer and Hearst to "increase the circulation of their newspapers." Yet one rhetorical question should render ineffective such an assessment. When was money ever a major factor in any of Hearst's decisions? Historian H. Wayne Morgan pictured him as wanting a "chance for fame, enshrinement in history books, and a kind of power." And in a similar vein biographer W. A. Swanberg described Hearst as "the most megalomaniac of men, supremely sure of his own greatness" and wishing to emulate his heroes—Caesar, Napoleon, Washington, Jefferson, and Lincoln. Yet Hearst may have revealed the simple truth of his actions during an interview with Damon Runyon in 1938:

"Ah, well, we were young. It was adventure." [2]

But after the 1896 election Hearst had problems of his own; with the defeat of Bryan on November 4, he faced the formidable task of economic survival. As Business Manager Charles Palmer had earlier predicted, the *Journal* did offend the Eastern commercial and economic establishments. Although recognized as the leading Democratic newspaper in the nation, with impressive, if not awesome, circulation numbers, it had clearly suffered a downward turn in advertisements and was losing money at a minimum of $100,000 a month and possibly as much as $2 million annually. In fact, Pulitzer anticipated weekly, if not daily, a Hearst announcement of bankruptcy. He therefore instructed certain *World* staff members to keep an accurate account of *Journal* promotions and outlays, expenditures and losses—more specifically, a precise estimate of the *Journal's* economic status. Pulitzer received a memo that "Mama" Hearst was drawing "the line" of indebtedness for her son at $5 million, most of which, according to *World* calculations, "was already spent." [3]

Hearst, while seemingly oblivious to money losses, was ever confident in his business formula for success. As in the case of the *San Francisco Examiner*, large monetary investments both in personnel and programs had elicited the desired financial results by the fourth year. Since the *Journal* was just beginning year two, Hearst recognized the immediate necessity for "fence mending." Hence he strove diligently to placate the political "targets" of the Bryan "crusade" as well as ameliorate the acrimonious rhetoric of the previous summer and fall. As a result, President-elect McKinley and Republican campaign manager Mark Hanna received favorable and, at times, "rave" reviews in the *Journal* during the four-month "honeymoon" between the presidential election and the forthcoming inauguration (November 3 to March 4). In fact, Hearst—with his typical flair for the dramatic—hired a *"Journal* Train" at considerable cost to transport Republicans and McKinley supporters from New York City to Washington, D.C., at the "record-breaking" speed of "228 miles in 249 minutes." He also devoted several pages to the McKinley inaugural festivities, which were described in detail by former Republican senator John J. Ingalls of Kansas together with several *Journal* staffers. [4]

More importantly, however, Hearst was determined to identify the *Journal* with the people of New York. He wanted them to consider it a voice against injustice, the protector of the poor and downtrodden, the defender of the average citizen against public corruption and corporate greed. Consequently, during the bitterly cold winter of 1896–97, when a fire destroyed a huge tenement house just after Christmas, Hearst provided food and shelter for forty families; he then established "the *Journal's* Relief Fund," encouraging contributions by listing the names of individual donors. Again in February, the *Journal* contributed $1,000 to "aid the cold and hungry," while persuading the Metropolitan Opera House to sponsor a "charity benefit" for the "starving and homeless," which raised more than $5,300. As a militant spokesman for New Yorkers, the *Journal* vehemently attacked the utility trust and demanded "dollar gas" to ease household costs. And even though the mayor and city commissioners were forced to renege on a contract at higher prices, Hearst was unable to pressure other local and state leaders into providing cheaper prices or instituting "gas socialism" through public incorporation.[5]

Hearst also targeted the news to attract diverse constituencies. While *Das Morgen Journal* continued to receive popular acclaim within the German community, the *Evening Journal*, under the expert leadership of Brisbane, adopted the slogan of New York City's "Home and Family Paper." And, much like the *Examiner* on the West Coast, it concocted contests and games that involved the readers as well as featuring stories that appealed to local interests. Always the showman and innovator, Hearst, together with his alter ego Brisbane, captured reader concerns. They understood the American psyche—an ingrained competitiveness that exalted athletic prowess (hence the popularity of such physical sports as football, baseball, and boxing), a lurid fascination with criminal trials that hinged on the decision by twelve jurors, a continuing obsession with feminine beauty (together with the unfathomable mysteries of the female mind-set), and an intrinsic yearning for the titillating details of human weakness, whether having to do with a scandalous divorce or a brutal murder or a "foul" betrayal by an elected official. The *Evening Journal* continually focused on such stories and news items. At the same time, it emphasized the Hearst formula of reader participation and identification. For example, during July and August, 1897, Hearst and Brisbane promoted summer vacations on Long Island for poor tenement children, paid for by reader contributions, which the *Evening Journal* matched dollar for dollar. During this same time frame they also sponsored a "free" month-long European trip from "Nice to Naples" for ten bicyclers, who qualified by mustering the most votes for themselves in a popularity contest. In ballots provided by the *Journal* papers, readers cast more than 6.5 million votes in fewer than two months.[6]

Crime and passion, no matter how bizarre and grotesque, were the most pervasive themes in every *Journal* paper. Hearst seemed to be especially fascinated with police work, with sleuthing and the vagaries of the criminal mind. He created a special "Murder Squad" from within his staff, challenging them to outwit and outthink the less ingenious New York police. Late in June, 1897, a case containing all the ingredients of a Hearst melodrama presented itself. Out of the depths of the East River surfaced the severed remains of a human male, "wrapped in white oil cloth tied with similar twine." Hearst and Brisbane immediately went all-out to solve this "unique mystery," with the *Evening Journal* headlines offering a $1,000 reward for "information or clews [sic], theories or suggestions" leading to the arrest of the perpetrators. Within three days, with Hearst enthusiastically directing the "Murder Squad," two *Journal* reporters discovered the dismembered body to be that of a Turkish bath masseur, William Guldensuppe. They then presented the police with evidence that led to the arrest—and eventual conviction—of Guldensuppe's former mistress, Mrs. Augusta Nack, and her new paramour, a handsome barber named Martin Thorn, who had decided to eliminate any possible competition. For a week New Yorkers avidly read about every gruesome detail of the victim's murder, his bloody dismemberment "in a bathtub"—with graphic illustrations—as well as the clandestine method of his disposal in the East River. Hearst protected the *Evening Journal* scoop by renting the entire building in which Mrs. Nack resided and assigned members of the "Murder Squad" to guard the entrance against the possible intrusion by rival reporters, while New York City detectives (using information supplied by the *Evening Journal*) elicited her confession. Hearst was delighted. By upstaging the police and scooping all opposition papers, he had personified the new slogan for his organization: "While Others Talk, the *Journal* Acts." [7]

Hearst, however, reserved a special responsibility for the *Morning Journal*, that of enlightening readers through stories and editorials about state and national concerns. But with his decision to make the *Journal* an active participant in the community, rather than just a recorder of the news—typified by the slogan "While Others Talk, the *Journal* Acts"—Hearst entered into a dangerous realm of newspaper activity, one that he euphemistically called "The New Journalism" (although soon acquiring the catchier terminology of "Yellow"). Hearst thus became a militant activist who generated power and influence through the *Journal* columns, specifically, he asserted, to aid the poor and disadvantaged, to effect change for good government, to crusade for a better America—with, ironically, a "superior regard for the truth."

And therein arose the problem, therein lay the danger. Hearst alone became the decision-maker concerning what was best for Americans to read, the judge and jury as to a positive or negative presentation of issues and characterization of individuals. Under the benevolent guise of "The New Journalism" he raised funds for the family of a slain New York City policeman; he aided the poor and the homeless during the dreadful winters of 1896–97 and 1897–98; and he provided helpful solutions for labor strikes in Ohio and Massachusetts.

More and more, however, he involved the *Morning Journal* in politics. On the local level he vigorously advocated a charter for Greater New York City (approved by voters in 1897), the passage of laws providing for "dollar gas," municipal ownership of public franchises, favorable working conditions for laborers including an eight-hour day, as well as increased appropriations for the upkeep of streets and parks, public schools, and rapid transit. On the national front Hearst continually criticized the McKinley administration for favoring big business to the detriment of the average American by discouraging foreign competition through the Dingley Tariff of 1897 (hence, higher consumer prices) and for failing to enact tougher antitrust legislation to curb huge corporations.[8]

Hearst also extended the realm of "The New—or Yellow—Journalism" to on-the-spot investigations of international events. Despite considerable cost he sent correspondents to all parts of the globe. In 1896 and 1897 he assigned Richard Harding Davis to Moscow for the coronation of the Russian czar; Stephen Crane and Julian Ralph to Athens for the Greco-Turkish War; Mark Twain to England for the sixtieth anniversary of Queen Victoria's reign; Joaquin Miller and a boatload of journalists to Alaska for the fabulous Klondike gold rush; and ex-senator John J. Ingalls to Carson City, Nevada, for the Bob Fitzsimmons-Jim Corbett heavyweight title fight.[9]

More and more, with the continuing growth in circulation, Hearst used the *Journal* as a propaganda tool to sway readers to his point of view, as a powerful bludgeon against politicians and individuals who differed with his programs or violated his sense of justice. And, in so doing, he quickly realized the awesome power of the *Journal* to mold public opinion. During the fall of 1897, for example, he helped direct voter approval—through daily polls—toward the winning *Journal* candidate for mayor of New York City, Robert A. Van Wyck. Within this same time frame he also leveled journalistic assaults and legal suits against a prominent paving contractor and a city commissioner as well as helping convict (for assault) a city policeman named Hannigan. And with each success his confidence abounded and his belief in such actions became more justified.[10]

Hearst was intently concerned about improving every aspect of the

Journal, about updating methods of production and streamlining techniques of presentation. Fluidity of style soon became more apparent;
headlines, sometimes two to three inches in height, covered the front page
uninterrupted, no longer restricted by seven separate columns; and editorials now prominently appeared, with circled captions, that briefly summarized the contents for the reader. As early as October, 1896, Sunday
editor Morrill Goddard was printing an eight-page, multicolored comic
section called "The American Humorist," in which Richard Outcault displayed "the yellow kid," a young street urchin who lived in a New York
slum known as "Hogan's Alley." Within several months Rudolph Dirks
developed the "Katzenjammer Kids"—that is, after Hearst displayed the
Bilder Bucher collection he had acquired during his twenty-month European trip in 1873–74 and enthusiastically encouraged its promotion.

By December, Goddard began adding other supplements, also in color,
such as "The American Woman's Home Journal" and "The American
Magazine," both of which contained the ever-popular stories on sporting
events, beautiful women, eccentric millionaires, prominent celebrities,
and theater activities by noted drama critic Alan Dale as well as tales
about animals (e.g., "Jungle Folk in the Zoo"). And in March, 1897, Goddard—with Hearst's encouragement—revolutionized graphic presenta-
tions by utilizing halftone photographs in print and, together with
beautifully crafted illustrations, made the Sunday *Journal,* now ranging in
size from fifty-two to eighty pages, a showpiece for its readers. Equally significant, in his game of one-upmanship with rivals, Hearst stymied the
World's attempt to prevent the *Journal* from obtaining Associated Press
news information. On April 2, for $500,000, he purchased the *Morning
Advertiser,* which had an AP franchise, and thereby thwarted this "ingenious scheme" by Pulitzer to eliminate the *Journal* as competition.[11]

Hearst was ever sensitive to the American metabolism of the 1890s
that craved recognition by the world community, that exuded pride both
in individual and collective achievement, that reveled in the greatness of
the United States and its people. He therefore identified the *Journal* with
national purpose and chauvinistic impulses. In the Sunday supplements
he began each display with the word "American"; he coined a new motto
for the masthead: "An American paper for the American people"; and, especially in editorials, such words as "patriotism," "nationalism," and "destiny" appeared frequently. At times he literally waved the American flag at
Journal readers, on one occasion urging them to "cut this one out" and
"decorate your home." He also recommended that the Fourth of July be
recognized as a national holiday, then exemplified this suggestion by

spending thousands of dollars in a *Journal* celebration on that day. And he continually campaigned, beginning late in the spring of 1898, for a "National Policy," which included a five-point agenda: the annexation of Hawaii, the building of an isthmian canal through Nicaragua, the maintenance of "a mighty navy," the acquisition of strategic bases in the Caribbean, and the establishment of "great national universities" at West Point and Annapolis. But, without question, Hearst believed that the culmination of all such expectations rested in American intervention in Cuba and the freeing of its people from a "tyrannous" Spain, actions that would establish the United States as a formidable power in world politics.[12]

Within a week after the McKinley victory in November, 1896, Hearst was already gearing up for a new crusade, one he was emotionally dedicated to winning, one that would erase the stigma of defeat. "*Cuba Libre*" became the byphrase throughout all *Journal* offices. Prior to the Bryan campaign Hearst had laid the groundwork for his journalistic assault. Because of Spanish tyranny and misrule, Cuba—once regarded as the "Pearl of the Antilles" and the seat of government for much of New Spain—had become a land of fire and famine, an example of savage cruelty and wanton barbarity. Early in 1896 General Valeriano Weyler, an able officer who was appointed captain-general of Cuba, was ordered to put down an ongoing rebellion of almost a year. Systematically he began destroying the effectiveness of the insurrectionists. First he selected a province heavily occupied by the rebels, then sent an overwhelming number of troops to eliminate all resistance. Upon encountering opposition, he imposed a "reconcentration" of the populace into garrison towns. In other words, he herded civilians into camps bereft of food supplies and sanitary facilities; thus disease and death were ever constant.

Hence, the *Journal* displayed even greater invective and character assassination than during the Bryan campaign. With almost daily accounts reporting Cuban atrocities, General Weyler was introduced to the American public as "Butcher" or "Wolf" Weyler who burned people alive, a "mad dog" who feasted on the flesh of his victims, a "destroyer of families," an "outrager of women," a "pitiless exterminator of men." Hearst also welcomed news with any anti-Spanish slant, once again seemingly unconcerned about its origin or authenticity. He often accepted stories handed to his reporters from the Cuban Junta in New York City, whose objectivity was, at best, questionable. To guarantee a steady flow of information he sent *Journal* "special correspondents" to Cuba with instructions to document the valiant resistance of the rebels against overwhelming odds as

well as to describe, in grisly detail, their suffering at the hands of Spaniards. And when noted Western artist Frederick Remington telegraphed,
soon after arrival early in 1897, that "everything is quiet. There is no trou-
ble here. There will be no war. I wish to return," Hearst allegedly replied:
"Please remain. You furnish the pictures and I'll furnish the war." [13]

And that was exactly what Hearst did. But he had help; Joseph Pulitzer
was a most accommodating adversary. In a bid to defeat the brash "California upstart" in the battle for circulation numbers and newspaper dominance, Pulitzer applied all of the *World's* resources. In other words, he
lowered his standards to those of "Yellow Journalism" or "New Journalism," thereby "playing the game" that Hearst had surely improved upon, if
not invented. Or putting it another way, biographer Swanberg observed
that Pulitzer "violated most of the journalistic principles that he had up-
held for years." Over the next eighteen months, cost was no longer a factor;
pride and expediency now held sway. Nothing could be more humiliating
to the "Napoleon of journalism" than being defeated by a "callow youth,"
who was, he asserted, a "public menace." Pulitzer therefore opened the
World pocketbook, sending a bevy of correspondents to Cuba who, in
1896, began sensationalizing the news, always with a pro-Cuban slant,
and usually without verification. On May 17, 1896, for example, James
Creelman, an able and imaginative writer with an "enthusiasm" for the
dramatic, provided a classic account of the inflammatory journalism of
the period, so much so that Hearst soon purloined him from the *World*.
From the comfort of his hotel in peaceful Havana, Creelman wrote:

> Blood on the roadsides, blood in the fields, blood on the doorsteps, blood,
> blood, blood! The old, the young, the weak, the crippled—all are butch-
> ered without mercy. . . . Is there no nation wise enough, brave enough, and
> strong enough to restore peace in this bloodsmitten land? [14]

Hearst surely had the answer to Creelman's question. He outper-
formed Pulitzer in every department. He outspent him as if money were
an endless commodity. He whisked away the *World's* best talent, including
Creelman; he "enriched" the Cuban tourist business, one observer noted,
by inundating the island "at various times" with thirty-five special correspondents and artists; and he maintained a steady, incessant drumbeat for
"Cuba Libre"—with, of course, American intervention in the name of hu-
manity as the ultimate solution. And as for the "New Journalism" or "Yellow Journalism," which emphasized on-the-spot reporting with "a
superior regard for the truth," Hearst disregarded facts. At times he vigorously supported fictionalized accounts, earnestly believing, like the

knight-errant Sir Galahad in search of the Holy Grail, that his cause was just and that only a successful conclusion would justify the *Journal's* gallant crusade.[15]

Thus the battle for American journalistic supremacy escalated in 1897, with Cuba as the best enticement to attracting reader interest. Most of the "special correspondents," besides needing an interpreter because of their inability to understand or speak Spanish, could not wangle a "passage" into the provinces where the Cuban rebels were fighting; consequently they engaged in historical fiction. They manufactured battles that never happened; for example, "Havana, despite the insurgents' total lack of artillery, fell three or four times over," historian/journalist Walter Millis noted. And as for reporting atrocities, the more inhumane the better. Hence, an eager American public devoured brutish tales about nuns raped and murdered; hospital sick and wounded, together with their doctors and nurses, savagely slaughtered; captured rebels set on fire by amused Spanish soldiers; prisoners at Morro Castle (at the entrance of Havana Harbor) either torn apart by ferocious dogs or dumped into the bay as food for ravenous sharks.[16]

But Hearst demanded more than a steady drum roll of Spanish atrocities, of brutal horrors, of bloody reprisals whether by Cuban rebels or their "heartless tyrants." As a keen observer of the American psyche, he understood that readers needed to identify with a specific event, to sympathize with a tragic martyr, to rejoice with the triumphs of a heroic figure; therefore, he determined that the *Journal* would provide the public continually with some stimulant, some "outrage," to arouse sympathy as well as anger for the Cuban underdogs. On February 12, 1897, for instance, *Journal* correspondent Richard Harding Davis began earning his $3,000-a-month salary. In collaboration with artist Frederick Remington, who sketched a naked young woman being examined by three Spaniards, he produced a shocking story, with the front-page headline "DOES OUR FLAG SHIELD WOMEN?" It was historical fiction at its best—or worst. At Havana, Davis wrote, the Spaniards decided to exile three young girls who had given aid to the insurgents. Three "detectives" searched them twice before leaving, but, after allowing them to board the American ship *Olivette*, undressed them "even to the length of taking off their shoes and stockings," as Spanish officers, "with red crosses for bravery on their chests and gold lace on their cuffs, strutted scowling about the deck."

On the following day the *World* announced that the story was a *Journal* "invention," that the girls "had been searched by women matrons while the policemen waited outside." Yet Hearst continued this "shocker" for three more days, with one story announcing: "War is a dreadful thing, but there are things more dreadful than even war, and that is dishonor." In fact, Davis and Remington, who furnished rather lame excuses for their actions, were neither reprimanded nor dismissed. As *Journal* reporter Willis Abbot cogently observed, "it was characteristic of the Hearst methods that no one suffered for what in most papers would have been an unforgivable offense, and I never heard the owner of the paper, in public or in private, express the slightest regret for the scandalous 'fake.'" [17]

So during the next six months of 1897, although little military activity occurred in Cuba, the *Journal* continued its propaganda barrage—and it was effective. Late in February, after correspondent Murat Halstead reported that dentist Ricardo Ruíz, a naturalized American, had died (presumedly tortured for thirteen days) in the "dark and silent cells" of a Spanish prison, *Journal* colleague George Eugene Bryson "discovered" a heart-rending message to "his wife and children." Then in March, through the continued efforts of the *Journal*, newly appointed Secretary of State John Sherman arranged the release of Dr. Ruiz's wife and five children to the United States, whereupon she journeyed to Washington, D.C.—with Hearst paying all expenses—as a sympathetic public applauded the "TELLING HER STORY TO PRESIDENT MCKINLEY AT THE WHITE HOUSE." Again, in April, the *Journal* denounced Spain for arbitrarily imprisoning seventy-four Americans, including "a young Arkansas boy" named Ona Melton, who had been cast into a Spanish dungeon for almost a year. The *Journal* published a front-page account of "His Life in the Spanish Prison," where "over forty of his fellows had been executed." And in May, even though the rainy season was beginning in Cuba, thereby curbing military hostilities, the *Journal* focused on the reign of "Butcher" Weyler, whose *reconcentrado* policy was plaguing Cubans with famine and disease and death. [18]

As the rainy season continued to limit the output of atrocity stories during the summer of 1897 and as the McKinley administration punctuated its diplomatic ineptness concerning Cuba by inaction and "lack of public focus," Hearst became more and more frustrated. Despite a tremendous outlay of funds as well as arduous efforts by *Journal* staffers, his "crusade for Cuba" was floundering, if not running aground. Then it happened. One sultry day in mid-August, while at his desk thumbing through a "mound of dispatches," he casually looked at a telegram that read:

Havana.

Evangelina Cisneros, pretty girl of seventeen years, related to President of Cuban Republic, is to be imprisoned for twenty years on African coast, for having taken part in uprising of Cuban political prisoners on Isle of Pines.

Hearst, characteristically drumming his fingers on the desk when mulling over an idea, sitting as usual with legs crossed, and whistling softly, pushed a bell that signaled for Sam Chamberlain "to come here for a moment." Hearst then excitedly exclaimed while handing the wire to his editor: "Sam! We've got Spain now!" And suddenly all of his imaginative showmanship and creative genius burst forth in a series of staccatolike directives. "Telegraph to our correspondent in Havana to wire every detail of this case. Let's get up a petition to the Queen Regent of Spain for this girl's pardon. Enlist the women of America. Have them sign the petition. Wake up our correspondents all over the country. Have distinguished women sign first. Cable the petitions and names to the Queen Regent. Notify our minister in Madrid."

Then Hearst explained his brainstorming. "We can make a national issue of this case. It will do more to open the eyes of the country to Spanish cruelty and oppression than a thousand editorials or political speeches." In fact, he reasoned, as if anticipating a debate, "the Spanish Minister can attack our correspondents, but we'll see if he can face the women of America when they take up the fight! This girl must be saved, if we have to take her out of prison by force or send a steamer to meet the vessel that carries her to Africa—but that would be piracy, wouldn't it?" [19]

Immediately the *Journal* offices resembled a "Chinese fire drill," with Hearst and his reporters displaying the "New Journalism" or "Yellow Journalism" at its zaniest. "With the precision of exploding firecrackers," John Winkler recollected, staffers carried out his orders expeditiously, with the creative James Creelman serving as coordinator. To all parts of the world, as well as throughout the United States, hundreds of telegrams revealed the tragic tale of a young Cuban girl who dared oppose the fiendish "Butcher" Weyler. In Evangelina Cisneros, Hearst had discovered the Holy Grail; she would be the symbol of Spanish oppression, the catalyst to propel the McKinley administration past the "slow processes of diplomacy." [20]

Both as producer and director, Hearst could not have been more pleased with the results. For the next three weeks Evangelina Cisneros dominated the pages of the Hearst papers. More than fifteen thousand letters and telegrams inundated the *Journal* offices. The Queen Regent of Spain, Maria Cristina, received pleas from such prominent women as Varina Jefferson Davis, widow of the Confederate States of America president, the mother of President McKinley, the wife of Secretary of State John Sherman, the widow of ex-president U. S. Grant, the daughter of ex-president John Tyler, Mrs. Mark Hanna, and American Red Cross founder Clara Barton. Soon the Sisters of Notre Dame and the Superior of the Order of Visitation also joined the chorus of appeals, together with many prominent New Yorkers. Consequently, the *Journal* filled several pages with names (in small type) of women petitioners; then published a "Roll of Honor" specifying well-known women "whose hearts bled for Miss Cisneros." But especially compelling was a petition to Pope Leo XIII from Julia Ward Howe, author of the "Battle Hymn of the Republic"; one *Journal* headline read befittingly: "Her Eyes Have Seen the Sorrow." [21]

Hearst further choreographed this drama by playing the story to the fullest. The *Journal*, mostly through the words of Marion Kendrick and former Cuban correspondent George Bryson, painted Evangelina Cisneros as "a pure flower of maidenhood" who had "defended her honor against a beast in uniform," the "venal" military governor of her prison, Colonel José Berriz. As a reward for her bravery, this "most beautiful girl in the island of Cuba," who "was reared in seclusion and, almost a child in years," who "is [as] ignorant of the world as a cloistered nun," was "threatened with an early death." She was now enduring a precarious existence in a crowded cell at the Casa de Recojidas, "the vilest prison in Cuba," scrubbing floors, sleeping on "bare boards," eating a bowl of mush at meals, amid the most hardened criminals and "abandoned women of Havana." [22]

To keep this story "alive" before the public, Hearst received unexpected help, especially after manipulating certain facts. As early as August 3, 1897, General Weyler had expelled George Bryson from Cuba for such unwarrantable activities as attempted bribery to obtain Cisneros's release; however, on August 21, the *Journal* blared front-page headlines—with an accompanying story by Creelman—that "WEYLER RESENTS THE JOURNAL'S CISNEROS APPEAL BY EXPELLING BRYSON." As a result, Weyler pleaded his case before Pulitzer, presenting, of course, a much different story and set of circumstances. The rival *World* bewailed, once more, the *Journal's* sensationalism and fabrication tendencies, noting that "the Spanish in Cuba have sins enough to answer for, as the *World* was first to show." The writer then admonished: "But nothing is gained for the Cuban cause by inventions and exaggerations that are past belief."

Hearst was unfazed. The *Journal* replied the next day in its huge Sunday edition that "the women of America will save her [Cisneros] yet, in spite of Weyler and the *World*." Thus the two powerful New York newspapers once again engaged in verbal sniper fire, as Americans throughout the nation, by means of the AP wire service, briefly enjoyed the controversy, even as the Cisneros story was losing its luster.[23]

But not for long! Hearst was not about to let this story die. "He took the whole affair with the utmost seriousness," Willis Abbot remembered. "His was the driving force that kept going the prodigious wave of publicity. If ever for a moment he doubted that he was battling a powerful State to save the life and liberty of a sorely persecuted girl martyr, he gave no sign of it"; for during these "sensationalism" days in the *Journal* offices, Abbot noted, "it was the one dominating, all-compelling issue of the moment for him and he brooked no indifference on the part of his employees."

Even as the controversy was raging, Hearst was concocting an alternative plan. On August 28, *Journal* correspondent Karl Decker, under the assumed name of Charles Duval—and loaded with Hearst money—arrived in Havana as a replacement for Bryson. What happened during the next month was easy to follow. At first Decker tried bribery to effect Cisneros's release, but with no success. He then decided to "break her out." With the help of two men, an American shipper named William McDonald and Cuban rebel Carlos Carbonelle, he rented a house directly across from the Casa de Reconjidas prison. He then visited Cisneros to alert her of his intentions. The two of them, after mulling over several possible escapes, finally agreed on a workable plan. On the night of October 6 Decker and his two coconspirators climbed to the roof of their rented house, projected a long ladder to the second-floor parapet of the prison, and reached the cell window of "Evangelina's room" (she had tied a white handkerchief around one of the iron bars to indicate that "the coast was clear"). Decker, upon applying a heavy Stillson wrench to the bars and bending them upward, dramatically recounted: "She gave one glad little cry and clasped our hands through the bars, calling upon us to liberate her at once."

And they did. Within five minutes they had whisked her across the teetering ladder to the street below and a waiting carriage. Then Decker dressed Evangelina in the garb of a young sailor—a blue shirt with flowing tie, a coat and trousers, "her hair plastered to her head under a large slouch hat." Through the dark and narrow streets of Havana, with pistols drawn, the conspirators drove to the harbor, where, undetected by Weyler's armed police, Evangelina boarded the steamer *Seneca*, which soon sailed for New York—and freedom.[24]

What a fantastic story! It was as exciting as any romantic novel. And no wonder! Decker, "a clever and daring correspondent," wrote the script—of course, with Hearst's approval. As Willis Abbot later revealed, Hearst instructed Decker "to rescue the girl at any cost"; therefore, *Journal* "money bought her way out of prison," Abbot candidly asserted. "But to exonerate the guards, as well as furnish newspaper material, an elaborate plan of rescue was worked out, including the rental of a house next door to the prison, and bridging of the chasm between by a plank across which the youthful heroine was spirited to liberty." Then, "disguised—needlessly—as a boy she was brought to New York." [25]

Regardless of the facts, Hearst was determined that the "Crusade for Cuba" occupy center stage before the American people and that the second act of his play continue with equal vigor. On October 9, with the help of the AP wire service, Evangelina Cisneros and the *Journal* took New York, and the nation as well, by storm. For the next six days her story was front-page news. One *Journal* headline bragged how cunningly she had escaped, "Despite Weyler's Spies, the Guards in the Streets and the Cordon About the City." Another presented two large illustrations side by side—one of a beautiful young girl, the other of a gaunt, haggard woman—with the caption underneath reading: "Miss Cisneros Before and After Thirteen Months' Incarceration." And still another captured the essence of Hearst policies, that of self-promotion and public approbation; it read: "An American Newspaper Accomplishes at a Single Stroke What the Red Tape of Diplomacy Failed to Bring About in Many Months." Hearst then continued these plaudits of affirmation with pictures and quotes of prominent Americans "Who Joined with the *Journal* to Free Miss Cisneros." [26]

But showman Hearst still needed a strong third act; for, as he acknowledged to Creelman, "Now is the time to consolidate public opinion." Through the arduous efforts of the *Journal* staff and Hearst's uncommon disregard for money, the finale was spectacular. On October 14 a huge headline, dramatically recording the events of the previous day, read: "EVANGELINA CISNEROS REACHES THE LAND OF LIBERTY." Hearst assumed all expenses, housing her in a suite of rooms at the Waldorf-Astoria and hiring an interpreter to see to her every convenience. The next day he brought in Karl Decker, alias Charles Duval, specifically to fill the *Journal* pages with the thrilling, fictionalized account of the "heroic" escape from "hated Recojidas prison." And then two days later (October 17) Hearst arranged, with Creelman dutifully carrying out precise instructions, a special extravaganza for all New York. That evening, Evangelina Cisneros emerged from the Waldorf, dressed in an expensive white couturiere gown—in no way reflecting any evidence of a torturous imprisonment. "On the arm of d'Artagnan Decker" and accompanied by Mrs. J.

Ellen Foster of the Ladies' Cuban Relief Association of New York, she entered a waiting carriage that proceeded slowly downtown, amid growing crowds of people, behind an honor guard of soldiers, police, and white-uniformed naval cadets, all marching to the cadence and tunes of several bands. At Madison Square they observed an electrical transparency over the *Journal* uptown office at Broadway and Twenty-sixth, which glittered brilliantly: "*Journal* Wants Cuba Free." Then, to a standing ovation, they entered Delmonico's, the famous restaurant then at Fifth Avenue and Twenty-sixth, where Creelman had arranged a dinner reception for them with a number of local dignitaries. Even though New York mayor Robert A. Van Wyck was unable to attend, constituencies from the DAR., the Holland Dames, and the Ladies' Cuban Relief Association, together with members of the Cuban Junta, were much in evidence, as were a number of curiosity seekers.[27]

But where was Hearst? The mastermind of this whole event, "the man who footed the bills," was nowhere to be found—and for good reason. Biographer Swanberg stated that Hearst "was like a surgeon who could not bear to have his finger lanced," that the "blaze of publicity which he had poured on Miss Cisneros, Decker and the *Journal* was too warm for his shrinking nature." In this evaluation Swanberg was undoubtedly correct, at least according to all who knew this enigmatic, at times unpredictable genius.

Yet Hearst did make a brief appearance that must also have been even more puzzling to Evangelina Cisneros. At some point during the dinner reception Hearst drove his newly acquired French racing car in front of Delmonico's and "ran inside." He "found" Evangelina (whom he had never met), journalist Frederick Palmer recorded, standing "among the palms, shyly shook hands with the heroine whom his wonder machine had created, and then excused himself and hastened away in his automobile."[28]

The Hearst extravaganza did not end with his departure. After a "great dinner" and several glowing speeches praising the *Journal* for striking a blow against Spanish tyranny by saving the "Flower of Cuba," the participants moved across the street onto the vast expanse of Madison Square, where a crowd that totaled 120,000 was gathering. On a wooden stage constructed for this occasion, the honored guests (including economist Henry George) delivered their words of praise for Cuba, while denouncing Spain for its iniquity. Although most of the assembled thousands could not hear the speakers, not even Evangelina who "made a stammering, half-crying speech in English," the night was a "rousing" success. Hearst's preparations entertained the crowd with scores of searchlights and several bands, then lit the New York skies with an impressive display of fireworks (which even as a boy fascinated him). Promoter and showman Hearst could not have been more pleased, because high above the platform, for all to see, was an enormous sign electrically lit and glowing in the night: "THE JOURNAL'S WELCOME TO EVANGELINA CISNEROS." [29]

Because of such generated momentum the Cisneros melodrama would continue its theatrical course for almost a week. Even though rival New York papers devoted far less coverage to the "Cuban girl's story," usually omitting any reference to the *Journal* while relegating it to a back page, their editors could not ignore the fact that President McKinley received Evangelina at the White House on October 23. Nor could they dismiss completely another well-staged Hearst drama in Washington that Saturday evening—a mile-long parade from the Livingston Hotel (where Hearst had made exclusive accommodations for Cisneros and Decker) down Pennsylvania Avenue to Convention Hall, from which "a thousand electric stars flashed" on a "steel-girded firmament." After a crowd of more than seventy-five thousand people cheered the Cisneros contingent en route, some twenty thousand jammed inside the auditorium as bands played "The Star-Spangled Banner" and "America," followed by orators delivering emotional, flag-waving speeches. In summing up the night's events, the *Journal* once again engaged in the Hearst policy of self-adulation by pointing out that "Karl Decker and Evangelina Cisneros and the *New York Journal* had pulled the plug" that had bottled up "delirious patriotism, pent up too long." [30]

Hearst, after so many demands on the *Journal* staffers and because of such expensive outlays in support of the Cisneros story, decided upon a brief respite before his next move for "*Cuba Libre*." And surely a "breather" was in order. Early in October, 1897, a "reform" Spanish government, headed by Praxedes Sagasta, had achieved power. By late November it had repudiated the Weyler methods for ending the Cuban rebellion, replaced him with General Ramón Blanco, and at the same time proposed its own plan for peace—eventual autonomy, although through a "formidable and complex system." In turn, the McKinley administration was hoping to give Spain time to realize its expectations. [31]

For what was supposed to be a lull in newspaper activities during the late fall of 1897, Hearst was extremely busy. His schedule was still much the same: sleeping throughout the morning, working at a furious pace during the afternoon before returning to his new living quarters—all of the third floor at the "small but fashionable Worth Hotel"—across

Twenty-fifth Street from his previous residence at the Hoffman House. He then changed into formal attire for his patented evening at a Broadway play or musical followed by dinner, often at Delmonico's, before heading back to the *Journal* offices to approve the early edition format.

But something changed this pattern, at least temporarily. Hearst had met the beautiful Willson sisters, sixteen-year-old Millicent and eighteen-year-old Anita, who were part of a dancing troupe known as "The Merry Maidens." They had been performing at the Herald Square Theater in a Broadway musical, *The Girl from Paris*, which, not so incidentally, received a "rave" notice from a *Journal* drama critic. Hearst, despite continual warnings from "Mama," who had a strong "prejudice against people of the stage," proceeded to escort both young women—although attracted to the lovely Millicent—through "the perils" of New York nightlife, apparently unconcerned over the speculation and gossip afforded by such activities. In fact, the sisters sometimes accompanied him on his after-midnight sojourn to the *Journal*, patiently sitting "among the statuary in his office" as he frustrated the night editors and staffers with last-minute changes.[32]

Hearst also rediscovered that important news was occurring locally; therefore, he focused his journalistic creativity and imaginative talent on such concerns. After voter passage of a Greater New York charter in 1897 (which the *Journal* had vigorously endorsed), the city was about to become the second largest metropolis in the world through the incorporation of Brooklyn, the Bronx, Staten Island, and Queens; accordingly, its population would increase from approximately 2,000,000 to 3,388,000. Of course, city officials realized that a celebration was not just appropriate but also expected; however, they could not agree on a workable plan, much less provide funds for such an expensive undertaking.

Enter William Randolph Hearst! The *Journal*, he assured the city fathers, would gladly organize all festivities for inauguration day on January 1, 1898—and assume all costs. Consequently, he received carte blanche approval from them. So once again Hearst would reflect the American psyche concerning celebrations and identify with the average citizen "by taking his own pulse." As in the past, he reverted to popularly proven techniques for success. He immediately raised money by initiating a "*Journal* Campaign Fund" that listed contributor names and the amount of each donation. He even collected more than $7,000 from guests while giving a sumptuous Christmas dinner (at his own expense) for the five thousand newsboys working for the *Journal*. With the help of his staff, Hearst easily persuaded scores of societies and organizations, particularly those representing the city's many ethnic groups, to participate in an elaborate parade, offering twelve expensive prizes—including solid silver loving cups, elaborate vases, and a Roman urn—to those who displayed the "best" float, carnival costume, military organization, singing group, and musical feature. And, of course, all New Yorkers were invited to march in celebration, as bands would lead the way from Union Square to City Hall, where thirty-six searchlights would make that beautiful marble building, even in the dark of night, "gleam so white and clear." Then, at the stroke of midnight, the ringing of bells and a chorus of voices and the raising of the Greater New York flag, followed by Henry J. Pain's fantastic fireworks display, would signal the dawn of the greatest city in the greatest nation in the modern world. Such were the elaborate dreams and detailed plans of Hearst.[33]

Yet the hard facts of reality almost turned this enormously complex undertaking into disaster. Although the *Journal* praised the whole enterprise as a "huge success," in which "One Hundred Thousand People Joined the *Journal* in Its Stupendous Celebration of the New Metropolis's Generation," rival papers painted a more objective picture. During the evening of December 31 a freezing rain, at times changing to snow, turned the streets into a miserable mess of ice and sludge. Parade participants, despite such inclement weather, marched cheerfully to City Hall, surrounded on all sides by onlookers exhibiting a "sea of undulating umbrellas." Many New Yorkers decided to insulate themselves from the cold, filling the saloons in Manhattan—and glasses as well—to overflowing; consequently, any number never realized when the festivities began or ended, but an indulgent police force made few arrests. At the Broadway Central Hotel, however, some fireworks were set off, causing horses drawing one of the floats to bolt into one of the marching bands, thus injuring fifteen people and "flattening a tuba and several smaller brasses." But the parade participants went bravely forward and, without further mishap, arrived at City Hall Plaza, where a dozen choral groups raised a cacophony of sounds while vying for first-place singing honors; however, at the approach of the New Year, in the eerie light of a misty night, with thirty-six searchlights and five hundred magnesium bulbs illuminating a hazy sky, they led the crowd in the familiar strains of "Auld Lang Syne."

Hearst then completely surprised—and awed—the huge throng with a spectacular climax. From three thousand miles away, Mayor James Phelan of San Francisco, at the behest of Hearst and the *Examiner*, pressed a button at Golden Gate Park, triggering an electrical impulse that, at the stroke of midnight, "propelled the blue and white flag of Greater New

York whipping up the staff of the City Hall cupola." And while a battery of cannons roared a one-hundred-gun salute and hundreds of Pain's rockets spiraled into the misty sky abursting, the crowd of one hundred thousand faithful cheered as New York City became "a dripping reality." Even the rival *Tribune* grudgingly admitted the success of the evening, stating that "no one could hold a Roman candle to Hearst when it came to staging a spectacle." [34]

Throughout most of January, 1898, the *Journal* continued its focus on local concerns. It helped arbitrate a labor strike, campaigned for "cheap gas and antitrust legislation," and alerted the public of the *Journal's* vigilance against crime—Mrs. Nack, who was responsible for dismembering former lover William Guldensuppe, was, at last, entering Auburn Prison to serve a fifteen-year term. And in editorials and designated stories the *Journal* demanded civic improvements, especially in regard to schools, mail service, parks and lighting, streets, and bridges. [35]

But Hearst never lost sight of the all-compelling issue that was most affecting his journalistic life, the "Crusade for Cuba." *Journal* staffers continually frequented the offices of the New York City Junta (jokingly referred to as the "Peanut Club" because of the limitless supply of peanuts proffered to them), sniffing for some rumor or gory tidbit from Cuba and, with luck, for information of spectacular consequences. On February 8, Hearst had his story. [36]

7 | The *Journal's* War

∽

Enrique Dupuy de Lome, the Spanish minister in Washington, had a difficult task representing his country, especially with the *Journal* and the *World* infecting the American public daily with an anti-Spanish virus. An experienced and dedicated diplomat, a proud, "chilling person," to some a "vision of [past] empire and faded glories," he did not understand, and "had grown to hate" William McKinley—and therein lay his downfall. The president, in presenting his annual State of the Union message to Congress early in December, 1897, had devoted considerable space to U.S.-Spanish relations regarding Cuba. Although detailing the history of the 1895 rebellion, its horrors and affronts to the civilized world, he advised caution and patience while being purposely vague in the administration's recommendations. But de Lome, reacting badly to the message, wrote an indiscreet private letter to a friend. Within the next month Cuban spies in Havana intercepted his note and, realizing the explosive nature of the contents, sent it to the Cuban Junta in New York City, who exultantly offered a translated version to the press.

But only Hearst was willing to accept this volatile information without verification. Thus on February 9 the *Journal* exploded this bombshell, "the sensational [scoop] of the year," printing a facsimile of the letter (with translation) in emblazoned headlines: "THE WORST INSULT TO THE UNITED STATES IN ITS HISTORY." And why? At one part in the letter, de Lome commented on the McKinley message as follows:

> I consider it bad.... Besides the natural and inevitable coarseness (*groseria*) with which he repeats all that the press and public opinion of Spain have said of Weyler, it shows once more what McKinley is: weak and catering to the rabble (*dibil y populachero*) and, besides, a low politician (*politicastro*) who desires to leave a door open to himself and to stand well with the jingos of his party.[1]

Hearst was now in an element all his own, one he had created and fine-tuned. With him directing every aspect of the "crusade," the *Journal* was once again agog with excitement. He daily initiated one "Extra" after another for immediate news on the street, applying his talents to the makeup of sensational headlines, to deciding the placement of stories, to exacting from *Journal* cartoonists and artists illustrations that graphically depicted his views and sentiments about Spain. And, each day, Hearst fashioned a history for New Yorkers and the nation through headlines: on February 10, "JOURNAL'S LETTER GETS DE LOME HIS WALKING PAPERS"; on February 11, "JOURNAL'S LETTER FREES COUNTRY FROM DE LOME"; on February 12, "THREATENING MOVE BY BOTH SPAIN AND THE U.S."; and on February 15, "SPAIN REFUSES TO APOLOGIZE, ARMS 6 MERCHANT VESSELS." Concerning the sensational journalism of these exciting days, one historian succinctly quipped that Hearst "snooped, scooped, and stooped to conquer." [2]

Even so, after a week of such sensationalism, the story began to die of its own inertia, especially since the Spanish government, besides accepting de Lome's resignation, agreed on February 15 to send an apology to McKinley. But, again, timing was everything. At 9:40 that evening the American battleship *Maine*, which had entered Havana Harbor on January 25, blew up and sank, with the loss of 2 officers and 264 sailors. And from that moment forward, war was inevitable. Across the nation the rallying cry was: "Remember the *Maine!*" [3]

The *World* and *Journal* thus intensified their loud, incessant drumbeat for war. By 6:00 A.M. on February 16 both had an "Extra" on the street. The huge *Journal* headlines surely typified the emotion of the hour: "WARSHIP MAINE WAS SPLIT IN TWO BY AN ENEMY'S SECRET INFERNAL MACHINE." Yet in this contest for circulation, through creative sensationalism, Hearst had few equals. When the *World* sent a tug and "expert divers" to Havana specifically for investigating the cause of the *Maine* disaster (a journalistic project that Spain rightly prevented), Hearst countered with a "$50,000 REWARD! For the Detection of the Perpetrator of the *Maine* Outrage!" Then on February 17 both papers published a "suppressed cable"—which later proved to be a fake—from Captain Charles D. Sigsbee, commander of the *Maine*, to Secretary of the Navy John D. Long, stating that "the explosion was not an accident"; in fact, one *Journal* headline blatantly announced that Assistant Secretary of the Navy Theodore Roosevelt was in complete agreement, an assertion he vehemently denied. And no matter that an outstanding journalist such as E. L. Godkin of the *Nation*, as well as several New York newspapers, termed his "behavior" as "disgraceful," Hearst had a cause to be won; and, equally gratifying, circulation had increased dramatically—"more than a million a day." [4]

For Hearst the next two months were high adventure. His reporters and editors scripted their own stories of exciting historical fiction whenever facts did not substantiate what Hearst pridefully began referring to as "The *Journal's* War." On February 17, even as McKinley was appointing a Naval Board of Inquiry to determine the cause of the *Maine* catastrophe, the *Journal* declared (along with a graphic illustration) that a "sunken torpedo," if not a "hidden" Spanish mine, had induced the explosion. On February 20 it compounded such fiction, the headline blatantly claiming, "JOURNAL HERE PRESENTS, FORMALLY, PROOF OF A SUBMARINE MINE." And again on February 25 the *Journal* produced for its readers a "secret map" locating specifically every mine in Havana Harbor, even though Spanish prime minister Sagasta denied its existence. During these tense days late in February, a host of divers miraculously materialized in Cuba, examining the *Maine* wreckage and supplying "positive proof" for all *Journal* stories, although Spanish authorities were effectively preventing such activities by all freelance investigators. [5]

For this "crusade," however, Hearst employed a multifaceted plan of attack that would culminate in American intervention. For a continual fount of information he expended tremendous sums of money. To Cuba he sent his most "creative" journalists, those who had few, if any, qualms about reporting unfounded rumors or uncorroborated stories as factual. Hence, the *Journal* team consisted of such apostles of venom and make-believe as Alfred Henry Lewis (the character assassin of Hanna in 1896), George Eugene Bryson, Karl Decker, James Creelman, William E. Lewis, and Julian Hawthorne. To complement their stories were such talented artists as Frederick Remington and William Bengough, who, through their illustrations, also applied imagination. And to provide food and transportation as well as an open communication channel to Key West, Florida, some ninety miles from Havana, Hearst placed at their disposal two fast yachts, *Buccaneer* and *Anita*, together with the tug *Echo*. [6]

Hearst also continued his pattern of reader involvement. Consequently the *Journal* initiated a "*Journal* Monument Fund" to "honor the nation's dead"; over the next five months, donations totaled more than $100,000. At the same time *Journal* staffers continually quoted "outraged" citizens—ministers, prominent citizens, and politicians at all levels of government—who abhorred the senseless loss of American life through "Spanish treachery." And, whenever possible, the *Journal* elicited reader sympathy. For instance, the Spaniards in Havana quickly buried the American dead after the *Maine* catastrophe because of the rapid decomposition of corpses in a torrid climate. On February 19, however, the *Journal* reported that authorities, displaying a bitter hatred toward Americans, interrupted the funeral procession of the *Maine* victims; then it claimed four days later on the front page (accompanied by several grisly illustrations) that the "BODIES OF DEAD HEROES [WERE] ON HAVANA WHARF" with "VULTURES HOVERING OVER A GRIM FEAST." Yet equally unsettling was a series of stories in mid-March by Julian Hawthorne that triggered public sympathy and shocked American sensibilities. In graphic detail he described—and *Journal* artists just as graphically depicted—the appalling horrors of the Spanish *reconcentrados*, especially the high mortality rate of Cuban women and children (estimated as high as forty thousand) in the Weyler "death camps." [7]

Yet Hearst could not push the McKinley administration into accepting what he considered to be an inevitable conclusion. He therefore applied increased journalistic pressure. On March 1, 1898, he sponsored a congressional commission, composed of three warhawk senators and two representatives, to "gather all the facts" in Cuba and "tell them to the people." He upped the tempo for war, with six to eight of the *Journal's* sixteen pages devoted daily to a demand for action. Editorials, exclusive stories, and *Journal* polls continually pointed out that Americans were united in their desire to defend the nation's honor, while questioning the patriotism of those who still sought a peaceful solution to the Cuban problem; Davenport cartoons, depicting Hanna and McKinley, were especially vicious. And when a Naval Board of Inquiry erroneously reported late in March that an "external explosion" caused the destruction of the *Maine*—in 1976 Admiral Hyman G. Rickover, under the auspices of the U.S. Navy, presented overwhelming proof that the explosion occurred from spontaneous combustion in one of the ship's coal bunkers, which was next to a powder magazine—the *Journal* response was emotional and intense. Hearst was especially pleased in promoting the slogan of the year: "Remember the *Maine*, to hell with Spain!" [8]

With the *Journal* and *World* clamoring for war, with a jingoistic Congress reflecting the popular will, President McKinley was unable to withstand such public pressure. After Congress pushed through an appropriation bill of $50 million for national defense on March 9—without a dissenting vote—and after the report of the Naval Board of Inquiry eighteen days later, McKinley sent the Spanish government in Madrid a request, which turned out to be an ultimatum. Specifically he suggested (but actually demanded) an immediate armistice in Cuba, an end to the *re-concentrado* camps, and American mediation between the Cuban rebels and Spain. To this blatant attempt by McKinley to interfere in their internal affairs, Spanish government officials reacted negatively. Yet they hoped to avoid war and therefore agreed to end the *reconcentrado* policy. They then asked the pope to request a suspension of hostilities in Cuba, whereby they would satisfy McKinley's "request" while "saving face" with their own people. On April 9, however, after the pope refused to intervene, the Spanish government caved in completely to all American demands. And the next day U.S. Minister Stewart Woodford in Madrid exultantly cabled the president: "I hope that nothing will now be done to humiliate Spain [further], as I am confident that . . . you will win the fight on your own lines."

McKinley, an astute politician, was not blind to the realities of the time or the mood of the American people, for as fictionalized Irishman Mr. Dooley said (through his creator, humorist Finley Peter Dunne) to side-kick Mr. Hennessey concerning the president's attentiveness to public opinion: "McKinley has his ear so close to the ground that he gets it full of grasshoppers." Well aware that Assistant Secretary of the Navy Theodore Roosevelt was not too secretly announcing—to anyone who would listen—that "McKinley has no more backbone than a chocolate éclair" and ever cognizant that the public was demanding Cuban intervention, the president was not about to jeopardize, much less ruin, his chances for reelection in 1900. And even though Mark Hanna, as well as many business leaders and party supporters, did not favor war, McKinley finally decided to give way to the popular will. On April 11 he urged armed intervention to free Cuba, and two weeks later, on April 25, Congress passed a war resolution.[9]

For the next four months (from April 19 to August 21, 1898), the *Journal* provided even more excitement, as 1.2 million to 1.3 million readers attested to daily. While Congress was debating McKinley's message to fight Spain, Hearst dramatically promised to sound the *Journal's* whistle—"Five Long Blasts"—to alert New Yorkers to the "Notice of War." But giant headlines, three to four inches high, allowed for greater theatrics; the first eight pages of the sixteen-page daily edition, designated by Hearst as the "War Extra," enthralled readers by discussing heroes and villains, expectations and fears; and rumors, running rife through the pages, received the stamp of authenticity and the drama of immediacy by an opening phrase, "By Special Cable to the *Journal*. (Copyright, 1898, by W. R. Hearst)."[10]

But during the last week in April, the *Journal* added to the prevailing excitement. Hundreds of dispatches and rumors abounded throughout its pages. The American "WAR FLEET" was possibly on its way "to bombard Havana." East Coast cities were preparing against an anticipated attack by the Spanish Navy. "Troops [were] to invade Cuba Saturday [April 30]," even as McKinley was calling for "80,000 volunteers" to enlist. And "by special cable" from Hong Kong—although Hearst had no correspondents in the area—the *Journal* reported for almost a week that Commodore George Dewey, with his Asiatic Squadron, was going to engage the Spanish fleet in Manila Bay "today or tomorrow." [11]

Then, almost immediately, the United States won a decisive victory, and the public—together with Hearst—had an authentic American hero. George Dewey, a short, ruddy-faced Vermonter nearing age sixty, frosty-haired with a matching mustache, was not especially impressive in appearance, sometimes considered as "an elderly commodore" to whom Assistant Secretary of the Navy Roosevelt had entrusted the Asiatic Squadron at Hong Kong. But early in the morning on May 1, 1898, Dewey achieved celebrity status by the boldness of his actions. Undeterred by Spanish mines and threatening coastal defenses, he intrepidly sailed into Manila Bay and attacked an undermanned, demoralized Spanish squadron that seemingly was anticipating defeat. At the tense moment of attack, Dewey gave the American public its second catch phrase of the war by turning to the captain of his flagship and calmly saying: "You may fire when ready, Gridley." Both he and his commanders did just that. After six hours of fighting, the Americans won an overwhelming victory, completely destroying the Spanish squadron, with the loss of only one man (due to heat stroke). [12]

What thrilling, fun-filled times these were in 1898—days that Americans would not soon forget! The United States became a nation of flags and fireworks and military marches. Overnight, Dewey had electrified the American people with his victory at Manila Bay. How quickly he assumed the status of a cult hero. Everything seemed to bear his name, from hundreds of babies to cigars to milkshakes and cocktails. A varied assortment of clothes and accompanying accessories also carried his stamp—neckties with stickpins, cuff buttons, watch charms, even a Dewey rabbit's foot. As a *coup de grâce* to such admiration and adulation, one pharmaceutical company produced a Dewey laxative with an appropriate slogan, "the 'Salt' of Salts."

And what an incredible feeling of unity and patriotism! Throughout every town and hamlet in the United States, Americans marched and sang to the beat of bands that played the stirring music of Sousa's "Stars and Stripes Forever." When McKinley called for volunteers, more than two hundred thousand young men, who had listened to Civil War veterans recount the heroics of more than thirty years past, rushed to the colors. In this ambiance of patriotic fervor, who would ever forget that millionaires such as the Vanderbilts and J. P. Morgan and Hearst offered their yachts to transport troops to Cuba, that Democrats and Populists contested with Republicans to demonstrate their confidence in the future greatness of the United States, that a large number of blacks volunteered for service, and that Southerners, momentarily suppressing past hatreds emanating from the Civil War, vied with Northerners to enlist in the military. For example, General "Fighting Joe" Wheeler, a former Confederate great, became a leader of an American force in Cuba; however, he had difficulty, at times, in concealing previous sympathies. When rushing into battle near Santiago and seeing the enemy retreat, "his old nostrils suddenly began to quiver as he smelled gunpowder again." Then he yelled enthusiastically to his men: "Yippee! The Yankees are running. Dammit! I mean the Spaniards." And who would ever forget that Theodore Roosevelt was second in command of a volunteer cavalry unit known as the "Rough Riders" and that William Jennings Bryan and his friends formed an army group fittingly dubbed the "Silver Battalion"?[13]

During this first month of the war Hearst was gloatingly ecstatic, with every success spurring an even further range to his imagination and creativity. Upon news of Dewey's victory, the *Journal* announced in three-inch-high headlines on May 2 to its 1,645,498 readers: "VICTORY, Complete! . . . Glorious! . . . THE MAINE IS AVENGED!" Within the week, "exclusive" accounts of the battle, as well as graphic illustrations by *Journal* correspondents and artists—although not one was present—filled the morning and evening editions, and then were told again and again, each story usually accompanied with a picture of Dewey surrounded by American flags. "HOW DO YOU LIKE THE JOURNAL'S WAR?" Hearst exultingly asked New Yorkers on May 9 and 10. And what was delaying a direct confrontation with Spanish forces in the Caribbean? Hearst seemed to be prodding the McKinley Administration to act decisively, just as he had prior to the war declaration. Day after day in May, the *Journal* raised the expectations of its readers, with headlines proclaiming that "Invading Army Sets Sail for Cuba," that "Great Naval Battle Is Due Today," that "Grand Expeditions to Put a Quick End to War." What fantastic, exciting fiction![14]

But make no mistake; Hearst was as earnestly dedicated to the crusade for Cuban liberty as to his newly found hero. In May, out of the vast rumor mill generating in the *Journal* offices, an alarming report suddenly began circulating that a powerful Spanish fleet under the command of Admiral Manuel de la Camara was preparing immediately to sail for Manila via the Suez Canal. Hearst was greatly perturbed concerning this threat to Dewey; hence, as "a piece of heartfelt, practical patriotism combined with a Napoleonic stroke of advertising," he concocted, James Creelman asserted, an extremely expensive scheme (at an estimated cost of more than $100,000), which would have produced enormous international repercussions with England if successful. To carry out his wishes Hearst once again relied on the dependable—and loyal—Creelman, who was on a *Journal* mission in London. He cabled these astonishing instructions:

> Dear Mr. Creelman:
>   I wish you would at once make preparations so that in case the Spanish fleet actually starts for Manila we can buy some big English steamer at the eastern end of the Mediterranean and take her to some part of the Suez Canal, where we can then sink her and obstruct the passage of the Spanish warships. This must be done if the American monitors sent from San Francisco have not reached Dewey and he should be placed in a critical position by the approach of Camara's fleet. I understand that if a British vessel were taken into the canal and sunk under the circumstances outlined above, the British Government would not allow her to be blown up to clear a passage and it might take time enough to raise her to put Dewey in a safe position.
>
> Yours very truly,
W. R. Hearst

But fortunately for those involved, Admiral Camara proceeded too slowly to have any effect on military operations, thus depriving Hearst of a journalistic coup that, if carried out successfully, would probably have amazed even him.[15]

Hearst, however, continued to be a man of ideas—and always expensive ones. Yet, what would a knight-errant be without a quest? To President McKinley late in May, 1898, he proposed raising a volunteer cavalry regiment to fight in Cuba—along the same lines that Theodore Roosevelt had helped organized the "Rough Riders." But the Hearst presentation had certain distinguishing features. He was willing to provide arms, equipment, and mounts "at his own expense," the estimated cost easily amounting to $500,000. Nor was he, unlike Roosevelt, seeking any special favor. "I am conscious of a lack of special qualifications to direct even in a minor capacity such a body of men," he candidly acknowledged, "and do not, therefore, request any other position in the regiment than that of a man in the ranks."

Although McKinley turned down this request, Hearst was not discouraged; he already had another offer on its way, one that would be more difficult to refuse. This time he switched military branches; for he cared not to differentiate between the armed services as long as he was allowed to participate. He thus submitted to the U.S. Navy his 138-foot steam yacht *Buccaneer* "without any conditions whatever." Specifically, he proposed to equip, arm, and service the ship "during the continuation of the present war"; he would enlist sailors, who would be "fully armed and uniformed ... in accordance with naval regulations"; and he would pay their wages. All that he asked in return was an appointment "either as commander or second in command" of the vessel, subject to passing "certain examinations" that demonstrated his qualifications. As a consequence, on June 4, Acting Secretary of the Navy Charles H. Allen accepted this proposal with one slight modification: Hearst, while appointed an honorary ensign in the U.S. Navy, would not be a member of the ship's complement. Three days later, a small detachment of soldiers from Camp Tampa took possession of the *Buccaneer*, thereby completing the transaction.[16]

So now the excitement intensified in the *Journal* newsrooms, once again reflecting the ebullient spirit of its leader. Everyone "who had influence enough," Willis Abbot admitted, "became a war correspondent. The office was depopulated." And surely his assessment was correct; Hearst immediately assigned nineteen writers and illustrators to the several war zones. But the Caribbean was especially alluring; Hearst saw to that. In fewer than two months he spent more than $500,000 on "essentials." Hearst, like Roosevelt, was not about "to miss the fun." First he chartered, biographer John Winkler noted, "two yachts, an oceangoing tug, six steam vessels, a Brazilian cattle boat and a Red Cross boat," partly for his own convenience and luxury but mainly for swifter communications; therefore, both day and night, *Journal* dispatch ships made their way to the nearest cable station at Kingston, Jamaica. After all, the name of the game was "scoop the opposition," which accounted for innumerable "Extras" on the streets, hence greater circulation and more advertisements.[17]

The Hearst communication system, whether producing actual or fictional stories, was so well organized and effective that rumors began circulating that rival papers had "hired queues of boys to stand in front of *Journal* bulletin boards to obtain the earliest news and rush it to their offices." The acid-tongued and often ill-tempered Scotsman Arthur

McEwen, together with the sometimes mischievous Arthur Brisbane, who was ever cognizant of reader entertainment, decided to test such hearsay statements, much to the chagrin of the *World*. On June 8 the *Journal* published a "dispatch" from Cuba, stating that during a naval bombardment "Colonel Reflipe W. Thenuz, an Austrian artillerist of European renown ... was so badly wounded that he has since died." The next day the *World* reported, in "all its twenty or more editions," Abbot laughingly recollected, an equally official-looking "dispatch" that stated: "On board the *World* dispatch boat *Three Friends*, off Santiago de Cuba, via Port Antonio, Jamaica.—Colonel R. W. Thenuz, an Austrian artillerist well known throughout Europe ... was so badly wounded that he has since died." McEwen and Brisbane were ecstatic. To the delight of New Yorkers, they crucified the "distinguished" *World* editors by pointing out that the story was a hoax, that their famous Reflipe W. Thenuz was, appropriately, a "disguised anagram for 'We Pilfer The News.'" Nor did McEwen and Brisbane let the matter drop, their teasing and ridicule continuing unmercifully. For the next month they periodically referred to the *World*'s dependence on the *Journal* for news by suggesting that a monument be erected for the *World*'s "hapless colonel," that readers contribute to a memorial fund with "Confederate notes, Chinese cash, repudiated bonds, everything that looked like money and was in fact worthless." Then, in the July 10 Sunday edition, they capped this prank with a full-page cartoon, which depicted the theft of the Thenuz story by frantic *World* editors. For years the ruse remained a "classic" in Printing House Square; but, more importantly, amused readers increased *Journal* circulation as well as substantiating Hearst's boastful logo: "If You Don't Read The *Journal*, You Don't Get The News." [18]

In the meantime, the events of war transpired somewhat slower in the Caribbean than in the Pacific, even though the outcome was just as decisive. Early in May, Admiral Pascual Cervera, the commander of the Spanish Atlantic naval squadron, decided not to risk an engagement with the American North Atlantic fleet and, therefore, sought protection in the port of Santiago de Cuba, on the southeastern edge of the island. Admiral William T. Sampson and Commodore Winfield Scott Schley (pronounced "sly"), who commanded the American naval forces, tried to block Cervera's exit by sinking the collier *Merrimac* in Santiago's channel. On June 3, after an unsuccessful attempt, they decided to wait until the Spanish squadron tried to escape. War correspondents, eager to write about heroes (or villains), elevated the two American commanders, who were continually at odds and of questionable judgment, to celebrity status by depicting, in a popular catchphrase, that the U.S. Navy was "as strong as Sampson and as Schley as a fox." [19]

With the Spanish naval threat practically eliminated, the American invasion of Cuba quickly became a reality. On June 13, after numerous delays and amid great confusion, an expeditionary force of approximately sixteen thousand men finally sailed forth from Tampa Bay—an action the *Journal* had been predicting for more than a month. Then from June 20 to 25 the troops, still in much disarray and in lack of leadership, disembarked near Santiago without incident or opposition, because the Spaniards were even more inept. And quickly the battle was joined. [20]

Not nearly as much confusion existed at the *Journal* offices, however; for its leader, on a "gallant quest," was fully in charge. Since the McKinley administration, as a political "pay back" for the vicious Bryan campaign of 1896, had blocked his every effort to fight for Cuban liberation, Hearst decided to lead his own expeditionary force, both as admiral of the *Journal* squadron and general of its troops. While cost was never a consideration, preparation was everything. Late in May he chartered the rather sizable steamship *Sylvia* from the Baltimore Fruit Company and stocked it not only with such essentials as food and drink and medicine, but, even more important in a tropical clime, with a large supply of ice. Hearst, who constantly amazed colleagues and companions with his resourcefulness and imagination, decided to equip the spacious *Sylvia* with a printing press, along with all the accoutrements and personnel necessary for publishing a daily newspaper if, perchance, such an occasion should arise. As "staff advisers" he invited such trusted associates as the reliable James Creelman, who had just returned from London, longtime friend from Harvard days Jack Follansbee, New York nightlife companions Millicent and Anita Willson, and superintendent of the *Journal's* mechanical operations as well as loyal companion George Pancoast.

John C. Hemment was the exception to this entourage. A gifted professional photographer who was experimenting with motion pictures, he so impressed Hearst that he was allowed to bring enough equipment and materials, Hemment noted, "to start an ordinary photograph supply shop." Consequently, he and several assistants had ample space designated aboard the *Sylvia* to ply their trade effectively, including a darkroom with the latest duplication processes. Hearst then attended to one last detail. To avoid any misunderstanding with the McKinley administration, he obtained permission from Secretary of War Russell A. Alger to enter the war zone, although having to endure a mild rebuke for his past political actions. [21]

So what Hearst considered to be the grandest adventure in his life began. By the second week in June, 1898, the *Journal* expedition sailed southward from New York. While the American expeditionary force under Major General William R. Shafter headed toward Santiago de Cuba, the *Sylvia* proceeded to Kingston, Jamaica, arriving on June 17. Once again, as when competing with Pulitzer and the *World* for more readers, Hearst was in his element, happy "as a schoolboy," commanding his troops to endure any hardship and peril, Hemment asserted, so that the American people could experience "the events at the seat of war with all the vividness and accuracy possible to camera and pen." At the same time Hearst dreamed of finding himself in the midst of an ongoing battle; hence, he and Jack Follansbee bought two polo ponies at Kingston in anticipation of being effective cavalrymen.[22]

Hearst, although assigning more than twenty correspondents and illustrators to accompany the U.S. Army and Navy, decided to be an active participant instead of a mere observer. On June 18, after a leisurely trip to the outskirts of Santiago de Cuba, he began setting up a work schedule, albeit a flexible one. Almost immediately Hearst, together with Hemment and Creelman, met Admiral Sampson on the flagship *New York* and was extended every courtesy. The next day, at Guantánamo Bay on board the leased steamship *Seguranca*, he located General Shafter, who granted his party "permission to enter the [American] lines at any point." Then on June 22 Hearst witnessed the landing of several regular and volunteer army regiments near Siboney, some ten miles southeast of Santiago. And several days later he accomplished a primary objective, visiting with General Calixto García, the aged Cuban *insurrecto* who was the commander of the Santiago de Cuba region and whom Hearst much admired.[23]

As a result of these experiences, Hearst appointed himself as a war correspondent for the *Journal* during the next several weeks, a position that fostered fond experiences and cherished memories. To *Journal* readers he soon began sending exclusive stories under his signature, which overall received favorable reviews but, more importantly, revealed his feelings and mind-set. In his first article of June 27, Hearst rather dramatically stated that "it is a satisfactory thing to be an American and be here on the soil of Cuba" where "the struggle for the possession of the city of Santiago and capture of Cervera's fleet seem to be only a few hours away." He then vividly painted a scene in words for his readers. From "a rough green ridge" overlooking the area, he wrote, "we can see dimly on the sea the monstrous forms of Sampson's fleet lying in a semicircle in front of the entrance to Santiago harbor, while here at our feet masses of American soldiers are

pouring from the beach into the scorching valley where the smell of stag-
nant and fermented vegetation ground under the feet of thousands of
fighting men rises in the hot mists through which vultures, that have already fed on the corpses of slain Spaniards, wheel lazily about the thorny,
poisonous jungle of Santiago." This story was somewhat melodramatic
even for the historical fiction printed in the *Journal* over the past year, but
"it is," the *New York Times* editorialized, "straightforward, clear, and readable, with the exception of a little nervousness at the start." [24]

But Hearst had not completed his report; he soon recorded his impressions of the American military commanders. Admiral Sampson was, he
noted, "a quiet, conservative man with thin features and almost snow
white beard, and melancholy eyes." He was also a "stiff, severe kind of man"
whom Hearst did not appreciate. As a consequence, the *Journal* began referring to him as a "tea-going admiral—a rear admiral, always in the rear."
General Shafter was another matter, however. A huge hulk of a man,
weighing an estimated three hundred pounds, described aptly as a "sixty-
three year old fat and gouty veteran who looked like three men rolled into
one—or, as a quip said, a floating tent," he did not look or act the part of a
military leader. Distracted often by a painful case of gout, he had developed no plan of attack for the American expeditionary force except to dis-
embark near Santiago de Cuba and thereafter engage the enemy. He was
the epitome of confusion inundated with illness. But Hearst liked Shafter,
hence describing him as "a bold, lion-headed hero, and massive as to
body—a sort of human fortress in blue coat and flannel shirt." [25]

A meeting with General Calixto García, however, was easily one of
Hearst's most treasured memories. Together with Creelman and
Hemment, he visited the aged, white-haired Cuban hero at a modest
headquarters in Siboney. After brief but cordial amenities, García, striking in appearance with a "square-cut beard" covering "an equally square-
cut chin," and mopping perspiration from a brow that displayed "a large
scar" as a reminder of previous sacrifices for his country, presented Hearst
with a tattered, bullet-pierced battle flag bearing the lone star of Cuba. As
Hemment was taking picture after picture, García announced emotionally: "I present to the *New York Journal*, in commemoration of its services to
liberty, the headquarters flag of the Second Department of the Republic.
You see upon it the marks of Mauser bullets. This flag has been borne
through many battles, and hundreds of brave men have died under it. Its
colors are faded, but is the best thing the Cuban Republic can offer its best
friend." Deeply moved, Hearst graciously accepted this treasured gift
amid the resounding cries of "*Viva Cuba Libre!*"—but not to such an ex-

tent as to commemorate the occasion with a photograph. Consistent with past actions, the painfully shy Hearst still avoided the camera and limelight.[26]

Although conditions in Cuba were at times pretty dismal—the mud constant from intermittent rainstorms, the heat insufferable because of such high humidity, the mosquitoes noisome and the sand crabs irritating, the food and drinking water often questionable—Hearst was ecstatic in this strange, eminently dangerous environment, even ready to feed "his men raw meat," biographer John Winkler asserted, if such an action would rouse them "to extraordinary efforts." In fact, Hearst thrived in this chosen land of "his crusade." Dressed in rumpled flannels, he in no way attracted attention except for his favorite panama hat, "with a gaily-colored band"; otherwise, he was nondescript, happily following the American troops as they slogged through the junglelike foliage outside Santiago de Cuba. The thirty-five-year-old Hearst, not wanting "to miss the fun," continued to push toward the battlefront.[27]

Hearst did not have long to wait. On the morning of July 1, while tagging along with Roosevelt's Rough Riders at El Pozo (on the outskirts of Santiago), he and Hemment and Follansbee were on horseback when shells began exploding nearby. Suddenly an American officer in charge of a skirmish line yelled out: "What in hell are you fellows doing? Don't you see you are drawing the fire from those [Spanish] batteries? For God's sake, men, get off your horses!" Hearst immediately reacted, turning to Hemment and then smilingly said: "Well, I guess possibly we are drawing the fire."[28]

In the midst of this skirmish, Hearst and Follansbee, along with Hemment photographing the action, watched the U.S. Army advance. By that afternoon, en route to San Juan Heights overlooking Santiago de Cuba, the American infantrymen attacked the heavily fortified village of El Caney. But unbeknownst to Hearst, James Creelman was carrying on his own private war. While accompanying an army brigade commanded by Major General Adna R. Chaffee, he realized that "whatever of patriotism or excitement was stirring others in that place of carnage had got into . . . [his] blood too." As a result, he led a bayonet charge against a well-protected fort and successfully overran its defenders without personal mishap. But, upon seeing a red-and-yellow Spanish flag "lying in the dust" just outside the bastion, he ran outside and picked it up, then tauntingly "wagged it at the entrenched village" below. For his foolish audacity, he received a painful bullet wound in the shoulder and the captured Spanish battle flag draped across his prostrate body.[29]

Over the next few hours Creelman, at times in a semidelirious state, lay helpless along a roadside that turned into a makeshift hospital. Then he sensed someone beside him; it was, he later wrote, "Mr. Hearst, the proprietor of the *New York Journal* . . . who had provoked the war and had come to see the result with his own eyes." So once again Hearst, as a war correspondent, was in his element. Wearing his favorite attire—rumpled flannels and a panama hat—with a revolver in his belt, and armed with pencil and notebook, he could not have been more thrilled with his situation. The day had been one of continual excitement and stimulating exhilaration. Soon after daybreak he and his *Journal* party had ridden on horseback with Colonel Honore Laine of the Cuban Army (hired as a *Journal* correspondent), usually at a safe distance from the fighting but still in danger of sniper fire. While experiencing the personal risks of individual soldiers and witnessing the ultimate sacrifice of many, he had rejoiced in the triumph of the military and the thrill of victory. But now he was living the ultimate dream—after the battle of El Caney, interviewing a wounded hero, who was one of the *Journal's* own. With painstaking care Hearst wrote down word for word Creelman's story, which was interrupted only by twinges of pain. When the task was completed, Hearst solemnly stated to Creelman: "I'm sorry you're hurt." Then, with his "face radiant with enthusiasm," he announced: "But wasn't it a splendid fight? We must beat every paper in the world." And with that comment he mounted his horse, intent on providing the American public with the latest news from the fighting front. The byline would be his, not Creelman's. The day was complete.[30]

After the capture of San Juan Heights on July 1, the capitulation of Santiago de Cuba was only a matter of days, if not hours away. The end of the fighting in Cuba was rapidly approaching. After all, the U.S. Army was imperiling the Spanish fleet; therefore, Admiral Cervera fatalistically decided to engage the superior American naval forces waiting just outside the harbor. On Sunday morning, July 3, he steamed forth to imminent destruction; within hours, the carnage was over and the victory complete.[31]

Early the next morning (5:00 A.M.), July 4, 1898, Hearst and the *Journal* "crusaders" sailed aboard their flagship *Sylvia* to view the aftermath of this remarkable American victory and describe it to an eagerly awaiting public. What a memorable day! They first came alongside the partially sunken armored Spanish cruiser *Vizcaya*, its girders "twisted into every conceivable grotesque shape," its superstructure "totally demolished." While Hemment took some masterful pictures of "the terrible havoc that shot and shell had wrought," Hearst, Jack Follansbee, George Pancoast, and several of the crew went aboard to explore conditions below decks and collect "a great many souvenirs, consisting of Mauser rifles, revolvers, and bunches of keys." Next, the *Sylvia* approached the *Almirante Oquendo*, a sister ship of the *Vizcaya*, "still on fire and smoking badly," the heat so blistering, Hemment noted, that "it was impossible to board," especially since its magazines might "explode at any moment."

Hearst, however, described the wreck of the *Oquendo* to *Journal* readers as a "shocking sight," with "dead Spaniards ... floating all about in the water, stripped to the waist as they had stood to man their guns." Then, revealing his unadulterated patriotism once again, he concluded: "We steered nervously among the bodies, feeling much pity, and some satisfaction, too, that the *Maine* had been again so well remembered."

As they proceeded toward a third cruiser, the *Infanta Maria Teresa*, a large party of men along the shore, at first glance believed to be Cubans, began "waving a white flag ... to attract attention." But Hearst soon realized that these men, "stripped to the waist," were Spanish sailors wanting to surrender. Not one to miss such a journalistic coup, he excitedly exclaimed to George Pancoast: "Let's get them." So Hearst, Follansbee, Pancoast, and Hemment immediately lowered the *Sylvia's* launch and headed toward them, making "a demonstration with our firearms," Hearst noted. Then, as "the poor, cowed fellows, with great alacrity, waved a white handkerchief or shirt in token of surrender," Hearst "jumped overboard, swam ashore," and accepted their surrender. Without any difficulty the *Journal* captors took their prisoners, twenty-nine in all, aboard the *Sylvia*, whereupon director Hearst added a grand finale to his script. With Hemment snapping picture after picture, he "persuaded" the Spaniards—with food and drink in sight as conducives—to give "three cheers for the Fourth of July" and again for "George Washington and Old Glory." After several hours Hearst delivered his prisoners to the American cruiser *St. Louis*, then demanded—and obtained—a receipt from "the officer of marines in charge" that stated: "Received of W. R. Hearst twenty-nine Spanish prisoners." He then "forwarded" this treasured possession to the *Journal* for publication, before having it framed for his office wall.[32]

Because General Shafter proceeded without energy or enthusiasm, the battle for Santiago de Cuba dragged on until July 17. But Hearst in no way emulated the American commander. He met with and briefly interviewed Spanish fleet admiral Cervera as well as Captain Antonio Eulate of the sunken *Vizcaya*. In the *Journal* he attributed heroic dimensions to naval constructor Richmond Pearson Hobson (upon his release as a prisoner of war), who had attempted unsuccessfully, early in June, to bottle up the

Spanish squadron by sinking the collier *Merrimac* across the channel of Santiago de Cuba Harbor. Most importantly, however, Hearst was determined to publish a newspaper exclusively for American servicemen; on July 11, 18198, he began printing the Cuban edition of the *New York Journal*, "issued at Siboney"—a forerunner of *Stars and Stripes*. After several productions, which included distributing forty thousand copies to soldiers and sailors in the Santiago de Cuba area, he closed all operations at Siboney and returned to the United States aboard the *Sylvia*, landing at Baltimore on July 17 and arriving in New York the next day.[33]

Director Hearst now choreographed the final act of the *"Journal's* War," which necessarily encompassed scenes of celebration and festivities in praise of the United States, its returning heroes, and, of course, the *Journal*. He prepared New Yorkers for a number of patriotic extravaganzas and fascinating sideshows. First of all, he defended New York's 71st Regiment, which a *World* correspondent, supposedly noted author Stephen Crane, had accused (on July 15) of becoming "demoralized" and retreating during the American assault on San Juan Heights. Hearst immediately seized this opportunity to lambaste his major competitor once again. On July 17 the *Journal* headline read: "SLURS ON THE BRAVERY OF THE BOYS OF THE 71ST. The *World* Deliberately Accuses Them of Rank Cowardice at San Juan." The article then pointed out that the "*World's* "dastardly lie" had conveniently omitted that, during the battle, the regiment had sustained seventy-three casualties, approximately "eight per cent," which was "one man in every twelve . . . struck by a Spanish bullet." Again on July 20, under his own byline, Hearst testified to the gallantry of the 71st (even though he was not an eyewitness to their actions on July 1), the *Journal* headline reading: "EDITOR OF THE JOURNAL'S PERSONAL EXPERIENCE OF THE SPLENDID HEROISM OF THE SEVENTY-FIRST."

In a straightforward but glowingly laudatory account he described the conditions of men wounded and dying on the battlefield, of the terrible fate endured by American soldiers that bloody day. Yet, "under these circumstances," Hearst fictionalized, "the men of the New York regiment were cheerful, as well as brave. Their only questions, asked of the wounded and the men bearing the wounded, were," he concluded, "'What is going on at the front?' and 'When will we have a chance to get in?' There was not the first sign of an inquiry as to when they were going to be permitted to get out."

As further verification, Hearst printed the corroborating testimony of *Journal* correspondent Edward Marshall, who had been wounded several days before the battle and also had not been present. So no matter what strategy the *World* applied during the next week, the *Journal* continued unrelentingly its brutal assault, so much so that Pulitzer, "heartily sick of the war" and the shenanigans of the California "upstart," retreated from this unequal contest, fully routed once again.[34]

With the competition in disarray, Hearst was freed up to indulge in his favorite brand of showmanship, specifically a dramatic ceremonial crescendo to the grand finale of the *"Journal's* War." On July 23, 1898, the *Journal* published a cablegram from naval hero George Dewey thanking Hearst for "truly a fitting memento"—a rear admiral's flag—commemorating his "great victory" at Manila Bay. Within the next few days Hearst announced that the well-publicized *Journal* Monument Fund, begun five months earlier to honor the *"Maine* martyrs," had reached an astounding $103,000, once more reflecting the public mood in these halcyon days of victory. To complement such pride and patriotism the *Journal* interspersed its pages with Hemment's marvelous pictures of the Cuban campaign, as well as striking illustrations (whether accurate or fictionalized) by Frederick Remington, J. A. Coggin, and other *Journal* artists demonstrating American prowess and valor in battle. Then in August, with the return of soldiers and sailors, New Yorkers celebrated their arrival with parades and marching bands.

But Hearst, unrivaled in showmanship and the wherewithal to expend large sums of money on favored projects, fashioned the conclusion to his liking. On August 9 he hosted a *"Journal* Carnival Night" at Manhattan Beach in Brooklyn, inviting as guests the heroes of the Santiago campaign and "at least 100 of the wounded men at Bellevue Hospital." Although the public had to pay a nominal admission fee, which was to go to the Monument Fund, Hearst shouldered the burden of expenses. He hired Henry J. Pain, the "Fireworks King" (whose services he had used as a climax to the Greater New York Charter celebration on January 1, 1898), to entertain the crowd. What a fun-filled night! On a three-hundred-foot stage Pain produced two truly magnificent fireworks displays: "The Blowing Up of the Maine" was, by its very nature, dramatic, but "The Battle of Manila," unveiling twenty glowing battleships (being maneuvered on wheels) with cannons booming, was a "masterpiece." Then, for the finale, Pain constructed a special fireworks, outlining two soldiers on a pedestal with their rifles aimed, and underneath, the fiery words, Journal Monument Fund. As the crowd watched in wonder and awe, a young Victor Herbert directed his band in a rendition of "The Star-Spangled Banner," a fitting patriotic end to a Hearst extravaganza.[35]

But for the pièce de résistance Hearst planned, as biographer Swanberg noted, "an unparalleled patriotic event," which in turn would enhance the stature of the *Journal*—and its owner—even more. Upon learning that the American fleet under Admiral Sampson was ordered to celebrate its victory over Spain by sailing up the Hudson River on August 20, Hearst decided to appropriate this historic occasion for the *Journal*; in other words, he maneuvered public information to appear as if he had arranged the entire affair. In a open telegram to Mayor Robert A. Van Wyck, he urged that August 20 be designated "a complete holiday, abandoning all business save that of cheering the Navy that has made America a bigger country and the American nation a bigger nation." Van Wyck, although sympathetic to the idea, sadly lamented to having "no legal authority to proclaim such a holiday." But Hearst remained undaunted. He instituted his usual modus operandi, whose rate of success was phenomenal. As in the past, he directed staffers to gather hundreds of endorsements from prominent businesses such as Lord and Taylor, Constable and Company, and Macy's. In turn, he obtained glowingly chauvinistic statements from numerous political figures, including Governor Frank S. Black of New York, Governor Foster Voorhees of New Jersey, and New York Republican boss Thomas C. Platt. Then, to the annoyance of many, especially rival newspapers, he "adopted" the American fleet for a "*Journal* Holiday." On August 19 the *Journal* headline read: "JOURNAL'S PLAN FOR FULL HOLIDAY ADOPTED. ALL NEW YORK MAY GREET OUR HEROES."

But Hearst was not done; his imaginative showmanship was now fully unleashed. On August 20 he lofted the *Journal's* huge hot-air balloon over Grant's Tomb, which overlooked the Hudson. He informed readers that the "*JOURNAL'S WAR BALLOON SIGNAL CODE*" of colored confetti would monitor the progress of the fleet—red to alert onlookers when the ships were departing from Staten Island, green and then white to denote their progress up the river, and "brilliant showers of red, white and blue, followed by all colors of the rainbow" to signal their arrival opposite Grant's Tomb. Then the *Journal* dispatch ship *Anita*, "proud of her war record in carrying the news from Cuba," would escort the fleet the rest of the way. As a further help to New Yorkers, Hearst published a full page of illustrations that marked the Spanish "shell hits" on the American ships. "TAKE THIS PAGE OF THE JOURNAL WITH YOU TO THE PARADE TO-DAY," Hearst instructed. Readers could thus identify the *New York, Oregon, Iowa, Brooklyn, Indiana,* and *Texas,* thereby giving a fitting "WELCOME TO THE SEA KINGS." Enthralled with fireworks, he most likely would have ended the day with a magnificent fireworks display; but "Pyrotechnist Pain" had already embarked on a "*Journal-Examiner* Train" for a cross-country tour to display his glowing productions at Los Angeles, Oakland, San Francisco, Portland, Salt Lake City, Denver, and Kansas City.[36]

So on August 20, 1898, without mishap, the impressive parade of ships thrilled New Yorkers—made complete with the Hearst touch. While tugs and small craft dotted the route, tooting whistles in a celebrative cacophony of sounds, while an estimated crowd of one million people applauded and cheered the victorious sailors, the *Anita*, conspicuously bedecked with *Journal* banners, seemingly directed the fleet in its route up the Hudson. As a consequence, the next morning's headlines read: "ADMIRAL SAMPSON PRAISES THE JOURNAL" and "HOW THE JOURNAL SECURED THE HOLIDAY FOR THE PEOPLE." Hearst could not have been more pleased with the outcome. Besides glorifying the navy—one of his favorite themes—he had increased dramatically the growth of the *Journal*, claiming on August 21 that its daily circulation had outdistanced the nearest competition, the *Petit Journal* of Paris, not the *World*, by 213,751 copies.[37]

Hearst thus concluded his crusade for Cuba with a fitting climax. And even though historians would continually debate his role in the Spanish-American War, whether he initiated the war in competition with Pulitzer for newspaper circulation or merely mirrored and abetted the chauvinistic attitude of the American people, Hearst had no doubts. The crusade for *"Cuba Libre"* had been the *"Journal's* War," the grandest adventure of his life. The *Journal* had become a dominant force, a journalistic power that had raised heroes and created villains, that had helped undo a once-powerful nation, that had swayed public opinion and influenced national policy with its "New Journalism." So the knight-errant readied himself for the next great crusade, possibly one that would demand of him public service on behalf of the American people.[38]

8 | Political Activist

⁊

In 1898, with the conclusion of what U.S. Ambassador to Britain John Hay called "a splendid little war," the American people basked—and reveled—in the resounding victory over Spain, in the wondrous glories of an emerging empire, in the triumphant applause for a vibrant New World democracy. The idea of Manifest Destiny, of American chauvinism and expansion, surely held sway. On July 7, 1898, President McKinley signed a measure that annexed the Hawaiian Islands, thereby extending American civilization and influence into the Pacific. Then, by the Treaty of Paris on December 10, 1898, the United States acquired even more territory. Spain agreed to relinquish Cuba, to cede Puerto Rico and an island in the Ladrones (ultimately Guam) to the United States, and to allow the Americans to occupy "the city, bay, and harbor of Manila" until some final disposition of the Philippines could be decided. And on February 6, 1899, with the treaty ratified by the Senate, the United States officially became a world power. Hence, such key words as "duty" and "destiny" seemed to characterize, to be emblematic of, American foreign policy, with the unfurling of "Old Glory" over foreign lands signifying an extension of democracy.

Even greater economic changes in American life had occurred. Since the Civil War the growth of national wealth had been astounding. The United States had become the greatest industrial power in the world, with giant trusts or corporations dominating their fields of endeavor, continually undermining competition or eliminating it altogether. By the 1890s, for example, Standard Oil Company monopolized 98 percent of all oil refining in the world; four huge business organizations—Swift, Armour, Cudahy, and Morris—controlled the lucrative meat-packing industry in the United States; American steel corporations produced as much tonnage as Great Britain and Germany combined; and railroads, with huge investments in land and buildings and rolling stock, clearly dominated transportation, especially with little competition nationally. The rise of the city also encouraged this trend toward "bigness." Urbanization produced a demand for raw materials and manufactured goods as well as a huge—and cheap—labor pool for numerous businesses. And such men as John D. Rockefeller, J. Pierpont Morgan, Andrew Carnegie, Jay Gould, Cornelius Vanderbilt, James J. Hill, Collis P. Huntington, George Pullman, Marshall Field, and James B. Duke soon became household names, recognized as captains of industry, who inspired envy or hate by establishing profitable businesses and amassing immense fortunes. The Spanish-American War further escalated prosperity, with American goods and foodstuffs much in demand. So the trend toward "bigness" through consolidation continued unchecked, culminating with the formation of the $1.4 billion U.S. Steel Corporation on April 1, 1901.[1]

William Randolph Hearst was well aware of the progress and accomplishments of the United States, of the pride and prosperity enveloping the nation. At the same time he recognized the accompanying problems affecting an emerging world power as well as the demand to curb certain privileges of the rich and to prevent intolerable abuses of the poor. Especially in New York City, where immigrants were arriving daily by the thousands, where overcrowding and rapid growth overwhelmed government, where the needs of its residents were many and the solutions to their problems painfully few, urban demands seemed to magnify in intensity. Yet reforms were often slow in coming. Republican state boss Thomas Collier Platt had effectively influenced New York politics for almost two decades. Tammany Hall, controlled by the Democrats through such "chieftains" as John Kelly and Richard Croker, had helped direct the affairs of New York City even longer. To effect change thus ran counter to the wishes of such men who had entrenched themselves and their organizations and who were determined to maintain their power; they would not easily surrender positions so strenuously fought for and so dearly cherished.[2]

So what could reformed-minded political leaders, local, state, and national, do? How could citizens, either individually or collectively, help influence their surroundings and determine their fate? Hearst confidently supplied the readers of the *New York Journal* with answers. On the last day of the old century, December 31, 1899, he announced in an editorial that "Government by newspaper . . . will be realized in the twentieth century," that "government by the people through popular organs" would accurately express "popular will." After all, he expounded, no politician was ever as closely in touch with the American people as the *Journal*. For instance, in the crusade to free Cuba after 1895, newspapers provided the leadership while the politicians followed. After all, while public leaders were ree-lected at "the end of two, four, or six years," the "ballots" affecting a newspa-per were "counted every morning." Hence, Hearst reasoned, "an honest, earnest, able press will become in fact the people's voice, with the elected representatives merely executors of its dicta." He then announced some-what piously and, to a certain extent, hypocritically that a newspaper "can-not be hired like a lawyer to defend wrong or protect evil, for no money can compensate it for the loss of that public support which is its life. Its aims are high, its ethics pure." Consequently, he concluded, "we shall see the press fulfill its noble calling, and as the mouthpiece of the people, rule, regulate, and reform the world." [3]

Hearst thus revealed to anyone who would listen—associates, sub-scribers, competitors, politicians, future biographers—his thoughts and, more specifically, his intentions. Since the *New York Journal* had acquired the greatest circulation in the world and the *San Francisco Examiner* had decimated all competition on the West Coast, he was readying himself to impact the American political scene even more. After all, had he not forced a reluctant President McKinley and an ambivalent Congress into a "righteous" crusade against Spain? Beginning late in the spring of 1898, had he not enunciated five propositions, called the *Journal's* "National Pol-icy"—construction of a Nicaraguan canal, annexation of Hawaii, the maintenance of "a mighty navy," the acquisition of strategic bases in the Caribbean, and the establishment of "great national universities" at West Point and Annapolis? And had not a majority of these suggestions, through a fervent campaign that enlisted thousands of *Journal* readers as advocates and "petitioners," been adopted by Congress? Or were not these issues in the legislative process of becoming so? [4]

Hearst, through a continual trial-and-error approach since his days in San Francisco and later in competition with Pulitzer in New York City, especially during the Spanish-American War, had perfected a journalistic formula for success and from which his newspapers seldom if ever devi-ated. First and foremost, stories had to be well written, the subject matter embellishing a certain shock value or appealing to baser human emotions or eliciting mystery and intrigue almost beyond human comprehension. To attract even more attention—and induce further reader in-quiry—huge black headlines (from one to four inches high) depicted the crux of the story together with graphic illustrations or cartoons and fantastic photographs. In other words, Hearst journalism had to educe from its readers, acerbic-tongued Arthur McEwen observed, "the gee-whiz emotion." Or, as one biographer noted, any article that did not raise the reader "out of his chair and cry, 'Great God!'" was considered "a failure." But the Hearst method of investigative reporting changed significantly during the Bryan campaign of 1896, and even earlier with certain staffers in San Francisco. Hearst began printing stories that were without foundation and verification or that were totally false. And why? His causes became crusades, his objectives ultimate victory, no matter what the methods, no matter how despicable the means.

Hearst reworked and polished his campaign formula to perfection during the Cuban crusade in 1897–98. Whether the issue was local or national, his editors followed prescribed standards. First, they directed reporters to interview hundreds, at times thousands, of people—politicians, businessmen, labor bosses, ministers, ethnic group leaders, women, and prominent individuals in all fields of endeavor. They next assigned one or two gifted writers, such as James Creelman, Julian Hawthorne, Willis J. Abbot, Alfred Henry Lewis, Winifred Black, or Arthur McEwen, to present the story from the *Journal's* point of view. Partly as an attention-getter, yet as a means of demonstrating sincerity for his latest cause, Hearst flamboyantly offered impressive monetary sums in the form of matching funds or large rewards. On occasion, to bolster the *Journal* crusade, his editors rented a convention or concert hall for a staged mass meeting (of course, bankrolled by Hearst) and provided front-page coverage for the participants at the event. They also published polls periodically that further established credibility that their cause was popular with the people, even though election results sometimes proved otherwise. Then the Hearst editors, systematically and daily, publicized accounts, backed by numerous supportive testimonials, favorable interviews, and petitions supplied by the *Journal*—but none in opposition. And the editorial page, whose format Hearst changed in 1898 to appear more like the front page, with bold-face and italicized type, became a "bully pulpit" for every crusade. As a consequence, Hearst orchestrated, managed, and at times manipulated the news for his readers, oblivious to charges that such "yellow journalism" lacked objectivity. After all, he believed that his pulse was the same as that of the American people. And therein lay the danger.[5]

Hearst, in actuality, was a public relations man promoting circulation, a huckster concerned with newspaper advertisements, an entertainer of the masses, a showman extraordinaire, rather than a journalist. He plied his readers with contests, puzzles, prizes, and free gifts. He intrigued them

with unsolved murders and bizarre jury trials; he entertained them daily
with a two-to-three-page coverage of sports, especially yachting and scull-
ing, boxing and baseball, football, biking, and horse racing; he piqued their
curiosity constantly with stories about beautiful women, the fabulously
rich, the nationally and internationally famous; and he amused them with
multicolored comic strips and biting political cartoons. For the pedestrian
and mundane, indeed the less adventurous, he published weather fore-
casts, business news, and, beginning in 1899, a daily obituary column.
And on special occasions, such as election-return nights, national holidays, and parades welcoming local or national heroes, he provided garishly
lighted displays on the street and huge balloons in the sky, with accompanying band music and choral groups, all topped off by the Hearst pièce de
résistance—a glittering fireworks display. All such improvisations and
techniques served as a window dressing not only to increase newspaper
circulation and further the number of advertisements but also to ensconce
his political agendas in a seemingly innocent, nonconfrontational setting.[6]

By August, 1898, with his journalistic formula thoroughly understood—and practiced—by *Journal* staffers, Hearst had to wrestle with
presenting news to the public that was far less exciting in content than the
events leading up to, and including, the Spanish-American War. But he
was equal to the challenge; he demanded of his editors an exciting newspaper. And it was. On August 4, for instance, even as the war was ending,
General Shafter dispatched to the port of New York—of all places—two
ancient freighters, the *Seneca* and the *Concho*, overcrowded with wounded
and fever-ridden veterans of the Cuban campaign. Either because of personnel incompetence or army carelessness, the water supply in one was
not just woefully inadequate but "putrid," while the medical care in both
was deplorable. The *Journal* immediately charged Shafter with criminal
negligence, that he knowingly relegated the "heroes" of the Santiago campaign to the "horrors" of "death ships." Hearst thus embarked on another
crusade as this story quickly developed into a full-blown scandal. The
conquerors of Cuba, en route to Camp Wikoff at secluded Montauk
Point on the eastern end of Long Island, became "an army of convales-
cents," partly reduced to such a weakened state because of coarse army ra-
tions and, at times, "spoiled beef." Such diseases as typhoid, yellow fever,
and malaria—so prevalent in Cuba—also decimated their ranks. Conditions at Camp Wikoff, as well as other army bases, were deplorable, the
men "dying like sheep," the *Journal* announced, suffering from food poisoning and inadequate housing, from ever-present pestilence and "criminal"
neglect.[7]

Readers were able to discern easily between the *Journal* villains and heroes. With reports from Cuba that as many as five hundred troops were stricken daily with fever and dying from neglect in ill-equipped hospitals, that camps were poorly managed and the suffering intense, the *Journal* charged General Shafter with a "pitiless" disrespect for his men. Nor was Secretary of War Russell A. Alger any better. He was a businessman-politician without the leadership abilities so necessary for a rapidly expanding army, a vain and, sometimes, lazy individual who welcomed praise but was unable to accept personal accountability. Hence, the *Journal* characterized him as "the blameless secretary" who intended "to hold field officers responsible." In contrast, Major General Nelson A. Miles, a Civil War veteran who gained fame as an Indian-fighter in besting the Sioux sachem Sitting Bull and the Apache chief Geronimo, became the "darling" of the *Journal*. Despite a monstrous ego and an irascible disposition, this "brave peacock"—as Theodore Roosevelt referred to him—who designed his own uniforms embellished with "a chestful of medals," had protected the health of his men, the *Journal* expounded, during the conquest of Puerto Rico. Miles was also bluntly outspoken, especially in regard to his evaluations of Shafter and Alger; therefore, this ongoing army controversy endeared him to the Hearst editors and staffers for many months to come.[8]

At the same time, the *Journal* involved its readers with specific urban problems and sordid mysteries. During August and for most of September, 1898, New Yorkers became aware that as many as twenty-five thousand students were in danger of being "turned away" because of inadequate facilities. Whether in San Francisco or New York City, Hearst had always crusaded for improved public schools—teacher salary increases, student encouragement, up-to-date textbooks, and better facilities. As a result, the *Journal* campaigned for a huge bond issue, which the city school board agreed to launch early in 1899. In the meantime the *Journal* editors suggested several options to remedy overcrowding, such as using church facilities or the Grand Central Palace as schoolrooms. On September 20 the board decided to rent the necessary space for classrooms, reenforcing once again Hearst's idea of "government by newspaper."[9]

With equal fervor the *Journal* titillated its readers with a gruesome murder that was reminiscent of the Guldensuppe tragedy in 1896. On September 13, 1898, in the watery depths of a dreary millpond at Bridgeport, Connecticut, a young man stumbled on the fragments of a human form. The local police, upon further investigation, recovered the remains of a "beautiful young woman," whose body had been "skillfully" dismembered, wrapped with cloth, and, to prevent detection, anchored at the bottom of the pond. For several weeks *Journal* readers followed a tortuous trail of clues, which ultimately revealed that a Dr. Nancy Guilford, with the help of her husband, also a physician, had panicked when a young patient named Emma Gill had unexpectedly died after surgery. The doctors thus "sought to cover up the crime," the *Journal* announced, "by carving the body into sections and disposing of the remnants in the river." When Hearst reporters learned that at least three other unexplained murders of young women had occurred in the Bridgeport vicinity over the past twenty years, the possibility of a serial killer became even more intriguing. Although four suspects, including her husband, were arrested, Dr. Guilford (referred to by the *Journal* as "Old Nance") escaped capture, fleeing first to Toronto and then to London. For three weeks the Hearst papers followed every morbid detail of the case—of course, with graphic illustrations of the surgical tools employed and the techniques applied in the hideous mutilation. During the first week of October, British police apprehended "Old Nance," who was returned to the United States to stand trial—and the chase was over.[10]

It was high time, because Hearst had committed the *Journal* to a new crusade. In mid-September, 1898, much to his chagrin, state Republicans, at the behest of party boss Tom Platt, discarded Governor Frank S. Black, whose administration had "come under fire" for misusing a $9-million Erie Canal improvement fund, in favor of Colonel Theodore Roosevelt of the famous Rough Rider regiment. Hearst considered himself partly responsible for this nomination; after all, the "*Journal's* War" against Spain had created a number of heroes. He was therefore determined to eliminate this newest political phenomenon from further public consideration.

For the next six weeks Hearst worked to elect a Democratic governor, applying his journalistic "success formula" to the campaign. Late in September, 1898, with the nomination of Augustus Van Wyck, whose brother was mayor of New York City, the *Journal* immediately endorsed him; and then an orchestration of the news began. Brutal Davenport cartoons appeared with frequent regularity, characterizing Roosevelt as the tool of Platt, a puppet who danced to the New York boss's tune. Day after day *Journal* editors provided ample newspaper space for Van Wyck (usually pages 1 and 2), while Roosevelt, who spoke to large, enthusiastic crowds, received little political coverage, except for negative reports. For example, on October 15, the front page of the *Journal* presented two stories side by side, one headline reading "CROKER TELLS WHY VAN WYCK SURE OF ELECTION" and the other, in smaller print, describing a scheduled Roosevelt rally, stating, "No Crowd" and therefore "No Speech." As the campaign progressed, the *Journal* editors "ran stories" (often on page 1) about gambling wagers on the governor's race, which, of course, favored Van Wyck, progressing from even money on October 13 to ten-to-eight odds on October 28. As further substantiation for such betting, they published several "*Journal* Polls" that showed Van Wyck carrying the state by a plurality ranging from 53,000 votes on October 12 to over 70,000 on October 30–31.

Then, during the week prior to the election on November 8, Hearst stepped up the campaign tempo. Such typical front-page *Journal* headlines, together with persuasive editorials, characterized the Hearst barrage: on November 1, "SOLDIERS VOTE FOR VAN WYCK"; on November 3, "The Demagoguery of Roosevelt" (an editorial); on November 4, "76 OF EVERY 100 OF THE 71ST [NEW YORK INFANTRY] ARE FOR VAN WYCK"; on November 7, "VAN WYCK WILL WIN . . . A RURAL TIDAL WAVE"; and on November 8, "DON'T WASTE YOUR VOTE! VOTE FOR VAN WYCK." [11]

But on November 8, 1898, despite the *Journal's* vigorous efforts, Roosevelt narrowly won by 17,194 votes—possibly because Democratic Tammany chieftain Richard Croker alienated New Yorkers during the last week of the campaign by criticizing the popular chief judge of the state Court of Appeals Joseph F. Daly. As a result of the election, Hearst was extremely distraught. "I guess I'm a failure," he wrote his mother. "I made the mistake of my life in not raising the cowboy regiment I had in mind before Roosevelt raised his. I really believe I brought on the war but I failed to score in the war. I had my chance and failed to grasp it, and I suppose I must sit on the fence now and watch the procession go by." Hearst continued this unrelenting self-flagellation to Phebe. "It's my own fault. I was thirty-five years of age and of sound mind—comparatively—and could do as I liked. I failed and I'm a failure and deserve to be for being as slow and stupid as I was." Then he concluded: "Goodnight, Mama dear. Take care of yourself. Don't let me lose you. I wish you were here tonight. I feel about eight years old—and very blue." [12]

Hearst did not remain dispirited for long, however—and for good reason. Before the end of November, 1898, he had decided to become a more active participant in politics; therefore, he unshackled himself from the daily routine of his newspapers. He appointed his alter ego, the brilliant Arthur Brisbane, as "publisher" of the *Morning* and *Evening Journals*, with "full authority" to make whatever decisions necessary; the loyal and talented Sam Chamberlain as second in command on the morning paper;

and the experienced Richard Farrelly, whom he had hired away from Pulitzer in 1896, to the same position on the evening one. Hearst was also pleased that, with daily circulation continuing at 1,250,000 copies, advertising had increased dramatically; on December 17, the *Journal* was recognized by the John Wanamaker department stores as "first among newspapers" in advertising. And in an uncharacteristic bent toward economizing, such as placing Brisbane on salary rather than commission, Hearst confidently wrote his mother that the *Journal*, through his reorganizational methods, would save $5,000 a month. Then he concluded: "I believe the advertising can be increased $300,000 so that for the year of 1899 I will show you a *profit* on the *Journal*." [13]

Hearst thus successfully applied his creative genius and proven sales techniques to the *Journal* advertisement growth. For several months late in 1898 and again in April, 1899, he offered "help and situation" ads "for free." He then reverted to the reliable "prize and puzzle formula," whereby subscribers received impressive, at times fantastic gifts for doing business with the *Journal*. During a year's time, participants acquired a thermometer-calendar set, a penholder and pencil and letter opener (all of sterling silver from Tiffany's), opera glasses, and a camera, as well as souvenirs of the Spanish-American War—"a five-peseta piece taken from the [Spanish] flagship *Cristobal Colon*" and a five-inch-by-nine-inch bust of Admiral George Dewey—"Have the Hero at Home." Hearst also attracted subscribers with monetary rewards, such as $100 to $200 in weekly gifts for participants who found "superfluous words" (from seven to fourteen) in the Sunday "Wants" and a "$500 REWARD For The Best Story Of JOURNAL 'WANT' ADVERTISING SUCCESS." As a result, the *Journal* claimed unprecedented achievements, exultantly stating on May 11, 1899, that the number of "Wants" over the previous year was 8,645. [14]

Since circulation was all-important, Hearst continued through Brisbane to entertain readers with intrigue and scandal. Three stories had long-lasting appeal. From late in September, 1898, to February 19, 1900, the *Journal* devoted considerable space to the "Great Poisoning Mystery," wherein a local resident named Mrs. Kate Adams unwittingly took cyanide of mercury pills from a bottle given to her. With Hearst offering a $5,000 reward for the arrest and conviction of Mrs. Adams's murderer, both the New York police and *Journal* reporters pursued a long and convoluted trail of clues for months, at length discovering a set of circumstances that pointed to Newark chemist Roland Burham Molineux as the sinister culprit. For more than a year New Yorkers (including Hearst, who was fascinated by murder mysteries) eagerly followed the legal maneuverings and a complicated court trial that eventually culminated in the conviction of Molineux.[15]

Equally interesting both to Hearst and New Yorkers was the ongoing War Department scandal that exposed the U.S. Army's "commissary delights" endured by soldiers during the Spanish-American War. The topic of concern was the diet of American troops in the Caribbean campaign, specifically cans of fresh meat labeled "roast beef," which actually meant that it was boiled. At best, it was stringy and tasteless, repulsive to the eye and nauseating to the nose. In fact, it was so unpalatable that Roosevelt, in his *Autobiography*, advised the Rough Riders "to take every opportunity of getting food for themselves," and General Miles, before an investigative committee, "dropped" the graphic epithet "embalmed beef."

As a result, the *Journal* had a reporters' field day. Not only were soldiers "fed ancient beef . . . six years old," but "diseased meat" that had been preserved with "boric and salicylic" acids, all with the knowledge of Commissary General Charles P. Eagan and with the approval of Secretary of War Alger. In fact, the *Journal* asserted, the Beef Trust—specifically Armour & Company—had "conspired" with General Eagan to "unload" meat—usually beef but at times "horse"—by the thousands of pounds, upon "Uncle Sam's Soldiers."

And when the commissary general foolishly assailed the *Journal* before the War Investigation Commission in Washington, stating that if "I [were] a man of wealth or means I would take this subject up myself . . . [and] put journalistic knaves, purloiners of the secrets of the Government, behind the bars where they belong," Hearst was ecstatic. He dramatically replied on the *Journal's* front page: "NOW, GEN. EAGAN, YOU CAN SUE THE JOURNAL, FREE. This Paper Will Pay All Expenses in Court Fees and Your Lawyers' Bills if You Will Prosecute It for Treason." Eagan, as a result of such continual hammering by the *Journal*—and by James Gordon Bennett's *Herald*—as well as a disgraceful performance before the War Investigation Committee, was relieved of command and dismissed from the service. Then in July, 1899, with the resignation of Alger from the Cabinet, the story had run its course. But as far as Hearst was concerned, it once again proved the dynamics of "government by newspaper."[16]

Equally enjoyable to avid *Journal* readers was the titillating and, to some, outrageous story about a newly elected Utah congressman, who seemed appropriately named Brigham H. Roberts because of the uniqueness of his situation (having three wives). Staunchly maintaining that polygamy was "good, pure, and holy," he became the focus of a *Journal* crusade (from late December, 1898, through much of 1899) that intended to disqualify him, "both legally and morally, from sitting in the national house of Congress." Roberts thus experienced the full weight of the Hearst-Brisbane journalistic success formula. To substantiate the righteousness of its cause the *Journal* sent reporters across the nation to interview hundreds of individuals as well as collect an immense amount of data on Utah Mormonism.

Brisbane also dispatched ace journalist Winifred Black to query Roberts and his three wives at Salt Lake City. Then he "managed" the information in an effective campaign. First came petitions of protest against Roberts and what he represented. With "2,000 polygamous marriages in two years," Utah was a "shameful" situation. Mormon women, through their scriptural teaching, approved of their station in life (even "wife-whipping"), thereby propelling a Winifred Black headline to read: "Crush the Harem; Protect the Home." The president of the Church of Jesus Christ of Latter-Day Saints reportedly had five wives and forty-nine children; therefore, "Utah Women [Were] for Roberts and Polygamy."

Petitions rolled in to the *Journal*. The legislatures of Kansas, New York, and Massachusetts first protested, then Colorado, Wisconsin, and Illinois. Such religious sects as Baptists, Methodists, and Free Baptists of Rhode Island, together with the Pastors' Association of Chattanooga, vigorously opposed the induction of Roberts, as did numerous members of Congress, including Speaker of the House Thomas B. Reed of Maine.[17]

Then in March, 1899, the crusade lost momentum, with the *Journal* focusing, for the moment, on other issues. But early in October, Brisbane renewed the *Journal's* "Holy War Against Polygamy"—and this time to a successful conclusion. As with Evangelina Cisneros in the fall of 1897, he allowed women to lead the assault. On October 6, at the American Female Guardian Society, a representative group of New Yorkers—with the backing of the *Journal*—protested "against the seating of the polygamist Brigham H. Roberts." Each day the crusade gained momentum, with headlines reading, "Women of America Enter the Fight." Then Brisbane opened offices throughout the city so that New Yorkers could register their indignation by signing a protest—prepared by the *Journal*—that demanded the rejection of Roberts. And on December 1, when Congress received this petition with more than six million names, the battle of "government by newspaper" was, in essence, a fait accompli. On December 20 the *Journal's* front-page headline triumphantly gloated, "ROBERTS' LAST

HOPE GONE" (although the House of Representatives, through the Tayler Committee, did not officially exclude him from Congress until January 20, 1900).[18]

In 1899, with each successful crusade, Hearst became more aggressive and militant in his quest for "government by newspaper." Since the *Journal* "obviously" reflected the ideas of the national Democratic Party as well as the sentiments of the American people—how could anyone think otherwise?—he renewed his campaign soon after the November elections of 1898 for completing the five planks of the *Journal's* "National Policy." The United States had already annexed Hawaii, was building a strong navy, and, from the pending peace treaty with Spain, undoubtedly was going to acquire strategic bases in the Caribbean. But, during the ensuing year, the building of "great national universities" at West Point and Annapolis received little congressional attention, and the digging of a Nicaraguan canal "under American auspices" encountered fierce opposition, even though the *Journal* pushed vigorously for its adoption.

By the end of 1898, however, Hearst, as well as the American public, became patently aware of the Philippine Islands; hence, he added an all-important plank to the "National Policy"—U.S. expansion rather than imperial exploitation. In signed editorials on November 10 and December 16, 1898, Hearst announced that the *Journal* and the Democratic Party must continue to stand for "the Jeffersonian principle of national expansion" and, therefore, "the retention of ALL the Philippines." As in the past, he considered his pulse and that of the public as one; consequently the *Journal* bombarded readers daily with testimonials endorsing his stand. Businessmen pointed to the potential markets for trade and commerce; the clergy urged the spread of Protestant beliefs; politicians proclaimed the extension of democratic institutions and American values; and *Journal* editorials often quoted a Hearst dispatch during the Battle of Santiago in June, 1898, that appealed to the patriotic fervor of Americans: "Let no peace be granted until the American flag is nailed to the flagstaffs of Porto [sic] Rico and the Philippines—not simply hoisted there, but nailed." Yet Hearst, putting aside all rhetoric, earnestly believed that the Democratic Party, by embracing the policy of expansionism, would endear itself to the public and be triumphant in the presidential election of 1900.[19]

For the Democratic Party to be successful, however, Hearst insisted that it must also be more progressive in character, that it must attempt to reform government and strive vigorously to alleviate, if not eliminate, the economic, political, and social abuses of capitalism. So on February 5,

1899, he presented a platform, titled "An American Internal Policy," that Democrats both on the state and national levels should immediately adopt. First and foremost should be the "DESTRUCTION OF CRIMINAL TRUSTS" that, through the "monopolization of the natural resources" of this country, had become "more powerful than the people's government." The magnates of oil, steel, copper, beef, and timber, together with the railroads, he argued, had eliminated competition and squelched economic enterprise. In fact, the *Journal* frequently registered weekly, and sometimes daily, consolidations and mergers affecting particular industries and trade associations. Another plank of the "American Internal Policy" also concerned trusts. "THE PUBLIC OWNERSHIP OF PUBLIC FRANCHISES" involved combinations dealing directly with consumers on state and local levels, especially water, gas, and rapid transit rates. In essence, Hearst was advocating "water and gas socialism" because "the values created by the community should belong to the community." He next proposed two future amendments to the U.S. Constitution, "A GRADUATED INCOME TAX" (Sixteenth Amendment, 1913), which would allow "every citizen to contribute to the support of the government according to his means, and not according to his necessities," and the "ELECTION OF SENATORS BY THE PEOPLE"—better known as "Direct Election of Senators" (Seventeenth Amendment, 1913)—which would extricate the U.S. Senate, often referred to as the "railroad lobby," from the pejorative reputation of being "the private property of corporations and bosses." And the fifth plank, one always foremost on Hearst's agenda, urged the "NATIONAL, STATE, AND MUNICIPAL IMPROVEMENT OF THE PUBLIC SCHOOL SYSTEM." After all, "every government, general and local, should do its share," Hearst announced, "toward fitting every individual to perform" the duties of citizenship.[20]

But Hearst had by no means exhausted his reform program. Within six weeks (March 19, 1899) he added a sixth plank, "CURRENCY REFORM." Since the Money Trust, headed by Morgan and Rockefeller, was increasingly in control of "all American industry," thereby keeping "the masses poor" and thwarting democracy, the "nation's government" should issue and control its own money, and, if necessary, establish a banking system "regulated by the people and not by the banks"—a nascent idea that culminated in the Federal Reserve Act of 1913. Then again, early in June, Hearst proposed a final plank to his "American Internal Policy," titled "NO PROTECTION FOR OPPRESSIVE TRUSTS." Alarmed by the rapid growth of "combinations"—increasing in number from 356 with a total capitalization of more than $5.8 billion in the middle of March, 1899, to 419 with assets approximating $7.4 billion by May 27—he urged the *Journal's* constituency and the Democratic Party to curb the growth of "the Trust Frankenstein." Such powerful organizations, which no longer could be termed as "infant industries," were responsible only to themselves and their stockholders, he asserted, rather than displaying any concern for the well-being of the average American.[21]

Immediately following the Spanish-American War Hearst found such attitudes and activities prevalent in corporate America—and especially in New York City. Whether sincere in purpose or using the *Journal* politically for personal gain, Hearst did unleash brutal attacks against the local Gas Trust (Amsterdam Light and Gas Company) in the spring of 1899, fervently advocating municipal ownership while driving down the price of gas for consumers, at least temporarily, from $1.10 per thousand cubic feet to as low as 50 cents. For almost two years he also waged a bitter crusade against a Water Trust (Ramapo Company) that was negotiating a forty-year contract to supply water to New York City at what the *Journal* considered "exorbitant rates." Hearst, in another example of "government by newspaper," pressured the mayor and council to forestall further bargaining, thereby allowing the city to obtain control over its water supply (municipal ownership). And again, beginning in the spring of 1899, Hearst campaigned for rapid transit—an underground system of street railway—"built and owned by the city." His actions were consistent with his words; he initiated a bond drive (pledging the *Journal* to $5 million in subscriptions) that helped raise more than $22 million in a four-day period (April 17–20).[22]

Ever cognizant of circulation growth, which in turn translated into profits through expanding advertisement revenues, Hearst continually sought to identify with New Yorkers, to ingratiate the *Journal* with the needs of the city—and always with showmanship and fanfare. When bitter winter weather caused intense suffering, he provided, again without concern for the extraordinary expense, *Journal* meals and housing for the hungry and dispossessed, *Journal* coal for the freezing, even *Journal* transportation for those needing a ride to the work place. And, of course, for any charitable project, he characteristically created a "*Journal* Relief Fund," oftentimes mentioning the names of contributors. At Thanksgiving and Christmas he sponsored huge holiday "feasts" for the poor and needy. Whenever a dispute between management and labor arose, he often proffered the services of the *Journal* to mediate all grievances "fairly"—although inevitably coming down on the side of the workers. And in times of an impending crisis or local tragedy, he directed the *Journal* in an all-out effort, both in staff energies and personal finances, to effect a favorable result.

On May 25, 1899, for example, Hearst learned that four days earlier someone had abducted a year-old boy named Marion Clark from his home. For the moment the police had several "leads," but no arrests were forthcoming. So Hearst and the *Journal* intervened, "offering $2,000 for the return of Baby Clark and no questions asked"—yet no one responded. He therefore assigned a top priority to the story, directing a number of staffers to search for clues, publishing life-size pictures both of the little boy and his nurse, and posting another $2,000 reward for information leading to the arrest of the persons responsible. After a week of intense activity a woman in a nearby community discovered "Baby Clark" and his abductor, specifically as a result of "the *Journal* pictures." With their quick apprehension by the local sheriff, Hearst provided funds for a "special *Journal* train," dramatically returning the child to his grieving parents. New Yorkers voiced their approval.[23]

But Hearst, along with Brisbane, seemed to breathe into the *Journal* a "let's-see-you-top-this" mind-set that excited the mundane and thrilled the imaginative. A city reception heralding the return of Admiral George Dewey proved to be an excellent case in point. During the second week in May, 1899, Hearst learned that the "Hero of Manila," because of recurring illnesses, had been ordered to return home for a triumphant tour of the nation, the first stop scheduled to be New York City on July 4. Mayor Robert A. Van Wyck immediately appointed a "Committee of 1,500"— soon to be cut to a mere 1,100—to plan an appropriate welcome.

Probably because of the upstaging by the *Journal* during the Sampson celebration the previous August, Hearst was a conspicuous omission. But no matter! Only on rare occasions had anyone ever denied him anything, much less thwarted his ambitions. Hence, he resourcefully initiated "A PEOPLE'S TRIBUTE TO ADMIRAL DEWEY," whereby any citizen could contribute "a silver ten-cent piece—simply that and nothing more"—that, along with similar gifts, would be melted into "a great vase or loving cup" appropriately titled "The *Journal*'s Dewey Cup." Dimes immediately rolled in by the tens of thousands, with the *Journal* often publishing the names of individual donors. At the same time Hearst dispatched John C. Hemment, who had gained renown for his photography during the Santiago campaign, to record by pictures and words the historic return of "America's greatest hero."[24]

Because of continuing health problems, however, Admiral Dewey was forced to delay his return until late in September, 1899, all of which allowed Hearst time to devise and improvise. He surely needed to be more innovative, especially since the Reception Committee had carbon copied past Hearst extravaganzas. Banners and flags and streamers would adorn buildings and skyscrapers as well as decorate the parade route. A number of bands and choral groups would continually enhance the festivities. Henry "Pyrotechnist" Pain, a mainstay in any Hearst spectacular, would light up the city and harbor with "100 colored skyrockets" and "500 aquatic fireworks" including "flying fish and sea serpents" as well as "a picture in fire of the *Olympia* [Dewey's flagship] 1,000 feet square." At every function during the three-day celebration [September 28–30], public officials and prominent New Yorkers were assigned certain positions and specific duties, whether in several parades or on the reviewing stands or at official dinners (thus incurring strong objections from Governor Roosevelt for obvious slights by Democratic mayor Van Wyck). And in a "parade of ships"—Dewey's fourteen warships headed by the *Olympia*—up the Hudson River past Grant's Tomb, "only" five specified vessels, would transport the mayor and council, official guests, and numerous city department heads, and "be allowed to remain out of the line of the procession; all others will follow in single column behind the wake of the *Olympia*." [25]

Of course, Hearst realized the import of such directives; the Reception Committee obviously was determined to exclude him from active participation in the festivities as well as prevent a recurrence of the *Anita* incident the previous August, wherein the Hearst dispatch boat, emblazoned with huge *Journal* banners, had seemingly led the way for the Sampson "parade of ships." Yet, despite this obvious snub, he remained undeterred and undaunted, having already formulated an ingenious script "of welcome for Dewey" that was typically Hearst—imaginative and expensive. On September 10, 1899, the *Journal* announced that, with more than a million people about to view this "monster celebration," it was establishing seven bureaus "at advantageous points throughout the city, where every stranger is invited to go for information about New York and the great parades." It had also compiled a "*Journal's* Handy Reference Book" that provided a street directory as well as general information about the city. In addition, through "many weeks" of intensive staff efforts, the *Journal* had assembled a mammoth list of boardinghouses and rooming houses, together with listed prices. And with the purchase of a September 24 Sunday *Journal*, a reader would receive "the only true portrait of Admiral Dewey," 20 by 28 inches in five colors. [26]

But Hearst was not done; he still had other surprises in store. On

William Randolph Hearst's mother, Phoebe Apperson Hearst. (*Courtesy of The Bancroft Library, University of California at Berkeley*)

George Hearst about 40, father of William Randolph Hearst. (*Courtesy of The Bancroft Library, University of California at Berkeley*)

A young Willie Hearst. (*Courtesy of The Bancroft Library, University of California at Berkeley*)

William Randolph Hearst, now called Will, prior to entering St. Paul's School, 1879-80. (*Courtesy of The Bancroft Library, University of California at Berkeley*)

Will Hearst at Harvard, 1882. (*Courtesy of The Bancroft Library, University of California at Berkeley*)

Famous Orrin Peck painting of Hearst executed in 1894. (*Courtesy of the Hearst San Simeon State Historical Monument, San Simeon, California*)

Hearst, as he appeared at the time of
the Spanish-American War (1898).

Homer Davenport sketch of Hearst
as the new owner of the New York
Journal, July 21, 1896.

Frederick Remington's "imaginative" depiction of Spanish officers searching a young woman on the Olivette—part of the crusade for "Cuba Libre."

Bold front-page headlines in Hearst papers on February 17, 1898, soon after the sinking of the *Maine*.

Spanish sailors captured by Hearst after the naval battle outside of Santiago de Cuba, July 4, 1898.

Typical of Hearst crusade to reform business monopolies. Ace cartoonist Frederick Opper satirizes coal trust in 1902.

The only wedding picture to run in Hearst's New York *American*, April 29, 1903, page 9, of Congressman Hearst's marriage to Millicent Willson.

New York American

RUSHED WITH ORDERS

Government Weather Report.

No. 8,253. WEDNESDAY. NEW YORK, NOVEMBER 8, 1905.—16 PAGES. WEDNESDAY. PRICE ONE CENT. TWO CENTS.

W. R. HEARST ELECTED MAYOR

Tammany, by Every Process Known to Criminals, Seeks to Steal the Election---Violence and Frauds Unparalleled in City's History Marked the Battle for Decent Government.

We have won this election. All Tammany's fraud, all Tammany's corruption, all Tammany's intimidation and violence, all Tammany's false registration, illegal voting and dishonest count have not been able to overcome a great popular majority. The recount will show that we have won the election by many thousands of votes.

I shall fight this battle to the end, in behalf of the people who have cast their votes for me and who shall not be disfranchised by any effort of criminal bosses.

WILLIAM RANDOLPH HEARST.

Beautiful Millicent Hearst in 1906. (*Courtesy of The Library of Congress, Washington, D.C.*)

Hearst at age 43 in 1906. (*Courtesy of The Library of Congress, Washington, D.C.*)

Hearst in frock coat campaigning for Governor of New York, 1906.

DISTRIBUTING CAMPAIGN LITERATURE.

American cartoonist T. S. Sullivant depicts Tammany Hall's "Big Tom" Foley "clubbing" his way to victory, October 28, 1907.

WILLIAM RANDOLPH HEARST AND HIS LITTLE SON.

Campaign picture of candidate Hearst and his son, George, affectionately called "Buster."

Hearst, Millie, and Arthur Brisbane in Chicago for Independence Party national convention, June, 1908, where Hearst was the convention chairman and keynote speaker. (*Courtesy of The Bancroft Library, University of California at Berkeley*)

Hearst family in late October, 1909, (*left to right*) William Randolph Hearst, Jr., William Randolph Hearst, Millicent Hearst holding one-month-old John Randolph Hearst, and George Randolph Hearst.

September 27, the day of Dewey's scheduled arrival, as a million and a half visitors converged on the city, Hearst attracted huge crowds by displaying in the window of the *Journal* building at Twenty-third and Broadway the magnificent Dewey Loving Cup, recently created from seventy-two thousand melted dimes. Then at eleven the next morning, two hours before Dewey was scheduled to lead the "parade of ships" from his anchorage to Grant's Tomb, the *Journal's* dispatch boat *Long Island,* "radiant in flags and bunting"—and with two huge flags embossed with the words "*New York Journal*"—appeared before the *Olympia.* On board was the renowned sixty-member Banda Rossa, resplendent in scarlet uniforms, whom Hearst had hired to serenade Dewey and his crew. At the conclusion of a stirring two-hour concert, as the *Olympia* was weighing anchor, Dewey graciously responded—as Hearst had calculatingly anticipated. The *Journal* probably told it best: "The *Journal's* dispatch boat *Long Island,* with a company of distinguished guests, occupied a post of honor at cable's length from the *Olympia* during the entire parade, and was the only newspaper vessel in the warship division. By common consent this position was conceded to the *Journal's* boat. The newspaper was in the front line during the entire Spanish war, and it was only appropriate that in a celebration of the greatest victory the *Journal* should have the best place." Hearst had indeed demonstrated once again his excellence as a master showman, as a superb purveyor of one-upmanship.[27]

Enough of parades and celebrations, of political agendas, of newspaper deadlines! Hearst had not been on vacation for more than three years; now it was time. Although continually involved in *Journal* operations, he still arranged every aspect of a five-month trip to Egypt; much like his mother when on tour, he, too, was a director. On November 1, 1899, he sailed for Alexandria on a Pacific & Orient steamer, with brief respites at London, Paris, and the small Italian port of Brindisi on the Adriatic. Then, by December, he had passed through Cairo up the Nile to Luxor. For traveling companions he invited the glamorous Willson sisters, Millicent and Anita, together with their parents. In letters to his mother, however, he failed to mention any guests, especially since Phoebe—she added an "o" to the spelling of her name in 1899—had never approved of his frequent attraction to showgirls.[28]

For Hearst, this vacation proved to be a rejuvenation in body and spirit, an elixir of health. Although at times complaining to his mother that Cairo was "sort of a Mexican village," that the pyramids were "disappointing," and that the Nile was "pretty fair, but a little too much like the Sacramento [River]," he soon announced that "I am well and happy and having a really glorious time . . . [that] the freedom from work and worry is delicious and I am having more rest and enjoyment than I have had for a long, long time." Then in Nubia, west of the Red Sea in Egypt and Sudan, he discovered another passion—Egyptology. Near a camp "in the hills" he had bought a number of prehistoric jars, which "would be," he wrote his mother, "good Museum stuff" for their future collections. He indeed had Phoebe's genes. So in March, 1900, after four months of obsessive buying, he began an enjoyable homeward trip, allowing for five days at Rome and more than a week in Paris. In a letter to Phoebe he reported: "I am happy and well. My nervousness is gone, my stomach is getting into good condition, I sleep well and life is worth living again. . . . I shall be home soon now and ready to work hard once more."[29]

Early in April, 1900, upon his return to New York, Hearst did exactly that, plunging himself into the vortex of Democratic politics. He had ultimately decided, although an uncharacteristic action on his part, that personal involvement through active political participation was the only way to achieve certain goals for "his America." Actually he had already prepared the way for such a move. Soon after the 1898 November elections, he had proclaimed that the *Journal* was the national "voice" of the Democrats. He had therefore promoted as the party platform for foreign affairs the *Journal*'s "National Policy," especially the "digging" of a Nicaraguan Canal, which would be owned and fortified by the United States, and "expansionism without imperialism," which meant "keep the Philippines." Then in February, 1899, and thereafter, in editorial after editorial, he had advocated an "American Internal Policy"—the domestic platform of the party—which emphasized the "destruction of criminal trusts" by such reforms as direct election of senators, a graduated income tax, and federal control of banking.

But, most important of all, Hearst needed someone to carry out this agenda. To that end, to be "solid with a power in politics," he settled on William Jennings Bryan. Late in August, 1899, he disclosed future plans by asking his mother to entertain Bryan, who was en route to California. "He is really a fine man, although an extreme radical," Hearst wrote. And whether he "is elected president or not, he is and will continue to be dictator of the radical wing of the Democratic Party, and it is pretty important that he should be very close to me and to the *Journal*." If you will "give" Bryan and his wife "a pretty good time," Hearst pleaded, "you will do more than I can do with the support of the *Journal* to get Bryan's close friendship."[30]

Hearst, while participating in local and state Democratic functions only in a perfunctory way, was maneuvering for party status that would elevate him nationally, that would challenge his abilities and prevail upon his imagination. He soon acquired such stature. In mid-April, 1900, James K. Jones of Arkansas, who was chairman of the National Democratic Committee, decided to involve Hearst strategically in the forthcoming presidential campaign. With Bryan's approval, the National Association of Democratic Clubs, meeting in Washington on May 19, elected him president after the resignation of Governor Benton McMillin of Tennessee.

Soon after acceptance, Hearst agreed to assume an immediate and even more formidable task. If Bryan, upon renomination, intended to win in November, the Democrats needed a major journal in the Midwest. Hearst thus promised to publish a newspaper in Chicago by July 4, "if the leaders will recognize," he stipulated, "that I am doing it for the party's sake, not for money."[31]

So, as simply as that, the *Chicago American* was born, provided that the Hearst organization and Hearst money were equal to the task. Both were. But what a tremendous six-week undertaking! Immediately the black-bearded, Satanic-looking Solomon Carvalho, who was the *Journal's* extremely efficient business manager, directed this newest crusade. He rented the old Steuben Wine Company building at 216 West Madison Street, near Franklin, and began its renovation with eight hundred men working round-the-clock in three shifts. Because of a temporary shortage of freight cars—and time being a factor—he was forced to send the huge newspaper presses from New York City aboard luxurious Pullmans. Soon thereafter Hearst and Brisbane arrived, along with cartoonists Homer Davenport and Jimmy Swinnerton, as well as a host of *Journal* "old reliables." Hearst quickly added to this nucleus by raiding rival papers, at times doubling or tripling the salaries of area reporters, printers, and pressmen. In this way the job was done.

On July 4, 1900, after Bryan dramatically wired Hearst to "Start the Presses," the first edition of Hearst's *Chicago American* rolled forth, its front page producing a congratulatory message from Bryan to Hearst. In part it read: "The fact that your paper was established not merely to make money, but because of your desire to aid the Democratic leaders that you should duplicate in Chicago this year the splendid work done by the *Journal* and the *Examiner* in '96, ought to commend the paper to the friends of democracy. And I am confident that a large circulation awaits the *Chicago American*." That evening at the Democratic National Convention in Kansas City, hundreds of delegates waved "Extras" of Hearst's *Chicago*

American "in triumph," while preparing to nominate Bryan for president the next day.[32]

At the same time Hearst, although aware of the tremendous financial drain facing him in the Chicago operation, was unwilling to economize at the expense of the *Journal*. To outdistance all competition, he had installed on April 7, 1900—at a cost of $200,000—the latest high-speed presses from R. Hoe & Co., with the capacity to print 288,000 eight-page papers an hour. Then the next day he initiated a rather ingenious project that further drained his pocketbook but that increased circulation and endeared the *Journal* to its constituency. He sponsored an all-expense-paid-trip contest that presented twenty-four (the number soon to be expanded to fifty) high school male students from the Greater New York area the opportunity to "SEE A PRESIDENT NOMINATED." After vigorous competition over a six-week span, in which more than a thousand participants wrote a three-hundred-word extemporaneous essay titled either "How Is Our Country Governed?" or "What Is a Republic?", a panel of "three distinguished professors" chose the winners, half of whom attended the Republican National Convention at Philadelphia in June and the other half the Democratic National Convention at Kansas City in July.[33]

During this same time period Hearst decided to file an injunction against the American Ice Company "to relieve," as the *Journal* asserted on May 8, "the poor and suffering from the soulless greed and grip of one of the meanest forms of monopoly." This crusade against the Ice Trust, which had doubled the cost of one hundred pounds of ice in one year from 30 to 60 cents, soon had far-reaching political ramifications. The *Journal*, while following its usual campaign techniques of orchestrating the news through arranged daily testimonials against the Ice Trust, suddenly discovered on May 15 startling information of volatile proportions. Mayor Robert A. Van Wyck and Tammany interim chief John Carroll (in the absence of Croker), both of whom two weeks previously had inspected ice plants in Maine and then had prevented the importation of competitive products, owned eight thousand shares and five thousand shares respectively of the American Ice Company. Further investigation also disclosed that Judge Augustus Van Wyck, the mayor's brother, together with a number of city officials and local Democratic Party officeholders, also held a minimum of five hundred shares each, the overall worth—by *Journal* estimates—approximating $1,550,000.[34]

For six weeks Hearst waged a first-class crusade, reminiscent of the campaign against General Weyler and Spain. Almost daily Davenport pictorially assassinated the Ice Trust and Van Wyck with his cartoons. On the front page and editorially the *Journal* beseeched, indeed demanded, that Governor Roosevelt appoint a special grand jury to investigate the insidious connections between the Ice Trust and public officials, that the New York County district attorney indict "MAYOR VAN WYCK, THE CRIMINAL OFFICIAL," and that Congress protect the people with stricter antitrust measures. Then came a "spontaneous" referendum, with the *Journal* collecting thousands of signed petitions asking Roosevelt, as governor, to remove Van Wyck. And even though the mayor escaped a trial and prosecution, "the leading Democratic paper," the *Journal* proudly announced, had condemned "wrongdoing even among its own party chieftains." In other words, Van Wyck was "dead" politically. At the Democratic National Convention at Kansas City early in July, the delegates, upon seeing him appear on the convention floor, hissed at him and then yelled: "Ice! Ice!" To which spectators immediately echoed: "Ice! Ice!"

The vaudeville team of Burton and Brooks, to the delight of Hearst, probably best expressed the sentiments of New Yorkers, who had witnessed the *Journal's* bitter fight against the Ice Trust. They entertained their local audiences with two verses of this rollicking song:

New York City's daily papers are always full of boast;
Of reform they've bragged about day after day,
Sensation is the news that pays, no matter whom they roast,
But they do it in a diplomatic way.
Now, for instance, take the JOURNAL, much good work it has done.
And no doubt you have heard it said,
There's more news in the JOURNAL than the Herald, World, and Sun;
Though called "yellow," we know better, for it's read.

CHORUS
The Herald and World, the Sun and the Times all look
Glum, glum, glum;
Every battle the JOURNAL has started to fight it has
Won, won, won;
For the good of the people, the rich or the poor, it is
Run, run, run;
And whatever the JOURNAL has said it would do, it has
Done, done, done.

II.
Now, the JOURNAL gave us cheaper gas, but for it had to fight,
And will soon freeze out the Mayor's big Ice Trust;
It turned a searchlight on the magnates, which put them to flight,

And to give us cheaper ice they'll find they must.
The terrific heat of summer has filled many a pauper's grave,
For luxuries they can't afford the price of ice.

CHORUS
Now the Herald and World, the Sun and the Times all look
Glum, glum, glum;
Every battle the JOURNAL has started to fight it has
Won, won, won;
The American Ice Trust it surely has put on the
Bum, bum, bum;
For whatever the JOURNAL has said it would do, it has
Done, done, done.[35]

Early in July, after the nomination of Bryan along with vice-presidential running mate Adlai E. Stevenson of Illinois, Hearst immersed himself in the campaign. As in 1896, his newspapers became blatant editorials for the Democrats, with news orchestration following the pronounced Hearst-crusade formula. For example, beginning late in July, the *Journal* published monthly and, as election time neared, weekly polls both nationally and statewide predicting a victory for Bryan. Testimonials endorsing the Democrats appeared daily, some stretching the credulity of readers—"Republicans deserting McKinley" (August 20 and September 16); "Andrew Carnegie indicates to *Journal* reporter that he will support Bryan" (August 24); poll "gives Illinois and Ohio [McKinley's home state] to Bryan" (September 19); "McKinley cousins to vote for Bryan" (September 30); "Seven Bryan Girls Refuse To Marry Republican Voters" (October 30).

Hearst also assigned his best correspondents to cover the campaign, such as James Creelman and Max Ihmsen reporting on Bryan and Winifred Black on Mrs. Bryan. And, as expected, political cartoonist Homer Davenport was at his acerbic best in depicting Republican nominees McKinley and running mate Theodore Roosevelt as the tools of the trusts, as the representatives of greed. Hearst, however, unlimbered still another cannon in his arsenal of political diatribe and graphic invective. Frederick Burr Opper, relatively unknown until this campaign, initiated a series of cartoons titled "Willie and His Papa," in which he portrayed McKinley as a small boy, gargantuan dollar-covered trusts as "Papa," and Republican national campaign director Mark Hanna as a devious, skulking nursemaid.[36]

Yet this campaign, in contrast to that of 1896, was significantly different. The enthusiasm for the candidates, the ardor for combat by the party faithful, seemed to be missing. Possibly voters had become too well acquainted with their leaders; in other words, McKinley and Bryan "sprang" no surprises on them this second time around. Or perhaps the major issues espoused by the Democrats—coinage of silver at a ratio to gold of sixteen–to–one, expansionism without imperialism, regulation of trusts—lacked the exciting luster and emotional depth to spark real controversy and, as *Journal* political editor and Bryan confidant Willis Abbot put it, "did not click" with voters. But whatever the reasons, with the nation having recovered significantly from economic depression (the Panic of 1893), with Americans still reveling in a triumphant victory over Spain as well as their newly acquired empire, the feverish aura of a crusade, the drumbeat for change, did not surface—nor would it.[37]

Nowhere was the tempo of a waning campaign, a lack of interest by the electorate, more evident than in the pages of the *Journal*. Whereas Bryan and Stevenson had received an inordinate amount of newspaper space on the front pages and in editorials after their nominations at Kansas City in July, such prominent exposure all but disappeared during a crucial five-week span beginning on September 10. The *Journal* inevitably reflected—and sometimes marshaled—public opinion, especially with an excellent pulse-taker such as Hearst at the helm. On the previous day (September 10) a destructive hurricane had devastated the small Gulf Coast Texas city of Galveston, killing and drowning five thousand to eight thousand people; therefore, a new crusade of relief and charity for victims of this horrible tragedy took center stage. The *Journal* immediately assigned such gifted writers as Winifred Black and Gertrude Atherton to report the storm's ravaging effects. Because their stories of destruction were so staggering, Hearst reacted impulsively, once again disregarding costs, by organizing three "Hearst Relief Trains," one from each of his newspapers, with food and clothing and medical supplies for the beleaguered sufferers. He then encouraged readers to contribute to a Galveston Relief Fund, which would help shoulder the expense for orphans at a "Hearst Hospital" in Houston, Texas. He also persuaded stage performers to "give benefits" and donate the proceeds to the Relief Fund. His most impressive coup, however, was that of inducing Mrs. John Jacob Astor, the leader of New York's fashionable "400," and the Duchess of Marlborough (née Consuelo Vanderbilt) to sponsor a Charity Bazaar at the Waldorf-Astoria, a social triumph on October 15 that was topped off with a speech by Mark Twain.[38]

But the distinguishing feature of this 1900 campaign was the emergence of Hearst as a political activist. During May and June, while striving arduously to implement the *Chicago American* by July 4, he worked through intermediaries to effect his platform goals—but to no avail. On all but two planks he agreed with Bryan; and, to a certain extent, really just one. The dynamic Nebraskan had accepted the *Journal* proposition of "expansionism without imperialism," except adversely advocating, as far as Hearst was concerned, the independence of the Philippines. But the money plank was a different matter. On June 2 *Journal* correspondent James Creelman, who had good rapport with Bryan, relayed that Hearst was contributing $10,000 to $15,000 immediately to the Democratic campaign, with the possibility of increasing the amount "by a little plan" to $40,000. But all such activity could be for naught, Creelman wrote to Bryan. "We cannot, cannot, cannot and will not, will not, take up '16 to 1' in the East." He therefore urged Bryan not to mention silver specifically but "simply reaffirm the [Chicago] platform of 1896 in general terms and devote the new platform to new issues." To such advice the Democratic candidate remained obdurate in his position—and Hearst would remember.[39]

Without any real support—or voice—in the Democratic Party except through his newspapers, Hearst decided to carve out an agenda of his own, a strong base from which he could operate. During his career he had always been the outsider, continually challenging well-established, comfortably entrenched forces both in business and politics; however, with a team of his own choosing, he had always won. Nothing had changed. After state Democratic leaders excluded him from a "seaside conference" late in July, Hearst set his own course of action; he would use his presidency of the National Democratic Clubs as the vehicle for admittance, if not acceptance.[40]

But Hearst first needed an organizational secretary who would do his bidding. After consulting with Bryan and Democratic National Committee chairman James Jones, as well as Creelman and Willis Abbot, he selected the curly-haired, somewhat rotund Max F. Ihmsen, who for the past several years had been a *Journal* correspondent in Washington. Energetic and seemingly indefatigable, dedicated and unquestionably loyal, with a flair for organization and detail, Ihmsen was an ideal choice. He immediately established a national headquarters at 1370 Broadway, New York City, obtained lists of Democratic county chairman in every state, then sent them application forms for club membership together with a Democratic campaign booklet, devised by Hearst, that was well illustrated by Homer Davenport. After constant written contact with them,

Ihmsen proposed, with Hearst's approval, a national convention of Democratic clubs at Indianapolis on October 3. And with Bryan, Stevenson, and Jones, as well as a bevy of prominent party leaders agreeing to attend, Ihmsen sought both publicity and results. As a consequence, the *Journal* tracked his accomplishments daily, which, if reported accurately, were astounding. For example, the *Journal* announced on September 2 that "More Than 1 Million Democrats Enroll"; on September 9 that the number had increased into a "Mighty Army" of 1.5 million; and on September 22 that "200,000 voters [en]listed in 3 days." [41]

Then on October 3, 1900, approximately 3,500 delegates descended on Indianapolis for the Democratic Club National Convention. For Hearst it was a learning experience. Painfully shy before the public and extremely self-conscious about his high, reedy voice—to the point of causing a "nervous stomach"—he was not present for the opening session, thus forcing Democratic chairman James Jones to call the meeting to order. Yet, despite his noticeable absence, this convention was, in many ways, a personal triumph. Speakers freely praised him for his "splendid work" that, through his own personal expense, had resulted in the formation of 7,353 clubs. But even more satisfying were the "tumultuous outbursts of applause," cries of "Hearst! Hearst! He is a good fellow," resounding throughout the convention hall, when delegates learned that he had agreed to match every dollar that the clubs or individual members contributed to the national campaign. [42]

Hearst thus determined to become a part of the public picture, a player in the political game, even though on unfamiliar turf. And, by sheer force of will, he did participate. On October 16 and 17, during the Bryan campaign "swing" into New York City, Hearst accompanied his candidate through the immense crowds, endured hours of handshaking and small talk, and survived lengthy dinners followed by a seemingly endless number of speeches. [43]

Yet the thought of being a follower, of being merely one of the crowd, was anathema to Hearst. So once again he played the game of one-upmanship. Early in October he prevailed on Bryan to rearrange his campaign schedule and return to New York City for a "grand reception" hosted by the Association of National Democratic Clubs. This time he was determining the agenda and the state Democratic leaders were the onlookers.

Consequently, on October 27, Bryan experienced the "Hearst treatment" of creative extravaganzas and flamboyant showmanship. At 2:45 that afternoon Hearst, together with the loyal Ihmsen and the dynamic

Creelman, met Bryan at the train station and, "arm in arm," escorted him immediately to quarters at the Hoffman House. Then at 5:30 P.M. the "treatment" began in full. At the elegant Green Parlor of the Hoffman House, Hearst arranged an elaborate dinner for Bryan, who was joined by his wife and forty guests, including such local Democratic dignitaries as Tammany chief Richard Croker, leader of the 1896 "gold Democrats" David B. Hill, and Mayor Robert A. Van Wyck (of Ice Trust infamy) as well as the Ihmsens and Creelmans and old Harvard crony Jack Follansbee. What a lavishly expensive outlay! While an orchestra played tasteful dinner music in a room that was "decorated," the *New York Tribune* noted, "with palms, ferns, white chrysanthemums and autumn leaves," the guests enjoyed such chef's delights as *huitres, potage, Saucisson de Lyon*, and *Ris de veau a l'Ecarlate*. As an added touch, Hearst had each table "banked with roses," on which were souvenirs of "little silver baskets with candy in them."[44]

But the extravaganza had just begun. Bryan was scheduled to speak five times that evening, the finale culminating at Madison Square Garden. So at 7:40 P.M. Bryan and Hearst embarked in a carriage on what the *Journal* described as "BRYAN'S GREATEST RECEPTION." In the park across the street from the Hoffman House two bands, each of one hundred pieces, entertained assembled crowds. Then down Broadway, lined on both sides by eager sightseers and Democratic Club members, Bryan and Hearst went to scheduled rallies, first with Italian Americans at the Broadway Athletic Club (8:00 P.M.) and then with German Americans at the Cooper Institute (8:30 P.M.).

In the meantime, the New York sky was all aglow. Hearst had once again relied on Professor Henry "Pyrotechnist" Pain to unleash his extraordinary artistry with fireworks. For hours thousands of New Yorkers watched in dismay as rockets screamed into the night sky, bursting into glittering stars and luminous flowers. As the evening progressed, Pain displayed an amazing creativity—a portrait in fire of Bryan, a spectacular representation of "Old Glory," another flaming picture showing the Fred Opper cartoon "Willie and His Papa," and still another glittering six-hundred-square-foot creation depicting a Davenport cartoon of "the trusts."

By 9:30 P.M., after two more stops en route, the Bryan and Hearst entourage arrived, as scheduled, at Madison Square Garden, its tower ablaze with four thousand lights, its massive stage covered with flowers and enveloped with hundreds of American flags hanging overhead. Hearst could not have been more pleased. As an eighty-piece band played stirring, pa-

triotic music, they made their way through the huge crowd of eager onlookers and party faithful. Such a setting was exactly what stage director
Hearst had choreographed as a fitting climax to this final campaign drama
of 1900. After ten minutes of what had to be unadulterated hell for him in
trying to calm the boisterous crowd, he finally was able to call the meeting
to order and, as prearranged, to introduce Anson Phelps Stokes, a wealthy
and prominent New Yorker, as permanent chairman.

Feeling relatively safe now amid the group on the platform and no
longer in the terrifying spotlight of public attention, Hearst enjoyed the
rest of the evening immensely. Bryan, in the concluding speech of the
night, graciously acknowledged the tremendous efforts of those responsible for this spectacular affair. He also noted that the National Association
of Democratic Clubs had raised $26,000 in campaign contributions, an
amount its president had promised to match. So Bryan called on the
crowd to "give three cheers" for the shy but appreciative Hearst.[45]

All such efforts by Hearst, no matter how herculean, were to no avail.
On November 6, 1900, McKinley defeated Bryan once again—and far
worse than in 1896—sweeping every state in the North and East and
Midwest, while losing only the "Solid South" and the western silver states
of Colorado, Nevada, Idaho, and Montana. He even carried Bryan's Nebraska (including his home precinct). He therefore won the electoral college vote almost two to one, 292 to 155.

Hearst was not surprised. The Republicans had rightly appealed to the
American voter through the slogan "The Full Dinner Pail," which emphasized the increased prosperity emanating from the Spanish-American
War and such economic policies as the gold standard. They had also endorsed the foreign-policy concept of empire—"Keep the Philippines"—through the emotionally patriotic slogan "Don't Haul Down
The Flag." Hearst, in turn, had backed a candidate who did not heed his
advice on major campaign issues, who did not realize that he had his finger on the pulse of the American people. He would not make that mistake
again. In the next presidential crusade the Democratic candidate would
have to be someone with whom he could identify, whom he could influence and trust. Who better than William Randolph Hearst?[46]

9 | Running for President

∽

Beginning in 1901, William Randolph Hearst was fast approaching a crossroads in his life. Although the owner and editor-in-chief of four powerful newspapers in the United States, with a daily circulation approaching the two-million mark, he was, to a certain extent, at loose ends within the Hearst publishing empire. For the first time in fourteen years, since first rehabilitating the *San Francisco Examiner* in 1887, he had no specific duties, no all-encompassing routine. He had removed himself as the hands-on leader of the *Morning Journal* with the appointment of Arthur Brisbane to that position late in 1899. He had then applied his astounding energies and organizational talents to the election of a Democratic president in 1900, but to no avail. And he gradually realized, as the campaign continued to its inexorable conclusion, that no one, other than himself, would—or could—shoulder the domestic and foreign policies that he had advocated over the past two years and that were paramount, he believed, to the betterment of the United States and the American people.

So what was Hearst to do? Except for his father and William Jennings Bryan, whom he had come to admire to the point of adoration, his "contempt for politicians was rather far-reaching—even all-inclusive." In fact, Willis Abbot observed, "I do not recall ever hearing him express any real admiration for even the men he supported for office." Yet Hearst, despite what Ambrose Bierce described as an "extreme diffidence" at public gatherings, despite a pronounced inability to sway an audience with oratory because of a high-pitched voice and ineffectual delivery (partly due to a slight lisp), and despite a limp and unimpressive handshake, ultimately decided to test the public arena, "to see if I can do better." In the 1900 campaign, as president of the National Association of Democratic Clubs, he had demonstrated, with the formidable assistance of Max Ihmsen and

James Creelman, a remarkable talent for political organization, for bringing diverse groups together and getting things done. Hearst had also
broadened his communications and propaganda base considerably with
the establishment of the *Chicago American*; however, he realized that further acquisitions in large cities would be extremely advantageous to him as
a national candidate, especially since each of his papers ostensibly bore
both name identification and stamp of ownership—"copyright by W. R.
Hearst" appeared repeatedly throughout the pages of every edition. And,
through sheer force of will, he had "played the game of politics" throughout the 1900 campaign as effectively as his aversion to faceless crowds and
speaking engagements would allow, acquainting himself with Democratic
state and national leaders as well as the party faithful. He even changed
his appearance, forgoing a penchant for expensive plaids and gaudy cravats and natty straw hats for "the usual uniform of American statesman-
ship, combining the long-tailed frock coat and the cowboy's soft slouch
hat."[1]

Hearst, besides establishing an impressive political base in preparation
for future campaigns, had synthesized and refined his political philosophy
into arguments that would appeal to the patriotism and pocketbook of average Americans. He was, he asserted, "a Jeffersonian Democrat" who believed in "equal rights for all and privileges for none." As his newspapers
reflected, he would be "a fearless, forceful fighter" for the "underdog"—laborers seeking better wages and shorter hours in the marketplace, farmers
concerned continually with mounting surpluses and falling prices, immigrants disadvantaged by economic and political systems so different from
their previous experiences, small businessmen and consumers battling
ever-rising costs in corporate America.

Hearst, a millionaire by inheritance as well as through personal efforts,
would be a crusader against his own class, against the "greed of plutocracy."
In front-page headlines, in cartoons, in editorial after editorial, he had
railed against the "criminal trusts" that exploited the people for their own
selfish ends. He had advocated such reforms as lower tariffs, which would
bring competition into the marketplace; direct election of senators, which
would curb corporate control of the Senate (often referred to as the "railroad lobby"); and stringent antitrust laws, which would have sufficient legal "teeth" to provide enforcement against such mammoth corporations as
Standard Oil and U.S. Steel. All that the people needed was a resourceful,
courageous political figure who would lead them in a "new spirit" intent on
abolishing privilege, a vigorous, intrepid champion who would "restore democracy in the United States." An ambitious, self-reliant William Ran-

dolph Hearst, at age thirty-eight, began dedicating himself to be the embodiment of such a movement.[2]

But after such arduous presidential campaigning during the summer and fall of 1900, Hearst needed to reinvigorate both his physical stamina and mental well-being or, vernacularly speaking, to "recharge his batteries." Such revivification meant just one thing to Hearst: travel to faraway places. So in December, 1900, he sailed for Europe, then to Egypt, accompanied by the four Willsons, sisters Millicent and Anita together with their parents—of whom Phoebe Hearst thoroughly disapproved; they were, especially Millicent, "so common." But she loved her Will despite his choice of female companions and his obvious disregard, bordering on contempt, for the mores of society. She also understood certain quirks of his character that triggered specific responses. For instance, she allegedly remarked that "every time Willie feels bad, he goes out and buys something." If this observation was correct, Hearst must have been terribly dispirited. During the next four months in Europe he "ravaged" a number of private collections, acquiring priceless tapestries and antique furniture and exquisite works of art, especially of German, French, Italian, and Egyptian origins. Late in the spring of 1901 he returned to New York City, rejuvenated in health and spirit, laden down with enough "loot" to occupy an empty warehouse.[3]

Hearst, although no longer the hands-on manager of the *Morning Journal*, still helped shape its policies and, at times, projected his imaginative ideas into print that fascinated and enthralled the American public. The summer of 1901 was a case in point. Late in May, Hearst—using Jules Verne's theme of *Around the World in Eighty Days*—"dreamed up" an international global race that pitted three seventeen-year-old American schoolboys, representing the Hearst newspapers in San Francisco, Chicago, and New York City, against two distinguished Paris journalists, Gaston Stiegeler of *Le Matin* and Henri Turot of *Le Journal*. After rigorous competition in which local teachers chose a representative of their public school system, William Clark Crittenden emerged as champion for the *San Francisco Examiner*, Charles Cecil Fitzmorris for the *Chicago American*, and Louis St. Clair Eunson for the *New York Journal*. Then at precise starting dates on May 20–21 (each contestant was being timed to the exact second), the three "HEARST NEWSPAPER BOYS" raced around the world, two going west and one east by rail and boat, en route to Yokohama, Vladivostok, Moscow, London, Dublin, and back to their home base. Foreign journalists Stiegeler and Turot followed the same itinerary, but began in Paris.[4]

Each day for the next two months the Hearst newspapers entertained their readers. Besides the participants writing daily accounts of their adventures, accompanying journalists and professors in each entourage described the wonders of distant lands and the difficulties of foreign travel. Politicians—U.S. senators, governors, mayors, foreign dignitaries, and even President McKinley—greeted the world travelers en route and wished them bon voyage. The Hearst newspapers, in turn, provided excellent maps that pinpointed the exact location of each contestant as well as detailing the next step of the journey. Hearst, ever the promoter of gamesmanship, offered $1,000 to any reader of his newspapers who predicted the winner of this 25,000-mile race and who guessed the closest finishing time. And when Charles Cecil Fitzmorris, representing the *Chicago American*, ended his "globe encircling journey" in the record time of "60 DAYS, 13 HOURS, 29 MIN., 42 4-5 SEC."—breaking the previous world's mark by eight days—thousands of Chicagoans greeted him in a massive parade, of course orchestrated by Hearst, replete with prancing horses and marching bands, ceremonial speeches by the "acting governor" and mayor, topped off with a lavish dinner and huge reception, all at the publisher's expense. Then the next day Hearst newspapers awarded a $1,000 prize to John J. Hakenstrom of Chicago, who missed guessing the actual time by "one-fifth of a second."[5]

During this summer of 1901 Brisbane and Hearst also directed crusades that both gratified and cheered *Journal* readers. When a terrible heat wave inundated Greater New York early in July, claiming 210 victims and prostrating 400, the *Journal* was at the disposal of the citizenry. As a "voice" for the people, it persuaded city officials to open recreational piers all night, maintain public baths until midnight, and continually spray water into the streets for needed relief of the sweltering populace. Because the intense heat prostrated so many New Yorkers, the *Journal* provided auto transportation as a service to already overburdened hospital staffs. For those suffocating in overcrowded apartment buildings, reporter Dorothy Dix obtained city permission for "respectable people" to sleep on park benches. But upon learning that such accommodations required "rent" payment, Hearst attorneys brought suit against Park Commissioner George C. Clausen, demanding that such property as "seats" be free of charge. Within a week the *Journal* won a popular victory, proudly proclaiming itself the "pater of the people."[6]

Hearst was, in the parlance of a gambler, "on a roll." Emboldened with success and confident of public support, the *Journal* selected even more formidable opponents for the continuing summer crusade. When the

Seventh National Bank abruptly closed its doors late in June, 1901, *Journal* attorneys filed suit for $1.2 million against those directors and officials who had robbed "THE SEVENTH'S DEPOSITORS." Within ten weeks, because of constant publicity and legal pressure, the *Journal* triumphantly reported that the "BANK LOOTERS ARE INDICTED AT LAST."

Even against less prestigious thieves, Hearst and Brisbane were equally adamant and unyielding. They targeted illegal gambling "dives" that were rife throughout the city. For months Justice William Travers Jerome had headed a public task force, known as the "Committee of Fifteen," in trying to deter, if not eliminate, this "cancer." But law officers, upon raiding such establishments, soon discovered that "phone operators" within the police department had "tipped" the gamblers. The *Journal* thus unleashed its trained corps of sleuth reporters, who soon uncovered damning evidence that a number of officers, reputedly including Deputy Police Commissioner William Devery, had accepted bribes and "payoffs" ranging from $250 to $500 a month.[7]

But on September 6, 1901, one incident erased this summer of journalistic success and good intent. At a little past four that afternoon, twenty-eight-year-old Leon Czolgosz, the son of Polish immigrants, shot William McKinley, who was attending the Pan-American Exposition at Buffalo, New York; eight days later, the president died. As the nation mourned over this senseless act, Hearst became a major target of the American people's frustration through illogical vilification. For more than a year one popular *Journal* feature had been Frederick Opper's "The McKinley Minstrels"—a brilliantly conceived political cartoon series that ridiculed the president and Mark Hanna for protecting huge corporations and "greedy" trusts against the needs of the American people. This previous criticism of a martyred president now angered a bereaved nation. Even more damaging, however, was an ill-advised editorial by the acid-tongued Ambrose Bierce, who—unknown to Hearst—had written a prophetic quatrain early in February, 1901, concerning the assassination of William Goebel, the Democratic governor-elect of Kentucky. It read:

> The bullet that pierced Goebel's breast
> Can not be found in all the West;
> Good reason, it is speeding here
> To stretch McKinley on his bier.

To exacerbate an already volatile public mood, rumors abounded linking Hearst and his newspaper to the assassin—Czolgosz had a *Journal* edition in his coat pocket that was highly critical of McKinley. And then from all sides a crescendo of venomous censure and verbal invective inundated

Hearst and the *Journal*. Foremost among the detractors was Paul Dana, editor of the *New York Sun*, who charged the Hearst papers with "encouraging anarchists" with "yellow journalism" techniques, the ultimate folly being the death of McKinley.[8]

Hearst, who was in the *Chicago American* newsroom on September 6 when first learning about the assassination attempt, quietly remarked to editor-in-chief Charles Edward Russell: "Things are going to be very bad." And he was right. In New York, Chicago, and San Francisco, mobs seized Hearst newsboys, trashing or burning their copies; public libraries and private clubs canceled their subscriptions; and competitors did a hatchet job on him, labeling him as the "teacher of anarchists." So bad did daily existence become that Hearst cynically remarked one day to trusted friend and editor Andrew M. "Andy" Lawrence: "They can't hang me." But with threats on his life mounting in number, he began to wonder. He therefore began to "pack" a pistol or keep one nearby on his desk; and any gift-wrapped box, without the name or origin of the sender, he had burned, for fear of a bomb.[9]

Hearst, although willing to accept personal criticism without retaliation (he believed that public censure was one of the risks for any high-profile personality), was disinclined to allow his newspapers to suffer; therefore he, together with Brisbane, applied both journalistic techniques and proven experience to save his somewhat shaken newspaper empire. For example, during the eight days that McKinley tenaciously clung to life, the *Morning Journal* devoted front-page coverage to his condition as well as numerous articles and editorials lamenting such a dastardly attack on an American president. After McKinley's death on September 14, the *Journal* ran a full-length editorial (on the first and last pages) titled "FAREWELL TO A GOOD AMERICAN," eulogizing McKinley, his accomplishments on behalf of the United States, and his service to the American people.

Five days later, after what turned out to be the equivalent of a national funeral, the Hearst New York newspapers launched blistering attacks on "THOSE WHO HATE THE JOURNAL." Artistic (referring to cartoons) and literary criticisms of McKinley and Hanna were not personal attacks, editorials persistently reiterated, but rather a defense of the masses against greed and cupidity, indeed a fight for the principles of political democracy and economic freedom. Various competitors, "the hired bravos of the plutocratic press," had viewed this shocking incident of a "murdered president" by a "madman" as a vehicle "for transmitting the public grief and horror into enmity" against all Hearst journals and for trying to destroy the major Democratic Party newspapers in the United States. Several *Journal* editorials also decried that Paul Dana of the *New York Sun* was nothing more than a "flunkey" of the "predatory" rich, his accusations "a cowardly lie told by a fool."[10]

With such rebuttals still not totally deflecting the public wrath, Hearst and Brisbane continued their assault to restore confidence in, and good will toward, the *Journal*. They applied successful techniques of previous crusades, orchestrating testimonials from numerous newspapers across the nation that characterized Dana and the *Sun* as "jealous" and "foul" and "contemptible" while praising the *Journal* for its courageous stance on behalf of the toiling masses. They also used statistics effectively; the Sunday *Journal* circulation for September 22—eight days after McKinley's death—was 4,496 more than for the preceding week, 68,125 more than for the corresponding time in August, and 100,624 more than for the previous year. The *Journal* was therefore "at least SIX MILLION A MONTH MORE than the circulation of any publication on God's green earth, not excepting the *Daily Mail* of London or the *Petit Journal* of Paris." But to erase any lingering reminder of an association between McKinley and the *Journal*, Hearst decided to rename his New York papers; on November 11, 1901, he changed the masthead to the *Journal and American*. In less than a year it would read simply the *New York American*, and the transformation would be complete.[11]

Just prior to Christmas, in a letter to his mother, Hearst summarized the terrible pressures of the past months. "I expect to have a hard time this coming year. I mean much work, much unpleasant economy," he candidly assessed. "But I will pull through I am pretty sure, for I do not believe another calamity like the McKinley one can overtake us. There is still about sixty thousand dollars per year advertising out of the *Journal* but I believe most of it will come back." Hearst then revealed the personal strain of this struggle for journalistic survival: "I would feel better if I could only get a good rest. I am tired and don't sleep well and my stomach is in a constant state of rebellion. I think I have enough in my storage batteries for another year of work and then I am going to take a long vacation and not look at a newspaper."[12]

But Hearst—and alter ego Brisbane as well—aspired to a lofty personal goal: that of high political office. And since the *Journal and American* was, without question, the acknowledged embodiment of Hearst's ideas, they were determined to endear his newspapers to the American voters, especially those in Greater New York. Since the Bryan campaign of 1896 they had established a proven formula for success, one that during the next ten months they would follow religiously. In regard to promoting the good deeds and public services of the Hearst newspapers, they really had no journalistic equals, at least not as long as Phoebe's money held out and his flamboyancy prevailed. For example, in December, 1901, they began a Christmas crusade for children. Columnist Ella Wheeler Wilcox cajoled well-to-do New York bachelors into "making the city's destitute little ones happy." The *Journal and American* persuaded merchants to donate money and toys, listing each donor and the amount contributed. And, throughout Christmas Day, Hearst employees in twenty-two "*Journal* Santa Claus wagons" tirelessly distributed four hundred thousand gifts to more than seventy thousand tenement children. Again, in the eastern United States during the bitterly cold winter of 1902, fraught with icy snow and tenement fires, the *Journal and American* seemed to be omnipresent in relieving starvation and suffering. On February 9, at nearby Paterson, New Jersey, monstrous flames, fanned by wintry gales, destroyed most of the business district. The very next day a "*Journal* Relief Train" arrived and distributed six thousand meals (consisting of coffee and sandwiches), furnished ten heated railroad cars to shelter the hungry and homeless, and continually provided "strengthening" food to firemen and soldiers "along the guard lines." Then for the next three weeks heavy, blizzardlike snows inundated New York City, crippling every means of transportation, idling food and fuel services, and incapacitating most of the population. Immediately "*Journal and American* Traveling Kitchens"—wagons dispensing "hot coffee and substantial sandwiches"—appeared regularly at three stations in the downtown areas of City Hall and Union and Madison squares, feeding as many as four thousand daily as well as providing a night's lodging for the cold and weary.[13]

Hearst and Brisbane also realized that to secure the lasting loyalty and ardent devotion of voters the *Journal and American* must embrace issues that were not only popular to the masses but that reflected necessary democratic reforms for working-class Americans, who especially seemed to need a fearless champion to represent them. Both men surely endorsed this philosophy and fit comfortably into such a niche; attacking the "establishment" had always been an essential ingredient for their New Journalism. Consequently they promoted a number of short-term, popular reforms, such as cheaper fares and better safety precautions for local railroads, more fire escapes and security regulations for New York tenements, and lower prices for such necessary consumer items as meat and coal.[14]

The *Journal and American* (whose masthead would be reversed to

American and Journal beginning in April, 1902, and then shortened to *American* on October 20), embarked on two long-range crusades of significant import for Hearst. As early as February, 1902, the *Journal and American* initiated still another campaign to eliminate corruption within "New York's finest." Yet, even though concerned over charges alleging that police appointments were for sale according to rank, the *Journal and American* concentrated more on the morale of rank-and-file officers. And that meant better hours with equal pay—or, more specifically, a three-platoon system of eight-hour work shifts daily instead of two platoons of twelve hours. Over the next six months Brisbane followed the Hearst patented formula of news orchestration. Testimonials from women, clergymen, politicians, and well-known citizens endorsed the *Journal* plan. Petitions (eventually numbering more than three hundred thousand), which appeared daily both in the morning and evening papers and which readers could easily cut out and sign, flooded the offices of city officials and the governor. Then Hearst money fueled the seemingly ever-growing demands for shorter workdays—huge mass meetings to garner support and "whip up" enthusiasm, a "special *Journal* train" to Albany carrying three hundred prominent leaders as lobbyists for the "*Journal* bill," and a constant repertoire of stories concerning police heroism and individual sacrifice and ardent devotion to duty, even at the expense of home and family.[15]

With equal verve and enthusiasm the *American and Journal* supported the beleaguered anthracite coal miners in Pennsylvania, not only associating Hearst with the causes of the American workingman but also identifying him as "a national spokesman for the labor movement." On May 12, 1902, after President John Mitchell of the United Mine Workers (UMW) ordered 140,000 workers to strike for better pay and shorter hours as well as union recognition, the *American and Journal* quickly sided against the coal operators. Hearst, who had always supported organized labor, understood both the immediate and long-range effects of this struggle, informing Brisbane that "the strike gives us an opportunity to offset the widespread attacks [from the McKinley assassination] and to again lead a fight for labor unions and the needs of the poor." He and Brisbane therefore orchestrated the news once again, their objectives those of mobilizing public opinion as a potent weapon against the rich and powerful magnates of industry; of instilling strength and solidarity in the ranks of the UMW; and, most importantly, of anointing Hearst as the champion of the American workingman.[16]

Over the next five months Hearst and Brisbane were remarkably suc-

cessful. And no wonder! Many of the same ingredients in this crusade for
the miners seemed to parallel those of *"Cuba Libre"* in 1898—the arrogance and tyranny of the rich and powerful attempting to maintain their
dominant positions; the downtrodden, toiling masses seeking to alleviate
their economic poverty and political despair; reluctant state and national
leaders unsure of their constituencies and hesitant to enter the trouble-
some arena of controversy; and a crusading newspaper and its publisher
unifying the American electorate into an awesome force of public opinion
to fight against injustice.

Hearst and Brisbane specifically had to underscore the differences between the two sides, to accentuate the positives of the underdog miners,
and to villainize the actions of the industrial overlords. And that was exactly what they did. On May 17, less than a week after the strike began,
the *American and Journal* proposed arbitration between the conflicting parties. The operative word was "mediate." Daily from May into mid-
October a steady drumbeat for settlement between the discordant groups
increased in proportion to the pain endured by men out of work and their
families starving; Americans, facing the prospects of a frigid winter without coal, were also of paramount concern. The *American and Journal* editorials were constant in their demands upon the industrial magnates, the
Opper cartoons, titled "Nursery Rhymes for Infant Industries," devastating in their ridicule. Then came the testimonials of citizens across the nation as well as petitions and mass meetings endorsing the *American and
Journal* proposal for immediate arbitration.

But on July 17, 1902, after George F. Baer of the Philadelphia and Reading Coal and Iron Company, who was the recognized leader of the mine
operators, imperiously responded to such pleas by stating that "the rights
and interests of the laboring man will be protected and cared for—not by
labor agitators, but by the Christian men to whom God in his infinite wisdom has given the control of the property interests of this country," Hearst
and Brisbane had a field day. Accordingly, they intensified their campaign
against such appalling arrogance and brazen conceit. They presented
"documented evidence" that the coal companies, together with associated
railroads, had knowingly formed a monopoly, thereby violating the Sherman Anti-Trust Act and systematically eliminating competition. Hearst
specifically asked the Roosevelt administration to intervene, but the president refused to break this impasse. Hence, the *American and Journal* petitioned Congress, state governors (especially of Pennsylvania and New
York), and members of legislative bodies throughout the country "to end
the coal trust tyranny." Yet no movement or action occurred. Conse-

quently Hearst brought suit against the coal barons. He also increased political pressures nationwide by stepping up the petition campaign. And, as a coup de grâce, he proposed a "blue-ribbon" mediation committee including such men as John Cardinal Gibbons of New York, former postmaster general and prominent businessman John Wanamaker, and former vice president Adlai Stevenson.

Results were soon forthcoming. In September, with winter fast approaching, with coal prices rising, with a congressional election at hand, and with the *American and Journal* crusade for the miners gaining more advocates with each passing day, Roosevelt decided to intercede. By October 15 the impasse ended, the miners agreeing to return to work with the understanding that a seven-member presidential commission would settle the dispute.[17]

Hearst was delighted with the outcome; as in the crusade to free Cuba, "government by newspaper" had once again proved effective. He had also benefited; this struggle for the working man had broadened his perspectives and had heightened his ambitions. To Brisbane he confided: "The strike has taught me that we must enter the political process to force that process to change, to acquire a conscience for the social evils in America and a willingness to correct them."[18]

With these ideas in mind Hearst decided how best to enter the political arena, how best to realize his ambitions. After New York Democrats met at Saratoga to select their slate of candidates for state office on September 29–30, 1902, congressional caucuses convened in their respective districts two days later (October 2). During the previous two weeks Hearst had laid plans to run for Congress, as masterfully as an experienced Broadway stage director. Brisbane had negotiated with Charles Francis Murphy, a former dock commissioner who had recently emerged as Richard Croker's successor as head of Tammany Hall. Brisbane, although supposedly offered the Democratic Party nomination for the Eleventh Congressional District in midtown Manhattan, immediately withdrew in favor of his "boss," who, in turn, promised to commit considerable monetary funds as well as the influence of the *American and Journal, New York Evening Journal,* and *Das Morgen Journal* to the election of all state Democrats. This agreement, if successful, would serve both individuals well: Murphy would have his first Tammany victory and considerable patronage power in Greater New York, while Hearst would achieve a first step toward his ultimate goal, the presidency. Hence, on the night of October 2, 1902, the Democratic Congressional Convention of the Eleventh District, meeting at the Horatio Seymour Club on Eighth Avenue, unanimously nominated William Randolph Hearst (who, in keeping with the custom of the time, was not in attendance) as their candidate. Consequently, Tammany members of the Eleventh appointed a delegation to inform Hearst of their action and await his reply.[19]

On the afternoon of October 6 the anticipated political anointment of Hearst occurred when fourteen rough-hewn Tammany politicos, led by former state senator Thomas O'Sullivan, arrived at Democratic headquarters in the Hoffman House; they were meeting, for the first time, this newspaper colossus who had led the fight to free Cuba, this awesome crusader who had been warring, without letup, against the most powerful coal magnates and railroad titans in the United States. What a shock! Before them stood a tall, youthful man in his late thirties, pale-blue-eyed and ashen-faced, nervously fingering a manuscript that was obviously an acceptance speech. With an *American and Journal* reporter present to record this "historic" moment, he began reading almost inaudibly—even in the small reception room—to a disbelieving audience, his thin, reedy voice, with an accompanying lisp, reminiscent of Ambrose Bierce's description "like the fragrance of crushed violets made audible." During the next ten minutes of uninspiring rhetoric he presented his campaign platform, which was essentially the *Evening Journal's* and the *American and Journal's* "Internal Policy" of the past three years: direct election of U.S. senators, government ownership of certain public utilities, and the destruction of criminal trusts. Indeed, his purpose in seeking higher office was, he asserted, not to aid the rich and powerful, such as J. P. Morgan, who were amply represented in Congress, but to "forward the interests of the seventy millions . . . of typical Americans who are not so well looked after."[20]

Hearst sincerely believed that, as a man of purpose and conviction, he could rid the nation of numerous political ills and previous wrongful turns, thereby restoring, as journalist Lincoln Steffens recorded in an interview, "democracy to the United States." Despite his innate shyness, his dislike of politics, he performed like a seasoned veteran over the next month. After all, organizing a campaign or crusade had always been one of his strengths, indeed a stimulus to his imagination. Although the Eleventh District was safely Democratic, he sometimes attended ten to fifteen meetings a day. Countless lithographs of him appeared on billboards—and even on ashcans. To attain the ultimate goal, that of high political office, he suppressed his dislike for a profession fraught with perilous pitfalls and unknown quagmires. He forced himself to mingle with a constituency eager to meet him, greeting one and all with a newly developed "firm handshake," then performed such necessary but previously revolting activities (to him personally) as backslapping and baby-kissing.[21]

The *American and Journal* and *Evening Journal* daily recorded this congressional campaign, one in which Hearst once again proved to be a showman extraordinaire. His intention was not just to win impressively but to surpass in vote count all previous victories. He therefore directed this canvass to a masterful conclusion. On October 16, while the *American and Journal* front pages trumpeted the "GREAT COAL CONSPIRACY LAID BARE," a story on the fourth page announced that seventy-five thousand men in the United Board of Building Trades had endorsed Hearst. At the same time Tammany chief Murphy, now with seemingly abundant monetary resources, energized his men with a voter-registration drive, promising to turn out a record ballot on election day. Then Hearst brought in celebrities and political "bigwigs" to attract huge crowds, to build a crescendo of excitement and enthusiasm. From California, former governor James H. Budd and Mayor Eugene E. Schmitz of San Francisco, both having received vigorous support from the *Examiner*, arrived to repay campaign debts, as did union leaders Peter Dienhart, George J. Thompson, and John Daly of Chicago. And from across the nation came such Democratic notables as former vice president Adlai E. Stevenson of Illinois; state party leader and former governor David B. Hill of New York; U.S. Senators Charles A. Culberson of Texas and Edward W. Carmack of Tennessee; former judge M. V. Gannon of Chicago, who was the past president of the Irish National League; and old friend and compatriot James K. Jones of Arkansas, who was still chairman of the Democratic National Committee.

On the night of October 27 this assemblage of notables gathered at Madison Square Garden for a "Democratic Congressional Rally under the auspices of WILLIAM RANDOLPH HEARST." And once again a Hearst spectacular unfolded as planned. An overflow crowd of more than tem thousand, each participant provided with a tiny American flag, was entertained by Fancuilli's eighty-piece 71st Regiment Band, directed by Mayor Schmitz (an accomplished musician), and regaled for several hours by partisan oratory. During the schedule of events Hearst spoke bravely for ten minutes, even though his voice was "not of great penetrating quality," the *Times* reported, "and could not be heard by one-tenth of the vast assemblage." The crowd, however, "was sympathetic and sat patiently, those in the rear and entirely out of earshot applauding vigorously whenever they saw those in front doing likewise." Only on one occasion was any disruption evident; out from the audience, the *Times* reporter noted, a foghorn voice bellowed good-naturedly, "Oh, how I wish you had my voice." But Hearst droned on in high tenor without further mishap or delay. And soon everyone was joyously happy; Hearst always produced a rousing finale. Once again Henry "Pyrotechnist" Pain thrilled the crowd by setting the Manhattan sky ablaze for more than an hour with a "continuous bombshell display [seen and heard for miles], showing compound effects in red, white, and blue, electric vermillion and emerald colors."[22]

For the next week the *Evening Journal* and *American* instructed their readers about the forthcoming election. Yet, while predicting a Democratic sweep with gubernatorial candidate Bird S. Coler as winner over incumbent Republican governor Benjamin Odell by a statewide plurality of thirty-five thousand votes, both papers featured Hearst as the prime party participant, as the obvious and true leader of the Democratic crusade on behalf of workers and toilers everywhere. Cartoonists Davenport and Opper, along with accompanying editorials, were vicious in their assaults, linking together the "coal barons" and "criminal trusts" with Republican candidates. For two consecutive days a Hearst petition and complaint to the Interstate Commerce Commission against those railroads supporting the mine owners received front-page coverage. Both newspapers also reminded voters of Hearst's crusades on behalf of New Yorkers, such as a three-platoon system for the police and the bitter fight against the Ice Trust in 1900 (known as the Ramapo scandal).

As in all Hearst crusades, the formula of daily testimonials appeared with regularity, specifically featuring one congressional race, that of the Eleventh District. "Hearst is the champion of the rights of the people," Adlai Stevenson of Illinois announced; "I only wish I could nominate Mr. Hearst for president," former governor Budd of California proclaimed; "Democrats everywhere recognize the importance of the contest in the Eleventh District of New York. All eyes are turned to your candidate," Mayor Schmitz of San Francisco echoed. Then on election night, to celebrate the anticipated Democratic landslide—with Hearst as the announced voter catalyst—an *American* airship, high above Madison Square, and bulletin boards atop the Flatiron Building, the *American's* uptown and Harlem offices, and the Democratic congressional headquarters at 435 Eighth Avenue, were to signal the election returns to eager New Yorkers. Between announcements, guests and onlookers were to be entertained with bands and motion pictures and fireworks.[23]

On election night, November 4, 1902, Hearst was ecstatic; he could not have been more pleased with the results. He defeated Republican opponent Henry Birell by an overwhelming vote of 26,953 to 10,841. As the largest congressional vote-getter in Greater New York, he was responsible, the *American* and *Evening Journal* implied, for helping win sixteen of eighteen congressional seats for the Democrats. And even though Governor Odell was reelected by approximately 14,000 votes, Bird Coler carried Greater New York, the *American* proclaimed, by a plurality of 120,720, noting that Hearst and new Tammany chief Murphy were, in large part, responsible. Hearst, however, assessed the results of the month-long campaign even more optimistically. In a note to Brisbane he jubilantly wrote: "This is just the beginning of our political actions. Our social aspirations have a greater chance than ever to be realized." [24]

Only one incident marred this otherwise perfect night. At 10:10 P.M., as a photograph of newly elected congressman Hearst flashed on the screen above Madison Square, where a crowd of forty thousand had gathered, one of Pain's nine-inch firebombs inexplicably exploded, triggering other huge rockets prematurely. In the wake of the resulting carnage, eighteen men and boys lay dead and an estimated one hundred injured; a policeman named Dennis Shea had his head almost blown off. Lawsuits against Hearst would follow and, like the McKinley accusations, would plague him in future campaigns. [25]

But this accident in no way forestalled the accelerating momentum. Hearst and Brisbane, because of their continual successes in newspaper crusades and their unusual insight regarding the mentality and psyche of the American voter, were already laying plans to capture the Democratic Party nomination for the presidency in 1904. They immediately assigned to Max Ihmsen the onerous but necessary task of organizing Hearst leagues and clubs throughout the country; his successes in organizing the National Association of Democratic Clubs in the 1900 campaign provided the blueprint for the Hearst assault against all presidential party opponents. Then, ever so gradually, they built the crescendo of even greater name recognition as well as real, or manufactured, popularity. Intermittently during November, 1902, articles appeared praising Hearst for his leadership in the previous campaign, at the same time suggesting that higher office awaited him. With predictable regularity from November, 1902 to July, 1903, the Hearst suit against the coal barons appeared, directed specifically at the arrogant George Baer, demanding justice on behalf of union miners and average Americans for violations of the Sherman Anti-Trust Act.

During the wintry season of 1902–03 the Hearst papers, whose publisher had always been civic-minded, were especially magnanimous in supporting the poor and lame and dispossessed. On several frigid nights early in December as well as in January, "*New York American* and *Journal* wagons" fed coffee and sandwiches to "a thousand famished waifs" and innumerable street people. The *American* also created a "Surgical Bureau" to provide immediate medical assistance for crippled children, numbering almost one hundred within a week. Again at Christmastime, the *American* arranged to distribute toys to forty thousand children within the inner city, with Hearst, the *American* announced, playing "Santa to many thousands." And again in January, 1903, with fuel prices soaring, Hearst bought one hundred tons of coal and then sold it, at cost, for nine cents a pail to several hundred thousand freezing and appreciative New Yorkers.[26]

In February, 1903, Hearst began elevating his presidential campaign to a wider constituency. While still advocating local measures such as eight-hour shifts for city police (the three-platoon system), he stressed reform issues of national concern. To diminish the legislative power of the "criminal trusts" he presented a resolution to Congress for the "popular [direct] election of senators," which Brisbane soon began referring to as the "Hearst Resolution." Throughout the country during the next two months the six Hearst newspapers (the sixth one, the *Chicago Examiner*, began producing a morning edition in December, 1902) pushed this crusade forward in their patented modus operandi—news orchestration with daily testimonials by prominent citizens, editorials accompanied by Opper cartoons, a staged mass meeting, and a continual count of state legislatures, numbering thirty-one by April 12, that had partly or completely adopted the "Hearst Resolution" for direct election of senators.

At the same time Hearst decided that his full name looked and sounded more presidential; hence, by 1903, he signed all of his editorials William Randolph Hearst—and all of his newspapers complied. For example, typical headlines in the *American* read: on January 3–4, "Hawaii Democrats Cable Their Congratulations to William Randolph Hearst"; on January 14 (front page), "William Randolph Hearst, of New York, filed a sworn statement and petition."

Increasingly offers to speak at prestigious Democratic functions throughout the nation poured in; he "regrettably" turned down every one of these engagements, but sent an emissary, who read his prepared remarks; he then published them (in toto) in the editorial section. His voice and delivery were far less effective than his written words. As a result, in Columbus, Ohio, at a February 12 dinner honoring former presidents Jefferson, Jackson, and Lincoln, Max Ihmsen delivered a Hearst speech (and apologies) before "1,000 cheering Democrats"; at a Jackson Day gathering on March 16, to the Iroquois Club of Chicago, Hearst sent a speech that was read to an "appreciative" audience; and again on April 20, at a huge Jefferson Dinner of the Jackson County Democratic Club in Kansas City, Missouri, he extended "regrets"—in a long letter—because of a "necessary trip to California." [27]

All the while Max Ihmsen was busily at work, his prodigious efforts gradually materializing and then rapidly maturing. At several state and national labor conventions, union delegates passed resolutions praising Hearst for his efforts on their behalf. Prominent citizens such as ex-governor Budd of California, Adlai Stevenson of Illinois, former mayor J. E. T. Bowden of Jacksonville, Florida, newspaper editor Josephus Daniels of Raleigh, North Carolina, and Mayor John Bible of Ionis, Michigan, endorsed him for president. Then weekly, beginning in mid-April, 1903—and soon thereafter almost daily—union leaders, prominent Americans, as well as "concerned" citizens began forming "Hearst for President" clubs (or leagues) in towns and cities across the country.[28]

Hearst, however, still lacked one important personal requisite for becoming a serious presidential contender: a wife and accompanying family. So at 11:00 A.M. on April 28, 1903, at Grace Episcopal Church in New York City, Hearst (just one day before his fortieth birthday) married twenty-two-year-old dancer Millicent Willson, a statuesque, dark-eyed beauty. Since 1897, he had dated her continually, with her older sister Anita usually as chaperone. He had escorted them to Cuba in 1898 and, subsequently with their parents, on two European-Egyptian trips in 1899 and 1900. Increasingly thereafter he and Millicent had become regular patrons of the theater nightlife of New York City, with Hearst determined to marry her despite "Mama's" opposition to showgirls.

What an unusual, uncharacteristic Hearst event this wedding turned out to be! The *American* and *Evening Journal*, unlike their usual coverage of prominent weddings, placed the story on page nine, partly because Hearst, in his desire for personal privacy, barred photographers from taking snapshots inside the church—only a formal picture of Millicent sitting and Hearst standing immediately to her right was allowed after the ceremony. Instead of a huge extravaganza, so typical of previous Hearst productions, the setting was intimate, with only thirty close friends and relatives attending; father of the bride George H. Willson gave "Millie" away, while older sister Anita was the one bridesmaid, and Orrin Peck, Hearst's boyhood friend who still maintained an artist's residence in Munich, Germany, was best man. Yet Phoebe Hearst, although sending the bride a brooch consisting of "a beautiful set of emeralds," was noticeably absent. Her niece and confidante Mrs. Ann Apperson Flint later revealed:

"She went to bed. She was terribly upset." Although devoted to her "dear Boy," Phoebe had always hoped that he "would marry someone she could care for—and respect." Despite this conspicuous void, the wedding proceeded without incident. The bridal party went to the Waldorf-Astoria for a brunch and then hurried to a 3:00 P.M. sailing to Europe on the *Kaiser Wilhelm II.* After arriving at Paris in May with a considerable entourage, including Orrin Peck and editor of the *San Francisco Bulletin* Fremont Older and his young wife—even on his honeymoon Hearst could not refrain from being the consummate tour director—he wrote Phoebe a detailed account of the wedding day. While exuberant and upbeat in his description, he did foretell, in an attempt at humor, the eventual outcome of this momentous occasion in his life by stating: "Our wedding was cheerful and not to be mistaken for a funeral." [29]

For the next several months Hearst and his bride took an extensive honeymoon, yet always at his pleasure and direction. While in London he nurtured a growing enthusiasm for racing cars, so much so that he cabled his trusted and able business manager Solomon Carvalho to examine a British magazine *The Car;* as a consequence, Hearst produced an American rendition called *Motor* in January, 1904. In the meantime he purchased a "fast" car, then toured France and northern Italy, sharing with Millie such treasured sights of past visits as the gothic cathedral in Milan. Of course, like his mother, he could not resist the expensive temptations to own valuable works of art and precious antiques, continually filling a warehouse in New York City to overflowing. The Hearsts next traveled to Mexico City, where President Porfirio Díaz, an old friend and business acquaintance of George Hearst in the 1880s, entertained them regally. They then visited briefly with lifelong college chum Jack Follansbee, who was still managing more than 150 vaqueros on the Hearst million-acre Babicora Ranch in Chihuahua, before proceeding to the Hacienda de Verona at Pleasanton, California, for a necessary meeting with Phoebe Hearst. Despite her maternal determination to control his social behavior and an irritating disdain for his showgirl mentality, Hearst loved her dearly—and, besides, he needed her continued financial support for further journalistic acquisitions as well as his forthcoming presidential campaign. Although no one recorded in detail this summit meeting between mother and son, Phoebe graciously "threw a magnificent birthday party for Millie," eventually receiving her into the family "with cool grace," especially after George Randolph Hearst, the first of five sons, was born on April 10, 1904. [30]

Hearst, with political portfolio now intact and financial base secure, turned up his presidential campaign a notch. He hired the taciturn, bespectacled Lawrence J. O'Reilly as his private political secretary; he encouraged Max Ihmsen to even greater organizational efforts regarding the "Hearst for President" clubs; and he orchestrated with Brisbane a personal "crusade" for the Democratic presidential nomination. Hence, testimonials on his behalf and formation of Hearst clubs and leagues daily appeared in his six newspapers throughout the country, his popularity seemingly increasing and swelling ever higher.[31]

Hearst realized, however, that deeds must accompany, if not equal and exceed, the propaganda of his newspaper empire, that the public must identify him not only with popular causes but also with righteous ones. Ever alert for a good story and unusually in tune with the American psyche, Hearst sought once again to find the pulse of voters. While on his honeymoon he seized on one story, believing that it would play well in many areas of the nation. Early in May, 1903, local authorities at Kishineff, in the far-off Bessarabian province of southwestern Russia, persecuted and slaughtered thousands of Jews. Hearst immediately registered his "horror" by sending to Brisbane a front-page editorial that appeared in all his newspapers. He appealed to Americans, "irrespective of origin or religion," to demonstrate their charity, to "contribute in some measure to the relief of the impoverished and grief-stricken survivors at Kishineff." In turn, he donated a $1,000 check for the beginning of what Brisbane dubbed the "HEARST RELIEF FUND." Each day, from mid-May to July 7, 1903, as contributions (eventually amounting to $34,620.49) rolled in, the *American* listed the names of donors and the amounts given—and consistently at the top was "Wm. R. Hearst ... $1,000."[32]

As the "dog days of summer" ended and New York City voters began concentrating on the hotly contested race for mayor between Tammany Hall nominee George B. McClellan, Jr., and incumbent Seth Low, Hearst decided to stage another of his spectaculars that would intrigue the imagination of voters, that would draw attention to, as well as aid, his presidential aspirations. On October 12, 1903, he embarked on an eleven-day, whistle-stop tour of the West, reminiscent of the Bryan campaigns of 1896 and 1900. At considerable expense Hearst, who was always comfortable in the roles of tour guide and stage director, hired a train—*The Hearst Special*—to transport a party of thirty-five guests, including three senators and seventeen congressmen, as well as ten wives, to visit the three contiguous American territories that anxiously awaited statehood—Arizona, New Mexico, and Oklahoma. With Max Ihmsen and Hearst's midwestern campaign director A. M. "Andy" Lawrence (temporarily on a leave of absence from the *Chicago American*) responsible for scheduling and news coverage, Hearst achieved a publicity coup that relegated other political stories to the back pages of his newspapers.

Leaving Chicago at 8:00 P.M. on October 12, the "Hearst congressional delegates" made their way to Kansas City, Santa Fe, and Albuquerque, and on to the Grand Canyon, Phoenix, and Tucson. On their return trip eastward they visited El Paso and Roswell, New Mexico, en route to Oklahoma City, Ardmore, Shawnee, and Guthrie, the first territorial capital of Oklahoma. At each stop they received a clamorous outpouring of affection and appreciation, especially with the "Hearst congressional delegation" announcing individually and in chorus that all three territories deserved statehood.

Hearst then took leave of his party because of a scheduling engagement in Georgia. And on October 22, "from noon until nearly midnight," William Randolph Hearst, accompanied by Georgia congressman James M. Griggs and Max Ihmsen, was the "guest" of Atlanta—proceeding first to the governor's mansion for a formal greeting, going next to the state fair grounds for a barbecue and brief remarks before "throngs" of eager onlookers, then visiting students at the Georgia School of Technology, to which he had "recently" contributed $5,000, before attending a reception and dinner as the honored guest of the three Atlanta newspapers and Mayor Evan P. Howell. And with the announcement that presidential clubs were being formed on his behalf, Hearst returned to New York, pleased and delighted with the responses to this eleven-day campaign.[33]

For the next three weeks Hearst, through Brisbane, monopolized the headlines of the *American* and *Journal*. Although Democratic candidate George B. McClellan, Jr., with the all-out support of Tammany Hall, won the mayoral race in New York City on November 3 by more than sixty thousand votes, both newspapers credited Hearst as the catalyst for victory. Orchestrated testimonials appeared. "No man is giving the Democratic ticket greater support than William R. Hearst," the Twenty-ninth Assembly District resolution stated in print. "REASONS FOR THE DEMOCRATIC VICTORY—Representative Hearst Made a Prediction of 60,000 to 80,000 Plurality," another headline read. And "due to his efforts" the "NATIONAL DEMOCRACY," including such party leaders as Democratic National Committee secretary Charles A. Walsh, Tammany chief Charles Francis Murphy, and New York state senator Patrick H. McCarren, "BESTOWS PRAISE ON W. R. HEARST." Still another headline characterized the hundreds of telegrams received and printed, as if in concert, during the two weeks after the election.[34]

In the meantime Hearst was off to Washington, a full year after his election—not until 1933, with the passage of the Twentieth Amendment, was this lengthy time lapse changed to January 3. The first session of the Fifty-eighth Congress, convening on November 9, 1903, was a major disappointment to Hearst. Instead of receiving celebrity status as the most prominent newspaper editor in the nation as well as a leading presidential contender for the Democratic nomination, Hearst was relegated to the obscurity of a freshman congressman in the minority party, one who was expected to be seen, but seldom, if ever, heard; forty-five-year-old John Sharp Williams of Mississippi, the House Democratic minority leader, saw to that. Although the *American* at first praised him as "a man of great learning ... of great strength of character and strong convictions," that assessment soon changed after Williams denied the "freshman from New York" a position on the House Labor Committee. He was thus introduced to the Hearst newspaper technique of influencing public opinion: telegrams and letters from union leaders nationwide, requesting, indeed demanding, Hearst's selection to that committee inundated him. Reluctantly, Williams acceded to such "backhanded pressure." But no more! He was, as his biographer put it, "determined to be the leader of the minority in reality as well as in title." Hence, when Hearst next asked for a seat on the prestigious House Ways and Means Committee, the answer was an unequivocal, resounding "no." [35]

As a result, Hearst seldom attended Congress for the first three months of the second session (December 7, 1903–April 28, 1904); in fact, except for several days early in December, he did not participate in any congressional business until February 1 and 2, 1904, and then only to present two resolutions to committees. He quickly developed a disdain and eventually a hatred for the minority leader, who relegated him and other freshman congressmen to an "inferior" status—no seniority, no power, therefore limited active participation. And for the action-oriented Hearst, who was accustomed to the role of leadership, merely to sit in the House chamber, listening to hour after hour of courteous parliamentary procedure ("Will the gentleman yield for a question?" Or "Does the gentleman move to limit debate?"), and endless polemics, followed by the deadly dull routine of countless petitions and personal resolutions and private bills, was frustrating and boring beyond belief. After all, since John Sharp Williams was refusing to use Hearst's multiple talents and leadership abilities for Democratic causes in the House, William Randolph Hearst would be equally contemptuous of him. As a consequence, Hearst, who leased an impressive residence on Lafayette Square just opposite Pennsylvania Avenue and the White House, often assumed the role of absentee renter as well as congressman. Not until March and April, 1904, did he demonstrate any enthusiasm for the art of legislation—and then only in committee with a coterie of followers known as the "Hearst Brigade." He thus advanced his own causes, such as an eight-hour day for labor and antitrust legislation against the coal barons and associated railroads. [36]

Outside of Congress, however, Hearst continued at a furious, even frenetic, pace for the Democratic nomination. He was especially omnipresent in his generosity to New Yorkers during the holiday season of 1903. At his direction the *American* and *Journal* sent "Hearst" turkeys, by the "wagonloads," to be distributed among the poor and needy at Thanksgiving. Immediately thereafter he donated $1,000 to the "*American's* Great Christmas Fund" to buy "toys and useful articles" for the children of Greater New York; his name always headed the list of contributors, which ran daily in both newspapers. Then on Christmas Eve he and wife, Millie, with the help of hundreds of Hearst employees, played Mr. and Mrs. Santa Claus to an estimated one hundred thousand people, mostly children, providing hot dinners, warm clothing, and "thousands of toys and tons of sweets." At the same time, and at considerable expense, he also sponsored a city basketball tournament for fifteen hundred public school children, which was held at Madison Square Garden on December 26 and 27, with the multiple winners receiving specially designed, solid-silver "Hearst cups." And if such activities were not enough, dozens of "Hearst *American* Coffee Wagons" distributed sandwiches and coffee and "steaming edibles" to thousands of homeless throughout the frigid winter months of 1903–4. [37]

Such charitable community activities had always been a hallmark of Hearst journalism; but now the *New York American* and *Journal* began crediting him publicly with every possible endeavor during this presidential campaign. In fact, they became raging advertisements for his nomination, a "bully pulpit" for his ideas and accomplishments. Every day during the first four months of 1904 the Hearst name occupied the headlines. Typical captions of praise were: "DELEGATES FROM 70,000 BRICKLAYERS THANK W. R. HEARST IN CONVENTION," stated one on January 19. "CHURCHES SHOULD THANK MR. HEARST." "A HEARST VICTORY! CRY POLICEMEN'S WIVES!" proclaimed two others on February 24 and 26, concerning the three-platoon police reform. "HEARST SUIT WON! COAL TRUST BEATEN! read another on April 5. [38]

On several other pages, however, the *American* and *Journal* applied the Hearst crusading technique of news orchestration to the utmost, of using testimonials that appeared to be a national referendum by the masses, a democratic groundswell by those previously excluded from the political system. The quiet industry of Max Ihmsen now began manifesting itself. Two editions of the *American* reflected an exciting drumbeat to elect Hearst, albeit a slanted picture of his growing popularity. On February 11 the headlines of four articles read as follows: "BANK PRESIDENT [in Jackson, Mississippi] TELLS WHY HE IS FOR HEARST"; "Tennessee's Delegates to St. Louis Will, It Is Said, Be for Hearst"; "Florida Bank Clerks Combine in Forming a William R. Hearst Club"; and "[The Memphis News] Mentions Seven States as Certain for Hearst Through the Labor Vote." On February 27, these headlines appeared: "A THOUSAND UNION MEN CHEER THEIR CHAMPION"; "Leading Iowa Banker Endorses New Yorker"; "Union Men in the Bronx Form New Hearst Club"; "Jersey City Voters Form a Hearst Club"; and "PORTAGE COUNTY, O[HIO] DECLARES FOR W.R. HEARST."

Of course, endorsements by prominent Americans also added to this aura of Hearst electability. J. G. Johnson of Kansas, who was chairman of the Executive Committee of the Democratic National Committee, asserted that "Kansas is solid for William Randolph Hearst. There is no sentiment there in the ranks for any one else." Young millionaire philanthropist J. G. Phelps Stokes of New York enthusiastically joined "in the approaching campaign" because "Mr. Hearst has maintained, and, I think, rightly, that industrial issues (such as the 'trust' issue) are at present of paramount interest and importance to the American people." Tom Watson of Georgia, the Populist vice-presidential nominee in 1896, "heartily" endorsed Hearst because "for a dozen years he has never faltered, never given ground, never surrendered a principle. Not in all things do we agree, but in the honest, earnest, persistent purpose to bring about better conditions for the common people [we do]." Yet, surprisingly, William Jennings Bryan, upon returning from Europe after a two-month assignment by the *American*, announced that he was "not urging" Hearst's nomination, "or any one else's," but noted (the headline read) that "HIS FOES OPPOSE W.R. HEARST." [39]

Because of this continual daily barrage of Hearst campaign propaganda, a number of conservative Democratic Party leaders, as well as longtime local bosses and machine politicians, who had, at first, looked on his pursuit of the nomination with amusement, now became concerned—and for good reason. Hearst, as always, was spending huge amounts of money, reputedly as much as $2 million. His organization, with Max Ihmsen and Andy Lawrence as campaign managers, was formidable. And now Hearst was adding two more newspapers to his journalistic empire that potentially might sway Democratic voters in two important delegate-rich states. On December 12, 1903, he bought the *Los Angeles Examiner*, which operated presses capable of turning out forty-eight thousand twelve-page papers an hour, the *American* proclaimed exultantly, "in the largest [newspaper] building in the United States." On February 7, 1904, he also purchased a five-story edifice to house the *Boston American*, "the second largest plant in the country," which would be ready for operation within the unbelievably brief time of six weeks. And when its first edition appeared, as promised, on March 21, Hearst had, at his command, eight newspapers that "spoke" daily to more than two million readers in five of the nation's most populated cities. Then, early in 1904, when Democrats began organizing in every state to choose delegates to their national convention in July, the Hearst contingents, many of whom were union laborers and the dispossessed and those previously excluded or ignored by the political process, were militantly enthusiastic for their candidate, reportedly armed with a ready supply of cash for any endeavor or emergency.[40]

Conservatives within the Democratic Party, who had suffered the "radicalism" of Bryan for the past eight years, were not about to allow an outsider to lead them into another presidential debacle. This millionaire newspaperman from New York had promoted, one political observer noted "a thoroughly demagogic movement ... by stirring up the worst feelings of the lower element of the population . . . with lavish disbursements"—and he must be stopped. As a first step, the Democratic National Committee, meeting in Washington, D.C., on January 11–12, 1904, surprised the prevailing predictions for a national convention site by selecting St. Louis over Chicago and New York City. And why? "Conservative trust leaders" of the National Committee wished to eliminate "any advantage of the Hearst boom" that might occur, the *American* announced; therefore, they did not choose Chicago, with its strong labor movement and two Hearst newspapers, or New York City, where the *American* and *Evening Journal* reigned supreme. In fact, the committee toyed with a proposal of opting for still another city if Hearst, perchance, should purchase a newspaper in St. Louis within the next thirty days.[41]

Party conservatives, whom Bryan referred to as the "reorganizers," ultimately had to decide on a candidate under whose banner they could all unite. After a brief trial run late in the fall of 1903 failed to ignite any enthusiasm for former president Grover Cleveland, they fixed on Judge Alton B. Parker of New York as the "safe and sane candidate." He had received considerable recognition for being the foremost Democrat to win statewide office in the 1900 election. His most prominent supporters in New York were August Belmont, reputedly "the representative of Wall Street," and ex-governor David Bennett Hill, whom the Bryan forces would never forgive for his remark in the 1896 campaign, "I am a Democrat still, very still." Together with Cleveland and transportation financier Thomas Fortune Ryan, they helped organize the Parker forces nationally, but they especially concerned themselves with winning delegates in New Jersey, Connecticut, Pennsylvania, and New York against the militant Hearst battalions.[42]

At the same time the Parker forces were determined to discredit Hearst, to hold him up to ridicule and disdain, to destroy his image as a potential presidential candidate. Thus the program of vilification began unabated. Hearst, even though proclaiming himself to be "a conservative" with identical purposes as those of "Washington, Jefferson, Jackson, and Lincoln," was pictured as more radical than Bryan, a socialist reformer who intended to change the basic structure of government, a reckless demagogue who catered to labor unions and the baser instincts of "the masses." In the *Louisville Courier-Journal*, renowned editor and publisher "Marse" Henry Watterson questioned, in disbelief, that "any sane Democrat" would vote for "Mr. Hearst, a person unknown even to his constituency and his colleagues, without a word or act in the public life of his country, past or present." The *New York Times* described his quest for the presidency as "stupefying impudence," because he was nothing more than "the mere cat's paw of Bryan." Senator Edward Carmack of Tennessee was even more acerbic, announcing that Hearst's nomination would "ruin the party," that all would be "lost, including our honor." And former gubernatorial candidate John W. Kern of Indiana, after a bitter struggle for national convention delegates, angrily asserted that "we are menaced for the first time in the history of the Republic by the open and unblushing effort of a multimillionaire to purchase the presidential nomination. Our state has been overrun with a gang of paid agents and retainers" for whom "I have nothing but contempt." Without question, he concluded, "the Hearst dollar mark is all over them." [43]

Despite such scurrilous attacks in opposition newspapers, the Hearst crusade for the presidency went merrily along during the first months of 1904, each day's headlines in the *American* and *Evening Journal* building momentum and excitement. On February 29 the Hearst journalistic empire jubilantly announced: "First Delegates [six in number from Ohio] for W.R. Hearst." On March 11 the count increased to fourteen, with Rhode Island's eight-man delegation "solid for Hearst." Again, on March 31,

South Dakota came through with eight more votes, the count increasing to twenty-two. And again on April 8 "KANSAS ENDORSES HEARST," with all twenty delegates under unit rule—and now the number reached forty-two. Equally encouraging were the many glowing reports of success—whether truth or rumor—that were interspersed among the delegate counts. Typical of the articles were: on February 21, "Hearst Will Sweep Country"; on March 3, "Florida Will Send Hearst Delegates"; on March 14, "Italians in Every State for Hearst"; on March 23, "STRENGTH OF HEARST FELT AT PRIMARIES IN SARATOGA COUNTY [N.Y.]"; AND ON APRIL 5, "ARKANSAS NOW CARRIED FOR HEARST." [44]

But in April, 1904, the Hearst crusade suddenly lost its momentum as the numbing facts of political reality became discouragingly clear. At the New York State convention on April 18, the Hill-Belmont faction of "safe and sane" conservatives rode roughshod over Tammany Hall and the Hearst battalions, winning all seventy-eight votes for Judge Parker. On May 6, Connecticut, with fourteen delegates, followed suit, as did Indiana, less than a week later, with thirty more. And since party regulars at the forthcoming southern state conventions either controlled or were influential in decision-making, the Parker political juggernaut rolled relentlessly on, confident that such leaders as House minority leader John Sharp Williams of Mississippi and Senator Joseph Weldon Bailey of Texas, who had received a generous amount of criticism in Hearst newspaper editorials, would deliver their states for Parker. [45]

Late in May and early in June, the Hearst campaign managers revived somewhat; unexpected victories as well as the imponderables of a national convention rejuvenated their flagging spirits. In May the Hearst forces prevailed in California, Washington, Iowa, Minnesota, and the Arizona Territory. Then within the space of six days (June 6–12) the Idaho, Colorado, and Illinois conventions pledged to Hearst, and reports—not of the propaganda-crusade variety, but reliable—indicated that the delegations from the New Mexico and Oklahoma territories (where Hearst had visited during the fall of 1903) were preparing to pledge to him. And from Nebraska also came heartening news: William Jennings Bryan, openly hostile to the Hill-Cleveland-Belmont faction representing Parker, was in control of the delegation. With a number of states coming to the convention "uncommitted" or endorsing a "favorite son," and with Hearst arriving with approximately two hundred delegate commitments, Bryan, as well as those opposed to the conservative "reorganizers," might be counted on to cast their ballots in favor of Parker's foremost adversary, William Randolph Hearst. [46]

So on to the national convention at St. Louis Hearst and his militant partisans proceeded, hopeful of bringing about a startling upset, of producing a new leader for "the Democracy." And what better way to impress and influence the delegates than a Hearst spectacular, with impressive displays and free mementos and rollicking activities? On July 2, 1904, the Hearst production began. Preceded by a host of employees and volunteers, he occupied two floors of the Jefferson Hotel. Then at "seven minutes to one," the *New York Times* noted, a boy leaned over the balcony "and deposited there a large and thoughtful picture of William Randolph Hearst." Everyone in the crowded lobby exclaimed: "Ah! They're off!" Within two minutes Hearst pictures were everywhere, covering all possible spaces on the walls and corridors, while in front of the hotel a huge electric sign, spelling "HEARST HEADQUARTERS," illuminated the whole area for a block. As delegates and curiosity-seekers pushed their way into the Jefferson during the next week, Hearst volunteers campaigned on his behalf, distributing huge piles of literature about his life and ideology, discussing his stances on the issues, while at the same time handing out thousands of buttons bearing his likeness "in a pensive pose." Upon arrival, the California delegates, loud and boisterous, each waving an American flag, continually jangling a bell in their van, chanted over and over again:

> Boom! Boom! Boom!
> First! First! First!
> California! California!
> Hearst! Hearst! Hearst!

Hearst once more was in his element, fascinating and entertaining the throngs of delegates in a desperate attempt to sell himself as a man of the people, as the only Democratic candidate with the money and organization necessary to win a national election.[47]

But the major participants had already decided the eventual outcome of this convention. Bryan, upon being asked to nominate Hearst, refused, thereby causing a bitterly disappointed Max Ihmsen, a *New York Times* reporter noted, to take "refuge in a large but somewhat acid smile." Tammany chief Charles Francis Murphy, although despising Parker and his convention managers Hill and Belmont, would also have nothing to do with Hearst—the *American* and *Evening Journal* had not only been critical of recent Tammany dealings but also of its foremost celebrity and ally, New York City mayor George B. McClellan, Jr. Earlier in the year Murphy had been disdainfully outspoken, stating to one of former president Cleveland's closest friends, Daniel S. Lamont of New York, that Hearst "cuts no figure whatever."

And as for the leader of the Parker campaign, David Bennett Hill, who ironically might have been Hearst's stepfather in 1895 if the gossipy "public cupids" had been accurate about Phoebe Hearst and him, the "radical" young publisher was anathema to him and conservative Democrats, a constant reminder of Bryanism and eight years of Republican rule in the White House. They therefore spread stories "painting him [Hearst] as an unrivaled voluptuary" with all the negative attributes of a Lothario or a Don Juan. One political cartoon pictured him on a yacht sailing and "cavorting along the Nile with a hundred Broadway nymphs."

The Hill-Belmont faction, however, was much more concerned with convention strategy and momentum. Upon arrival in St. Louis, the Pennsylvania delegates, with sixty-eight votes, declared in favor of Parker; soon thereafter New Jersey and Virginia followed suit. No longer was the nomination in doubt, that is, unless some unforeseen incident occurred.[48]

Even so, Hearst played out his part in this unfolding convention drama without any sign of letup or defeat. While displaying "no heart for making a fight" concerning a credentials dispute in the Illinois delegation, he urged his followers to support specific planks, which were eventually included in the Democratic Platform—enlargement of the Interstate Commerce Commission, direct election of senators, jury trials in labor injunction cases, more stringent antitrust legislation, and lower tariffs. He also encouraged Max Ihmsen and Andy Lawrence to keep the boisterous Hearst battalions in full readiness for political combat, either to cheer for their "hero" or to demonstrate against the opposition. Then at midnight on August 8, 1904, their brief moment of triumph—as well as performance—occurred. After Delphin M. Delmas of San Francisco, a former ally of Senator George Hearst and reputedly one of the most renowned orators on the West Coast, spoke "eloquently" and at length in placing Hearst's name in nomination for the presidency, they burst forth upon the convention hall with all the hoopla and ballyhoo at their command. For forty-three minutes they marched and chanted and sang to the accompanying sounds of a Hearst band that played "America" and "Dixie" interchangeably. They cheered the raising of a six-foot portrait of their "hero" onto the platform; they jostled poles up and down that carried his name and picture; they waved American flags and pennants while occasionally keeping in step with the continuing music. The American summed up the Hearst extravaganza, several bold headlines announcing: "Extraordinary Applause For Congressman" and "CHEERS FOR HEARST NIGHT'S FEATURE AT CONVENTION."[49]

At four-thirty on the morning of July 9, "as the gray dawn was pushing through the convention windows," William Jennings Bryan addressed the weary delegates and, as far as Hearst was concerned, committed an unforgivable act of disloyalty and bad faith. In a forty-five-minute speech, which many observers considered both moving and eloquent, he defended his actions of the past eight years and pleaded with the convention delegates to "be merciful to your former leader." He suggested that several nominees, such as Hearst, were "good men" and deserved consideration, but not "any one" who worshiped "the god of gold," not, as everyone quickly realized, the Democratic front-runner, Alton B. Parker. Then at the crest of "his measured eloquence and the crowd's wild approval," when an endorsement of Hearst might have swayed the convention (as it would eight years later for Thomas Woodrow Wilson), he lamely seconded the nomination of little-known senator Francis Marion Cockrell of Missouri, who had no chance for victory.

And why Cockrell and not Hearst, who idolized Bryan, who had expended at least $7 million in his behalf during the 1896 and 1900 presidential campaigns, who had loyally endorsed the Bryan platform, including the unlimited coinage of silver? Biographer Louis Koenig put it best in writing that Bryan believed that Hearst was "weak in the South" and that "his foremost strength was among the more radical sectors of the party." But the real reason, Koenig concluded, was that "any endorsement of Hearst would have thrust the press lord into a posture of influence and power where his voice would, in the future, rival Bryan's." [50]

Immediately the convention began a roll-call vote. The results were both anticlimactic and expected. The sleepy and exhausted delegates performed their duties in a lethargic and perfunctory manner; the first ballot tallied at 5:45 A.M. While Hearst polled 200 votes and Cockrell a mere 42, Parker had 658, just 9 short of the necessary two-thirds majority. Then a bandwagon mentality inevitably occurred. The chairman of the Idaho delegation asked to change its six votes from Hearst to Parker; then Nevada, West Virginia, and Washington followed suit. Thus the Democrats selected their nominee. The final vote: Parker, 679; Hearst, 181. [51]

Hearst was bitterly disappointed. So much time spent, so much energy expended! And, equally devastating, the betrayal by the one man in political life whom he idolized—but never again. From this campaign he learned that his base as a congressman was not broad enough to initiate a successful national race, that he must continue expanding his powerful political organization. As a Jeffersonian Democrat who believed in "equal rights for all and privileges for none," Hearst had been denied the opportunity to be the intrepid champion of the "underdog," the embodiment of a "new spirit" against the "greed of plutocracy." He thus intended to bide his time, to await the propitious moment for launching another crusade on behalf of American democracy. It would not be long in coming.

10 | "Uncrowned Mayor of New York"

❦

In July, 1904, William Randolph Hearst returned to New York City after an exhaustive presidential campaign that had ended in defeat. But, as James Creelman recognized, he was now "not a force in prospect, but a force in being." Or putting it another way, Lincoln Steffens observed that Hearst had the capabilities of "arousing in some people dread, in others hope, but compelling in all an interest which of itself is significant." And no wonder! At his command and dictation was a journalistic empire of eight newspapers in New York City, Chicago, Boston, Los Angeles, and San Francisco that influenced and entertained more than two million readers. Already he was gearing up to enter the magazine arena with the publication of *Motor*; and, within a year, he would acquire *Cosmopolitan*. Other than President Roosevelt, he was arguably the best-known American, not just in the United States but in the world.

In fact, his image was beginning to take on mythical proportions. Here was a multimillionaire who was not only born to wealth but who had also created it, yet a man who embraced the Jeffersonian philosophy of "equal rights for all and privileges for none." He was unquestionably the enemy of corporate greed, of arrogant wealth, of his social set, those who would use this "democracy" for their own selfish ends. For instance, in New York City since 1898, the *American* and *Evening Journal* had viciously attacked the ice and coal and meat-packing trusts for their mendacious avarice and their unsympathetic feelings for the poor and downtrodden, for those nameless millions who were struggling to realize the fulfillment of the "American Dream." As a consequence, historian Louis Filler wrote that Hearst, through his newspapers, "more than any other man, was the absolute expression of all the blind need and ignorance and resentment which troubled the worker and farmer." His pulse was theirs; therefore, he followed his own inclinations and ambitions, confident that "government by newspaper" not only reflected the "popular will" but best represented the predilections of the American people.[1]

Hearst, in appearance and mannerisms, had not changed much over the past decade. At age forty-one, he was a large man (particularly for the early 1900s), at six feet, one inch and approximately two hundred pounds, who, although athletic, did not reflect physical strength because of sloping shoulders and a certain gangliness. His pale-blue eyes, "cold, sharp, and curiously close together," dominated his face, obscuring somewhat a clear complexion that was smooth and unwrinkled, a nose long and straight that rested beneath a broad brow topped off with blond hair, now darkening to brown, and parted down the middle. His high-pitched and lispy voice, his obvious shyness with strangers, his nervous finger-tapping prior to making a decision, as always belied the inner strength of the man. Over the years opponents had continually underestimated his tremendous organizational talents, his genius in understanding the American psyche, his determination to lead—and win—with an open pocketbook whenever necessary.[2]

In many ways Hearst was a creature of habit; alterations either in business activities or lifestyle occurred infrequently, if at all. People had always adjusted to his ideas and whims and desires. Why change? Married life, of course, required minor adjustments, although not many.

Remarkably energetic and work-oriented, Hearst maintained his frenetic newspaper routine, never of set scheduling but always of intense concentration. At his residence on Twenty-eighth Street and Lexington Avenue, he seldom arose before noon because of working late at night and into the early morning. His valet and majordomo, George Thompson—unsympathetically described as a "very blond" and "very fat" Irishman, with pale-blue frog eyes—was a devoted friend for thirty years who attended to every need. "George Tom," at his own discretion, arranged afternoon appointments. He screened individuals in order of importance: first, close friends such as Brisbane and George Pancoast and Jack Follansbee, who called him "W.R."; then trusted lieutenants such as Max Ihmsen and Solomon Carvalho and valued attorney Clarence J. Shearn, who referred to him as "Chief"; and eventually lesser lights in the Hearst organization or acquaintances who addressed him simply as "Mr. Hearst"—formality and decorum were a necessary part of leadership. Only his mother and wife called him "Will" or "Bill."

In turn, "George Tom" prepared meals to the boss's liking. Hearst was no epicure; he required, indeed demanded, that simple foods—bread, cheese, condiments, and pickles—always be on the table. Since boyhood, he had been continually plagued by a dyspeptic stomach and was "not too hearty an eater." And although loathing lavish parties and formal dinners, that is, unless he was the host and sponsor, he and Millie went to the theater "every night," often dining at Martin's or Delmonico's before or after a musical; it was their "chief diversion," she recalled, then added but "not opera, baseball, or racing." And, upon their return, no matter how late, the faithful "George Tom" was waiting, ready to do his master's bidding.[3]

Hearst should never have entered politics; he was ill-suited both in habit and temperament. He was a "loner," not a joiner, a booster, a glad-hander. Shy to the point of seeming indifference, he hated the faceless crowds. He neither smoked nor drank; hence, he had difficulty relaxing in unfamiliar surroundings or, like any good politician, happily mingling and mixing with his constituency. Even worse, "at the bare thought of making a speech," Creelman noted, "Hearst would tremble and grow pale." In fact, his list of excuses for refusing a speaking engagement at some major Democratic gathering became a source of amusement for "Hearst watchers," noticeably unrealistic, if not bizarre, and often eliciting both "laughter and jeers." But the need to lead was his Achilles heel, indeed a character flaw in a profession that necessarily focused on compromise and cooperation and alliances. After the summer of 1904 Hearst was ever so gradually moving toward a one-man-party position, wherein he, as undisputed leader, would be at liberty to command the vast regiments of leaderless Americans, surely with advice from his lieutenants, but never at their behest. More and more he loathed politicians of both parties; the dynamic Roosevelt and the Republicans, he believed, represented corporate America and the wealthy few, while the Democrats, with Parker and Hill in control, were a carbon copy. Except for his father and William Jennings Bryan and such former presidents as Jefferson, Jackson, and Lincoln, he had no political idols. Now all were dead, save one—a betrayer not only of him but of millions of Americans who were without a spokesman and defender.[4]

But for the moment Hearst was unwilling, or unprepared, politically to chart an independent course. He therefore played the expected game of party allegiance and full cooperation. After his defeat at the St. Louis convention, he immediately wired Parker a congratulatory note. Hearst was "A GOOD LOSER," the *American* headline read, pledging "loyalty to his party and its principles." He later admitted that "I did, as a matter of fact, shut my eyes, hold my nose, and support Judge Parker. . . . It is the one act of my political career that I am heartily ashamed of." Yet editorials in all

Hearst papers during the next four months were invariably one-sided, extolling Parker and Democratic issues as those reflecting the needs of the average citizen, while depicting Republican stances as base and false and ugly. The Hearst political cartoonists were particularly vicious, with Frederick Opper, T. S. Sullivant, and Robert Carter characterizing Roosevelt and the Republicans as the tools of "criminal trusts" and the oppressors of the American people.[5]

Yet the Democratic national campaign was a paradigm of inefficiency, abysmally organized and ineffectively run, its leadership having no sense of purpose or direction. Judge Parker, who disliked speechmaking and electioneering seemingly even more than Hearst, decided against a whistle-stop tour throughout the nation, a technique that Bryan had first introduced into presidential politics in 1896; instead, he planned to run his own campaign in a dignified manner, forgo the questioning and abuse that might befall a candidate on the "stump," and welcome Democratic leaders and curious voters to his family home at Esopus, New York. His vice-presidential choice, eighty-year-old Henry Gassaway Davis, a multi-millionaire and former U.S. senator from West Virginia, was a colossal mistake. The two had never met; and Davis, who was expected to contribute generously to Democratic coffers and, hopefully, to campaign vigorously, did neither.[6]

In New York State, whose electoral votes were essential for victory, Parker proved time and again to be a dreadful politician and an ineffectual leader. During July and August, 1904, he tried unavailingly to negotiate peace between such powerful rival leaders as ex-governor David Bennett Hill and State Senator Patrick McCarren of Brooklyn on the one hand, and Tammany chief Charles Francis Murphy on the other, offering to meet with them at Esopus to work out their differences. Then for several days in mid-September he thought of purchasing harmony by allowing Tammany to handpick the state Democratic candidate for governor, that is, until he undermined such negotiations by persuading old friend and colleague Judge D. Cady Herrick to accept the nomination. As for involving Hearst in the campaign, Parker did invite him to Esopus late in July, but never allowed him the necessary freedom to exercise his organizational talents and fund-raising abilities, the result of which had to anger and frustrate Hearst and his political lieutenants.

The Hearst newspapers reflected this growing disappointment and deepening disillusionment. While the *New York Times* ran stories about Parker and Davis on the front pages, the *American* usually relegated them to page four, at times giving Roosevelt and the Republicans equal, if not better, coverage. And why not? On September 15, for instance, instead of a huge fanfare and extensive publicity for the Democratic Party, the *American* noted simply that "Parker arrives in city on yacht at midnight." On October 3, at a political reception in his honor, Parker refused to address the audience; then to questions by a number of reporters he retorted: "I must observe the rule laid down at the beginning of the campaign, that I decline to be interviewed." And again on October 31, before a huge crowd at Madison Square Garden, the *American* reported that Parker, who finally agreed to take to the "stump" during the last ten days of the campaign, "Reads Speech" but "Didn't Smile." [7]

While the Parker campaign was self-destructing, Hearst prepared for life after the anticipated debacle—and his political course of action. Although Murphy was ready to "ditch" him as early as August 1 in favor of a more pliable congressman, those within the Parker camp persuaded the Tammany chief to endorse the uncontrollable publisher once again in the interest of party harmony. Hence, on October 3, 1904, Hearst was renominated in the Eleventh District of New York, a decision Murphy would soon regret. For the next month Hearst campaigned vigorously by proxy. In other words, he flooded his "safe Democratic district" with political literature and picture posters; he sent friends and allies to represent him, to offer condolences for his absence, and to deliver effectively one of his well-crafted addresses. He also used the *American* and *Evening Journal* as a means of spreading campaign propaganda throughout the city, reminding New Yorkers of the past accomplishments of William Randolph Hearst, his persistent legal suits against the Coal Trust on behalf of labor, his continuing demand for lower fuel prices to benefit average citizens, indeed his unswerving devotion and service to the Democratic Party.

No matter that betting odds favored Roosevelt over Parker at four or five to one, no matter that Democratic debacles both on the state and national levels were at hand, Hearst was determined to turn out a record vote at the polls for himself and a majority in his district for Parker and other Democrats. And he did. On November 9 the *American* recorded the results of the election, with bold front-page headlines blaring: "ROOSEVELT LANDSLIDE! EVERY DOUBTFUL STATE REPUBLICAN!" In a follow-up story on page two, a reporter noted that Hearst polled significantly higher than either Parker or D. Cady Herrick, but pointed out that even in defeat the Democratic standard-bearer received his highest vote majority from Hearst's congressional district. [8]

In the wake of these Republican victories, the *New York American* and *Evening Journal* attempted to provide proper solutions to the Democratic defeat, with Hearst leading the way in harsh condemnation as well as optimism for the future of his party. In a full-page editorial on November 13, 1904, he denounced the "sham Democratic leaders" who had displayed an "inordinate thirst for power," men who had discarded the Jacksonian principles of protecting the average citizen against imperious wealth and corporate oppression. Instead of addressing major concerns affecting basic American needs—trust control, government ownership of utilities, and high tariffs—such "disloyal" leaders had cynically distrusted placing government "into the hands of the people." But in Massachusetts, Michigan, and Missouri, Democratic gubernatorial candidates had kept faith with their constituents and had won out over the Republican "tidal wave." Democrats unquestionably embraced the best issues, Hearst asserted, but had no spokesman nationally to espouse them. Of course, the inference for a progressive Democratic leader was obvious, especially with the editorial signed in bold letters "WILLIAM RANDOLPH HEARST." [9]

To promote a continuing public interest in his candidacy and maintain political momentum, Hearst needed to find, or create, issues that would justify his patented, high-visibility crusades. He did not have long to wait. Early in December, 1904, he returned to Washington for the last session of the Fifth-eighth Congress. With the "Hearst Brigade" well organized, at times numbering as many as twelve congressmen, he became, as one astute observer put it, "the captain of the forces of social discontent." With his efforts for an eight-hour day for labor hopelessly stymied, he immediately pushed for a measure to increase the powers of the Interstate Commerce Commission, specifically to "curb" the "outrageous" costs exacted on the public by the "railroad trust." Although having introduced a bill (H.R. 13778) the previous spring, he soon attracted attention by dubbing it the "Hearst bill."

In turn, he introduced to the House his patented crusade techniques. For the next two months, petitions from across the nation inundated the Committee on Foreign and Interstate Commerce; Hearst newspapers, especially the *New York American* and *Evening Journal*, published testimonials praising the "Hearst bill" as a "model" to eliminate the "rate evil." And Hearst willingly testified, and was cross-examined at length, before the Commerce Committee—although never defending his measure on the House floor—vigorously arguing that it would control railroad rates and thereby protect the average American "from oppression." When House minority leader John Sharp Williams attempted a parliamentary maneuver by substituting a less stringent measure for the "Hearst bill," the *American* and *Evening Journal* viciously blistered him, characterizing him as a man who was "intellectually bankrupt," as a House leader who was seriously compromising the Democratic Party, as the equivalent of the proverbial "fly on the wheel" who foolishly "seems to think it is the real power that keeps the wagon moving."[10]

Hearst, by advancing his own agenda without regard to the wishes of the House Democratic leadership, became a prime target for party discipline. And how better to do so than by public humiliation? The instrument for such punishment was Congressman John A. Sullivan, a second-term Democrat from Massachusetts. On February 13, 1905, Sullivan, in response to a critical article in the *American* that he had displayed an "indifference to the people's rights" in opposing the "Hearst bill," unleashed the pent-up anger of the Democratic leadership in a vicious, well-crafted speech. The members could not take seriously the "gentleman from New York," he asserted, who, while professing a "love" for his party, did not "attend one day in ten" and had answered, "out of fifty-five roll calls in the first and second sessions of the Fifty-eighth Congress . . . only nine." Indeed, Sullivan disdainfully inferred, the "gentleman" was no more than "a political novice whose only recommendation . . . [was] his inherited wealth" and whose "great ambitions" far outweighed his abilities, a man who had used his congressional position simply as "an opportunity to exploit . . . [his] candidacy for the presidency of the United States." And when the "statesman from Mississippi," Minority Leader John Sharp Williams, opposed a "will-o'-the-wisp" Populist measure by this "contemptible opponent," he had suffered "the lash of rancorous newspaper coverage." Thus "I will conclude," Sullivan dramatically announced, and "if by my remarks I have checked the scheme of political assassination which has been marked out by a Nero of modern politics . . . I believe I have performed a service to the House and to the country . . . by exposing the malice that inspires these newspaper articles which operate to create in the minds of the people false impressions of our public servants. [Prolonged applause.]"[11]

Sullivan, just prior to his summation, suggested that his speech might possibly expose him to the dangers of "yellow peril" journalism, "as disastrous to reputation as . . . is alleged to be to Christian civilization." Hearst was not one to disappoint; such invectives never seemed to upset him—but did arouse a retaliatory response. "Personally I did not inspire nor suggest the publication of that article," he calmly began, "but I am entirely willing to assume all responsibility for everything that appears in my newspapers, no matter whether I inspire or suggest them or not." As for "my" record of "action, or lack of action, on the floor of this House," Hearst rebutted, "I am proceeding here in the way that I think most effective to my constituents. I have heard incompetents speak . . . for hours for the mere purpose of getting their remarks in the Record; and I have heard the ablest speakers deliver the most admirable addresses on the floor of this House without influencing legislation in the smallest particular. [Applause.]" But, he reflected, "I do not know any way in which a man can be less effective for his constituents and less useful to them than by emitting chewed wind on the floor of this House. [Laughter.]"

Then came the bombshell! Hearst revealed that "a certain class of gentlemen . . . are peculiarly sensitive to newspaper criticism, and have every reason to be." Years previously, for example, his newspapers had criticized a former member, a "Mr. [Grove L.] Johnson" from California, "for subserviency to the Southern Pacific Railway." As a result, Hearst candidly stated, he had been viciously attacked on the House floor by Congressman Johnson, who "had been indicted for forgery." Now, Hearst announced, Congressman Sullivan had castigated him on behalf of the "respectable element" in the Democratic Party. "I had no desire, really, to criticize the gentleman from Massachusetts, and if I had, I should certainly not have done it in so puerile a way." But Hearst, because of this unwarranted, but similar assault upon his character and reputation, recognized the same pattern; he thus recalled that during his Harvard days in 1885 "a murder was committed in a low saloon in Cambridge . . . by the two owners," one of whom was named John A. Sullivan. They were forthwith "arrested and indicted by the grand jury for manslaughter and tried and convicted." Hearst then, by applying the same classic technique of Cicero in his oration against Cataline, asked if the gentleman from Massachusetts knew "anything about that incident, and whether, if I desired to make a hostile criticism, I could not have referred to that crime?"

Vigorous objections to the chair occurred immediately, interrupting further comments for several minutes. But eventually Hearst was allowed to continue, and once again he alerted the House leadership—and for that matter, any opponent—not to underestimate him. "I really have nothing further to say," he concluded, "except that I am proud to have incurred the hostility of that class of individual, and I shall make it my duty and my pride to continue to incur the hostility of that class of individual as long as I am in journalism or in politics. [Applause.]" [12]

Except for a few brief appearances thereafter, Hearst was done with Congress. Since December, 1904, he had been commuting regularly between New York City and Washington because local political events were impelling him upon a crusade almost as momentous as "Cuba Libre." The object of his concern was the mayor of New York City, the handsome and affable thirty-nine-year-old George B. "Little Mac" McClellan, Jr.—two years younger than Hearst—who had first been elected in 1903. To many Americans his family was a household name, his father the Union general who had created a formidable fighting force in 1862, known as the "Army of the Potomac," and then as the Democratic presidential nominee who had opposed Lincoln in 1864.

In certain aspects, McClellan's life seemed to parallel that of Hearst. Educated at an Ivy League college (Princeton), he had then proceeded after graduation on a two-year "grand tour" of Europe, whereupon he became a devotee of art—especially the works of the old masters—before returning for a brief career as a newspaper reporter. A lifelong Democrat whose family was well-to-do, he, too, had become a Tammany member and nominee, serving four terms in Congress before being drafted for mayor. And like Hearst, he added to the "luster but not the power of Tammany." [13]

But there the comparison ended, at least as far as Hearst was concerned. Although McClellan would eventually be recognized by many as one of the city's finest mayors—"a man of high character"—Hearst painted a far less favorable image of him in the *American* and *Evening Journal.* The major points of contention had to do, first of all, with McClellan's approval of the "Remsen bill," which permitted the New York Consolidated Gas Company to remove its manufacturing plant out of Manhattan while still supplying fuel for the people and, secondly, with the mayor allowing Tammany chief Murphy the power of appointment for most city positions. Both actions, Hearst believed, were reprehensible and definitely detrimental to New Yorkers. Not only had McClellan sided with the Gas Trust against the people, but he also had ensured the success of corruption and graft by surrendering the leadership of the city to Tammany. [14]

Together with the studied thought of Brisbane, Hearst launched a monumental crusade lasting almost a year, with the momentum of scandal, whether real or imagined, gathering strength with each passing day. Late in November, 1904, stories and editorials, along with accompanying cartoons by Opper and Sullivant, began appearing, lamenting the fact that New Yorkers were "dying from poison gas" and that an uncaring mayor was insensitive to their problems. Within a week the *American* and *Evening Journal* supplied answers to their readers, with front-page headlines blaring: "GAS TRUST COSTS N.Y. $9,000,000" (December 1) and "[CITY COMPTROLLER EDWARD N.] GROUT WILL PAY THE GAS TRUST $7,000,000" (December 2). Since Mayor "the Gas Man" McClellan had failed to carry out his oath of office by being "ever vigilant" for the people against corporate greed, New Yorkers needed a protector against inordinately high utility rates, against those who would shut their eyes to graft and corruption.

On December 3, William Randolph Hearst dramatically stepped into that role, with his attorney Clarence J. Shearn asking for an injunction against McClellan and city officials, the *American* announced, "To Stop the Giant GAS GRAB!" Hence, for the next two weeks this tabloidlike crusade was at full tilt, with stories about city officials blaming one another, with Comptroller Grout at first resigning his position and then reneging, while admitting that the "Hearst Suits to Stop the Gas Steal Are RIGHT." As usual in such patented crusades, a number of testimonials praising Hearst appeared daily, while comments condemning McClellan were almost equal in number. In fact, so venomous was the media blitz that both Tammany and McClellan speculated that Hearst was preparing to deprive the mayor of a second term by becoming an opponent in the fall of 1905.[15]

To offset such inferences, Hearst issued a statement on December 17, 1904, announcing his retirement from all officeholding, a singularly bold stroke demonstrating extraordinary political savvy, although not totally honest and aboveboard. "I am not a candidate for mayor of New York nor the presidency of the United States nor for any other office," he candidly stated. "I will retire because I think my political work will be less subject to misrepresentation and consequently more effective, if I am not myself a candidate." A *New York Tribune* article, in which Tammany chief Murphy alleged that Hearst was attacking the New York City administration "for personal and political reasons," was a case in point. "The only question," Hearst asserted, "is one of trust extortion and public corruption." He therefore proposed "doing all I can to prevent both, no matter whom it affects . . . whether the individuals concerned are Democrats or Republicans." Then he laid down a gauntlet that endeared him to reform-minded New Yorkers but that was a carefully veiled threat and an indication of future intentions. "'Turn the rascals out' is a good motto for Democrats," he concluded, "but 'let us first turn them out of the Democratic Party.'"[16]

Hearst, however, was already charting a new political course. Along with thirty-one-year-old Judge Samuel Seabury, a dedicated urban reformer who had also become disillusioned with the Democratic leadership, he was planning to counter the Gas Trust with a demand for city ownership of all utilities. As early as December 21, 1904, four days after

his "retirement" announcement, application forms began appearing daily
in the *American* and *Evening Journal*, whereby readers could enroll in the
newly established Municipal Ownership League (MOL). Within a week
more than a thousand people had enlisted—and a new crusade was well
on its way. Max Ihmsen began mobilizing the William Randolph Hearst
leagues of the previous presidential year into instruments dedicated to
ousting McClellan. Labor men in convention and local businessmen at a
mass meeting denounced the mayor while endorsing the "Hearst War on
the Gas Trust." And Brisbane agreed with Hearst that "since neither Republican [n]or Democratic leaders represented or cared about the needs
of the masses ... a third party, a radical or liberal party, could be successful
at all levels."[17]

To enlist recruits under the banner of municipal ownership required
stories denoting a wholesale corruption of city government, a continual
litany of abuses endured by the average New Yorker, indeed a blatant contempt for the rights of the people. So during the winter and spring of 1905
the crusade "for justice" intensified; Hearst and Brisbane saw to that. The
American and *Evening Journal* characterized McClellan as a "traitor to labor," a tool of Tammany known as "Mr. Murphy's little mayor," a negligent
public servant whose "police force is a farce," whose lack of concern permitted the "gas grab," and whose standard comment, when apprised of a
newspaper revelation about alleged corruption by some city official, was:
"This is a surprise to me."

The assault on Tammany chief Murphy was equally brutal. Time and
again he was referred to as a modern-day Boss Tweed, with "Graft ... the
Order of the Day in NYC." Through a construction company headed by
his brother, he had profited handsomely from city contracts, the *American*
proclaimed, with the photos of an expensive country estate and a newly
acquired $7,000 touring car as graphic evidence—the average cost of an
auto was $300. In turn, Tammany appointees had been well rewarded for
their services in the McClellan administration, Hearst reporters revealed,
by a "SALARY GRAB" amounting to "an increase of more than $200,000 in
the payrolls of the various departments." But even worse for the average
New Yorker, Murphy had reportedly concluded an agreement whereby
the Gas Trust could build outside the city (a new "Remsen bill") while his
construction company would benefit from lucrative contracts; New Yorkers could therefore anticipate much higher utility rates. As the ultimate in
ridicule, political cartoons by Opper, Sullivant, and George Herriman
daily demeaned McClellan and Murphy as "flunkies" of the Gas Trust,
while Jimmy Swinnerton attained even greater renown with a humor-

ously critical series of illustrations about the two men, titled "Some Manhattan Nursery Rhymes."[18]

As a result of this intensive propaganda campaign, Hearst and Judge Seabury together fashioned an organization of impressive numbers and significant wealth—with Hearst, as usual, the behind-the-scenes leader. Through the auspices of the Municipal Ownership League they conducted mass meetings (financed by Hearst) in which reform-minded participants established committees to investigate such city agencies as the police, transportation, and utility departments. They gathered signatures on a petition to "help fight for municipal ownership," then presented "107,000 names . . . nearly a mile and a half in length" to the state legislature at Albany. They created a speakers' bureau whereby hundreds of citizens volunteered to preach the gospel of city ownership of utilities and transportation. And on April 7, 1905, as the culmination of this five-month crusade, they brought in a rising political "star," mayor-elect Judge Edward F. Dunne of Chicago, who, besides praising Hearst for his civic virtue, explained to a crowd of twelve thousand eager listeners that "no force [was] so effective as Hearst papers" in the recent Chicago victory for municipal ownership. As a result, they formally established an executive committee on April 29, consisting of the youthful J. G. Phelps Stokes, C. Augustus Haviland, and Hearst, whose primary mission during the summer months was to visit and investigate European cities where municipal ownership had functioned effectively. In the meantime, Seabury, Phelps Stokes, and Ihmsen would be responsible for enlarging the League organization, while ferreting out Tammany men who reportedly had infiltrated local groups, specifically to undermine and thwart ultimate objectives of the League. And while Hearst was in Europe for the summer, they would also confer with like-minded political organizations to find a mayoral candidate whom they could support in the fall against McClellan and Murphy.[19]

Early in the summer Hearst sailed for Europe with family, in-laws, and friends on a long-overdue vacation. What a welcome interlude! As always, he was tour director and guide as well as art collector. For more than three months, while investigating municipal ownership in various European cities, he enjoyed his true passion: that of acquiring valuable treasures from the Old World, which, upon his return, temporarily found residence in another New York City warehouse. At the same time, Ihmsen alerted him to the ever-changing political situation concerning a "fusion" candidate for mayor, one upon whom such organizations as the Republicans, Municipal Ownership League, Citizens' Union, German-American leagues of Brooklyn and Richmond, and Workingmen's Municipal Ownership Association could all agree. The reports were not encouraging. Hence, on September 23, 1905, Hearst booked passage for New York on the Cunard liner *Lucania* and six days later docked, where a waiting throng of five hundred "friends, admirers, and district leaders of the Municipal Ownership League" gave him a "rousing welcome" with one intent in mind. The *New York Times* headline succinctly observed, "Hearst Asked To Run."[20]

Hearst, however, was in somewhat of a quandary concerning what political path to follow. Since his ultimate objective was the presidency in 1908, should he not strive for the strongest possible electoral base, which obviously was the governorship of the most populous state? Yet, the mayorship of New York City would surely place him in the Democratic Party spotlight as a major contender. Hence, for the next ten days, he maneuvered deftly, and with a certain savoir-faire, to keep his options open. He, together with Brisbane, anticipated that Charles Evans Hughes, a brilliant attorney who was receiving rave reviews for an effective, nonpartisan investigation of the New York insurance scandals, might be the Republican candidate for governor in 1906. Not a happy prospect! So Hearst, while resisting persistent pressure to run against McClellan, bided his time by publicly endorsing the nomination of several fusion candidates, especially Judge Seabury, but also State Senator John Ford. Yet secretly he was trying to persuade Hughes to enter the fray, pledging in every way on October 7 to "support him or, alternatively," to run "himself in order to split the opposition and ensure the election." Hearst would thus defeat McClellan, a possible Democratic presidential rival, and "box in" a likely Republican opponent, who would be serving—beginning in 1905—a four-year mayoral term.[21]

But on October 9 Hughes rejected the Republican mayoral candidacy; therefore, the decision quickly became obvious. The next day Hearst accepted the nomination offered by the Municipal Ownership League, stating he would "defer to" their wishes and "not shirk a task that presents itself to me as a public duty." For, he candidly pointed out, "the situation in this city is so grave, and the condition of the public in the face of organized bossism is apparently so helpless, that no man has a right to consider anything else, least of all his private affairs or personal inclination."[22]

With this letter of acceptance, the crusade for urban reform and basic justice against bossism and corruption by Tammany unobtrusively began. For the next four weeks, however, New Yorkers experienced an exciting, unforgettable campaign, one that fulfilled all the ingredients of a masterful story. As always, Hearst spent whatever the needs of the moment demanded, reporting his campaign costs to be $65,843, although estimates by others ranged as high as $200,000. Hearst, however, encouraged small contributions, which would ensure voter loyalty, promising personally to "double" the amount of "every dollar." Hearst campaign managers— Seabury, Brisbane, Ihmsen, and longtime friend Jack Follansbee—wisely reserved all of the best auditoriums and convention halls throughout Greater New York for scheduled meetings, much to the surprise, and chagrin, of the Republicans, who scrambled for roomspace after deciding to nominate William M. Ivins for mayor. They also helped maneuver the Municipal Ownership League members into selecting a city slate of officers with a definite Hearst stamp of approval—John Ford for comptroller and J. G. Phelps Stokes for president of the Board of Aldermen as well as former Democratic gubernatorial candidate Bird S. Coler for borough president of Brooklyn and Hearst counsel Clarence J. Shearn for New York County district attorney, who subsequently announced that his first official act would be "to put Murphy in jail." To strengthen their ticket against Tammany even more, they "arranged" to merge or "fuse" with certain Republican candidates—twenty of thirty-five running for the Assembly in Manhattan and nine of twenty-one in Brooklyn.[23]

Hearst, together with Brisbane, applied every technique of past journalistic crusades to win this all-important contest. Of course, the *American, Evening Journal*, and *Das Morgen Journal* became screaming campaign advertisements for Hearst and his brash band of urban reformers. For almost a month, front-page headlines presented an uneven yet extremely effective view of daily events. Each issue was rife with political cartoons—Swinnerton initiating a series on Murphy and Tammany titled "Ballads of Graft," Sullivant in a similar vein displaying "Honest Graft," and Opper detailing the "Wolves of New York." And at least one or two editorials daily compared Hearst and the need for municipal reforms and honest government with "Little Mac, the Gas Man," and his corrupt boss "The Contract Man, Murphy," both of whom represented "business as usual."[24]

This campaign, although resembling other Hearst crusade extravaganzas replete with brass bands and American flags and fireworks displays, was definitely different in attitude and makeup. An almost indescribable enthusiasm, an infectious ardor that only first-time political neophytes could conjure up and convey, was ever-present at each gathering of "the crusaders for municipal reform." Imagine fifteen thousand men and women, mostly young and fervently idealistic, waiting for hours in a steady rain to hear their candidate, then upon his arrival cheering for seven, ten, even fifteen minutes before allowing him to speak, creating a special passion and festive enthusiasm all their own by repeatedly calling out: "What's the matter with Hearst?" And then in chorus responding: "He's all right." Imagine the hilarity and excitement when thousands of men and women, marching in a "monster parade," chanted over and over again:

> Hoist, Hoist, he's not the woist;
> William Randolph Hoist, Hoist, Hoist;
> He's after the gas man last and foist;
> William Randolph Hoist, Hoist, Hoist.[25]

Hearst, too, became inoculated with all the excitement and drama. For the first time since childhood, when mimicking his mother's Chinese servants or attempting to replicate the roles of favorite actors before some of his schoolmates, he displayed no self-consciousness, no fear or dislike of crowds, no dread of meeting with and addressing the faceless throngs. In fact, he developed a method of public speaking that seemed to fit both his falsetto voice and diffident personality. He punctuated each brief and well-crafted talk with rhetorical questions that allied the audience with his spirit of reform. "Is there in this city a government for the people?" Cries of "No." And "if you left your private house with your private servant in charge [McClellan] and you came back and found that he had taken the pictures off the wall and the carpets off the floors, and the beds and the chairs and everything that belonged to you and had disposed of them, what would you do?" A cry of "Fire him!" Well then, Hearst called out: "Are you going to vote for the Gas Man?" Throughout the audience echoed a resounding "No."[26]

Even more effective was his persona of genuine sincerity and fearless dedication that affected not only his actions but crowds of devoted followers as well. As his attacks of vilification on Murphy and Tammany intensified, so did the number of threats on his life. But he seemed to revel in challenging his opponents and, whenever the opportunity presented itself, facing down the minions of Murphy. After all, this campaign was no race for a weakling. More and more, after each full day of scheduled campaign stops, he assumed the role of a knight-errant searching for the Holy Grail of municipal ownership. On the night of October 25, for example, a packed house was waiting patiently for him to arrive at New Star Casino at 107th Street and Park Avenue, when a Tammany "tough" tried to break up the meeting. Hearst, hearing about the fracas en route from another engagement, hurried into the hall to meet this adversary, then dramatically announced: "I am here to speak to honorable men, not to answer blackguards." [27]

As the election on November 7 neared, as McClellan pleaded with his followers to "work as you've never worked before," Tammany leaders realized that the Hearst threat to their political dominance of New York City was a reality, that they must exert every means at their disposal to ensure victory. Hearst newspapers revealed shocking stories pertaining to some of their activities. Registration illegalities bordered on the ridiculous if not the outrageous. The *American* reported that Murphy men had registered "floaters"—men who would "drift" from one election district to another and then be paid for their votes—as residents at a convent and an immigrant girls' home. Tammany lieutenants had also raised huge sums of money for bribery and, on occasion, physical violence; indeed, they were making "unblushing attempts to vote dogs, Chinamen, and dead men."

Lest such illegal activities were not sufficient to bring victory, Tammany politicos resorted, in desperation, to further chicanery. During the last week they mailed thousands of postcards to New Yorkers, the contents of which were so "defamatory" to Hearst that postal authorities confiscated 361,000 intended mailings. To remind voters of Hearst's past record as a radical, Murphy and Tammany distributed campaign literature suggesting that Hearst's vicious newspaper criticism of the late, lamented President McKinley had stirred a demented man to an act of assassination. And as a further reminder, Murphy hung banners citywide that were embossed with a McClellan likeness and an American flag underneath together with a similar one of Hearst under which was a red flag signifying anarchy and revolution. Then a caption read: "Under Which Flag Do You Vote?" [28]

With the election in doubt but with momentum building, Hearst focused all his energies on the last week of the campaign. To prevent or deter further Tammany malfeasance he offered rewards totaling $15,000 for the arrest and conviction of illegal voters, at the same time recruiting (as poll watchers) hundreds of volunteers for the newly organized New York Vigilance Committee. He also intensified his campaign schedule, speaking five, six, even ten times a day. At each stop he promised that under his administration a new era of prosperity, of urban reform, would envelop Greater New York—new schools, better pay for the average workingman ("$1.39 a day was unacceptable"), decent hours and wages for all city employees, 55-cent gas, an end to graft and corruption, and, of course, municipal ownership of utilities and street railways. Then repeatedly, after referring to McClellan's record of "broken promises," he vowed: "I will make no promises that I do not intend to keep." At the same time, to offset Tammany's personal attacks on his character and political "radicalism," the *American* and *Evening Journal* depicted him as a stable family man, publishing pictures of his parents, wife, and an especially endearing photo of Hearst and eighteen-month-old George "Buster" Hearst.[29]

But as always, with any creative play director like Hearst, a climax of dramatic proportions—a third-act showstopper—had to occur, which of course meant a Hearst extravaganza. So at 8:00 P.M. on November 5, the Sunday before the Tuesday election, Hearst promoted a political rally that outdid any previous one. To entertain a packed crowd in Madison Square Garden, estimated at 12,000 to 20,000 people and with another 20,000 standing outside in the street, he had hired a 120-piece orchestra under the leadership of the "famous American conductor, Mr. Nathan Franko, of the Metropolitan Opera House." Hearst, upon entering the Garden with a police escort at a little after eight, received an uproariously wild, standing ovation of seventeen minutes, men and women stomping the floor, waving American flags, throwing hats in the air, even lifting up babies in front of him to kiss. Finally the orchestra quieted them down by playing "America" and Liszt's "Second Rhapsody." But nothing could contain the enthusiasm of the crowd. In the midst of one musical rendition someone shouted out what had become a familiar chant during the campaign, "Everybody woiks for Murphy!" In keeping with the spirit of the moment, Conductor Franko began playing a popular tune of the day, "Everybody Works for Father," and thus thousands of voices sang the familiar words until substituting their own in the chorus:

> Everybody works but Murphy,
> He only rakes in the dough.

Even with more music interspersed with political speeches, the audience could not be contained; the people had come to hear their hero. So throughout the great hall, and outside as well, the chant went up in unison: "Hearst! Hearst! Hearst!"[30]

Hearst thus rose before them, standing tall and still, his face wreathed in smiles, as thousands cheered. The crowd hushed as he began to speak. "My friends, I do not desire to make a political speech on Sunday night. I only want to thank you for your kindness and your friendship." And, he humbly asserted, "I greet you tonight, not as Democrats or Republicans, but as friends. I greet you not as partisans, but as citizens deeply interested with us in the welfare of our fellow citizens, and in the progress and prosperity of our great city." With these opening statements Hearst captivated his audience, men and women listening and attuned to his every word. He thus spoke briefly of heroic men such as Samuel J. Tilden, who brought the "arrogant" and "corrupt" Boss Tweed to justice in the 1870s; of Abraham Lincoln, who placed his faith during a bloody Civil War in the "virtue and vigilance" of the American people; and of those before him, who would vote out "on Tuesday the corrupt corporations, the thieving bosses, the impudent puppets in power." Indeed, this huge audience should go to the polls, Hearst urged, dedicated to an Andrew Jackson credo, "Let us ask nothing but what is right, and submit to nothing that is wrong." And if "we ... fight the battle along those lines," he concluded, "we will win a glorious victory." Once again the crowd erupted, cheering wildly, as Hearst stood with his wife before them. This night he would long remember—and smile.[31]

Hearst arose early on election day, November 7, 1905, confident in the outcome, yet with a certain sense of foreboding. At 6:45 A.M. he walked to the polls, accompanied by Brisbane, and cast his vote, as a crowd of supporters gathered to applaud him. Then, after a few hours of sleep, he spent most of the day at his main election headquarters in the Hoffman House, where scenes ranging from pathos to outrage continually occurred. Hearst poll watchers and voters, bloodied and bruised, staggered in with tales of Tammany "toughs" trying, in vain, to bribe them before resorting to physical mayhem. While Max Ihmsen, who had publicly predicted such election violations, at times was emotionally distraught, Hearst remained outwardly "cool," advising his staff to "fix these men up and put others in their places." League pollsters also reported stories of ballot stuffing, of organized gangs "slugging every Hearst man" attempting to cast a ballot, of Tammany precinct chairmen allowing "floaters" to vote numerous times at a going rate of three to five dollars. Yet expectations for victory were still high; such roughhouse Tammany tactics could not so easily dampen this crusade for reform, this enthusiasm of the masses for municipal self-government against boss rule.[32]

The election was therefore extremely close. The Hearst forces were jubilant over the first returns, so much so that an early-morning American edition read: "W. R. HEARST ELECTED MAYOR." But then came reports about delays in counting, manipulation of ballots, and, even more preposterous, voting boxes (in precincts favoring Hearst) mysteriously dumped in the North River [that section of the Hudson River from about 51st Street to the Battery]. By the next day, however, the vote was announced: McClellan, 228,651; Hearst, 225,166; Ivins, 137,049. McClellan had won by a plurality of 3,485 votes.[33]

Hearst was not about to concede defeat, to allow the results of this "stolen election" to go unchallenged. With widespread reports of blatant voter irregularities in all city newspapers, he demanded an immediate recount. He also offered rewards, amounting to $27,000, for the conviction of "Murphy men" who had conspired to defraud. His followers, as well, were outraged, gathering 40,000-strong at a mass meeting at Durland's Riding Academy on November 11, specifically "denouncing the Tammany plot to nullify the election" and demanding vindication for honest government—meaning Hearst's promotion to mayor. But with Tammany threatening violence, Hearst urged against further demonstrations, vowing "to make it my business to see to it that the men engaged in the outrages of Tuesday last are punished" and that "the citizens who voted for honest government on that day shall not be disfranchised by the criminal methods of desperate and defiant bosses."[34]

Yet, even though a number of "Murphy men" would "celebrate Thanksgiving in Sing Sing" and even though Hearst would continually, through several attorneys including Clarence Shearn and Republican mayoral opponent William Ivins, seek the opening of voting boxes for a recount, McClellan would officially be declared mayor-elect on December 27, 1905, with revised figures giving him a plurality of 3,472 votes. But Hearst was, in no way, discouraged or downcast. This election had received nation-wide coverage; through the eyes of many, he had emerged as the "uncrowned mayor of New York City." He had given Murphy and Tammany Hall—unquestionably the most powerful urban political organization in the nation—"a black eye," weaning from them such basic support as immigrants and the working classes. And Hearst, even as Brisbane urged him "to leave politics and devote himself to his propaganda for the elevation of the masses," sensed the opportunity of the moment. He had reached the apex of his political career, universally recognized as a reformer who had fought for "enlightened" municipal government in behalf of downtrodden Americans, as a public man who had been unjustly denied high position by a corrupt and venal city boss. Thus on December 1, 1905, he wrote to Brisbane that "the masses look to reformers like you and me and Seabury and Hughes," then concluded: "We will run for governor as planned."[35]

During the next six months Hearst promoted himself whenever possible, keeping his name in the news, while providing Ihmsen, Phelps Stokes, and Judge Seabury with all the materials and manpower and funds necessary to organize the state in his behalf; they immediately began reinstituting the Municipal Ownership League under the banner of the

Independence League, as well as recruiting groups throughout the state that were dedicated to the principles of civic reform. Meanwhile, Hearst attended the opening session of the Fifty-ninth Congress, beginning on December 4, 1905; for a week he stayed to present bills and resolutions in which he fervently believed—direct election of senators, the strengthening of the Interstate Commerce Act by punishing those corporations that accepted rebates from the railroads, the creation of a federal parcel-post system, and the suppression of "criminal trusts." He also gained reappointment to the House Labor Committee, wherein he pushed for an eight-hour day for labor. Yet all such actions, while sincere, were mere posturings for his constituency, a political show with no hope of success; after all, as a member of the minority party in the House, he could accomplish very little, especially since the Democratic leadership had already relegated him to the unenviable position of persona non grata.

In mid-December, 1905, Hearst left the unfriendly confines of Congress, seeking more salubrious arenas and more appreciative audiences. Late in December, while wife, Millicent, participated in the "American's Santa Claus Fund" by helping distribute food and toys and clothing to thousands of hungry children and destitute New Yorkers, he journeyed to California, not to spend Christmas with "Mama" (who was presently residing in Paris) but to attend a reception and banquet in Los Angeles, honoring him as a "worker for the people." So great had his confidence grown from the experiences of the mayoral campaign that he even began granting interviews to opposition newspapers or to reporters who were knowingly inimical to him, expressing his views candidly on issues and individuals.

Without question Hearst was the acknowledged leader of the Independence League, enjoying the role of a political "martyr" who, like St. George, was now leading a surging movement, intent on slaying the dragons of corporate greed and malevolent bossism within both parties. Early in February, 1906, after enjoying a hunting vacation at his Babicora Ranch in Chihuahua for almost a month, Hearst "summoned" the major political lieutenants of his mayoral campaign—Seabury, Brisbane, Shearn, Ford, Phelps Stokes, Judge John Palmieri, Thomas Gilleran, Melvin G. Palliser, Augustus Haviland, Bird Coler, and Ihmsen—to his home at Twenty-eighth and Lexington to lay plans for the forthcoming gubernatorial campaign. As a result, on February 27, he led a city delegation of "five hundred prominent citizens," representing the Independence League—riding on a Hearst special train—to urge passage by the legislature and governor of such bills as municipal ownership of utilities and rapid transit as well as a mayoral recount in the recent New York City election. He then met with delegates attending the statewide convention of the Independence League, in which he enunciated seven platform "principles" for their new partnership and urged them to organize vigorously for a people's victory in November. But was he, himself, a candidate for governor or president? Not at all! That is, unless no one else could be found to represent the principles for which he had fought in the late mayoral campaign and, even then, only if the will of the people demanded it.[36]

Yet an unforeseen calamity, momentous and catastrophic in its enormity and devastation, sidetracked Hearst's personal quest for political supremacy, at least temporarily. At 5:13 A.M. on April 18, 1906, the citizens of San Francisco awakened to one of the most destructive earthquakes in American history (estimated at 8.2 to 8.3 on the Richter scale). For three days, with water mains ruptured, fires burned uncontrollably throughout the city as residents, dazed and terrified, searched for loved ones and personal belongings through the charred ashes of burnt-out buildings and the rubble of tumbled brick, twisted steel, and blackened timbers. Razed completely was the business district as well as the waterfront, manufacturing, retail, and wholesale areas. In fact, the "quake" demolished nine-tenths of the city, or as an "Extra" of the *San Francisco Examiner* so graphically described in its headlines: "300,000 ARE HOMELESS, HUNGRY, AND HELPLESS.... CITY TOTALLY DESTROYED."[37]

Hearst, upon first hearing a report about San Francisco, reacted like most Californians. Just another "quake"! Fifteen hours later, however, he responded quite differently after wire stories about the tremendous havoc and horrifying devastation began pouring into the *American* and *Evening Journal* newsrooms. Yet for those who, over the past fifteen years, had been continually amazed at the Hearst genius for organization and efficiency when a disaster occurred, his reactions seemed to be programmed and his orders readily anticipated; he directed his newspaper empire to aid San Francisco and its citizens in every way possible—humanely, without regard to cost, and, of course, flamboyantly. His first concern was the printing of a newspaper; the eight-story *Examiner* Building on Third and Market streets was a burnt-out shell and within a week would be dynamited. Despite a financial loss of a least $1 million, Hearst immediately tried to buy new presses from printing manufacturer R. Hoe & Co. But with none available, he was able to acquire some already sold, at double the price, that were en route to Salt Lake City. He also arranged for temporary newspaper offices across the bay at the *Tribune* Building in nearby Oakland—all these transactions amazingly accomplished within twenty-four hours. Consequently the *San Francisco Examiner* missed publication for only one day, April 19, 1906. And since no photos of the San Francisco disaster could, as yet, "be transmitted over telephone wires," the *American* and *Evening Journal* art departments used fakes, retouching pictures from the Baltimore fire of 1904.

At the same time Hearst organized missions of mercy for his former hometown. Within twenty-four hours after the disaster he hired twenty doctors and sixty nurses in Los Angeles to board a "Hearst Special Train" bound for San Francisco, filled with necessary supplies and medical equipment. Simultaneously, the *Los Angeles Examiner's* newly chartered steamer *Roanoke* arrived at Oakland early in the morning of April 21, its cargo containing much-needed provisions and groceries as well as "tents, cots, disinfectants, and other staples." And from as far away as Boston, New York City, and Chicago he organized seventeen "Hearst Relief Trains" loaded with more food and equipment and medical supplies.[38]

The Hearst extravaganza, however, had by no means ended. In New York City alone he raised more than $250,000 for "quake" victims through a "Hearst Relief Fund" that sponsored such charity "nights" as boxing carnivals and theatrical revues. From Los Angeles, whose citizens contributed $46,190.93, he sent *Examiner* employees to supervise such projects as a "W. R. Hearst Tent City" in Oakland, five "Hearst hospitals" in the Bay Area, and a "Hearst Bureau," which reported the status of area inhabitants to concerned relatives across the country—all for gratis to San Franciscans, although costing Hearst more than $100,000 in less than a month.[39]

For Hearst such long-distance promotion and directing was definitely unsatisfactory; he wanted to witness firsthand the results of the San Francisco catastrophe and to participate personally in salvaging the city. Late in April he made one of his rare appearances in Congress to propose two bills, one authorizing a federal appropriation of $2.5 million for "earthquake and fire sufferers" in California, and the other allotting funds to replace "public buildings" destroyed in the Bay Area. Then he and Millie journeyed by train to San Francisco, arriving by May 7.[40]

And for the next three months Hearst, as an experienced yet still eager "chief," once again enjoyed the thrill of being the hands-on editor of the *Examiner* who, from makeshift offices on Spear and Folsom streets, directed his staffers to seek out and slay the "giants and dragons" oppressing the people "simply for the fun of the thing." As a result, Hearst continually alerted San Franciscans of his immediate presence. In a Sunday editorial dated May 13, 11906, he graphically reported his impressions (which were printed in all Hearst newspapers) of the "fearful havoc" caused by the awesome "quake" and destructive fires, then dramatically—and somewhat effusively—predicted that "the rebuilding of a greater San Francisco is as well assured as that the sun now sinking beyond the Golden Gate will rise tomorrow above the snow-capped peaks of the Sierras." On the same day he sent a "trainload of sewing machines and dress goods" to nearby Oakland and Berkeley, specifically to clothe thousands of "sufferers." Over the next weeks, together with Millie, he presented a $100 bill to each "refugee babe" born in the Hearst Maternity Hospital (in all, twenty-five donations) and was especially appreciative after one "little lad" was named "W. R. Hearst Eby." At the same time he set up an "Examiner's Bureau" to provide legal assistance for individual policyholders whose insurance companies were trying to renege on payments; consequently, the Examiner boasted on May 25, "Bureau Helps 1,000 Policy Holders FIRST DAY." Nor did Hearst ignore the needs of Examiner employees who were members of the Photo Engravers' Union. Although at first considering wage cuts because of his own financial losses, he paid time and a half for overtime and promised "employment to as many extra men as possible" during such calamitous times.[41]

Hearst, however, was not content merely in rehabilitating the city and its people; he always liked to portray his newspapers as a sword of truth in defense of the public. His three-month stay in San Francisco was no exception. Mayor Eugene Schmitz, the union musician who had campaigned for Hearst in New York during the 1902 congressional contest as a payback for Examiner support in a victorious election bid, now came under heavy fire. Within less than a week after arriving, Hearst uncovered information that Schmitz had received bribes from Boss Abraham Ruef—the city's equivalent of Charles Francis Murphy of New York—and was also in the pay of the United Railroads of San Francisco. Hence, when the mayor introduced an ordinance allowing the "transportation trust" complete control over the city's famous trolley system, the Examiner headline of May 15 blared: "UNITED RAILROADS WOULD TRY TO LOOT THE STRICKEN CITY." Hearst thus mounted a crusade that helped nullify the existing contract and initiated the eventual downfall both of Schmitz and Ruef, especially after uncovering further evidence of their corrupt practices in numerous civic endeavors.[42]

By mid-August, 1906, Hearst could do no more for his home city; and, besides, matters in New York required his personal presence and immediate attention. He and Millie departed by train, stopping en route for two speaking engagements at Springfield and Petersburg, Illinois, before arriving in New York City on the night of August 20. And what an auspicious time it was for a crusading reformer to return! The richest, most populous, and arguably the most corrupt city in the United States reeked with the foul odors of injustice, a majority of its people suffering from low wages and poor housing and abject poverty, its rich and famous seemingly oblivious to the needs of the average American, and its city government controlled by a powerful, boss-run organization readily emphasizing election victories for resultant patronage rather than the improvement and betterment of its citizenry.[43]

Over the past year journalists and authors, called "muckrakers" by Theodore Roosevelt because of their propensity for delving into the seamier aspects of American life, reported in books, magazines, and newspapers the apparent breakdown of American society. Of course, Greater New York was an obvious focal point. And no wonder! In March, 1906, *Cosmopolitan* (now owned by Hearst) began publishing monthly the individual chapters of David Graham Phillips's *The Treason of the Senate*, the first one a political "shocker." Phillips charged that senior senator Thomas Collier Platt (R-NY) "had knowingly received thousands of dollars of the stolen goods of the insurance thieves" plaguing the state and that, in regard to junior senator Chauncey Depew (R-NY), the New York Central Railroad (operated by Cornelius and William Vanderbilt) "owned him completely."

State government officials seemed to be no better. Republican governor Frank W. Higgins, although supposedly representing a continuation of predecessor Benjamin Odell's administration, was unable to cope successfully with the widespread wrongdoing involving the gas, electric, and life insurance industries that directly affected the lives of New Yorkers; corruption between businessmen and public officials seemed to run rampant throughout the state, as one shocking disclosure after another destroyed the already flagging confidence in elected leaders. And, after the New York City mayoral race in 1905, McClellan was tagged as the Tammany "puppet," the beneficiary of a "stolen election" who could never hope to be reelected, even when he distanced himself from "boss" Murphy late in December, 1905.[44]

Yet, to more than eight hundred thousand daily readers, the *American* and *Evening Journal* provided, by far, the most alarming and, at times, discouraging discourse concerning the poor conditions under which New Yorkers were forced to exist. Huge corporations were not only portrayed as "criminally" irresponsible but also arrogantly uncaring, their major aims those of increasing profits for affluent stockholders as well as the protection of their own interests no matter what the means. Hence, New Yorkers read how the Gas Trust was trying to price its fuel at $1 per thousand cubic feet instead of 80 cents, although 29 cents was considered a legitimate return. Insurance companies were also gouging policyholders by refusing to meet contractual obligations, then subsidizing legislators and political leaders to avoid prosecution; as an example, the Hearst newspapers repeatedly linked New York County district attorney Jerome to the insurance and ice industries. The railroads, especially Vanderbilt's New York Central, were seemingly contemptuous of the Interstate Commerce Act, driving costs higher for consumers and small businessmen by granting rebates to such powerful trusts as the Louisiana Sugar Growers and John D. Rockefeller's Standard Oil Company. And once again the Beef Trust occupied headlines with its utter disregard for public health. After the publication of Upton Sinclair's *The Jungle*, which the *American* ran in serial form daily from the end of May to June 21, 1906, Americans reacted in outrage to repulsive stories describing the meatpacking process in the United States—of "tubercular germs" mixed in meat, of sausage produced from cholera-ridden hogs, of "potted ham" evolving from "pieces of pigskin . . . and bits of rope strands and other rubbish."[45]

But equally disconcerting to New Yorkers were shocking exposés that seemed to exhibit an erosion of societal values, a decay in the moral fiber of American life. The *American* and *Evening Journal* titillated their readers daily with such disclosures. But two stories in particular reflected this increasing breakdown of community. On the evening of June 25, 1906, at the Madison Square Roof Garden, a young millionaire from Pittsburg named Harry Thaw murdered Stanford White, one of the most renowned architects of the day, by firing two bullets point blank into the back of his victim's head. For the next three months New Yorkers learned every sordid detail about the forthcoming trial, the most sensational facts revealing that Thaw, who would plead "insanity" as a defense, had acted to protect his marriage; his wife, beautiful Evelyn Nesbit Thaw, had allegedly become involved in an illicit relationship with White. Less exciting but equally scandalous was the revelation that Bennett's *New York Herald* was abetting, through advertisements in its "Personals," the city's growing "massage-parlor" trade, which resulted in the "Red Light" trials of *Herald* men late in July, 1906. As a result, one *American* editorial compared the vice and corruption within New York society to the "parallel days of decadent Rome."[46]

Into such an ambiance of private despair and public concern William Randolph Hearst arrived after an absence of more than three months. He could not have expected—or appreciated—a more joyous homecoming.

Thousands of New Yorkers celebrated his arrival as a savior who would wrest their state from the malevolent giant of corporate greed, from the undemocratic depravity of boss rule. The *New York Times*, although anti-Hearst in coverage and editorials, seemed to catch the spirit and anticipation of the moment, repeatedly referring to him over the next three months as the "leader of the cause."[47]

Hearst did experience "one long ovation" for the next month. In his first interview with the New York press on August 21, he assailed the "rascals in office," such as McClellan and Jerome, "who serve their corporation masters slavishly and shamelessly." When informed that Murphy and Patrick McCarren, the Democratic boss of Brooklyn, were reportedly ready to endorse him for governor, Hearst replied: "I am opposed to boss rule in politics." Many New Yorkers enthusiastically applauded, agreeing with the *American* front-page headline that read: "MURPHY MAY BE FOR HEARST, BUT HEARST IS NOT FOR MURPHY." As a result, to the end of August, diverse organizations and groups continually sought Hearst's presence, such as "a committee of eleven" that represented five local boroughs of the old Municipal Ownership League, union leaders who beseeched him to speak to their members on Labor Day, even a delegation of "Bryan men" who, while visiting New York City, wanted to take a group picture with him.[48]

But Hearst devoted most of his time conferring with leaders of the Independence League; after all, since early in March, they had begun laying plans for his gubernatorial campaign. The indefatigable Max Ihmsen, as League president, had successfully organized hundreds of clubs throughout the state—and nationally, whenever possible, since 1908 was a presidential election year. Such council members as Seabury, Palmieri, Ford, and Shearn—but not Phelps Stokes who had resigned to join the Socialist Party—had also worked tirelessly for his election, along with Follansbee and Brisbane who, late in June, had initiated a weekly periodical known as *The New York Hearst's American Home and Farm*, which targeted the state's rural population. They also focused on the traditionally Republican, upstate New York area, encouraged by strong union support as well as the ardent backing of William J. Conners, publisher of the *Buffalo Courier* and *Enquirer*, who confidently predicted that Hearst would win the governorship by two hundred thousands votes. On September 3, Hearst officially opened his campaign at Syracuse and Watertown, delivering two addresses, the *American* announced, to boisterous Labor Day crowds estimated at fifty thousand people.[49]

The next step for the Independence League was a state convention, which the council had set for two days, beginning on September 11 in New York City. As for daily operation and dramatic orchestration Hearst was delighted with the outcome. At the first two sessions on day one, 1,611 enthusiastic delegates adopted a platform of his choice, including specific planks that he had advocated over the years either in his newspapers or in Congress: control of government by the people (and not bosses), "purity in politics" by a "free ballot and a fair count," direct election of senators, open nominations as well as party primaries, an end to criminal trusts, an eight-hour day for workers—even a plank protesting the persecution of Russian Jews at Kishineff—and municipal ownership of utilities and transportation, which was "not socialism or radicalism, but Americanism." On the second night the delegates agreed harmoniously on a "full state slate" of candidates—headed by Hearst for governor, Lewis Stuyvesant Chanler for lieutenant governor, and John Ford for attorney general—but with the provision that the League council would ratify the nominees only after consulting with Democratic leaders, who were meeting in state convention on September 25. Both the Independence League and the Democrats realized that, without fusion or some agreement on candidates, the Republicans would easily carry the state.[50]

Yet the delegates focused on Hearst; he was the catalyst for their hopes and dreams, the true "leader of the cause." So, on the night of September 12, 1906, they demonstrated their admiration for and devotion to him in the forthcoming crusade. As he entered Carnegie Hall, walking dramatically through the crowd toward the platform, the delegates rose in unison for thirty-five minutes of uncontrollable enthusiasm, reminiscent of the mayoral campaign of 1905. Although a fifty-piece convention band attempted to entertain the crowd, estimated at five thousand, with such stirring tunes as "America" and "Dixie" and "A Hot Time in the Old Town Tonight," men and women, waving American flags or Hearst pennants and pictures, exuberantly drowned out the music with tooting horns and chants of "Hearst! Hearst! Hearst!" From one side of the hall delegates from Brooklyn (accompanied by their own band) began singing "We Won't Go Home Till Morning," while those opposite them responded with the stirring melody "Red, White, and Blue." Then everyone on the hall floor decided to circle in review before their leader, where Hearst, onstage, tall and erect, stood smiling and obviously delighted. Eventually Chairman Ihmsen was able to quiet the tumultuous crowd long enough for them to listen to the "founder" of their new party. And no matter what he said, they reacted with unrestrained enthusiasm, indeed, the New York Times reported, with "one long ovation."[51]

Over the next two weeks the politics of fusion, of compromise and rec-
onciliation, was a paramount order of business for Hearst and the Independence League. Nor were they the only ones privy to this realization.
Democratic state leaders recognized that their only chance for victory
rested in Hearst's nomination. And no one understood this reality better
than Charles Francis Murphy. In the New York City mayoral election he
had been unable to prevent thousands of the Tammany faithful, especially
union workers and immigrants, from voting for the powerful publisher of
the *American, Evening Journal*, and *Das Morgen Journal*, despite the fact that
those newspapers had "blistered" him and Tammany in political cartoons
and editorials for more than a year. Murphy therefore "swallowed his
pride," one labor historian noted, "in hopes of winning against the
scandal-ridden Republican administration." He intended, of course, to
bargain for certain key positions on the ticket in recognition of Tammany
support. In turn, the Independent Labor Party readily agreed to endorse
Hearst, provided that the Independence League placed unionists on local
slates, as did the Central Federated Union, which was closely allied with
Tammany.[52]

When the Democratic state convention met at Buffalo on September 25, 1906, the leading participants had already "cut their deals" or were
in the process of doing so. And the delegates, as well as knowledgeable political observers, soon realized that Hearst, with Tammany support,
would be the nominee—but not without fierce confrontations and acerbic expressions that resulted in political attrition. Conservatives such as
McClellan, Jerome, McCarren, and Parker considered Hearst anathema
to the well-being of the body politic, a "demagogue" who had not only
separated himself from the Democrats but was presently, through "radical
ideas," sowing the seeds of party divisiveness and ultimate destruction.
Certain Municipal Ownership Leaguers (known as the "Committee of
100"), shocked by scenes of political trade-offs and unwilling to add the
word "compromise" to their vocabulary, accused Hearst of double-
dealing, of betraying their trust, of emulating the actions of a boss. Some
union leaders, particularly of the Independent Labor Party, also became
disenchanted after Hearst "reneged" on his promise and replaced their
nominees with Tammany men. And certain Independence Leaguers, after
seeing the same thing happen to more than half their state slate, such as
the removal of Ford for attorney general, became, as the *New York Times*
observed, "ten times more independent than he [Hearst] bargained for."[53]

But such contentiousness and disenchantment could not stop the
Hearst political juggernaut. On September 27 the Democratic delegates

agreed upon fusion with the Independence League by nominating him for governor; and with Lewis Stuyvesant Chanler as his running mate for lieutenant governor, a thirty-seven-year-old Democrat (and also Independence Leaguer) who had been elected in 1902 to the Board of Supervisors in predominantly Republican Dutchess County, Hearst seemed to be the odds-on favorite to win the governorship, especially with the Higgins administration riddled with scandal and the Republicans, without a candidate, in a state of disrepair.

But not for long! Meeting in state convention at Saratoga on September 25, Republicans somewhat reluctantly nominated for governor Charles Evans Hughes, the one man whose record could offset the Hearst crusade against corporate favoritism and government corruption. As chief council in the state insurance scandals during the fall of 1905 and later as President Roosevelt's choice to probe the illegal practices of the coal industry, Hughes had distinguished himself as a lawyer of integrity "free from entangling alliances with corporate wealth." He was, President William H. P. Faunce of Brown University noted, an "investigator without malice and without fear . . . through whose labor the public conscience has been quickened and purified." Consequently Hughes, like Hearst, would not be beholden to anyone in his party's power structure. In response, by telegram, to the Republican state convention on September 27, he announced: "I shall accept the nomination without pledge other than to do my duty according to my conscience. If elected, it will be my ambition to give the state a sane, efficient, and honorable administration, free from taint of bossism or of servitude to any private interest."[54]

Thus for the next six weeks the race for leadership of New York State raged, one that Hearst had eagerly anticipated and fervently welcomed. As in the past political campaigns, whether state or national, he attempted to reshape the persona of his opponent. In other words, he applied techniques in vilification that the staffs of the American and Evening Journal had deftly perfected over the years. Hughes, whom Hearst had urged to run for mayor in 1905, was recast as a villain of the people. Cartoonists Sullivant, Opper, and Davenport were especially brilliant in their "poison-pen" political diatribes; they pictured Hughes as the "tool of the Plunderbund," a pitiful suppliant of corporate moguls and Republican bosses who were intent on strengthening their own political bases, as well as enhancing their pocketbooks, to the detriment of "the people." Brisbane was also equal to the task. In one editorial after another, with accompanying cartoons, he linked Hughes to the "criminal trusts," as the "Plunderbund attorney" who had assisted in state investigations "only after being paid."

When Hughes denied ever being "a corporate attorney"—one who was on permanent retainer—Brisbane ridiculed him unmercifully for such spurious logic and deceptive arguments.

In much the same vein, but less harshly in his patented speeches, Hearst proudly reveled "in the enemies I have made"—whether moguls of industry such as Rockefeller, Morgan, and the Vanderbilts, or Democrats such as McCarren, McClellan, and former Tammany leader Richard Croker—all of whom supported Hughes. He therefore refrained from venomous, personal attacks on his opponent, relying on Clarence Shearn and John Ford to be his political "stalking horses." In other words, candidate Hearst would remain above the sordidness of campaign rhetoric, while they bludgeoned Hughes with vicious personal attacks on his character as well as qualities of leadership.[55]

Republicans were equally vicious in this bruising campaign for the governorship, dredging up information on Hearst or, when convenient, inventing stories. The *Times, Tribune,* and *Herald* were clearly the worst offenders, repeatedly using the words "hypocrite" and "demagogue" to describe him. And what was their evidence? Hearst claimed to be an advocate of an eight-hour day and higher wages for the laboring man, they asserted, yet allowed "slave conditions" to prevail for workers at the Homestake mine in South Dakota (neglecting to mention to readers that his mother owned it); he had hired "CHINESE CHEAP LABOR" on the "Hearst estate in California," they claimed (displaying a picture that was completely unidentifiable as to origin), while asking for stricter American laws for Chinese immigration; and, sanctimoniously, Hearst had railed against city bossism and political corruption, with the *American* on several occasions after the mayoral election of 1905 picturing Murphy in prison stripes, yet Hearst now was allied with him and Tammany. As rumors about Hearst became rife—and more farfetched—throughout rival newspapers, Brisbane and Hearst somewhat impishly established (early in October) a competition for the "Ananias Cup," which would "Be Awarded to the Newspaper Most Often and Most Ingeniously Publishing CAMPAIGN LIES." A month later, the *American* sarcastically announced that the *New York Herald,* "in a whirlwind finish of the most bitterly contested fight in the annals of journalism," was the winner.[56]

But Hearst's hypocrisy was, the *Tribune* claimed, even more damning. Although supposedly a strong advocate of the judicial process, he had "dodged" one lawsuit after another over the years; for instance, he was still refusing to pay claimants $3 million in damages for the fireworks explosion on the night of his congressional victory in November, 1902, that resulted in hundreds of injuries and eighteen deaths. For more than a decade, another story stated, Hearst had attacked corporations unmercifully as "criminal trusts," while amassing the largest journalistic empire in the United States. But, worse of all, the *Tribune* charged, he had avoided taking any responsibility for the death of President McKinley; his newspapers had inflamed the sick mind of the assassin Czolgosz. And what did Hearst do? Although denying any blame for this tragedy, he quickly changed the name of his newspaper, the *Tribune* claimed, to avoid any future association of his misdeeds by the public.[57]

Hearst, however, did not allow negative campaign propaganda to affect his performance, to sidetrack him from his ultimate goal; he had become inured to such acts of vilification, recognizing them as part of the political game. He therefore intensified his efforts for victory, exerting incredible energy and physical stamina over the next six weeks. Beginning on September 27 he staged six upstate trips—"whirlwind tours" that were three to four days in length—into the Republican heartland. In every town and city, boisterous crowds were impressively large, their lively cheers and obvious veneration intoxicating, their enthusiasm contagious, encouraging him to press his endurance to an even higher level. In New York City and Brooklyn as well as Buffalo, major unions endorsed his candidacy at huge mass meetings, labeling him as the "friend of labor" and pledging their all-out support. Murphy, despite Hearst's repeated denunciation of boss rule, demanded strict Tammany discipline right down the line in an all-out push for the Democratic ticket. And Independence Leaguers, consumed with the zeal for reform, treated him with adoration, men grasping his hand or touching his coat, women trying to embrace him, as police attempted to protect him in enthusiastic meetings filled to overflowing.

With victory seemingly within reach, Hearst increased the number of daily appearances, his managers arranging nine, twelve, even fifteen engagements in an already overcrowded schedule. Because of the demand for his presence he produced a "canned speech" of six minutes on a phonograph record, together with a silent movie of him giving an address and shaking hands with crowds of admirers; this innovative campaign technique seemed "to be satisfactory," the *Tribune* reported, especially with rural audiences who had seldom, if ever, witnessed this intriguing "Broadway" technology.[58]

With such displays of support that increasingly indicated a Hearst victory, Republicans both statewide and nationally reacted at first with concern that quickly turned to fear if not panic. Hearst, as governor of New York, could easily become the Democratic Party nominee for president in

1908, unquestionably a formidable opponent who, in the eyes of many Americans, was attaining stature as a folk hero. President Roosevelt had become increasingly interested in the outcome of this campaign, writing to close friend Henry Cabot Lodge that a Hearst victory would be "a very bad thing," one from which the Republicans might have difficulty recovering.

To eliminate that possibility the president planned strategies with Hughes and state Republican leaders to rally their troops and then deliver a late-hour political assault of devastating proportions. Their preliminary efforts, however, were somewhat disheartening. With campaign funds un-limited, they hired workers to enroll voters in the Republican strongholds of upstate New York, at the same time distributing biographical sketches and speeches of Hughes by the tens of thousands in an attempt to offset Hearst's reported popularity. They also enlisted national party "bigwigs" to electioneer throughout the state; for instance, on October 9, the *Times* jubilantly announced that Roosevelt was sending his "cabinet heavy-weights" into New York "to fight Hearst"—yet the results were negligible, having little noticeable effect on the campaign. Again on October 19, Speaker of the House Joseph G. Cannon of Illinois arrived for a brief tour, only to leave several days later "full of the gloomiest feelings as to Hearst's probable victory."[59]

In desperation, the Republicans were forced to "play their trump card." Roosevelt, applying the pressure of the presidency together with an appeal for party loyalty, persuaded Secretary of State Elihu Root, an upstate New Yorker, to represent him on behalf of Hughes. What a brilliant ploy! At Utica on the night of November 1, less than five days before the elec-tion, Root delivered an hour-long philippic that not only stymied the Hearst momentum, Secretary of War William Howard Taft cogently ob-served, but "left a picture of Hearst that . . . [would] be useful in all future time."

Before an upstate crowd Root was at his best that evening. As a Hearst partisan tried to disrupt the meeting and was being physically removed, Root dramatically called out to his supporters: "No, let him stay and learn!" And from that moment forward, he enraptured the partisan audi-ence, his voice gaining confidence and his words expressing conviction with each spoken phrase. His address was a masterpiece in character as-sassination, wonderfully insidious in its reconstruction of historical facts and deftly saturated with well-placed invectives. Hearst, he announced in his opening remarks, was "a demagogue," a man who posed as the friend of the workers and the enemy of trusts, while at the same time fashioning an enormously rich newspaper empire. Yet he had not used his wealth benevolently but rather "for sowing the seeds of dissension and strife and hatred throughout our land," pitting "capital against labor" and "wealth again poverty." For those distinguished public servants (both of the Democratic and Republican parties) who had differed with him on policy, Root pointed out to the crowd, Hearst was utterly contemptuous, his newspapers constantly belittling and denigrating his opponents, characterizing New York County district attorney William Travers Jerome as a "political Croton bug," Mayor George B. McClellan "an office thief, the dead cat in City Hall," Judge Alton B. Parker "a cockroach, a waterbug," former president Grover Cleveland "no more or less than a living, breathing crime in breeches," and President Theodore Roosevelt a man who "has sold himself to the devil and will live up to the bargain."

Nor were the consequences of such reprehensible slurs limited to the destruction of reputations, because in one instance, Root accusingly announced, Hearst's irresponsibility had led to murder. "For years, by vile epithets and viler cartoons, readers of the *Journal* were taught to believe that McKinley was a monster in human form, whose taking-off would be a service to mankind." As proof, Root proceeded to read the bitter quatrain by Ambrose Bierce that Hearst newspapers had printed early in February, 1901, soon after the assassination of William Goebel, the governor-elect of Kentucky:

> The bullet that pierced Goebel's chest
> Cannot be found in all the West;
> Good reason, it is speeding here
> To stretch McKinley on his bier.

To the stunned crowd Root thus proclaimed: "What wonder that the weak and excitable brain of Czolgosz [McKinley's assassin] answered to such impulses as these! He never knew McKinley; he had no real or fancied wrongs of his own to avenge against McKinley or McKinley's government; he was answering to the lesson he had learned, that it was a service to mankind to rid the earth of a monster." And then Root damningly proclaimed that "the foremost of the teachers of these lessons to him and his kind" was none other than "William Randolph Hearst with his yellow journals." In fact, Root concluded, Roosevelt in his first presidential message to Congress had accusingly denounced "the reckless utterances of those who, on the stump and in the public press, appeal to the dark and evil spirits of malice and greed, envy and sullen hatred." So "I say," Root solemnly concluded, "by the President's authority, that in penning these words, with the horror of President McKinley's murder fresh before him, he had Mr. Hearst specifically in mind. And I say, by his authority, that what he thought of Mr. Hearst then he thinks of Mr. Hearst now."[60]

Although obviously aware of this mortal blow to his campaign (the Republicans immediately distributed two million copies of the Root speech), Hearst displayed little outward concern to reporters, except when his campaign managers overscheduled him with sixteen speeches on November 2; in fact, he redoubled his efforts, on one occasion speaking past midnight, despite the hoarseness in his voice from constant overuse. Because of the Root onslaught, he was on the defensive during the last four days of the campaign. While *American* and *Evening Journal* cartoons and editorials depicted the secretary of state as "Root, The Rat" who was "the spokesman of the Plunderbund," Hearst repeatedly rebutted the charges against him as the desperate efforts of a "corporation attorney" and "trust servant" whose client was facing defeat.[61]

Nor did Hearst ever falter in this major quest for the "grail of public leadership," in his crusade for reform, spending at least $500,000 of his own money, while Hughes invested only $619. At each campaign stop, though tired and worn, Hearst stretched his endurance and upped his energy. He then followed a familiar routine and structured scenario that had become second nature to him. At every reception for him a regimental band entertained an overflow crowd of supporters, some of whom had been patiently waiting for hours. Always behind schedule, he would eventually arrive, walking into a meeting hall that was adorned with long strings of Japanese lanterns and other attractive trappings overhead, toward a platform stand profusely decorated with brightly colored balloons, American flags, and impressive pictures of the candidate. As the crowd applauded and cheered in wild enthusiasm, he stood tall and erect before them, acknowledging their welcome with a characteristic "faint smile." While waiting to be introduced, he sat "with eyes downcast," pensive and seemingly preoccupied. Then Hearst would rise to speak.

During the first weeks of this arduous campaign he had adopted an orator's pose, standing rather stiffly with "hands behind his back," a *Times* reporter noted, while delivering a "prepared speech without variation." But now he had learned to extemporize, keeping his thin, reedy voice at a lower pitch, applying words and statements that excited his followers, waving his arms or pounding the dais to emphasize determination or portray outrage. To disassociate himself from Tammany, at least in the eyes of his followers, he repeatedly denounced Boss Patrick McCarren of Brooklyn and the "fraud mayor" George B. McClellan and former Tammany "chief" Richard Croker, reveling "in the enemies I have made." He also reiterated his programs for "the people" that advocated "honest elections," better working conditions for labor, and municipal ownership of utilities and transportation. In closing, he urged them to go to the polls and thereby ensure a victory over Hughes by a margin of 200,000 votes. Then to the delight of his followers, as the band once again began to play, Hearst provided a much-anticipated crowd-pleaser: Henry "Pyrotechnist" Pain lit up the sky with "red fire and rockets." [62]

On Tuesday, November 6, 1906, New Yorkers went to the polls in what the *American* described as "perfect weather." Hearst casually strolled to his voting precinct a little after noon, greeting and shaking hands with supporters and well-wishers. But he was inwardly nervous about the outcome of his race—and he had reason to be. By midnight the verdict of the people was clear. Although he had received more than a 75,000-vote plurality in Greater New York, Hughes had carried the Republican upstate areas by even greater margins. In bold, black headlines, a 2:00 A.M. "Extra" of the *American* succinctly announced: "HUGHES ELECTED BY PLURALITY OF 50,000." [63]

So once again Hearst had seen the "grail of public leadership" barely elude his grasp. Would he ever possess it? For the moment, after this bitter defeat, the presidential race of 1908 seemed too elusive, too remote and far away.

11 | "Patron Saint" of the Independents

O n the night of November 12, 1906, six days after the election of Charles Evans Hughes as governor of New York, the successful candidates of the Independence League and the Democratic state ticket honored William Randolph Hearst with an impressive banquet at Delmonico's. They surely had ample reasons to do so. Because the just concluded contest for leadership in New York had far-reaching political ramifications—the winner being a likely contender for the presidential nomination in 1908—Hearst had attracted considerable attention from national periodicals, whose editors had, in turn, assigned prominent journalists to evaluate his life and ideas. Although James Creelman, who was no longer an employee of the *American*, wrote a favorable appraisal in *Pearson's Magazine*, Hearst suffered scathing criticisms in a four-part series by Frederick Palmer in *Collier's* and by Lincoln Steffens in *The American Magazine*, so much so that Hearst advised his mother that "those articles are outrageous.... Don't read them. Any kind of success arouses envy and hatred."

The Republicans had also reinforced these "muckraking" articles of character defamation with their own techniques of negative campaigning. They had concentrated most of their efforts, both in manpower and money, upon the governor's race. They had directed editorial writers and cartoonists to vilify Hearst as a base and ruthless politician, a "slanderbunder run amuck" who, in the name of reform, preached class warfare to immigrants and the economically deprived, indeed a reckless demagogue intent on destroying the basic fiber of American life. As a result of this strategy, they elected Hughes, but nearly all of the Independence League and Democratic slates for state offices emerged victorious—principally, Lewis Stuyvesant Chanler as lieutenant governor, William Schuyler Jack-

son as attorney general, and Julius Hauser as treasurer, as well as Samuel
Seabury and Otto Rosalsky as state judges. They therefore paid homage
to their "standard-bearer" who "deserved success" but had sacrificed personal ambition on their behalf.[1]

Hearst, although appreciative of such recognition, was unable to still
the disappointment of two bitter defeats during the past twelve months or
lessen his cynicism regarding the major parties and their leaders. As far as
he was concerned, the Republicans, while enacting a number of progressive initiatives in the Roosevelt administration such as more stringent
regulation of railroads, meat inspection, pure food and drug, and environ-
mental protection, still catered to the rich and powerful, their leaders in
Congress controlled by captains of industry, their major programs designed to protect the "criminal trusts," especially through high protective
tariffs and lax government enforcement.

On the state and local levels, Republican Party bosses jealously guarded
their political domains, keenly aware of their patronage influence as well
as the lucrative possibilities that might be derived therefrom. After all,
they had spent their lives working in, and perfecting, this system of favors,
whether by appointing cronies to important state committees such as insurance, banking, transportation, and finance, or by selecting judges favorable to their needs and concerns. What greater evidence did the American
people need, Hearst reasoned, than to witness the Republican leadership
in New York! Senators Tom Platt and Chauncey DePew were the embodiment of boss rule and corporate domination.

Yet the Democrats, Hearst acknowledged, were not any better. Bryan,
whom he had idolized and, through two national campaigns in 1896 and
1900, had loyally supported at considerable expense both in time and
money, had proven to be a "politician" in the worst sense of the word, a Judas whose betrayal of him at the 1904 national convention was responsible, Hearst contended, for the nomination of Judge Alton B. Parker. And
for what purpose? Bryan was fearful that Hearst, who espoused similar
political programs, would assume leadership of the progressive or "radical"
wing of the party and rival him for president in 1908. In regard to the
Democrats on the state and local levels, Hearst had suffered equally
wretched treatment. Tammany chieftain Charles Francis Murphy epitomized all that was wrong in American politics. Through ballot stuffing
and voter intimidation and blatant illegalities in November, 1905, he had
thwarted the "popular will" with the election of the "fraud mayor," George
B. McClellan, Jr., whose administration, Hearst's *American* claimed, rivaled that of Boss Tweed. And with judges seemingly "in the pocket" of

Murphy and McClellan, every legal attempt by Hearst attorney Clarence Shearn to force an "honest" recount of ballots had failed miserably. Then came the 1906 campaign against Hughes—and again a bitter defeat. Hearst, although partly to blame for certain Tammany disaffections by denouncing Brooklyn boss Patrick McCarren and others of like ilk, was contemptuously disappointed that such state Democratic conservatives as ex-president Grover Cleveland and Judge Parker and former Tammany chief Richard Croker openly endorsed Hughes rather than accept new leadership.[2]

Because of these experiences Hearst understandably formulated—and began espousing—a third-party mentality. Both Democrats and Republicans were servants of the "criminal trusts" rather than of the people, he asserted, their platforms a reflection of special interests, their candidates "chameleons" concerning controversial issues who were ready to "change the color of their political opinion with every varying hue of opportunism." Indeed, leaders of both parties had erected and nourished a system that emphasized maintenance of the status quo, that was geared to protecting their own selfish interests, that repeatedly discouraged innovation and reform. And anyone who threatened to disturb this formidable structure was termed a "radical," a person to be shunned and avoided, a danger to the democratic way of life. Yet those leaders were the ones, Hearst stated, who had betrayed the people. Instead of promoting liberty for Americans and alleviating the economic ills afflicting the average workingman, they had opposed progressive legislation and, at every turn, seemed determined to exclude reformers, such as Hearst, from the councils of Republican and Democratic leadership. Consequently a third party was necessary, Hearst candidly asserted, one whose "persistent purpose ... should be to maintain, or, where necessary, to reestablish the fundamental American ideas of independence in politics, honesty in public life, opportunity in business, and equality before the law."[3]

But no matter what his political predilections in November, 1906, Hearst, weary in body and disconsolate in spirit, realized the need to recoup his energies by distancing himself from the rigors of two exhaustive campaigns. As in the past he sought salutary recovery through travel—and eventually over the next five weeks he succeeded. After his "appreciation dinner" on November 12, he immediately departed for Mexico in a private railroad car *Constitution* with Millie and little George, together with a bevy of friends (that usually included Jack Follansbee), ostensibly to inspect mining and ranching properties. He was emotionally "on edge" because, upon arriving in St. Louis on November 16, he uncharacteristically became involved in an inconsequential public argument with young Joseph Pulitzer, Jr., shoving him aside before walking away. The next evening at San Antonio, Hearst somberly announced to reporters that "I will never again be a candidate." And after visiting Mexico City and the family's huge Babicora ranch in northern Mexico, he continued to seek solace by traveling to California. Although his mother was in Europe, he enjoyed his brief stay immensely. In a postcard to Phoebe while en route to New York, he reflected on his happy state of mind. He appreciated everything about "God-blessed California"—the sun and rain, the heat and mud. "Some people may object to the horned toad, the cacti and the tarantula," he effused ecstatically, "but I like them." In fact, he announced, "California is the best country in the world, and always will be." Then prophetically he exclaimed, "Vive le ranch! I am going to save up and build a cabin down at the ranch [San Simeon] just big enough for you and Millie and the baby and me."[4]

Hearst, upon returning to New York City on December 21, 1906, attended to pressing political matters. The newly elected state candidates of the Independence League and Democratic slate, who readily acknowledged his contribution to their victories, were to take office at the beginning of 1907. They wished to consult with "their leader" about patronage, especially what individuals had the best qualifications both in training and experience for specific positions. As soon as time permitted, Hearst also planned to attend the Fifty-ninth Congress during its waning days and, although a "lame-duck" Representative, introduce several bills that had no chance for enactment but would further identify him as an advocate of reform. But most important was, he believed, a viable opportunity to become the legitimate mayor of New York City, a position denied him over the past year, first because of election fraud and then by legal procedures initiated by Mayor McClellan. Incoming New York attorney general W. S. Jackson, a dedicated and appreciative "true believer," urged Hearst to petition his office immediately for a recount vote by examining the 1905 election boxes sequestered by the state. Hearst and Brisbane were so ecstatic about this request and so confident as to the eventual outcome that a New York American headline on December 31, 1906, blared forth: "VICTORY AT LAST."[5]

Hearst, while awaiting court action on the mayoral recount, busily attended to organizing a national party. Meeting at Gilsey House on January 4, 1907, he met with the Independence League council, whose members dutifully elected him chairman. He, in turn, instructed Max Ihmsen to concentrate on establishing clubs throughout New York before

branching out to other states. To strengthen their organization the council urged chapters to develop a camaraderie within the membership, to initiate social as well as political agendas that allowed for dances and dinners,
picnics and carnivals, theater parties and "ladies' nights," even a baseball
league with the winner receiving an impressive silver loving cup appropriately titled the "Hearst Trophy." Yet all such preparations would be for
naught, council members realized, without an eye-catching extravaganza
that proclaimed their intentions. Once again they looked to William Randolph Hearst, his organizational flair in general and his economic resources in particular.[6]

Hearst was surely equal to the task; however, his celebrity-status persona overshadowed all demands for reform—and, for that matter, the
League itself. For example, on March 2, 1907, after almost two months of
preparation, Hearst led a New York City delegation of Independence
Leaguers to Albany, their major objectives, the *American* announced, to
pressure the state legislature into considering four reform bills having to
do with "direct nominations, city debt, municipal ownership, and new ballot form." Two days later, 150 League delegates, representing almost every
county in the state, met in convention, the *American* reported, to begin the
organizational structure for a third party in New York together with a basic platform of principles. Yet Hearst monopolized most of the newspaper
headlines—his address to "cheering" delegates, his list of demands for
progressive legislation, his speaking engagements for the next week, indeed his "friendly talk" with, and observations about, Governor Hughes.
Ever so gradually the Independence League and the name "Hearst" were
becoming interchangeable.[7]

The League council, however, still struggled to maintain its identity.
While Ihmsen continued chartering new clubs in New York, Independence League candidates recruited followers in a bid to win various "county
and village" elections. Late in March, 1907, through the efforts of Hearst
attorney Clarence Shearn, the League achieved a place on the official state
ballot. Then during April and May, such League leaders as Attorney General Jackson, Shearn, and Ihmsen, together with Judges Seabury, Rosalsky,
Palmieri, and Ford, voiced their support for a national third party, proclaiming that neither the Democrats nor the Republicans were in tune
with the needs of the American people. Hearst echoed the same sentiments at a Jefferson Day dinner in his honor on April 13. But more than
any other program the League council pushed for a 1905 mayoral recount
that would install their acknowledged leader, they asserted, as the official
head of New York City.[8]

In the midst of this continuing third-party buildup, Hearst attended to family matters as well as pursuing personal wants and pleasures. On March 1, 1907, with the counsel and advice of real-estate expert Martin F. Huberth, he bought one of the "most prominent and desirable plots" on Riverside Drive at 105th Street, the *Times* noted, to "erect a handsome structure there in the near future." In the meantime he settled into new living quarters, also with the help of Huberth, renting the top three floors of the lush Clarendon apartment building on Riverside Drive at 86th Street. He then proceeded to redecorate the more than thirty rooms and a roof garden, approximately three-fourths of an acre in space, with many of his priceless art treasures—paintings, sculptures, artifacts, books, and furniture—acquired in previous travels to Europe and Egypt. When all was in readiness, he and Millie moved in, but not without the Hearst dramatic flair for the unique and unusual. They invited their closest friends to a "fancy dress" housewarming party, with Hearst greeting them in the garb of Napoleon and Millie in the clothes of a milkmaid. Then early in the summer Hearst, tired to the point of exhaustion, sought a remedial cure once again to rejuvenate his health and spirit—meaning a trip to Europe.

Surely the constant pressure of the past seven months was apparent. In Paris, Hearst wrote Phoebe, describing his frame of mind and present intentions; he had reached the psychological stage known as "burnout." During his stay in France he therefore planned to isolate himself from the world by ignoring all newspapers completely. "I don't know what is happening anywhere," he confessed. "I am not interested in the news." In fact, he concluded, "I have the same aversion to news that I once had for stewed pears after having got sick from them. My mental gorge gags at the thought of news."[9]

But Hearst could not hide indefinitely from his many duties and responsibilities. Nor did he really want to. By mid-August, 1907, he returned to New York City ready to fulfill a crowded political agenda. Although scheduled on August 23 as the major speaker at an Independence League two-day carnival and sports festival at Bergen Beach in Queens County, he had to cancel. On that same day the University of California at Berkeley dedicated a Hearst Building of Mines in honor of his father; therefore, together with Millie, little George Randolph, and Phoebe, he not only attended an impressive academic ceremony but also delivered a speech acknowledging the appreciation of the Hearst family. Then, after a brief stay with Phoebe, he and Millie departed by train for Virginia, arriving on September 2 just in time to deliver a major Labor Day address at the Jamestown Exposition.[10]

During all of September Hearst involved himself in every aspect and phase of Independence League politics. Yet the public spotlight still remained focused on him more than his party. Day after day, in accordance with a long-established policy of the Hearst newspapers, Brisbane orchestrated a series of testimonials from state and national journals that commented on the Jamestown speech. Some stories, while noting Hearst's praise of unions and advocacy of reforms for workingmen such as an eight-hour day, also noted his "conservatism" in proposing a closer relationship and a better understanding between "capitalists" and laborers. In other words, here was a "brand-new" Hearst, the *New York Times* implied, who was no longer hostile to business and wealth per se but rather to the evils emanating from corporations uncontrolled by government and unresponsive to the needs of the American people. In an interview to an incredulous *Times* reporter on September 15, Hearst repeated his "conservative" stance concerning management and unions as well as his ideas on gigantic trusts, stating that he had "always entertained" such views. Once again he preempted any publicity about Independence League functions and activities. And, of course, he continued to pique the curiosity of the national press by allowing the underlying and intriguing questions associated with his name to go unanswered. Would he run for the presidency in 1908? And if so, under what party banner?[11]

Reporters did not have long to wait, at least for one of these answers. At New York City late in September, 1907, the Independence League capped off six weeks of intensive preparations by holding a convention at Carnegie Hall to initiate the formal beginnings of a new national party. More than two hundred Independence League delegates, representing approximately thirty-two states and territories, participated on September 26 in a huge torchlight parade that ended in a festive celebration at Gilsey House, the League headquarters. The next day they concentrated on creating a party structure that was clearly understood and easily workable. To spread the blessings of the League programs to every state, they created a National Committee, consisting of a chairman, secretary, and treasurer, that received the appointive power to enlarge the overall committee membership to one person for each state or territory.[12]

Hearst had at last discovered a political organization that he fully appreciated and endorsed—and for good reason. The delegates obviously admired and adored him. He was their "patron saint" who had shouldered all expenses without reminder or complaint, who had recorded every League activity in his eight newspapers no matter how small or insignificant, who had led the fight for them in New York through two bitter campaigns. Gratefully they acknowledged Hearst as their leader, voicing approval when he presided over the two-day convention and cheering his introduction of every speaker. As a further mark of respect, they unanimously elected him national chairman of the Independence League. They then delineated his powers of office. Specifically, they endowed full patronage power to him, with authority to appoint members of every committee, such as Finance, Ways and Means, Rules and Regulations. If need be, he could replace the national secretary and treasurer of the League. And he was empowered to expand and "harmonize the action of the branches" throughout every state and territory. In other words, Hearst had become the personification of the Independence League, a position he relished.[13]

During the next five weeks Hearst anticipated putting his own popularity and leadership abilities to a major test. With the election of judges and a sheriff in Greater New York at hand early in November, he strove to enhance his own popularity and thereby increase the strength of the Independence League. To ensure the allegiance of the German population in the city, Hearst offered to the National German-American Alliance, meeting in convention on October 5, the services of his eight newspapers to promote a closer relationship between "our two countries." He also proposed an all-expense-paid trip to Berlin for "ten or twelve eminent [German-American Alliance] citizens" to cement stronger international ties. Then the next day he sponsored a two-day special train excursion to Boston for 230 national delegates, taking them as his guests to the Harvard Museum (which displayed German art and history in America) and treating them to a festive feast at the Westminster Hotel in Copley Square, where the governor of Massachusetts cordially welcomed them. Hearst was pleased with the outcome; the delegates boisterously toasted him as "our honored and esteemed friend."[14]

More importantly in this upcoming election Hearst concerned himself with offsetting the sizable strength of Tammany Hall. Although Boss Murphy had, through fraud and thuggery, "robbed" him of the mayorship, Hearst was equally aware that Republican candidate William Ivins had polled approximately 137,000 votes, which, if cast for Hearst, would have been more than enough to have ensured the mayoral victory. So even though the Republicans had viciously denigrated him in the 1906 gubernatorial race, Hearst still considered the idea of "fusion" with them because Ivins had strongly supported his demand for a mayoral recount and because of his personal disdain of and galling experiences with Tammany. He therefore opened negotiations with Herbert Parsons, chairman of the

Republican New York County Committee, to pursue the possibilities of "fusion." And while a number of politicos questioned the wisdom of such an unholy union, arch negotiator and Hearst confidant Clarence Shearn headed a League conference committee to pound out a compromise slate with the Republicans. They soon selected ten judicial nominees, seven of whom were League members. When they agreed on Max Ihmsen as their candidate for sheriff, Hearst's victory was complete. On October 11, 1907, the *New York American* front-page headlines exultantly proclaimed their unprecedented accomplishment: "INDEPENDENCE LEAGUE AND N.Y. REPUBLICANS UNITE ON A TICKET." [15]

With the quest for political control of Greater New York now imminent, Hearst geared up for all-out war; League prestige, as well as his own, was at stake. Rival newspapers, such as the *Times*, were reporting that city Republicans were defecting in large numbers, preferring defeat to a victory with Hearst and his "mongrel ticket." In turn, Tammany united against him and "fusion," with McClellan agreeing to work with Murphy "for a straight Democratic ticket." Hearst therefore mustered all the resources of his growing newspaper empire, applying his tremendous organizational talents and skilled advertising techniques in quest of victory. He immediately assembled the League candidates at Gilsey House, announcing particulars concerning the forthcoming election. He and Parsons had agreed that the Republicans and Independence Leaguers would conduct separate campaigns, with their party headquarters and designated meetings and "educational literature" completely independent of each other. Hearst promised to "go on the stump" for a vigorous week's tour through upstate areas, speaking on behalf of Independence League candidates running for the Court of Appeals before concentrating his efforts in Greater New York. To meet necessary campaign expenses he also committed an open Hearst checkbook, while instructing the nominees, "from Ihmsen down, that they must get out and hustle as they never hustled in their lives." [16]

But the key to success, Hearst realized, was the election of Max Ihmsen as sheriff of New York County. And to this end Hearst and Brisbane concentrated their energies and newspaper craftsmanship. They could not have chosen—much less have created—a more ideal opponent for Ihmsen than "Big Tom" Foley, a beefy ex-bartender from Brooklyn who had, through years of dutiful devotion to Tammany, become its candidate for sheriff. What a field day for the Hearst newspapers! For more than three weeks Foley received a concentrated journalistic focus, best described as character assassination both full and complete. Day after day Brisbane orchestrated stories and interviews, the most effective being from the Association of Methodist Ministers of New York (representing three hundred congregations), urging the defeat of Tom Foley, who was, they testified, nothing more than a "saloonkeeper and notorious political boss." Each day, without exception, cartoonists Frederick Opper and T. S. Sullivant wielded satirically vicious pens; one of the most effective creations—captioned by Opper "Distributing Campaign Literature"—depicted a grimacing, gargantuan hoodlum (tagged Foley) distributing clubs to Tammany thugs going into a polling place. Brisbane added significantly to these renditions of acerbic analysis, with editorials titled "Not a Matter of Politics, but Public Decency" and "A Divekeeper's Chance to Be Sheriff." In the *American* and *Evening Journal* he also printed damaging revelations that Foley owed the state "$5,000 in forfeited bail bonds" and that one of his aides was a fugitive from justice. Yet possibly the most effective campaign tactic—and surely the most humorous for Hearst subscribers—was a series of invective lyrics composed by staff writer James J. Montague that was titled "The Foley Campaign Song." It went liltingly like this:

> Get out an' vote the ticket, boys; get out an' work like sports;
> Put in the Ryan candidates; an' purify the courts!
> There's Bill the Bug, an' Tim the Thug, an' Three-Card-Monte Dan.
> Repeater Mike, an' Short-Card Ike, an' Ballot-Thief McGann,
> An' each an' every one of them's an honest gentleman
> Who's going to vote a hundred times for Foley.
>
> Get out an' vote the ticket, lads; we've simply got to win.
> We'll open all the jails if we can get our judges in!
> There's Strong-Arm Ed, an' Hold-Up Red, an' Beat-'Em-to-It Pete.
> An' Sneaker Slim, an' Sand-Bag Jim, an' dear old Slung-Shot Skeet.
> An' each is registered eight times on almost every street.
> So he can vote from dawn till dark for Foley![17]

On October 16, 1907, Hearst began a "swing around the circle," which meant speaking to audiences in Brooklyn, Manhattan, and Queens from three to six times a night. He continually denounced Tammany leaders Murphy, McCarren, and "fraud mayor" McClellan for undermining the election process as well as debasing American democracy by nominating a slate of "purchased" judges and a corrupt barkeeper for sheriff. In fact, Hearst addressed letters to New Yorkers in the *American*, urging them to support the candidates of "an honest alliance." Neither did his endurance ebb nor dedication waver during this hectic three-week period. For example, the night before the election (November 4), he braved a cold and wintry rainstorm, speaking to thousands of cheering partisans awaiting him at St. Peter's Hall, then zigzagging to stops in Brooklyn, and ending a long evening before "a great outpouring of Union Labor" at Durland's Riding Academy in Manhattan.[18]

Yet Hearst began to sense that the "fusion" forces, despite significant resources in money and energy and dedication, were losing. And he was right. The crowds at the Independence League rallies were boisterous and enthusiastic, but not quite as large as during previous campaigns. Union labor organizations that had received his unflinching support while in Congress and in all his newspapers over the years were rumored to be splitting their loyalties, with some locals reportedly calling him "a Judas" rather than "a Moses of the labor movement." His two years of bitter campaigns, of switching party allegiances, had also left political scars that neither rhetoric nor ideas nor actions could easily repair and heal. As the campaign continued to grind toward its inexorable conclusion, vitriolic attacks on his character and ugly insinuations about his ultimate ambitions increased in volume and intensity, so much so that three days prior to the election he announced being forever "out of politics" as a candidate.

More than anything else Hearst was witnessing once again the strength and influence of Tammany. He was combating a fraternal order that, for more than a hundred years, had reinforced its political power with repeated victories at the polls. Despite offering a $500 reward for the name of any illegal registrant, despite recruiting six thousand volunteer poll watchers, Hearst realized the futility of trying to alter the course of this election. The Tammany "chiefs" were too adept at enrolling "repeaters" or "floaters," with some "recruits" voting as many as ten to twenty times throughout the city. They also excelled at turning out their basic supporters—especially immigrants and laborers—in huge numbers, at discouraging opposition participation through intimidation, and, if need be, at falsifying returns and corrupting the ballot.[19]

So on November 5, 1907, Hearst was disconsolate and disheartened, anticipating another political—as well as personal—defeat. His instincts were on target. Weary from strenuous weeks of campaigning and bedridden with a severe cold, he decided not to venture from his residence on election day, even though "camera men and watchers," the *Times* reported, "waited for him in vain at [his] polling place." He knew that his vote would not matter significantly. Within hours, Tammany won overwhelming victories, and "Big Tom" Foley led the way with a twenty-thousand-vote margin over Ihmsen.[20]

Consequently, for the remaining two months of 1907, Hearst vanished from public view, as if exiled into political oblivion. Yet he remained optimistic. Whether ignoring the obvious decline in his own popularity or unwilling to accept the harsh realities of three successive political defeats, he maintained an unrealistic confidence in the future of an Independence Party, indeed an impractical idealism about his abilities to lead the American people in the "ultimate crusade" that would revolutionize politics. Through the inexhaustible efforts of Max Ihmsen and the newspaper genius of Arthur Brisbane, he intended to prevail—and emerge victorious. Respectable election returns in Syracuse, Buffalo, and Brooklyn, where the Independence Party had shunned "fusion," encouraged him to hope for a national third-party movement that would embrace the spirit of progressivism. An acceptable showing in Massachusetts, where Independence Party candidate Tom Hisgen recorded more than a hundred thousand votes for governor, emboldened him to anticipate, indeed to dream, that the seeds of unrest were arising among the people, that Americans were at last "eager to align themselves to an honest independent movement." Hearst, in writing to Ihmsen late in 1907, thus revealed his innermost ambitions. "I do not expect to win in 1908," he asserted, "but [I] do expect to control the executive branch in 1912." [21]

As a result, Hearst devoted a considerable amount of time to strengthening his political base during the first half of 1908. Almost instinctively, he instructed Max Ihmsen to exert even greater organizational efforts, first directing him to target southern states. As always, he bankrolled the entire quest for an extensive network of League clubs. He provided Ihmsen with an unlimited expense account, plus bonus money for increased membership totals, and authorized the hiring of a forty-five-man campaign force nationwide. He also lured John Temple Graves, the noted editor of the *Atlanta Evening Georgian*, ostensibly to bolster the *New York American*'s staff but principally to help energize his political operations.

In the meantime, Hearst focused on the Midwest and East. On January 11 he sent a lengthy letter to Independence Leaguers, who were rallying in state convention at Indianapolis, outlining a "declaration of purposes" for a new party and encouraging them to anticipate a national meeting in the summer. For a Lincoln Day birthday celebration on February 12 he agreed to deliver a major address to the Independence League faithful, who expectantly gathered at the Hotel Knickerbocker in New York City to hear their "patron saint"; however, a family crisis, coupled with a brief illness, forced him to cancel. [22]

Without hesitation Hearst abandoned all political ambitions to deal with a personal situation of major proportions. On January 27, 1908, Millie gave birth to a second son, William Randolph Hearst, Jr. But complications arose. A closed pylorus, the tube connecting the stomach with the small intestine, threatened the infant's life. For the next ten days the most noted pediatricians in New York could not correct the problem, eventually suggesting an operation that admittedly had an "infinitesimal" chance for success. As the Hearsts watched their little baby, now having contracted pneumonia, "wasting away," Jessamine Rugg Goddard, the wife of Morrill Goddard who was Hearst's brilliant editor of the *New York American Weekly*, offered her services. Accompanying her was an experienced practitioner of Mrs. Mary Baker Eddy's Church of Christ, Scientist, who prayed and cared for the baby continually into the evening and throughout the night. By the next morning, Bill, Jr., called little "Weeyum," was retaining milk—and the crisis was over. As a result of this "miracle," Hearst assigned Brisbane to write articles in defense of Mrs. Eddy and her church, which was under journalistic siege by *McClure's* magazine. In later years he also allowed Bill, Jr., as well as two of his brothers, to attend a Christian Science Sunday school, even though he was Episcopalian and Millie a Catholic.[23]

Yet nothing else deterred Hearst from resuming his political goals. At Chicago on Washington's birthday, he sounded the formal keynote for initiating a new national party. Independence Leaguers were not like the Republicans, who represented that class of Americans bent on avarice and wealth, he candidly exclaimed, or like the Democrats, who had become sectionalized and whose leadership rested mainly in the South. This new party, Hearst asserted, was free "of opposing cliques and warring factions," void of "selfish interests," and devoted to the "fundamental American principles" of liberty and justice, which meant restoring the "power of government to the people." He outlined a basic platform and instituted plans for the first national Independence Party convention, which would assemble at Chicago late in July.[24]

Hearst, while providing money and organization and publicity abundantly for his "new creation," realized that any presidential nominee needed a strong political base from which to operate. Of course, election defeats both for mayor of New York City and for state governor had denied him that advantage. But he still hoped to retrieve the mayorship, which Tammany had stolen from him, by replacing McClellan, who had served for more than two years. With dogged determination Hearst continued petitioning the New York judiciary to sustain his demand for a recount of the 1905 ballot boxes, which action, he confidently predicted, would declare him the winner. With the help of state attorney general

William S. Jackson and special counsel Clarence Shearn he pressed the matter.

Hearst did not have much longer to wait. On March 6, 1908, the state Court of Appeals directed Attorney General Jackson to open the ballot boxes and search for fraudulent evidence. On April 13 in New York City, Jackson began jury selection for the trial that would "AT LAST PUT TO TEST," the *American* headlines proclaimed, "M'CLELLAN'S TITLE TO OFFICE." Attorneys for McClellan appealed such proceedings, thereby delaying the recount until June 1.[25]

During this May interlude, Brisbane decided to launch another excitingly dramatic Hearst crusade, which both entertained and outraged *Evening Journal* and *American* subscribers. Once again the sordid election activities and criminal shenanigans of Tammany occupied front-page headlines, horrifying many by such abject behavior in elections, while eliciting smiles, if not laughter, from others at the ridiculous lengths to which "Chief" Murphy and his Tammany "braves" mocked democratic processes. But Brisbane wanted to fix in everyone's mind the unconscionable injustice perpetrated upon Hearst in the "stolen election" of 1905.

What a field day for the *Evening Journal* and *American* staffers! In story after story they shocked a dismayed public. "New York Is Easy," bragged election felon "Spunk" Brown, who admitted voting twenty times for "Big Tom" Foley in November, 1907. "I [also] voted eleven times in New York City that morning," twenty-year-old Richard White contritely acknowledged. From a Tammany leader "I received for casting those votes $22." Nor were they the only culprits. Throughout "Big Tom" Foley's Second Assembly District, one jailed participant confessed, illegals cast "more than 1,000 votes," with one using the credentials of a dead man.

Such examples were merely indicative of more outrageous crimes. Reporters uncovered that gangs of "repeaters" from New Jersey, some recruited from jails, had cast thousands of votes over the past three years. William George Van Horn of Newark confessed that Tammany lieutenant John F. Pickett, who was "the proprietor of the 'gas house gang's' saloon at First Avenue and Twentieth Street, had charge of small armies of repeaters . . . and with his own hands paid them for the work in cash." A more important charge had to do with the mayoral campaign of 1905. Repeaters confessed that, if Tammany had not hired them in such numbers, "Mr. Hearst would have had fully a 25,000 plurality."[26]

On May 27 this crusade by newspaper orchestration ended abruptly as Attorney General Jackson achieved court permission, four days ahead of schedule, to begin opening the 1905 ballot boxes. And again the drama mounted, the stakes so high that Hearst, who had departed for England on the Cunard liner *Lusitania* the previous day, cabled that he was "willing to give up his vacation" and "place himself at the disposition of [Supreme Court] judge Lambert." Every day New York newspapers followed the proceedings closely. The *American* was unquestionably the most flamboyant in its reports, also the most biased. Through headlines, however, readers sensed the crescendo of anticipation by the Hearst forces: "HEARST GAINS 27 WITH ONLY TWO BALLOT BOXES OPENED" (May 28); "HEARST GAIN JUMPS TO 85 IN RECOUNT" (May 30); "HEARST GAINS 11 VOTES AS RECOUNT BARES MORE FRAUDS" (June 9); "HEARST SHIFTS 90 MORE BALLOTS" (June 13); "HEARST GAINS 109 IN ONE DAY" (June 17); "RECOUNT SHOWS HOW TAMMANY VOTED BANDS OF REPEATERS" (June 19); BALLOT BOX STUFFING FOUND BY RECOUNT" (June 26); BALLOTS BY THE HUNDREDS FOR HEARST DESTROYED ON ELECTION NIGHT" (June 27).[27]

The legal decision, however, turned on the question of whether to allow the counting of ballots where the total votes cast in a district outnumbered those on the registration rolls. Shearn argued against their inclusion; such boxes were rife "with fraud"—101 precincts, to be exact. He demanded their exclusion; otherwise, as the *New York Times* observed, the "net increase" for Hearst was only 863 votes, far short of the necessary 3,472. On June 30, 1908, the court rendered its judgment in favor of McClellan. And even though Hearst cabled from London that "the result is satisfactory to me . . . that the fight was not to make me mayor, but to secure an honest count of the votes cast by the citizens," he was bitterly disappointed. His chances for high political office and national leadership were fading.[28]

Hearst, however, continued to maintain the outward composure of the ultimate leader, whose every action, whose every comment displayed a confident belief in the triumph of the Independence Party movement. Besides, he enjoyed the rarefied role of "patron saint," of dictating policy and controlling patronage, of savoring a new tune at party rallies titled "The William Randolph Hearst March." With Ihmsen conducting organizational expansion and Brisbane providing favorable publicity, Hearst shaped the Independence Party in his own image. Before leaving for Europe late in May, he had set an agenda that would guarantee the national party nominations: for president, Thomas L. Hisgen, a Massachusetts manufacturer of kerosene and axle grease who had fought Standard Oil in the marketplace and survived, and for vice president, John Temple Graves, a "stem-winding" orator from Georgia whom Hearst had hired the previous November. He had also agreed on a platform that was progressive in substance and that reflected every reform registered in his newspaper crusades over the past decade.[29]

Hearst, after touring England, France, and Germany for almost two months with Millie (their two boys stayed with Phoebe in California), returned to New York City aboard the Cunard liner *Lucania* on July 25, 1908. The marvelous reception they received rivaled that of visiting royalty. As their ship waited in the harbor to dock, reporters contrived ways to get aboard and flocked en masse to his stateroom. While refusing to grant any interviews, Hearst did answer one question of singular importance concerning his political intentions. Without hesitation he responded: "I have given my word that under no circumstances would I be a candidate. I cannot accept a nomination. This is final. I have made my decision, and will abide by it." When he and Millie finally disembarked, a cheering delegation of Independence Party members were waiting to escort them to a grand reception in his honor at a new headquarters at 17 Grammercy Park (which, of course, had been underwritten by Hearst). Then early the next day he and Millie rushed to board a special car on a train en route to Chicago. After all, on July 27, he was not only going to be the temporary chairman of the first Independence Party national convention but the keynote speaker as well. He was indeed basking in his celebrity status.[30]

The results of the next two days could not have been more to his liking. On July 27, at 8:25 P.M., after the convention had been called to order, Hearst—as had become his custom in campaigns—made a late entrance, walking down the aisle from the back of Chicago Orchestra Hall en route to his place on the raised stage. Delegates, recognizing him, responded as anticipated with a ten-minute ovation that "rocked" the building. Then, some twenty minutes later, after the national committee recommended him for temporary chairman and the delegates unanimously voiced their approval, Hearst moved forward to the podium, standing in appreciative silence to the cries of "Hearst! Hearst! Hearst!" ringing throughout the great hall. How he loved the adoration, the cheers, the approbation. It was reminiscent of the 1905 and 1906 campaigns. In his keynote address he stirred the vast throng of five thousand both to anger and dedication. To their continual applause and obvious approval, he "pilloried" party bosses, denounced all offers of "fusion" as insulting, and declared the Democratic and Republican leadership bereft of any new ideas that would benefit the average American. As a fitting end to the evening events, "union labor presented him a union-made gavel," the *New York American* reported, "and his own neighbors in New York [gave] a silver gavel, both of which were immediately consecrated to the uses of the National Independence Party."[31]

The next day, July 28, the convention continued on course just as smoothly. The delegates approved a platform for which Hearst had vigorously campaigned over the years and which was progressive both in spirit and substance. The party planks suggested reforms that reflected the ills of an embattled American society and government, proposals that U.S. congresses and state legislatures would wrestle with and eventually adopt. For unions and the laboring man, whom Hearst had always supported in his newspapers and as a congressman, the Independence Party advocated the exemption of labor unions from prosecution under the Sherman Anti-Trust Act of 1890, an employers' liability law and better protection for the lives and health of employees, and an eight-hour day for government employees. The delegates also endorsed ending the "blacklist" against union organizers, prohibiting competition of convict labor in the marketplace, and abolishing child labor.

With equal enthusiasm the delegates also addressed important economic reforms: a lower tariff, parcel post and postal savings banks, money to be "issued by government through a central bank," an antitrust law with severe criminal penalties, and government ownership and operation of telegraph companies "immediately" and of railroads "as soon as practicable." And to improve the American political system, the delegates endorsed legislation "against corrupt practices and the use of money at elections" (still a problem); the passage of initiative, referendum, and recall; a graduated income tax; and direct election of U.S. senators. Then, to no one's surprise, they capped off their second day of work, just as Hearst had orchestrated, by nominating fifty-two-year-old Thomas L. Hisgen of Massachusetts for president and John Temple Graves of Georgia for vice president.[32]

Despite such an enthusiastic political display before the public, Hearst privately acknowledged to Brisbane and Ihmsen that the Independence Party ticket had no chance of winning. The two major parties had more formidable slates, held together by entrenched political structures and well-established traditions. Late in June, 1908, the Republicans, in adhering to the wishes of their strong-willed leader, Theodore Roosevelt, had resolved their differences and united behind beefy Secretary of War William Howard Taft of Ohio for president. Less than a month later, in midJuly, just two weeks before the Independence Party convened in Chicago, the Democrats selected William Jennings Bryan, with only token opposition, as their nominee.[33]

Yet, while Taft was easily the odds-on favorite to win in November, Hearst still intended to push, as well as carry out, a strategic plan involving his own future presidential aspirations. His first order of business was to secure—and hopefully solidify—the union vote. Although the Independence Party platform had obviously courted the favor of the average laborer, one huge obstacle blocked the Hearst agenda. American Federation of Labor president Samuel Gompers feared that a division of the labor forces between the Democratic and Independence parties would necessarily result in a Republican victory; hence, he personally backed Bryan but refused to commit the AFL. Yet, while Gompers proposed fusion, Hearst adamantly opposed the idea, repeatedly acknowledging that the alliance with the New York Republicans in 1907 had been a mistake. "There are three stages of fusion—fusion, confusion, and diffusion," Hearst announced; and "either this Independence Party movement is necessary or it is not." During July and August the Hearst newspaper empire thus laid siege to Gompers, bombarding him with denigrating stories and scathing cartoons that questioned his credibility and integrity.[34]

But Hearst also wanted to settle an old debt, to his way of thinking one of blatant disloyalty and political betrayal. In other words, this campaign was also "payback time"—and William Jennings Bryan was the recipient. Hearst, besides conscientiously avoiding any personal or written contact with the Democratic nominee, thereby preventing any chance for rapprochement, pilloried his "former idol" at every opportunity. The Hearst newspaper empire, reaching daily more than two million readers in five major cities, was no longer a fervent crusader for Bryan but rather an abusive critic. Cartoonists Opper, Davenport, Sullivant, and Carter humiliated him with their lethal drawings, often portraying him in a Hearst characterization. Bryan resembled, Hearst asserted, Sir John Falstaff, the rather obese, sometimes witty, often jovial knight in Shakespeare's *Henry IV* and *The Merry Wives of Windsor*, who was bold in talk but cowardly in action, a political leader of failed campaigns who had "arrayed [himself] in a motley of modified professions and compromised principals, of altered opinions and retracted statements." But Bryan was an experienced politician who realized that every vote for the Independence Party lessened the chances for a Democratic victory. And that thought, alone, was especially satisfying to Hearst.[35]

While the three national parties were organizing for the final presidential push beginning on Labor Day in September, 1908, Hearst, too, was replenishing his energies and girding himself for a strenuous two-month canvass, especially after the Independence Party national delegates "persuaded" him to manage their campaign. He and Millie immediately traveled to California not only to "repossess" their two sons but also to enjoy life with Phoebe at her luxurious La Hacienda del Pozo de Verona near Pleasanton. And for most of August they did just that.

Besides appreciating the family's California properties—"the little rancho" at San Simeon always held a special fascination—Hearst also delighted in severing his connections with Bryan and the Democratic Party even further. On August 24, just prior to his departure for New York, he resigned from the Iroquois Club, the prestigious Democratic organization in San Francisco of which both he and his father had long been members. "I was pleased and surprised . . . to learn that the Iroquois Club was still in existence," he wrote, somewhat bemused, "for I thought that it had died the death and had been peacefully buried along with the last remnants of the defunct Democratic Party of California."

But with Bryan as the standard-bearer, who over the past sixteen years had "changed" the original principles of Jefferson and Jackson "so often that there is no recognizing" their tenets, Hearst no longer wished to be a member, his withdrawal reminding him of a story that reflected his present course of action. "There was a farmer who had a balky mule, and he couldn't make the mule go," Hearst explained. "A stranger came along and offered to help, and the farmer told him to go right ahead. The stranger had a bottle of turpentine, and he opened the mule's mouth and pushed back his head and poured about half of the bottle into the mule's stomach. The mule gave one startled gasp and struck out across the prairie, and was lost to sight. The surprised farmer stood for a while immersed in deep thought, and then said, 'Stranger, please give me the rest of that turpentine; I've got to catch my mule.'" In conclusion, Hearst thus reflected his state of mind as well as the predicament of many Americans who had previously supported Bryan and the Democratic Party. "I have always stood just where I stand now, squarely upon the principles of the founder of the Democratic Party [Jefferson] and the framer of the Declaration of Independence; but the Democratic donkey has gone galloping over the political prairie until it is lost to the sight of its original adherents. I am not in the race to catch that donkey," Hearst acknowledged, "and if you are, you will find that you have to keep plumb full of a different kind of turpentine in every campaign."[36]

At the end of this month-long respite in California, Hearst anticipated a hectic campaign; as usual, his political advisers and managers had overscheduled him. En route to New York, he stopped briefly in Chicago on August 29, 1908, providing reporters with multiple news items about the activities of the Independence Party, together with his protracted timetable. Two days later in New York City he staged a "remarkable demonstration," replete with cheering throngs and ample entertainment, in giving Thomas L. Hisgen formal notification that the Independence Party had nominated him for president; yet, as usual, Hearst occupied center stage by delivering a "stirring speech" against both "old parties," the *American* proclaimed, "in phrases that snapped as though thrown from a whip lash." He was then off to Indianapolis, where on the night of September 3—and "in rare voice" to encouraging cheers of "Hit him again! Go on, Hearst!"—he once again paid "his respects to Bryan" by raking him "fore and aft." On September 5 in Chicago he, together with Hisgen, spoke briefly to the Independence Party faithful en route to a Labor Day rally the next day at Davenport, Iowa. Hearst typically, before seven thousand union men, upstaged his presidential nominee, grabbing headlines across the nation by producing affidavits that revealed that Bryan, while in Congress, declared laboring men to be "a lot of public beggars."[37]

Hearst, in hopes of securing a more formidable base and further undermining Bryan, directed the Independence Party campaign upon a "southern swing" during the second week of September. He and Hisgen joined Graves for home-state rallies in Georgia before proceeding to Alabama, Tennessee, and Kentucky. But as the speaking tour progressed, Hearst realized that something was dreadfully wrong. He began to doubt the strength of the Independence Party movement, to question Ihmsen's estimates of having enrolled three million members in more than three thousand clubs. The crowds were discouragingly small, the rallies poorly attended, the participants distressingly unenthusiastic. For instance, on September 13 at Albany, Georgia, only a thousand people assembled to witness John Temple Graves receive formal notification of his vice-presidential nomination. And at each scheduled stop, Hearst sensed no exhilaration for the speakers, no dedication to his "new party," no emotion in his "crusade" for justice and independence for the average American. But the most telling evidence of all was the disquieting silence of former supporters, the conspicuous absence of cherished confidants. Such ardent reformers as Justice Samuel Seabury and Attorney General William S. Jackson had considered a third-party movement to be "foolhardy" and had deserted the "cause," while Lieutenant Governor Lewis Stuyvesant Chanler had "sold his birthright," Hearst announced, by agreeing to become the Democratic nominee for governor of New York.[38]

Consequently, on September 17, 1908, Hearst decided to instill new life into the Independence Party campaign; at Columbus, Ohio, he dropped one of his patented political bombshells, the Standard Oil let-ters. And why? Even in a losing cause, he wanted to emphasize the prevail-ing need for reform in American life, to demonstrate the importance of the Independence movement that, in comparison to the two major par-ties, was free of bossism and untainted by corruption. At the same time Hearst recognized the infinite possibilities of inflicting more damage on the political fortunes of Bryan. And, in so doing, he would occupy the cen-ter stage that he increasingly sought and savored. Without question, he recognized the explosive nature of such revelations as well as the fantastic "news" value to the Hearst empire; after all, his creative genius had master-minded and syndicated the techniques of shock and surprise, indeed had accustomed the public to the sensationalism of his "New Journalism."[39]

The Standard Oil letters were a reporter's dream. What happened was easy to follow, a simple story of theft for profit. As early as 1904 Willie Winkfield, whom Vice President John D. Archbold of Standard Oil Company had employed as a janitor for his offices at 26 Broadway in New York City, delved through correspondence files that involved Archbold and a number of prominent political personages. Winkfield and fellow worker Charlie Stump decided that certain newspapers might be willing to pay for such information. Although rebuffed by the *New York World*, they discovered a ready customer in the *American*. As a result, they rifled the Standard Oil files at night, took letters and telegrams to the *American* newspaper office to be photographed, and quickly returned them before morning.[40]

On September 17 at Columbus, Hearst changed the whole tenor of the 1908 campaign; he, rather than the presidential candidates, would be the focus of media attention. Hearst did not alert anyone in advance about the explosive information in his possession. Instead, in a scheduled speech, he somewhat matter-of-factly compared the differences between the na-tional parties. The Independence Party candidates from the very begin-ning had railed against the depravity in American politics, especially the "corrupt bosses and criminal special interests" who had "become more powerful than the people's vote," he candidly asserted. "We claim that the Democrats are today eagerly competing with the Republicans for trust fa-vor," specifically seeking financial advantages from the most hated corpo-rate head in the United States, John D. Rockefeller of Standard Oil. "I am not here to amuse you and entertain you with oratory," Hearst exclaimed, "but I am here to present to you . . . some facts that should startle and alarm . . . and arouse you to a fitting sense of the genuine danger that threatens our republic."

Nor had Hearst come "with empty assertions, but with legal evidence and documentary proof.... I am now going to read copies of letters written by Mr. John D. Archbold, chief agent of the Standard Oil [and] an intimate personal representative of Mr. Rockefeller." Hearst then proceeded to establish the validity of his charges, reciting documents that originated from Archbold to Senator Joseph B. Foraker of Ohio (who had been one of the leading contenders against Taft for the Republican presidential nomination in June) that detailed how Archbold paid him considerable sums—$15,000 and $14,500 during a three-week period in 1900—to fashion congressional legislation favorable to Standard Oil as well as to help undermine "dangerous" political candidates. Hearst next read a letter from Republican congressman Joseph C. Sibley of Pennsylvania to Archbold, part of which attempted, through innuendo and association, to damage Roosevelt. Sibley recollected the following conversation apparently occurring at the White House: "For the first time in my life I told the President some plain, if unpalatable truths, as to the situation politically, and that no man should win or deserve to win who depended upon the rabble rather than upon the conservative men of affairs.... Anything you may desire here in my power please advise." Hearst then ad-libbed to the audience, "You gentlemen, I, Mr. Hisgen—all of us are the rabble. Seekers after office cannot depend upon us; they need the conservative citizens, these magnates of the great criminal trusts."

But the Democrats were no better, Hearst accusingly asserted in completing this assault on the present political system. Bryan had also courted Standard Oil by appointing a Rockefeller "agent," Governor Charles N. Haskell of the Oklahoma Territory, as treasurer of the Democratic national campaign fund; Hearst thus implied—and would continue to do so—that Standard Oil, in "appreciation," contributed $300,000 to the Bryan candidacy.[41]

Although the audience surprisingly did not grasp the import of these documents, Hearst could not have been more pleased and delighted with the results. "The next day [September 18] when he stepped from the train at St. Louis," Mrs. Fremont Older recorded, "all the newspaper men in America seemed to be present inquiring about the [number of] letters" and the names of others who might be linked to this exposé. But like any experienced journalist, "with the story of the year," Hearst meted the information piecemeal to the press while allowing the drama of an evolving scandal to escalate. At St. Louis he read two Archbold letters, which revealed that Foraker had received an additional $50,000 "in accordance with our understanding." He also produced two "photographed" affidavits accusing Governor Haskell as the acting "agent" in negotiating an attempted $400,000 bribe of the Ohio attorney general in 1898–99 "to stifle prosecution of the Standard Oil." At Memphis on September 19 Hearst, to a "riotously enthusiastic" audience—and eagerly attentive reporters—exposed Democratic senator Joseph Weldon Bailey of Texas as one of the "Standard Oil wire-pullers and hired men" who had helped Archbold "organize" Congress.[42]

In the midst of this continuing furor, Hearst departed for New York City, where "his" Independence Party was holding a state convention on September 24. He had earlier agreed to accept his own invitation to be temporary chairman as well as the behind-the-scenes negotiator concerning specifics in the platform and the selection of party candidates. As "patron saint," he could do no less. The delegates therefore adopted the "salient" progressive planks approved at the national Independence Party convention at Chicago and named a slate headed by Hearst attorney Clarence J. Shearn for governor. As a fitting climax to this brief political drama, Hearst delivered the major address. Upon being introduced, he stood "silently" for ten minutes, the *American* recorded, as "the delegates rose as one man and cheer followed cheer." In an attempt to bring order, the convention band began to play, but the "outburst" continued for another five minutes. How Hearst treasured these moments! He then began to speak, once again denouncing those who had "betrayed" the American people. Governor Hughes had "served the privileged interests like the trained corporation lawyer that he is" and did not deserve reelection. Democratic gubernatorial candidate Lewis Stuyvesant Chanler was a "political turncoat," nothing more than a "pocket-piece of Charlie Murphy rubbed smooth by Murphy's soiled thumb"—and he, Hearst, would campaign against him. Bryan was even worse, having forsaken the party principles of Jefferson and Jackson by allying himself with lackeys of Standard Oil and other "criminal trusts." As still further proof of political corruption, Hearst entertained the crowd by reading two more Archbold letters, which implicated Senator John L. McLaurin of South Carolina as another Standard Oil accomplice. Then in solemn sincerity Hearst concluded: "Go forth, my friends, to battle. You have a mission to perform. . . . Make no fusion with fraud, no compromise with corruption."[43]

Back to the presidential campaign trail Hearst proceeded, now on a western swing, as reporters from across the nation flocked en masse after him, anxiously listening to his every word. He did not disappoint them. At Denver on September 30 Hearst read two more Foraker letters; he was attaining even greater celebrity status as thousands of people "waited in the street" or "jammed" an auditorium just to see or hear him speak. In Salt Lake City, Albuquerque, and El Paso Hearst continued his assault on both parties, presenting enough documentary proof each day to fuel greater interest, while whetting public anticipation by having already leaked to the *Times* that he had "Enough Oil Sensations to Last Till Election Day."

For the week of October 5–12, Hearst spoke in Los Angeles, San Francisco, and Berkeley, delivering his message concerning political corruption to fellow Californians, especially in regard to the Democratic ticket. Bryan had not returned a $300,000 "gift" from Standard Oil; vice-presidential candidate John Worth Kern was the "railroad pass candidate" and "debtor of bosses and corporations"—and "should get out"; and such party "statesmen" as Bailey, McLaurin, and Haskell had concluded lucrative financial deals with Standard Oil. At San Francisco and Berkeley, Hearst enjoyed his scheduled engagements immensely. Like an experienced actor, he "played" to his audiences. He built a sense of anticipation and drama in his speeches, punctuating them with "shocking" Standard Oil letters. The Native Son had returned in triumph.[44]

But Hearst did not tarry long in California. The Independence Party canvass was proving to be a disaster; Hisgen and Graves were ineffectual campaigners, especially with Hearst upstaging them at every speaking engagement. Yet the "patron saint" was determined to salvage the New York State organization. He had promised Shearn his unqualified support, a vow he was determined to keep. Hearst thus rushed "from the Pacific slopes," the *Times* announced, not only to settle disputes arising within the state party but also to campaign intensively. And that was exactly what he did. Except for a quick one-day trip on October 21 to honor Hisgen in his hometown at Petersburg, Indiana, Hearst electioneered with Shearn in upstate New York for almost a week (October 19-24). He then concentrated on the Greater New York area during the week prior to the election on November 3, contributing both time and money in what was obviously a losing cause.[45]

Hearst, although continuing to shock audiences with more Standard Oil letters, actually revealed the deep disillusionment of previous disloyalties, the personal scars of past elections. During the closing days of the campaign he focused on two themes: political subterfuge and party betrayal. On October 27, before a boisterous crowd of five thousand, he upbraided a former "crusader" for the people, Lewis "Tiddlewinks" Chanler, by applying an unusual campaign technique called "stereoptics." In a series of slides projected on a huge screen, Hearst displayed—to the delight of the assembled throng—political cartoons by Opper, Sullivant, and Carter that characterized Chanler at his worst, while an "Independence Quartette" denigrated him with satirical songs. Hearst then proceeded to read correspondence revealing the hypocrisy of Chanler, who had praised Bryan the previous night "from the same platform," yet had been a "recent foe" and highly contemptuous of him. To the approval of his listeners, Hearst denounced such utter political insincerity, concluding that "there is nothing more pitiful or more painful than first-class ambition with second-class ability."

But Hearst was even more contemptuous of, and equally unrelenting about, Bryan. Besides Hearst newspapers, in cartoons and editorials, depicting the Democratic nominee as a man of constantly changing beliefs who had become a tool of the "criminal trusts," Hearst denounced Bryan in speech after speech "for having surrounded himself with the worst enemies of the workingmen" and for abandoning Democratic Party reforms that were so essential to the average American. In his last speech on election eve, Hearst endorsed, at length, the progressive platform of the Independence Party. But he could not conceal his bitter disillusionment of the past twelve years. In summing up the reasons for "abandoning" the Democrats and forming a new national movement, Hearst released the following statement to the press, a satisfying coup de grâce to his flawed idol: "I admit frankly and freely that I have utterly and absolutely lost confidence in Mr. Bryan. . . . I have lost confidence in Mr. Bryan's ability, in his sincerity, in his political honesty and his personal honesty."[46]

The election of 1908 was anticlimactic—in other words, no upsets and few surprises. Just as the political pundits predicted, Taft defeated Bryan convincingly both in the popular and electoral college count—and Hisgen registered an infinitesimal vote, a little more than 83,000 out of almost 15 million cast. In New York, Hughes won an easy victory for governor over Chanler, with Shearn a distant third. And while the Republicans were victorious overall throughout the state, the Independence Party showing was abysmal.

Hearst had difficulty rationalizing this "humiliating" defeat. Although the Democrats and Republicans were obviously "corrupt," voters had rejected the Independence Party crusade that had stressed basic reforms. "The progressive battle is long from over," he wrote Brisbane two weeks after the election. "The people have been awakened to the injustices and inequities in American society. They are ready to act, I believe, to force a change."

Hollow words, indeed! Hearst, besides having no basis in fact for his statements, was an incurable optimist, seemingly unwilling to recognize the inevitable fate of third parties in American history. More importantly, he still enjoyed the game of politics, especially the excitement of a campaign and the approbation of the crowds; such experiences continued to color his judgment and influence his actions. In a final thought to Brisbane, he asserted: "There is so much that needs to be done to ensure the success of progressivism—let us do our share to ensure its success."[47]

In mid-December, 1908, six weeks after the Independence Party debacle, Hearst emerged from the shadows of election defeat, ready once more to do battle. His recuperation was relatively painless because he and Brisbane had previously forged for his political future a successful modus operandi. They intended to instill permanently in the minds of New Yorkers that the *American* and *Evening Journal* were the defenders of truth and the protectors of the people, or more specifically the foremost advocates of urban reform. Voters must necessarily equate any contributions effected by these newspapers with the name of William Randolph Hearst. What better way to prepare for another political campaign when the opportunity should arise?

As a result, the Hearst newspapers became fervent advocates for reform as well as staunch promoters of their owner's accomplishments. In January and February, 1909, headlines repeatedly trumpeted the triumph of the *American*'s fight for "80 CENT GAS" on behalf of New Yorkers. In following its prescribed "crusade formula," the *American* promoted a mass meeting that heaped praise on Hearst, then daily printed a "coupon" to register consumers with the newly established "American Gas Bureau," whereby, with the assistance of Hearst attorney Clarence Shearn, the public would receive refunds totaling $12 million. With regularity in the pages of the *American*, stories and editorials, indicative of the Hearst-Brisbane campaign ploy, also appeared. Such headlines were typical: "MASS MEETING COMMENDS W.R. HEARST'S LONG FIGHT" (January 15); "The New President of Cuba Cables Thanks to Mr. Hearst After 2d Birth of the Republic" (January 31); "U.S. Supreme Ct. Upholds Hearst Proof of Sugar Rebating" (February 24); "Goldhammer Fund [relief for a widow and her four children] Is Headed by Mr. Hearst with $500" (March 3).[48]

During the spring and summer of 1909 the tactics remained much the same; only the subject matter was different. As in the past the *American* continued to cater to the immigrants and the working classes in the inner city, to identify with the poor and downtrodden everywhere, by intermittently launching popular crusades or insisting on necessary urban reforms. On March 20, after a small boy was abducted, the *American* offered a $2,000 reward for information leading to his recovery, then upon his return four days later raised the amount to $10,000 for "the arrest and conviction" of the kidnappers. In April and May editorials continually demanded municipal ownership of railroads, "playgrounds for children" and "parks for people," equal pay for women teachers, and an eight-hour day for city workers. And in June and July, Hearst advocated, and contributed $500 to, a summer camp for several thousand newsboys, a community project that New Yorkers roundly approved of and praised. But the most ingenious idea was the establishment of an "American Information Bureau" on May 25, where New Yorkers, "free of charge," could find "answers to scientific, literary, and other 'bookish' questions," as well as receive aid, "upon request, in the simple problems of everyday life." This free information service was, the *American* proclaimed, "AN UNPARALLELED FEATURE IN JOURNALISM" that provided a trained staff of professional researchers for the Greater New York area. As a result, during the summer of 1909, the *American* closely identified with subscribers as "the newspaper that cares."[49]

Hearst, because of such grievous setbacks in state and national politics over the past three years, decided to position himself above the political fray, leaving his candidacy as a solution when all other possibilities had failed. Of course, he intended to choreograph and stage a production in which the only sensible choice would be William Randolph Hearst. Hence, with the help of Brisbane, Ihmsen, and Shearn, he chartered a calculated course leading to his future availability. On December 14, 1908, he addressed a nonpartisan banquet in New York City, stating that the Independence Party would succeed only with a truly progressive platform. For the next seven months the Hearst newspaper empire embarked on a national reform agenda, not unlike previous years, but more in the vein of quiet confidence and absolute certainty. Because President Roosevelt and Governor Hughes had "adopted" many of Hearst's ideas, the *American* proclaimed that railroad regulation, trust enforcement, and direct nominations at conventions (instead of a slate by party bosses) were becoming realities. Nor were postal savings banks, direct election of U.S. senators, and a graduated income tax—all to the benefit of the average American—far from legislative enactment. And woman's suffrage, *American* editorials predicted, "is sure to come."[50]

In the midst of all this journalistic rhetoric Hearst depended on Ihmsen and Shearn to reorganize and rebuild the Independence Party to fit his specifications—meaning complete control by its "patron saint." At the

Hotel Knickerbocker on April 17, 1909, the Third Annual Independence League banquet was representative of their handiwork. Of course, Hearst delivered the major address. When Judge Leroy R. Crane, in an introduction, "pointed out Mr. Hearst," the *American* reported, "as the most logical candidate for mayor in the coming municipal election," the audience responded with "great enthusiasm," the room reverberating to the cheers of "Hearst! Hearst!" In turn, the "patron saint" proceeded to recount the outstanding accomplishments of the Independence Party. But "the possibilities of achievement ahead of it," Hearst assessed, "are ten times as great as the record of achievement behind it." He then announced: "I intend to take an active interest in politics, as every good citizen should. But I have made a hard and fast agreement with ... [Independence League chairman Charles E.] Gehring that I shall not again be asked under any circumstances to run for office." Yet, he did not say specifically that he would never again be a candidate. And thereafter, with Judge Otto Rosalsky and Gehring and Shearn leading the way, the Hearst drumbeat began to increase in sound and intensity.[51]

To prepare himself for the rigors of an anticipated fall campaign, Hearst sailed to Europe in the summer of 1909, in what was becoming an annual ritual and vacation event. At the end of August, however, he returned to New York, renewed in spirit and invigorated in health, ready for one last battle—and immediately he established his presence. On September 3 Hearst set forth his ideas for the campaign. The Independence League, with "better candidates, better principles and, I believe, a greater number of voters," should support a full ticket. Yet he was not necessarily against fusion, provided that the Murphy forces were not included. As he announced on September 9, "Tammany Hall stands before the community as a convicted criminal." Hence, for the next two weeks, Hearst endorsed a "Committee of 100," composed of Republicans, labor unionists, and Independence Leaguers, to formulate a platform and select candidates upon whom they could all agree.[52]

But Hearst, in order to achieve his ultimate objective as a candidate, needed to marshall the Independence League forces through the dangerous quagmires of city politics. His task would not be easy. While building momentum for his own nomination, he must eliminate potential opponents without appearing to do so. Hearst relied on Charles Gehring, who represented the Independence forces on the "Committee of 100," to further their planned objective. At different times over the next two weeks (September 9-23) Gehring praised separately and together sixty-eight-year-old William M. Ivins, who was the Republican mayoral candidate in

1905 and thereafter a staunch supporter of Hearst, and fifty-two-year-old Henry L. Stimson, the U.S. attorney for the Southern District of New York who had successfully prosecuted the "criminal trusts" during his tenure in office. Gehring announced that both were acceptable to the Independence Party; however, he recognized that neither had enough overall support to win nomination. Hence, after much bickering over various candidates and platform planks, the *Tribune* announced, "HEARST MEN LEAVE 100." And all the while, Hearst-for-mayor stories—as well as rumors—continued to appear in the major New York newspapers with increasing regularity.[53]

With one part of the plan successfully concluded, Hearst then dispensed with another opponent rather easily and with relatively few repercussions. After the remaining members of the "Committee of 100," as well as the Republicans, in convention, nominated for mayor Otto T. Bannard, who as the president of the New York Trust Company and "a personal friend of President Taft" was "the ideal businessman's candidate," Hearst immediately rejected this rival. No Independence Party support would be forthcoming, he bluntly asserted, because of Bannard's "negative attitude," which resulted either from an "unwillingness to talk" about urban issues or, even worse, his "inability to think."[54]

Judge William J. Gaynor, however, was much more formidable—and could not be disposed of so cavalierly. An eminent jurist who had achieved a deserved reputation as a crusader against municipal corruption, he was a self-professed Democrat who had maintained an independence above party factions, a man of confidence and character who, like Hearst, had advocated labor reform and the municipal ownership of railroads. He was, without a doubt, the most attractive candidate available, a fact that Tammany chief Charles Francis Murphy readily recognized. So on September 29 the Democrats, in convention, nominated Gaynor with strong backing from Tammany.

To these fast-breaking political events, Hearst reacted in such a confusing and contradictory way during the first week in October as to defy logical explanation, that is, except for those who understood his intense desire for public office. He asked Gaynor to repudiate Tammany; otherwise, he and the Independence Party would not endorse him. What irony! In the gubernatorial election of 1906, Hearst had faced the same problem and resolved it to his own satisfaction. Judge Seabury, who had been a major player in state reform and a close confidant of Hearst but had rejected the third-party Independence movement in 1908, put it best: "Mr. Hearst, through his newspapers, has repeatedly praised Justice Gaynor and

pointed out that he was an ideal candidate for mayor." But "he is now unwilling that Justice Gaynor should succeed where he himself has failed.…
In other words, he will support Justice Gaynor only upon the condition
that Justice Gaynor will attempt to ensure his own defeat." And then
Seabury trenchantly observed: "It is not so long ago that Mr. Hearst saw
no impropriety in accepting for himself a Democratic endorsement."[55]

Yet Hearst, although at times uncertain as to tactics, remained resolute
in purpose. No question about it, he despised Tammany, but he also relished the opportunity to serve the public. He therefore jockeyed repeatedly to obtain a feasible position in the eyes of the voters. As late as
October 3, Hearst wrote Brisbane that "I can still support Gaynor because he is running on a platform made up almost exclusively of Independence League demands." Three days later a *Tribune* headline read
"HEARST FOR GAYNOR." And at each gathering and to every reporter, he
continued to reject the idea of his own candidacy—"it would not be best
for our principles."

But beneath the surface Hearst was orchestrating a "voluntary draft"
from the people. Charles Gehring commented to a *Tribune* reporter that
Hearst was still the choice of the Independence League and, at the appropriate time, would "not shirk his duty." Almost simultaneously, a paid political announcement appeared in the *Times* urging "voters of New York"
to nominate "Hearst for mayor." And on October 6, the Independence
League convention, which Hearst had purposely postponed for a week in
anticipation of a Tammany endorsement of Gaynor, assembled to elect its
own slate. The *Times* headline revealed the result: "HEARST MUST RUN,
CRY 3,000 LEAGUERS." The delegates appointed a "committee of five" to
implore their candidate—who was intentionally not present for his own
coronation—to be responsive to the popular demand. On October 8, in a
prepared letter, Hearst, bowing to their "will and judgment," accepted.[56]

In this "last fight" to achieve public office, Hearst applied the tactics and
techniques that had proven effective in past crusades. Although the *Tribune*, late in the campaign, claimed that he expended "relatively little effort
as compared to four years ago," his actions during the next twenty-four
days did not support that conclusion. As always, Hearst supplied whatever money was necessary for this costly campaign. After leasing the two
floors of the Hermitage Hotel as a central headquarters, he directed his
managers to rent the best available convention space in Greater New York,
deciding to concentrate on four or five major addresses each night rather
than, as in the past, following an exhaustive speaking schedule at ten to
twelve smaller meetings. The audiences at each of these political exhibi-

tions received the usual "Hearst treatment," the lecture hall decorated with balloons and bunting and flags, walls plastered with life-size pictures of their standard-bearer, uniformed bands entertaining the people until the candidate arrived, and at times the sky glittering and bursting with fireworks—a first-class production characteristically extravagant. And, for the first time in any of his canvasses, Hearst paid for full-page political ads in rival newspapers, one in the *Times* beginning with this headline: "WHAT MR. HEARST WILL DO IF ELECTED MAYOR."[57]

The *American* and *Evening Journal* were unblushing propaganda tracts for Hearst. Brisbane, an astute choreographer of campaigns, inevitably portrayed his candidate with motives and actions approaching sainthood while depicting the opposition as base and false and ugly. The New York City mayoral campaign of 1909 was no exception. At the behest of civic-minded reformers, of prominent newspapers such as the *Times* and *World*, and of those New Yorkers who needed a champion to defend their rights, Hearst had reluctantly entered the race to bring honesty to government, the *American* informed its readers. He alone could defeat the "Tammany tiger." He alone had the strength of character and the wherewithal to "turn the rascals out." As Brisbane proclaimed in one editorial after another, "The Only Way to Beat Tammany Is to Vote for Hearst." The *American* political cartoons were equally venal in their portrayal of the Gaynor-Murphy association, attributing base instincts to both men. At the same time, Brisbane published full-page testimonials praising Hearst, under such groupings as "prominent editors," the "country's press," German-American leaders, suffragettes, independent Democrats, ministers, and those registering an anti-Tammany resentment. Then, to impress upon the electorate that a politician should be a "good" family man, he published an endearing picture of Hearst and his three sons, with Millie holding their newest addition, one-month-old John Randolph Hearst.[58]

Hearst also applied his considerable knowledge and campaign experience on behalf of this "last fight." At Carnegie Hall on October 11, before an "enthusiastic" crowd of five thousand, he publicly accepted his party's nomination to "put the Tammany Tiger back into his cage and bolt the door." Without a "dissenting vote," the Independence delegates ratified the platform and ticket of the Republican-Fusionists in toto, except for substituting the name of William Randolph Hearst for Otto Bannard in the top position. Within this same time frame Hearst also instructed Gehring and Shearn to change, through the courts, the title—and symbol—of the Independence League to that of the Civic Alliance; Tammany had once again "infiltrated" League meetings and had "stacked" the Independence slate with their "own" candidates. Hearst thus prevented this attempted adulteration of his party.[59]

As another innovation in this campaign, Hearst assigned Brisbane and Shearn and William Ivins as "attack dogs," specifically to "stalk" and discredit Justice Gaynor. And they did so outrageously. The Tammany nominee, whom the *American* had praised continually over the past four years, was now a man of utter contempt. He was a "bad judge," Ivins exclaimed, whose "whole life" was "a chapter in political hypocrisy," a "self-seeker" who had soiled the bench by working on behalf of "racetracks and gambling." Shearn was just as vicious, charging that Gaynor had become "a partner" of the "Tammany ballot-box stuffers." And Brisbane assaulted equally the judge's character and principles, proclaiming him to be "the unblushing bride of Tammany."[60]

The campaign soon turned even uglier. In speech after speech Hearst sarcastically referred to the sixty-one-year-old jurist as "the old gentleman" or "my aged friend" and accused him of being the new "tool" of Tammany, "a leader of Murphy's hungry phalanx" of grafters and hoodlums. But Gaynor, whom the *American* described as "angry" and "irascible," bitterly resented these attacks on his heretofore splendid reputation and unchallenged public record; therefore, he soon proved the *American* assessment of him to be the understatement of the year. A master at vile invectives and political diatribes, he launched scathing philippics against Hearst that only an individual deeply hurt and bitterly disappointed could muster. Hearst was no longer a man of honor, having reneged, in front of witnesses, on a promise to support Gaynor. In turn, he had employed "blackguards" and "mud slingers" to besmirch his opponent's name, while hiring "a man [Ivins] at the rate of $50,000 a year to slobber over" him as if he were "a patent medicine or a painkiller of some kind." Hearst was also morally corrupt, Gaynor implied, having left California "for reasons well known to a great many people." In fact, he and his top editor Arthur Brisbane were, Gaynor angrily asserted, nothing more than "scovy ducks," shabby and disreputable men who whined about Tammany corruption. "Oh, dear me," he exclaimed, "how long since he [Hearst] was on the Tammany ticket!" Yet every time "he does not win, it is the same cry, 'Framed, ballot boxes stuffed; Murphy did it, Tammany did it!'" Gaynor surely agreed that some members in the national press had named his major antagonist correctly—"William 'Also-Ran' Dolph Hearst."[61]

Despite these vicious character attacks launched by Gaynor and Hearst, the outcome on this mayoral election of 1909 rested on a number of imponderables. The major newspapers were either for Gaynor or Bannard; however, the *American, Evening Journal,* and *Das Morgen Journal* served the largest readership in the city. While Bannard expected to tap the "conservative" vote, Hearst and Gaynor both advocated urban reform, especially municipal ownership of subways, improvement of schools and higher teacher salaries, "80-cent gas," better parks and playgrounds, and a more efficient police force through a "three-platoon" work schedule. Which political camp would progressives support? And even with such an all-out crusade against Murphy and bossism, Tammany was still an awesome political organization that was doing its utmost to rally the foundations of its support, the immigrants and laborers, to Gaynor and away from Hearst. And, of course, the presence of "Hearst the candidate" was truly an imponderable, a "lightning rod" that aroused strong emotions among voters, either of intense hatreds or fierce loyalties.[62]

Hearst, however, displayed no doubts about the outcome of the election, continually stirring the enthusiasm of his supporters by announcing, "I strongly suspect that I am going to be elected mayor this time whether I want to be or not." But no matter what the result, he treasured such poignant moments, such wonderful memories—of thousands waiting for hours in a pouring rain to hear his plans for reform, of the chant "Hearst! Hearst! Hearst!" resonating in a deafening roar throughout a convention hall, of faithful followers urging and pleading with him to lead them into battle against the oppressors of freedom and justice.[63]

On Saturday night, October 31, 1909, Hearst officially ended his campaign at Madison Square Garden, with the Civic Alliance and Republican-Fusion parties meeting in concert. Memories! Memories! An estimated forty thousand New Yorkers lined the streets for blocks, while inside the Garden, the *American* reported, sixteen thousand people, "the greatest crowd that ever jammed into the old building to hear a man speak," awaited their leader. When Hearst arrived, customarily late and marching down the center aisle toward the raised stage, the audience erupted with wild enthusiasm, women waving handkerchiefs and flags, men "tossing" their hats in the air and "stomping on" chairs, the boisterous din continuing without letup for thirty-two minutes until a 150-piece orchestra directed by an "old friend," Nathan Franko of Metropolitan Opera House fame, restored order with music. As the audience quieted, Hearst delivered his last speech as the leader on a party ticket. "My friends, the campaign is over," he began; therefore, "this is not, to my mind, a political meeting, but a patriotic meeting. I am not here to tell any man how to vote, but merely to urge him to consider the important issues, to rise above party feeling, and to do his patriotic duty."

Hearst then reviewed his reasons for embarking on this mayoral campaign, but, he emphatically asserted, his major objective was "to destroy the evil Tammany system and defeat the evil Tammany ticket." And what would be the result? As mayor, with the power to appoint "excellent citizens" as departmental heads, the city government would not only "be ably and honestly conducted, but ample support ... [would] be given to proper progressive measures." Hearst thus urged New Yorkers on election day to "abandon the fetish of party loyalty and vote, not for what is 'regular,' but for what is right."[64]

On Tuesday, November 2, 1909, New Yorkers delivered their verdict; Hearst was disappointed. Gaynor won with 250,387 votes, with Bannard second with 177,304, and Hearst trailing with 154,187. Yet, most of the Republican-Fusionist candidates defeated the Tammany slate. Hearst, in his concession speech, stated that he was "well satisfied with the result" because the "worst characters on the local Tammany ticket have been defeated." Some consolation! As in the gubernatorial election of 1906, he was largely responsible for the political victories of everyone except himself. At age forty-six, the knight-errant, after devoting ten years in strenuous search for the Holy Grail of public office, had failed once again in his quest.[65]

Hearst, although the Independence Party's state candidate for lieutenant governor in 1910, never again campaigned vigorously for political office. Instead, over the next three decades, he directed his energies and genius toward other fields of endeavor—and that change of focus may have been the tragedy of William Randolph Hearst. He would build the Hearst Corporation, an immense communications empire that at its height consisted of twenty-eight newspapers in seventeen cities together with nine popular magazines, all of which were closely allied with prominent news and photo services. But Hearst, whether disenchanted or disillusioned by his experiences in quest of the Grail, would alter his political outlook so that at times it bordered on the reactionary. He had been a sincere urban reformer who had advocated numerous changes on behalf of the American people, yet became a bitter critic of many progressive programs emanating from the Wilson and Franklin D. Roosevelt administrations—for example, his newspapers referred to the "New Deal" in 1933 as the "Raw Deal." He had been a champion of laboring men since first obtaining control of the *Examiner* in 1887; yet he lost touch with them as his empire expanded—labor unions would gradually become anathema to him.

After 1919, Hearst also became more self-indulgent. He built such monuments to his creativity as the breathtaking one-hundred-room Hearst castle on "Enchanted Hill" above the bay at San Simeon and the fantastic "Bavarian village" at Wyntoon on the McCloud River in northern California. He also fell in love with actress Marian Davies and, when unable to obtain a divorce from Millie, moved permanently to California, thereby separating from his family, except for special occasions. Hearst then decided to be a motion picture producer, a field in which he achieved more notoriety than success.

Indeed, from 1887 to 1910, Hearst was at his productive best, building a newspaper empire that would be known around the world, involving himself directly in the political activities of his state and nation, molding public opinion that, at times, helped fashion American domestic and foreign policies. Hearst later recorded what could easily have been the epitaph for his life. "Those were the wonderful days and happy achievements of youth," he wrote. "No grandiose performance of later years ever equaled them in satisfaction." And then he perceptively observed: "Life was not 'one damn thing after another' then. It was one wonderful adventure after another.[66]

Notes

Chapter 1

1. Vonnie Eastham, "The Life of Phoebe Apperson Hearst," MSS, in possession of author, Fort Worth, Tex., pp. 6, 10–12, 14–15 (hereafter cited as Eastham MSS); *San Francisco Examiner*, April 14, 1919, pp. 1–4.

2. *San Francisco Examiner*, April 15, 1919, p. 7; April 16, 1919, pp. 1, 6; April 17, 1919, pp. 13–18; April 18, 1919, pp. 1, 6; Eastham MSS, pp. 7–9, 16–28; Oliver Carlson and Ernest Sutherland Bates, *Hearst, Lord of San Simeon* (New York: Viking Press, 1936), pp. 282–83; Winifred Black Bonfils, *The Life and Personality of Phoebe Apperson Hearst* (San Francisco: John Henry Nash, 1928).

3. Bonfils, *Phoebe Apperson Hearst*, pp. 6–7, 10–11; Mr. and Mrs. Fremont Older, *The Life of George Hearst: California Pioneer* (San Francisco: John Henry Nash, 1933), pp. 33–97ff; Mrs. Fremont Older, *William Randolph Hearst: American* (New York: D. Appleton-Century, 1936), pp. 4–6; John K. Winkler, *W. R. Hearst: An American Phenomenon* (New York: Simon & Schuster, 1928), pp. 29, 33–34; John K. Winkler, *William Randolph Hearst: A New Appraisal* (New York: Hastings House, 1955), pp. 17–20; Carlson and Bates, *Lord of San Simeon*, pp. 5–8. Even in W. A. Swanberg, *Citizen Hearst: A Biography of William Randolph Hearst* (New York: Charles Scribner's Sons, 1961), pp. 4–6, which is by far the most objective of the seven biographical studies on Hearst, much of the legend persists—and several authors have erroneously placed the wedding at "Stedville" instead of Steelville.

4. Eugene Morrow Violette, *A History of Missouri* (Boston: D. C. Heath, 1918), pp. 33–39, 51–52, 61; Ray Allen Billington, *Westward Expansion: A History of the American Frontier*, 4th ed. (New York: Macmillan, 1974), pp. 212–13, 392–95; Frank L. Owsley, *Plain Folk of the Old South* (Baton Rouge: Louisiana State University Press, 1982), pp. 52–57.

5. In George Hearst, *The Way It Was* (New York: The Hearst Corporation, 1972), p. 5, the author stated: "The great grandfather of all the Hearsts came here in 1680. I do not know where he landed. . . . He was a Scotchman, that is, I take it for granted he was Scotch, because all the race were Scotch. My father's cousins, are all Scotch." Older and Older, *George Hearst*, pp. 2–3, corroborates the above information. Yet neither David Dobson, *Directory of Scottish Settlers in North America, 1625–1825* (6 vols.; Baltimore: Genealogical Publishing Co., 1985–86) nor George F. Black, *The Surnames of Scotland: Their Origin, Meaning, and History* (New York: New York Public Library, 1946) lists any surnames under Hearst, Hirst, Hurst, or Hyrst. In an extensive study, Grady McWhiney, "Virginia, North Carolina, and South Carolina Surnames,

Taken from Presbyterian Cemeteries, Gravestones and Church Membership Lists Prior to 1841," MSS in possession of author, has not found the surname Hurst or Hearst listed. On the other hand, Henry B. Guppy, *Homes of Family Names in Great Britain* (Baltimore: Genealogical Publishing Company, 1968), p. 249, notes that "the Lancashire Hearsts have taken the name of a town in the county." He also showed that in 1890, for every ten thousand names in Buckinghamshire, twelve Hursts appeared, while in Lancashire the number was seventeen. Charles Wareing Bardsley, *A Dictionary of English and Welsh Surnames* (Baltimore: Genealogical Publishing Co., Inc., 1980), p. 410, states that the surname Hurst or Hirst "has ramified in the most remarkable manner in the West Riding of Yorkshire, Hirst being the favored form." See also C. L'Estrange Ewen, *A History of Surnames of the British Isles* (Baltimore: Genealogical Publishing Company, 1968), p. 233; Michael C. O'Laughlin, *The Complete Book of Irish Family Names* (Kansas City, Mo.: privately printed, 1986), pp. 27, 202; Robert E. Matheson, *Varieties and Synonymes of Surnames and Christian Names in Ireland* (Dublin: Printed for His Majesty's Stationery Office, 1901), p. 46; Robert E. Matheson, *Special Report on Surnames in Ireland* (Dublin: Printed for His Majesty's Stationery Office, 1909), p. 54; and Edward MacLysaght, *The Surnames of Ireland* (Dublin: Irish Academic Press, 1980), p. 164.

6. For specific Hearst genealogy see Ralph Gregory, "George Hearst in Missouri," *The Bulletin* XXI (January 1965): 76; Billie Louise Owens and Robert Owens, *Sons of Frontiersmen: History & Genealogy of Rowland, Whitmire and Associated Families* (Canon City, Colo.: privately printed, 1976), p. 62; Older and Older, *George Hearst*, pp. 3–5.

7. Violette, *A History of Missouri*, pp. 51–52, 61, 66–72; Gregory, "George Hearst in Missouri," p. 76; Older and Older, *George Hearst*, pp. 5–8; Judith Robinson, *The Hearsts: An American Dynasty* (Newark: University of Delaware Press, 1991), pp. 33–34.

8. Gregory, "George Hearst in Missouri," pp. 76–77; Hearst, *The Way It Was*, pp. 5, 10; Herman G. Kiel, "Pioneers in Meramec Township, Franklin County, Mo., About 100 Years Ago," *Sullivan News* (Missouri), August 15, 1921. The deposition of Silas Reed, pp. 102–4, sets the Hearst property at 703 to 843 acres, while the deposition of James Halligan, p. 265, lists the amount at 775.34 acres, in *Hearst v. Halligan et al.*, Case 120 in Chancery, U.S. District Court, Eastern District of Missouri, September Term, 1876.

9. Hearst, *The Way It Was*, pp. 6–10, 40; Edmond D. Coblentz, ed., *William Randolph Hearst: A Portrait in his Own Words* (New York: Simon & Schuster, 1952), p. 24; Older, *Hearst*, p. 5; Older and Older, *George Hearst*, pp. 13–15, 18–19; Carleson and Bates, *Lord of San Simeon*, p. 5; Winkler, *Hearst: A New Appraisal*, p. 17; Robinson, *The Hearsts*, pp. 34–35. In Hearst, *The Way It Was*, the author admits that he did not know the date of his birth.

10. Deposition of George Hearst, *Hearst v. Halligan et al.*, pp. 131–51ff; Gregory, "George Hearst in Missouri," pp. 78–79; Hearst, *The Way It Was*,

pp. 9–10, 12; Eastham MSS, pp. 35–37. Older, *Hearst*, p. 5; Winkler, *Hearst: A New Appraisal*, pp. 17; and Swanberg, *Citizen Hearst*, p. 5, perpetuate the myth that George Hearst was poor. Robinson, *The Hearsts*, pp. 37–38, gives a more accurate assessment.

11. Hearst, *The Way It Was*, pp. 13–15; Older and Older, *George Hearst*, pp. 34–62ff; Robinson, *The Hearsts*, pp. 40–41; Rodman Wilson Paul, *Mining Frontiers of the Far West, 1848–1880*, Histories of the American Frontier Series (Albuquerque: University of New Mexico Press, 1963), pp. 12–13; William S. Greever, *The Bonanza West: The Story of the Western Mining Rushes, 1848–1900* (Norman: University of Oklahoma Press, 1963), pp. 13–19.

12. George Hearst to John Bidwell, Sacramento [sic] City,October 26, 1853, January 23, March 28, October 27, 1854, Incoming G-Ho, Box 130, Folders 43–46, John Bidwell Collection, California State Library, Sacramento, Calif.; William S. Byrne, *Directory of Grass Valley Township for 1865* (San Francisco: Charles F. Robbins, 1865), p. 76; W. W. Allen and R. B. Avery, *California Gold Book, First Nugget: Its Discovery and Discoverers and Some of the Results Proceeding Therefrom* (San Francisco: Donohue & Henneberry, 1893), pp. 326–46; Mrs. Rowena Turpen, "Miscellaneous Notes," MSS, California State Library, Sacramento, Calif.; Eastham MSS, pp. 51–52; George Hearst to Father [Judge Funk], March 19, 1858, Nevada City, Calif., in *Hearst v. Halligan et al.*, pp. 157–58; Hearst, *The Way It Was*, pp. 15–16; Gregory, "George Hearst in Missouri," pp. 81–83; Winkler, *Hearst: A New Appraisal*, p. 18. See Robinson, *The Hearsts*, pp. 41–45, for a slightly different account. Older and Older, *George Hearst*, pp. 64–67, is mostly fiction; however, it does have enough correct information to warrant reading.

13. George D. Lyman, *The Saga of the Comstock Lode: Boom Days in Virginia City* (New York: Charles Scribner's Sons, 1934), p. 53; T. A. Rickard, *A History of American Mining* (New York: McGraw-Hill, 1932), p. 98; Paul, *Mining Frontiers*, pp. 58–63; Greever, *The Bonanza West*, pp. 92–93; Grant H. Smith, *The History of the Comstock Lode, 1850–1920*, Geology and Mining Series No. 37 (Reno: Nevada State Bureau of Mines, University of Nevada, 1943), pp. 15–16; Dan De Quille (pseud.), *The Big Bonanza* (New York: Alfred A. Knopf, 1947), pp. 32–33; Older and Older, *George Hearst*, pp. 80–82. For letter (in toto) from Hearst to Funk, see specifically Robinson, *The Hearsts*, pp. 44–45.

14. Hearst, *The Way It Was*, pp. 16–17; Older and Older, *George Hearst*, pp. 87–90; Lyman, *Comstock Lode*, pp. 53, 74; Paul, *Mining Frontiers*, p. 63; Smith, *Comstock Lode*, pp. 16–17; Eastham MSS, pp. 52–53; Robinson, *The Hearsts*, pp. 45–47; *Pacific Coast Annual Mining Review, 1888*, p. 10.

15. Paul, *Mining Frontiers*, pp. 63–64; Smith, *Comstock Lode*, pp. 20–24; Eastham MSS, pp. 53–54; Wm. M. Lent and Geo. Hearst to Joe Clark, May 13, 1860, Sec. RG, Archives of Indian Wars, California State Capitol, Sacramento, Calif.; *San Francisco Evening Bulletin*, August 1, 1860, p. 3; *Panama Star*

Herald, August 16, 1860, p. 2; Hearst, *The Way It Was*, p. 18. See also Robinson, *The Hearsts*, pp. 49–50.

16. Hearst deposition, *Hearst v. Halligan et al.*, pp. 131–51ff; Eastham MSS, pp. 56–59; Gregory, "George Hearst in Missouri," pp. 61–62; *Nevada [City] Transcript*, September 12, 1861, p. 2; *Nevada [City] Democrat*, September 12, 1861, p. 2; Robinson, *The Hearsts*, pp. 49–52.

17. Ann E. Hatton Lewis, "Whitmires of South Carolina," reprinted from the *Atlanta Sunday American*, December 22, 1935, pp. 2–7; Owens and Owens, *Sons of Frontiersmen*, pp. 57, 61–63; Eastham MSS, pp. 30–31, 35–43, 46–49; interview with Mrs. Joseph Marshall Flint by William A. Swanberg, January 18, 1960, Columbia University Library, New York (hereafter cited as Flint Interview, January 18, 1960); Robinson, *The Hearsts*, pp. 28–31; Older, *Hearst*, p. 3; Swanberg, *Citizen Hearst*, p. 5.

18. Coblentz, ed., *Hearst*, pp. 24–26; Hearst, *The Way It Was*, p. 9; Eastham MSS, pp. 60–62; Older, *Hearst*, p. 6; Robinson, *The Hearsts*, pp. 52–53; Swanberg, *Citizen Hearst*, pp. 3–5.

19. Eastham MSS, pp. 37–62ff, discusses their relationship in detail. See also interview of Vonnie Eastham by Tom Scott, January 11, 1977, tape 76, Hearst Castle Archives, San Simeon, Calif.

20. Marriage Contract Book A, Nos. 1, 4, 5, and Marriage Book A, No. 2, p. 139, Crawford County Courthouse, Steelville, Mo.; Eastham MSS, pp. 63, 66–71; Gregory, "George Hearst in Missouri," pp. 84–85; Robinson, *The Hearsts*, pp. 53–54.

21. Eastham MSS, pp. 59, 72–77; *San Francisco Daily Alta California*, November 7, 1862, p. 1; *San Francisco Daily Evening Bulletin*, November 7, 1862, p. 3; *San Francisco Evening Bulletin*, November 7, 1862, p. 3; Robinson, *The Hearsts*, pp. 55–56; Swanberg, *Citizen Hearst*, p. 6; Older, *Hearst*, p. 6; Older and Older, *George Hearst*, pp. 100–101; Flint Interview, January 18, 1960.

22. Robinson, *The Hearsts*, pp. 59–61; Swanberg, *Citizen Hearst*, p. 7, Older, *Hearst*, p. 7; Winkler, *Hearst: A New Appraisal*, p. 20; Older and Older, *George Hearst*, pp. 101–2; John Tebbel, *The Life and Good Times of William Randolph Hearst* (New York: E. P. Dutton, 1952), p. 22. During November, 1862, the San Francisco newspapers make no mention of the Hearsts under the columns "Arrival at the Lick House," "Arrivals at the Stevenson House," or "Arrivals at the Russ House." Vonnie Eastham, whose research is exhaustive, did find that the San Francisco Directory for the year beginning September, 1862, lists the dwelling of a "George Hurst" to be 605 Broadway, the identical address of a "Dr. Vincent Gilcich, a physician." See Eastham MSS, pp. 72–78, for historiography concerning this question. In addition, both Tebbel, *Hearst*, p. 52, and Eastham MSS, pp. 79–85, maintain that Hearst was a twin. See also Robinson, *The Hearsts*, p. 60, for a discussion of the possibility of twins.

Chapter 2

1. Swanberg, *Citizen Hearst*, p. 7; Older, *Hearst*, p. 7; Winkler, *Hearst: A New Appraisal*, p. 20; Tebbel, *Hearst*, p. 20; Eastham MSS, pp. 80, 87–92ff; *Nevada [City] Daily Transcript*, June 13, 1863, p. 2. See also *Nevada [City] Daily Transcript*, June 19 to July 25, 1863, for conditions in that community.

2. *San Francisco Evening Bulletin*, July 28, 1863, p. 2; Eastham MSS, p. 94, states that "from the time Phebe's parents joined her until early 1866 when she moved into a mansion on the southwest corner of Chestnut and Leavenworth streets in San Francisco, there is no authentic record of her residing in the city. Where she lived during 1864–1865 is not known." See first four citations in note 1 for "Rincon Hill" references.

3. Direct Index to Deed Book, Crawford County Courthouse, Steelville, Mo.; Eastham MSS, pp. 93–94, citing "Marine Intelligence" column, *New York Times*, November 4, 1863; Older, *Hearst*, pp. 8–9; Winkler, *Hearst: A New Appraisal*, p. 20.

4. P. A. Hearst to Eliza Pike, July 2, 1865, Phoebe Apperson Hearst Papers, Bancroft Library, University of California at Berkeley (hereafter cited as PAH Papers); Older, *Hearst*, p. 9.

5. Older, *Hearst*, p. 9; Winkler, *Hearst: A New Appraisal*, pp. 20–21; Swanberg, *Citizen Hearst*, p. 8.

6. P. A. Hearst to Pike, July 2, 1865, September 18, 1866, November 18, 1866, December 9, 1866, February 20, 1867, March 29, 1867, June 27, 1867, September 15, 1867, PAH Papers.

7. P. A. Hearst to Pike, July 21, 1867, PAH Papers; Older, *Hearst*, pp. 15, 17; Coblentz, ed., *Hearst*, pp. 11–12; Winkler, *Hearst: A New Appraisal*, pp. 22–23; Swanberg, *Citizen Hearst*, pp. 11–12.

8. P. A. Hearst to husband, May 11, 1873, PAH Papers; Winkler, *Hearst: A New Appraisal*, p. 24.

9. Eastham MSS, pp. 94, 97–108, 110; Swanberg, *Citizen Hearst*, pp. 9, 12; *Sacramento Union*, December 7, 1865, p. 1; Winkler, *Hearst: A New Appraisal*, p. 21; Thomas Edwin Farish, *The Gold Hunters of California* (Chicago: M. A. Donohue, 1904), pp. 218–19.

10. Eastham MSS, pp. 121–23; U.S. Census, 1870, Population Schedule, Santa Clara County, Calif., p. 65; P. A. Hearst to Pike, February 10, 1869, January 26, 1870, PAH Papers; Winkler, *Hearst: A New Appraisal*, p. 22. Swanberg, *Citizen Hearst*, pp. 12–13, states, however, that the family "continued to live in style on Chestnut Street with servants and a handsome carriage."

11. Winkler, *Hearst: A New Appraisal*, p. 22; Rickard, *A History of American Mining*, p. 98; Farish, *The Gold Hunters of California*, pp. 215–19; Paul, *Mining Frontiers of the Far West*, pp. 180, 185; Greever, *The Bonanza West*, pp. 222, 239–40, 307–8; Michael P. Malone and Richard B. Roeder, *Montana: A History of Two Centuries* (Seattle: University of Washington Press, 1976), pp. 153–54; Otis E. Young, Jr., *Western Mining* (Norman: University of Oklahoma Press,

1970), pp. 272–73.

12. P. A. Hearst to Pike, June 26, July 5, July 29, October 18, 1868, January 8, 1869, PAH Papers; *San Francisco Alta California*, May 5, 1868, p. 2; *Panama Star Herald*, May 20, 1868, p. 4; Eastham MSS, pp. 111–12.

13. P. A. Hearst to Pike, September 15, 1867, February 10, June 20, 1869, PAH Papers; Older, *Hearst*, pp. 16, 22; Coblentz, ed., *Hearst*, pp. 12–13; Winkler, *Hearst: A New Appraisal*, pp. 23, 24; Tebbel, *Hearst*, pp. 326–27.

14. P. A. Hearst to Pike, May 26, 1870, May 22, 1871, PAH Papers; Older, *Hearst*, pp. 19, 25.

15. Older, *Hearst*, pp. 23–24; Winkler, *Hearst: A New Appraisal*, pp. 23, 24; Coblentz, ed., *Hearst*, p. 15.

16. P. A. Hearst to Pike, February 8, 1873, PAH Papers; Older, *Hearst*, p. 27; Winkler, *Hearst: A New Appraisal*, p. 24; Swanberg, *Citizen Hearst*, pp. 13–14.

17. P. A. Hearst to Pike, March 17, April 3, 13, 1873, PAH Papers; Older, *Hearst*, p. 27; Swanberg, *Citizen Hearst*, p. 14.

18. P. A. Hearst to husband, May 11, 1873, PAH Papers; Winkler, *Hearst: A New Appraisal*, p. 24.

19. P. A. Hearst to husband, May 11, 1873, PAH Papers.

20. P. A. Hearst to husband, May 17, 18, 1873, PAH Papers.

21. P. A. Hearst to husband, June 5, 15, 1873, PAH Papers.

22. P. A. Hearst to husband, June 29, 1873, PAH Papers.

23. P. A. Hearst to husband, June 30, July 13, 19, 1873, PAH Papers.

24. P. A. Hearst to Pike, September 26, 1873; P. A. Hearst to husband, July 25, 28, August 3, 8, 16, 1873; Willie to Papa, July 6, 1873, PAH Papers; Winkler, *Hearst: A New Appraisal*, pp. 4, 25, 71; Older, *Hearst*, pp. 28, 32.

25. P. A. Hearst to husband, August 16, 23, September 2, 9, 16, 20, 23, 1873, PAH Papers; P. A. Hearst to Pike, September 26, 1873, PAH Papers.

26. P. A. Hearst to husband, October 5, 14, November 8, 1873; P. A. Hearst to Pike, September 26, December 10, 1873; Willie Hearst to Papa, October 13, 18, 1873, PAH Papers; Older, *Hearst*, p. 32.

27. P. A. Hearst to Pike, December 10, 1873, February 10, 1874; P. A. Hearst to husband, December 3, 15, 20, 1873, PAH Papers; Winkler, *Hearst: A New Appraisal*, p. 25.

28. P. A. Hearst to Pike, February 10, 1874, PAH Papers.

29. P. A. Hearst to husband, November 21, December 3, 1873, PAH Papers. In Older, *Hearst*, pp. 33–34; Winkler, *Hearst: A New Appraisal*, p. 26; and Tebbel, *Hearst*, p. 57, the authors mention the story concerning Hearst and the eternal light. But they are incorrect in stating that Eugene (Genie) Lent was with him. The Hearsts first met the Lents in Paris after leaving Italy. See P. A. Hearst to husband, April 20, 1874, PAH Papers.

30. P. A. Hearst to husband, April 20, 1874, PAH Papers; Coblentz, ed., *Hearst*, pp. 15–18; Older, *Hearst*, pp. 32–33; Winkler, *Hearst: A New Appraisal*,

pp. 25–26.

31. Coblentz, ed., *Hearst*, pp. 18–19; Winkler, *Hearst: A New Appraisal*, p. 25.

32. P. A. Hearst to Pike, September 1, October 26, 1874; P. A. Hearst to husband (telegram), October 23, 1874, PAH Papers.

33. P. A. Hearst to Pike, December 27, 1875, January 5, 1877; P. A. Hearst to husband, April 30, October 26, 1874, PAH Papers; Older, *Hearst*, p. 35; Winkler, *Hearst: A New Appraisal*, pp. 26–27; Older and Older, *George Hearst*, p. 130.

34. P. A. Hearst to Pike, September 24, 30, November 13, December 1, 1876, PAH Papers; Older, *Hearst*, pp. 37–38; Winkler, *Hearst: A New Appraisal*, pp. 27–28.

35. P. A. Hearst to Pike, December 1, 15, 1876, January 5, 1877, PAH Papers; Older and Older, *George Hearst*, p. 149; Winkler, *Hearst: A New Appraisal*, p. 34; Tebbel, *Hearst*, pp. 42–43; Rickard, *A History of American Mining*, pp. 351–52.

36. Older, *Hearst*, pp. 40–42; Winkler, *Hearst: A New Appraisal*, p. 28.

37. W. R. Hearst to Father, January 12, 1879, PAH Papers. All other biographers state that this European tour began in 1879 instead of 1878. For further information see Older, *Hearst*, pp. 42–44; Winkler, *Hearst: A New Appraisal*, p. 28; Tebbel, *Hearst*, p. 43.

38. P. A. Hearst to husband, February 5, 1879; Thomas F. Barry Diary, May [26] to August 14, 1879; T. F. B[arry] to Mrs. Hearst, August 11, 17–27, 1879, PAH Papers; Winkler, *Hearst: A New Appraisal*, p. 29.

39. W. R. Hearst to Mother, September [?], 21, 27, 1879, PAH Papers; Older, *Hearst*, p. 44; Winkler, *Hearst: A New Appraisal*, p. 29; Coblentz, ed., *Hearst*, pp. 20–21.

40. W. R. Hearst to Mother, September 21, 27, [fall], 1879, PAH Papers; Older, *Hearst*, p. 44; Winkler, *Hearst: A New Appraisal*, pp. 29–30.

41. W. R. Hearst to Mother, September 21, 1879, PAH Papers; Winkler, *Hearst: A New Appraisal*, p. 30.

42. For evidence of Hearst's withdrawal from St. Paul, see Malcomb Kenneth Gordon to Henry [Crocker Kittredge], April 29 and May 20, 1950, Archives, Ohrstrom Library, St. Paul's School, Concord, N.H.; fax from Librarian David Levesque to Ben Procter, February 12, 1997, in possession of author. See also Winkler, *Hearst: A New Appraisal*, p. 30. For those who surmised incorrectly, see Ferdinand Lundberg, *Imperial Hearst: A Social Biography* (New York: Equinox Cooperative Press, 1936), p. 20; Carlson and Bates, *Lord of San Simeon*, pp. 39–40; Swanberg, *Citizen Hearst*, p. 22; Lincoln Steffens, "Hearst, The Man of Mystery," *The American Magazine*, November, 1906, p. 10; Tebbell, *Hearst*, p. 57.

43. William A. Bullough, *The Blind Boss & His City: Christopher Augustine Buckley and Nineteenth-Century San Francisco* (Berkeley: University of California

Press, 1979), p. 77; R. Hal Williams, *The Democratic Party and California Politics, 1880–1896* (Stanford, Calif.: Stanford University Press, 1973), pp. 22–26; Older, *Hearst*, pp. 45–46; Winkler, *Hearst: A New Appraisal*, p. 30. See W. R. Hearst to Mother, May, 1884, PAH Papers, in which he hopes that his father will shun politics.

44. Older, *Hearst*, pp. 46–47; Winkler, *Hearst: A New Appraisal*, p. 30; Swanberg, *Citizen Hearst*, pp. 23–24; John K. Winkler, *Hearst: An American Phenomenon* (New York: Simon & Schuster, 1928), p. 46.

45. W. R. Hearst to Father, December 30, 1882, April 19, 1883; W. R. Hearst to Mother, [spring], June 5, 1883, PAH Papers; Tebbel, *Hearst*, p. 328; Older, *Hearst*, p. 48; William Randolph Hearst, "Biographical File," Harvard University Archives, Cambridge, Mass., lists all of Hearst's courses for his freshman, sophomore, and junior years (fall, 1882, through spring, 1885).

46. W. R. Hearst to Mother, March [?], April [?], 24, 27, 1884; C. J. White, registrar of the Harvard Faculty, to W. R. Hearst, July, 1884; W. R. Hearst to Mother, April 29, 1884, PAH Papers; Samuel Eliot Morison, *Three Centuries of Harvard, 1636–1936* (Cambridge: The Belknap Press of Harvard University Press, 1965), p. 350; Samuel Eliot Morison, *The Development of Harvard University Since the Inauguration of President Eliot, 1869–1929* (Cambridge: Harvard University Press, 1930), pp. 156, 190, 197, 459.

47. W. R. Hearst to Mother, August, [fall], 1884, PAH Papers; Hearst, "Biographical File"; Older, *Hearst*, p. 51; Winkler, *Hearst: A New Appraisal*, p. 32; Frederick Palmer, "Hearst and Hearstism," *Collier's*, September 22, 1906, p. 20; Morison, *The Development of Harvard University*, pp. 75–76, 130–31, 133 footnote; Morison, *Three Centuries of Harvard*, pp. 351, 374, 403.

48. Carlson and Bates, *Lord of San Simeon*, pp. 40–41; Older, *Hearst*, pp. 49–51; Winkler, *Hearst: A New Appraisal*, pp. 31–32; Winkler, *Hearst: An American Phenomenon*, pp. 47–48, 57–58; G. R. Katz to W. A. Swanberg, December 15, 1959, WAS Papers; W. R. Hearst to Mother, [November, 1884], PAH Papers; George Santayana, *The Works of George Santayana, I: Persons and Places, Fragments of Autobiography*, ed. William G. Holtzberger and Herman J. Saatkamp, Jr. (Cambridge: MIT Press, 1986), p. 189; Winkler, *Hearst: An American Phenomenon*, pp. 47–48, 51–52; Swanberg, *Citizen Hearst*, pp. 25, 27.

49. W. R. Hearst to Mother, [November, 1884], [fall, 1884], PAH Papers; Older, *Hearst*, pp. 48–50; Winkler, *Hearst: A New Appraisal*, pp. 32–33; Winkler, *Hearst: An American Phenomenon*, 48–51; Santayana, *Persons and Places*, p. 189; Swanberg, *Citizen Hearst*, pp. 26–27. Mrs. Older, Swanberg, Winkler, and other biographers are incorrect in stating that Hearst worked on the *Lampoon* as cobusiness manager for two years. Hearst was first cited as cobusiness manager in the *Harvard Lampoon*, March 1, 1884, and reelected on October 17, 1884. See *Harvard Lampoon*, Series II, Vols. 7–8, 9–11, Harvard University Archives, Cambridge.

50. Older, *Hearst*, pp. 50, 51–52; Winkler, *Hearst: An American Phenomenon*,

pp. 51, 59–62; Winkler, *Hearst: A New Appraisal*, pp. 32–33, 35; Santayana, *Persons and Places*, pp. 189–190.

51. Three letters from W. R. Hearst to Mother, [fall, 1884, and spring, 1885], PAH Papers; Older, *Hearst*, p. 52; Winkler, *Hearst: An American Phenomenon*, pp. 50–51; Winkler, *Hearst: A New Appraisal*, p. 35; Swanberg, *Citizen Hearst*, p. 28.

52. Three letters from W. R. Hearst to Mother, [fall, 1884], PAH Papers.

53. W. R. Hearst to Mama and Papa, [fall, 1884]; W. R. Hearst to Mother, [November, 1884]; two letters from W. R. Hearst to Mama, [fall, 1884], PAH Papers; Winkler, *Hearst: A New Appraisal*, pp. 33–34; Older, *Hearst*, pp. 52–53; Winkler, *Hearst: An American Phenomenon*, p. 49; Carlson and Bates, *Lord of San Simeon*, p. 42; Swanberg, *Citizen Hearst*, pp. 28–29; Allan Nevins, *Grover Cleveland: A Study in Courage* (New York: Dodd, Mead, 1958), pp. 184–87; Florence Finch Kelly, *Flowing Stream: The Story of Fifty-six Years in American Newspaper Life* (New York: E. P. Dutton, 1939), pp. 239–40; James Creelman, "The Real Mr. Hearst," *Pearson's Magazine*, September, 1906, p. 256.

54. "Faculty Records," New Series, IV, 1884–87, MS, pp. 30, 68, 91, Harvard University Archives, Cambridge; W. R. Hearst to Mother, [spring, 1885], PAH Papers; Winkler, *Hearst: A New Appraisal*, p. 35; Older, *Hearst*, pp. 54–55; Swanberg, *Citizen Hearst*, pp. 32–33.

55. W. R. Hearst to Mother, [spring, 1885], PAH Papers; Coblentz, ed., *Hearst*, pp. 21–22; Winkler, *Hearst: A New Appraisal*, p. 38; Winkler, *Hearst: An American Phenomenon*, p. 58; Lundberg, *Imperial Hearst*, p. 20; Carlson and Bates, *Lord of San Simeon*, p. 43; Swanberg, *Citizen Hearst*, p. 33.

56. "Faculty Records," pp. 141, 215. While Swanberg, *Citizen Hearst*, p. 33, states that he was assured that Hearst did not return after the spring term, Older, *Hearst*, pp. 61, 63, incorrectly places Hearst at Harvard during the fall of 1885. Other biographers either followed Mrs. Older's misinformation or ignored the matter.

Chapter 3

1. *Tenth U.S. Census*, Schedule I: Population, San Francisco, Calif., p. 382; Williams, *The Democratic Party and California Politics, 1880–1896*, p. 4; Bullough, *The Blind Boss*, pp. 28–47ff, 55–62, 65–66, 72–95ff, 100–103, 277 (note 24); William Issel and Robert W. Cherny, *San Francisco, 1865–1932: Politics, Power, and Urban Development* (Berkeley: University of California Press, 1986), pp. 23–34, 102–3; Terrence J. McDonald, *The Parameters of Urban Fiscal Policy: Socioeconomic Change and Political Culture in San Francisco, 1860–1906* (Berkeley: University of California Press, 1986), pp. 19–32, 60, 93–96, 98–99; John S. Hittell, *The History of the City of San Francisco and Incidentally of the State of California* (San Francisco: A. L. Bancroft, 1878), pp. 381–404; Rockwell D. Hunt and Nellie Van de Grift Sanchez, *A Short History of California* (New York: Thomas Y. Crowell, 1929), pp. 425–32.

2. Bullough, *The Blind Boss*, pp. 37, 100–112; Hittell, *San Francisco*, pp. 235–37, 241–43, 245–49, 241–77ff; Williams, *The Democratic Party and California Politics, 1880–1896*, pp. 4–5, 7–20; Issel and Cherny, *San Francisco*, pp. 53–82.

3. Hunt and Sanchez, *A Short History of California*, pp. 436–50, 529–46; Bullough, *The Blind Boss*, pp. 66–67; Allen Stanley Lane, *Emperor Norton: The Mad Monarch of America* (Caldwell, Idaho: Caxton Printers, 1939), pp. 72–79, 80; Issel and Cherny, *San Francisco*, pp. 126–33; McDonald, *San Francisco*, pp. 123–25; Hittell, *San Francisco*, p. 443; Rudyard Kipling, *American Notes* (Freeport, N.Y.: Books for Libraries Press, 1972), p. 22.

4. PAH to husband, October 22, 28, November 12, 19, 1885, PAH Papers; J. P. Oliver to WRH, February 6, 1886, ibid.; WRH to Mother, [summer, 1885], WRH to Father, [summer, 1886], WRH Papers.

5. PAH to husband, October 22, 1885; W. R. Hearst to Father, November 23, 1885, WRH Papers; Williams, *The Democratic Party and California Politics, 1880–1896*, pp. 96–97; Swanberg, *Citizen Hearst*, pp. 31–32, 35; Older, *Hearst*, p. 58; Edith Dobie, *The Political Career of Stephen Mallory White* (Palo Alto, Calif.: Stanford University Press, 1927), p. 31.

6. Coblentz, ed., *Hearst*, p. 31; Swanberg, *Citizen Hearst*, pp. 26–27, 34; *Collier's*, February 18, 1911; Winkler, *Hearst: An American Phenomenon*, p. 59.

7. W. R. Hearst to Father, [1885], W. R. Hearst to Papa, January 4, 1885, WRH Papers; W. R. Hearst to Father, January 25, 1886, PAH Papers; Older, *Hearst*, pp. 61–62; Winkler, *Hearst: A New Appraisal*, pp. 4, 6, 36–37; Carlson and Bates, *Hearst, Lord of San Simeon*, pp. 44–45; Lincoln Steffens, "Hearst, The Man of Mystery," p. 11; W. A. Swanberg, *Pulitzer* (New York: Charles Scribner's Sons, 1967), pp. 102, 131.

8. W. R. Hearst to Father, [1885], WRH Papers; reprinted in Older, *Hearst*, pp. 61–63, and in Swanberg, *Citizen Hearst*, pp. 29–31.

9. Swanberg, *Citizen Hearst*, pp. 34–35, 53; Willard G. Bleyer, *Main Currents in the History of American Journalism* (Boston: Houghton Mifflin, 1927), p. 355; George Juergens, *Joseph Pulitzer and the New York World* (Princeton, N.J.: Princeton University Press, 1966), pp. 43–50; Winkler, *Hearst: A New Appraisal*, pp. 6–7.

10. James Creelman, "The Real Mr. Hearst," p. 256; Steffens, "Hearst, The Man of Mystery," p. 11; Older, *Hearst*, pp. 64–67; Swanberg, *Citizen Hearst*, p. 34.

11. Winkler, *Hearst: A New Appraisal*, pp. 39–40; Older, *Hearst*, p. 68; Carlson and Bates, *Lord of San Simeon*, pp. 44–46; Swanberg, *Citizen Hearst*, pp. 35–37.

12. W. R. Hearst to Pa, [December, 1886], WRH Papers; Winkler, *Hearst: A New Appraisal*, pp. 39–41; Williams, *The Democratic Party and California Politics, 1880–1896*, pp. 96–97; Swanberg, *Citizen Hearst*, p. 35; *San Francisco Examiner*, January 15, 1887, p. 1; January 19, 1887, p. 3; January 20, 1887, pp. 3, 5.

13. Steffens, "Hearst, The Man of Mystery," pp. 11–12; Winkler, *Hearst: A New Appraisal*, pp. 41–42; Swanberg, *Citizen Hearst*, p. 34; *San Francisco Examiner*, March 4, 1887, p. 2.

14. Steffens, "Hearst, The Man of Mystery," p. 6; Creelman, "The Real Mr. Hearst," pp. 256–57, 267; Carey McWilliams, *Ambrose Bierce: A Biography* (New York: Albert G. Charles Boni, 1929), pp. 173–74; NBC Radio address by William Randolph Hearst on U.S. foreign policy, [1940], in Metta Hake files, Hearst Castle Library, San Simeon, Calif.; Older, *Hearst*, pp. 49, 71, 76–77, 80–81; Winkler, *Hearst: A New Appraisal*, p. 43.

15. *San Francisco Examiner*, February 20, 1887, p. 1; March 5, 1887, p. 1; March 6, 1887, p. 1; March 7, 1887, p. 1; March 8, 1887, p. 1; May 3, 1887, p. 3.

16. In ibid., March 11 to March 17, 1887, p. 6, Hearst ran the same advertisement, then condensed it into two columns in ibid., March 21, 1887, p. 5; W. R. Hearst to Father, [March, 1887], PAH Papers; Williams, *The Democratic Party and California Politics, 1880–1896*, p. 77ff; Oscar Lewis, *Bay Window Bohemia: An Account of the Brilliant Artistic World of Gaslit San Francisco* (Garden City, N.Y.: Doubleday, 1956), p. 137.

17. Winkler, *Hearst: A New Appraisal*, p. 47; Older, *Hearst*, pp. 70, 72, 82; Swanberg, *Citizen Hearst*, pp. 43–44, 52.

18. Jerome A. Hart, *In Our Second Century: From an Editor's Note-Book* (San Francisco: Pioneer Press, 1931), pp. 82–89; John Bruce, *Gaudy Century: The Story of San Francisco's Hundred Years of Robust Journalism* (New York: Random House, 1948), pp. 201–3; Lewis, *Bay Window Bohemia*, pp. 133, 136–37; McWilliams, *Bierce*, pp. 173–77; Paul Fatout, *Ambrose Bierce: The Devil's Lexicographer* (Norman: University of Oklahoma Press, 1951), pp. 155–64; Walter Neale, *Life of Ambrose Bierce* (New York: Walter Neale, 1929), pp. 88–89; Richard O'Connor, *Ambrose Bierce: A Biography* (Boston: Little, Brown, 1967), pp. 153–58; *San Francisco Examiner*, October 27, 1887, p. 4; Steffens, "Hearst, The Man of Mystery," pp. 11, 15–16; Creelman, "The Real Mr. Hearst," p. 257; Winkler, *Hearst: A New Appraisal*, pp. 49–50; Older, *Hearst*, pp. 71, 79, 81–83, 85, 96–99; Carlson and Bates, *Lord of San Simeon*, pp. 49–51; Swanberg, *Citizen Hearst*, pp. 41–45.

19. Neale, *Bierce*, pp. 88–89; O'Connor, *Bierce*, pp. 153–57; Older, *Hearst*, pp. 76–77; Swanberg, *Citizen Hearst*, p. 43; Lewis, *Bay Window Bohemia*, p. 137.

20. Lewis, *Bay Window Bohemia*, pp. 133, 138ff; Steffens, "Hearst, The Man of Mystery," pp. 11–16; Older, *Hearst*, pp. 77, 81–83; Swanberg, *Citizen Hearst*, pp. 41–58ff. For ample evidence of changes in format as compared to the *Examiner* in 1886 and first two months of 1887, see *San Francisco Examiner*, March 4–31, 1887.

21. Concerning sports emphasis, see the *San Francisco Examiner*, March 14, 1887, p. 5; March 28, 1887, p. 5; April 4, 1887, p. 3; April 18, 1887, p. 3; May 2, 1887, p. 3; May 23, 1887, p. 3; then see ibid., June–August, 1887, p. 1; con-

cerning biographical sketches see ibid., May 5, 1887, p. 3; May 8, 1887, p. 3; July 1, 1887, p. 3; July 2, 1887, p. 3; concerning Jules Verne see ibid., May 25, 1887, p. 4; May 26, 1887, p. 1; then daily from May 28 to June 14, 1887; concerning Julian Hawthorne see ibid., June 26, 1887, p. 12 and thereafter; concerning H. Richard Haggard see ibid., July 2, 1887, pp. 9–10; July 4, 1887, pp. 3–4; concerning stage play songs see ibid., March 20, 1887, p. 12; March 27, 1887, p. 12; April 3, 1887, p. 14; April 17, 1887, pp. 9, 14; Lewis, *Bay Window Bohemia*, p. 133.

22. *San Francisco Examiner*, March 27, 1887, p. 1; March 28, 1887, p. 1; April 3, 1887, pp. 1–2, 4; April 7, 1887, p. 4.

23. Ibid., April 20, 1887, p. 1; April 21, 1887, p. 1; May 15, 1887, p. 2; May 16, 1887, p. 1; June 18, 1887, p. 1.

24. Ibid., March 27, 1887, p. 4; April 13, 1887, p. 1; June 1, 1887, p. 4; June 7, 1887, p. 8; June 26, 1887, pp. 4, 9; June 27, 1887, pp. 1, 4; June 29, 1887, p. 4; June 30, 1887, p. 4; Winkler, *Hearst: A New Appraisal*, p. 47.

25. *San Francisco Examiner*, May 19, 1887, p. 1; May 20, 1887, pp. 1, 4; May 21, 1887, p. 1; June 11, 1887, pp. 1, 4; June 16, 1887, p. 4; June 30, 1887, p. 3. For typical examples of *Examiner* editorial attacks on police corruption see ibid., May 27, 1887, p. 4; May 28, 1887, pp. 3–4; May 30, 1887, p. 4; June 1, 1887, p. 4; June 2, 1887, p. 4.

26. Ibid., April 16, 1887, pp. 1, 9; April 18, 1887, p. 4; May 13, 1887, p. 1; July 1, 1887, pp. 1, 4; July 2, 1887, pp. 1, 4; July 3, 1887, p. 2; see ibid., April 28, 1887,p. 4, for advertisement of $50 reward, which had previously been $10; concerning special trains see ibid., May 21, 1887, p. 1, and thereafter.

27. Winkler, *Hearst: A New Appraisal*, pp. 50, 86–87; George P. West, "Hearst: A Psychological Note," *American Mercury*, November, 1930, p. 301.

28. Coblentz, ed., *Hearst*, p. 280; Hearst to Mother, [March or April, 1887], Hearst to Father, [April or early May, 1887], Hearst to Father, [December, 1887], WRH Papers.

29. Concerning Folsom Prison see *San Francisco Examiner*, July 20, 1887, p. 1; July 21, 1887, p. 4; July 22, 1887, p. 1; July 23, 1887, p. 1; August 8, 1887, p. 1; August 14, 1887, pp. 1–2; concerning missing girl, the Clarice Shattuck case, see ibid., August 23, 1887, p. 1; August 24, 1887, pp. 3–4; March 4, 1888, p. 11; concerning one murder, the Louise Duckow case, see ibid., September 1, 1887, p. 1; September 2, 1887, p. 4; September 18, 1887, p. 4; March 4, 1888, p. 11; and the Henry Benhagon case, see ibid., October 25, 1887, p. 1, to November 4, 1887, p. 1; March 4, 1888, p. 12; and concerning young girls posing nude, the Ollie Hutchings case, see ibid., September 24, 1887, p. 1; September 28, 1887, p. 8; September 30, 1887, p. 4; October 1, 1887, p. 8; March 4, 1888, p. 11.

30. Concerning police corruption and Alfred Clarke see ibid., August 15, 1887, p. 4; August 21, 1887, p. 4; August 23, 1887, p. 4; September 15, 1887, p. 4; September 28, 1887, p. 4; October 11, 1887, p. 4; October 16, 1887, p. 4;

October 19, 1887, p. 4; October 24, 1887, p. 4; November 1, 1887, p. 4; November 3, 1887, p. 4; November 5, 1887, p. 4; December 20, 1887, pp. 1, 4; concerning educational issues see ibid., January 18, 1888, p. 4; January 19, 1888, pp. 4, 6; January 22, 1888, pp. 4, 11; January 24, 1888, p. 4; February 5, 1888, p. 13; February 7, 1888, p. 4; concerning tariffs see ibid., January 14, 1888, p. 4; January 27, 1888, p. 4; January 29, 1888, p. 4; January 30, 1888, p. 4; February 17, 1888, p. 4; concerning Chinese exclusion see ibid., December 29, 1887, pp. 4, 6; February 18, 1888, p. 4; and concerning strong defense see ibid., December 12, 1887, p. 4; December 17, 1887, p. 4; January 3, 1888, p. 1; January 4, 1888, pp. 4, 8; February 13, 1888, p. 4.

31. Concerning coupons see ibid., July 2, 1887, p. 1; July 3, 1887, p. 1; concerning newspaper quiz see ibid., January 23, 1888, pp. 1, 4; concerning small ads see ibid., December 28, 1887, p. 1 and thereafter; February 17, 1888, p. 4; concerning new branch offices see ibid., January 18, 1888, p. 4; January 20, 1888, p. 4; and concerning the Democratic National Convention see ibid., January 28, 1888, p. 1; February 4, 1888, p. 4; February 22, 1888, pp. 1, 4; February 23, 1888, pp. 1, 4; February 24, 1888, pp. 1, 4.

32. Lundberg, *Imperial Hearst*, pp. 33–34; Carleson and Bates, *Lord of San Simeon*, p. 48; *San Francisco Examiner*, February 27, 1888, p. 1; March 2, 1888, p. 1; March 4, 1888, pp. 1, 4, 10–12.

33. In 1888 and 1889 the *San Francisco Examiner* is replete with stories about the Chinese as well as unions and "working men." For specific references in paragraph see ibid., January 10, 1889, pp. 1, 4; January 27, 1889, p. 1; February 18, 1889, p. 1; February 21, 1889, p. 1; February 25, 1889, pp. 1, 4; March 3, 1889, p. 1; March 31, 1889, p. 1; July 1, 1889, p. 1. Concerning Samoa see ibid., January 20, 1889, pp. 1, 4; January 21, 1889, p. 4; January 27, 1889, pp. 9–10; February 17, 1889, pp. 1–2; February 18, 1889, p. 1; March 10, 1889, p. 1.

34. For typical examples of daily ads see ibid., March 21, 1888, p. 8; April 6, 1888, p. 8; April 21, 1888, p. 2; December 15, 1888, p. 8. For stories by reporters concerning women factory workers see ibid., March 18, 1888, p. 12; March 22, 1888, p. 4; on milk adulteration see ibid., June 18, 1888, p. 4; on underfunding of parks and schools see ibid., December 16, 1888, p. 3; February 1, 1889, p. 4; on fire hazards see ibid., January 13, 1889, pp. 1, 4; January 16, 1889, p. 1; April 2, 1889, p. 4; on gas overcharging see ibid., February 1, 1889, p. 8; and on cable car dangers see ibid., April 5, 1889, p. 1; April 6, 1889, p. 1; April 9, 1889, p. 4; April 10, 1889, p. 4.

35. For examples of serial stories see ibid. (re Hawthorne), March 11, 1888, p. 12; March 12, 1888, p. 8; March 14, 1888, p. 8; March 15, 1888, p. 8; March 16, 1888, p. 8; ibid. (re Stevenson), March 20, 1888, p. 4; March 23, 1888, p. 5; March 24, 1888, p. 5; March 25, 1888, p. 9; April 29, 1888, p. 14; and ibid. (re Haggard), May 12, 1889, p. 4, to June 29, 1889 (usually on p. 5). For lunatic asylum see ibid., May 6, 1888, p. 11; May 9, 1888, p. 4; May 11, 1888, p. 6; for

Salvation Army see ibid., September 30, 1888, p. 9; for church exposé see ibid., December 3, 1888, pp. 1, 4; December 4, 1888, p. 4; December 5, 1888, pp. 1, 4; December 8, 1888, p. 1; December 9, 1888, p. 2; December 10, 1888, p. 1; for Black Bart see ibid., December 10, 1888, p. 4; December 11, 1888, p. 1; January 5, 1889, p. 8; for "missing man" see ibid., February 13, 1889, p. 4; and "elixir of life" see ibid., August 11, 1889, p. 1; August 14, 1889, p. 1; August 15, 1889, p. 4; September 1, 1889, p. 4.

36. See ibid., April 8, 1888, pp. 1, 8; April 9, 1888, pp. 1, 6; April 10, 1888, pp. 1, 6; April 11, 1888, pp. 1, 6; April 17, 1888, pp. 1, 8; November 1, 1888, p. 4; November 2, 1888, pp. 1, 4; November 3, 1888, pp. 1, 4; November 7, 1888, pp. 1–4. See ibid., December 6–13, 1888, p. 1, as typical examples of free-gift advertisement in the form of books.

37. See ibid., February 25, 1889, p. 4, through all of March, 1889, p. 4—and often on p. 1. See also PAH to Husband, July 21, August 7, 1888, PAH Papers.

38. W. R. Hearst to Papa, [1889], W. R. Hearst to Poppy, [late in December, 1889], WRH Papers; Phebe to My dear Husband, July 21, August 7, August 11, October 16, 1888, PAH Papers.

39. See Older, Hearst, pp. 98–99, for a discussion of Nast. For examples of Nast's work see San Francisco Examiner, March 10, 1889, pp. 1, 4, 9; March 13, 1889, p. 1, as well as succeeding weeks. For "a trip to Paris" see ibid., May 30, 1889, p. 4; June 5, 1889, p. 1; June 9, 1889, p. 1; December 29, 1889, pp. 6, 11–20. For "Written in Blood" contest see ibid., August 16, 1889, p. 1; August 17 to September 7, 1889, pp. 1, 5; September 17, 1889, pp. 4–5. For three books and prizes see ibid., August 11, 1889, pp. 4, 10; August 12, 1889, p. 1, to September 30, 1889, p. 5.

40. San Francisco Examiner, May 26, 1889, p. 11; July 1, 1889, p. 4; July 9, 1889, p. 4; August 5, 1889, p. 4; October 19, 1889, p. 1; October 20, 1889, pp. 1, 6, 31, 37; October 21, 1889, p. 5. Concerning weather report see ibid., October 29, 1889, p. 1. See discussion of the grizzly in ibid., November 3, 1889, p. 11; November 4, 1889, pp. 1–2; November 5, 1889, p. 2; November 8, 1889, p. 1; November 10, 1889, pp. 3, 6. On valuable gifts for subscriptions see ibid., November 19, 1889, p. 6; November 25, 1889, p. 11, and in most of days thereafter.

41. Lewis, Bay Window Bohemia, pp. 138–39; Older, Hearst, pp. 99–100; Swanberg, Citizen Hearst, pp. 59–60; San Francisco Examiner, October 24, 1889, p. 6; October 25, 1889, pp. 1, 7; October 27, 1889, pp. 9, 12; October 29, 1889, p. 7; October 31, 1889, p. 7; November 1–8, 1889, p. 7. For other Annie Laurie stories see ibid., December 8, 1889, p. 11; December 11, 1889, p. 6; and December 22, 1889, pp. 11–12.

42. San Francisco Examiner, December 29, 1889; December 30, 1889, p. 6; December 31, 1889, p. 2; W. R. Hearst to Poppy, [late December, 1889], WRH Papers.

Chapter 4

1. Winkler, *Hearst: An American Phenomenon*, pp. 67–70, 75; Winkler, *Hearst: A New Appraisal*, pp. 44, 48–49; Hart, *In Our Second Century*, p. 87; Older, *Hearst*, pp. 96–104ff.

2. Hearst to Poppy, [late December, 1889], Hearst to Papa, [late 1889], WRH Papers; Phebe to My dear Husband, October 16, 1889, PAH Papers; Kelly, *Flowing Stream*, pp. 240–41; Winkler, *Hearst: A New Appraisal*, pp. 44–45, 48–49; Steffens, "Hearst, The Man of Mystery," pp. 6, 11–12.

3. In 1959 and 1960 W. A. Swanberg conducted approximately sixty interviews with Hearst employees, friends, and associates. Late in the 1980s he deposited his research in the Rare Books and Manuscript Library, Columbia University, New York (hereafter cited as specific interview and date). Dr. Henry Wexler Interview, January 26, 1960; Lee Ettelson Interview, [n.d.]; Mrs. William Randolph Hearst Interview, May 15, 1959; John Francis Neyland Interview, October 13, 1959; James Swinnerton Interview, November 2, 1959; Harry Hershfield Interview, September 10, 1959; C. J. "Joe" Hubbell Interview, November 1, 1959; Swanberg, *Citizen Hearst*, pp. 51, 54–55, 60, 64; Older, *Hearst*, pp. 96–97; Winkler, *Hearst: A New Appraisal*, pp. 51–52, 56–58; Older, *Hearst*, pp. 85–86, 98–99.

4. Wexler Interview, January 26, 1960; Swanberg, *Citizen Hearst*, pp. 70–71; West, "Hearst: A Psychological Note," p. 301.

5. Kelly, *Flowing Stream*, p. 239; Winkler, *Hearst: A New Appraisal*, pp. 49–50; Wexler Interview, January 26, 1960.

6. William Randolph Hearst, Jr., Interview, April 27, 1959; Neyland Interview, October 13, 1959; Swinnerton Interview, November 2, 1959; Winkler, *Hearst: A New Appraisal*, pp. 48–49; Kelly, *Flowing Stream*, p. 239; Swanberg, *Citizen Hearst*, pp. 48, 51, 52, 55; Older, *Hearst*, pp. 85, 87, 103.

7. Hearst to Father, December 24, 1889, Hearst to Father [1890?], WRH Papers; Mrs. Hearst Interview, May 15, 1959; Hearst, Jr., Interview, April 27, 1959; Mrs. Fremont Older Interview, October 8, 1959; Swanberg, *Citizen Hearst*, pp. 32, 33, 35, 52, 57; Carlson and Bates, *Lord of San Simeon*, p. 52.

8. Mrs. Hearst Interview, May 15, 1959; Winkler, *Hearst: An American Phenomenon*, pp. 70–71; Winkler, *Hearst: A New Appraisal*, pp. 48–49; Hart, *In Our Second Century*, pp. 87, 88–89; Carlson and Bates, *Lord of San Simeon*, p. 52; Swanberg, *Citizen Hearst*, pp. 51–52, 54, 70–71; Hearst, Jr., Interview, April 27, 1959; Neyland Interview, October 13, 1959; Evelyn Wells Interview, September 23, 1959; William W. Murray Interview, October 9, 1959; Princess Pignatelli Interview, November 3, 1959; Louella Parsons Interview, November 2, 1959.

9. Winkler, *Hearst: An American Phenomenon*, p. 84; Swanberg, *Citizen Hearst*, pp. 60–61, 65; Carlson and Bates, *Lord of San Simeon*, pp. 51, 59; Older, *Hearst*, pp. 97–98.

10. Kelly, *Flowing Stream*, pp. 240–41; "Pancoast Views 47 Years with

'Chief,'" *Editor and Publisher*, March 14, 1936, pp. 5–6, 24; "Pancoast, Mechanical Genius, Dies at 77," *Editor and Publisher*, March 18, 1939, p. 12; Will Irwin, "The Spread and Decline of Yellow Journal," *Collier's*, February 18, 1911, pp. 18–19; J. D. Goratatowsky Interview, April 27, 1959; Evelyn Wells Interview, September 23, 1959; John Dienhart Interview, November 12, 1959; Swanberg, *Citizen Hearst*, pp. 51, 54–55; Carlson and Bates, *Lord of San Simeon*, p. 51.

11. Swinnerton Interview, November 2, 1959; Swanberg, *Citizen Hearst*, p. 70.

12. Kelly, *Flowing Stream*, pp. 240–42; Swanberg, *Citizen Hearst*, pp. 48, 60; Wexler Interview, January 26, 1960; Martin Mooney Interview, October 28, 1959.

13. The author read and took voluminous notes on the *San Francisco Examiner* from January, 1885 to July, 1895. This paragraph is a condensation of that research.

14. Wexler Interview, January 26, 1960; Ettelson Interview, October 9, 1959; Mrs. Hearst Interview, May 15, 1959; Anita Day Hubbard Interview, October 15, 1959; Charles Mayer Interview, October 15, 1959; Steffens, "Hearst, The Man of Mystery," pp. 4, 6; Swanberg, *Citizen Hearst*, pp. 51, 54, 60.

15. *San Francisco Examiner*, January 1, 1890, pp. 1–44; January 2, 1890, pp. 1, 6; January 4, 1890, p. 1; January 5, 1890, pp. 1–2; January 6, 1890, p. 4; January 7, 1890, p. 6; January 26, 1890, pp. 1–3; January 27, 1890, pp. 1–2; Older, *Hearst*, p. 111; Winkler, *Hearst: An American Phenomenon*, p. 84; Winkler, *Hearst: A New Appraisal*, p. 52; Coblentz, ed., *Hearst*, pp. 46–48; Carlson and Bates, *Lord of San Simeon*, pp. 53–54; Swanberg, *Citizen Hearst*, p. 56.

16. Irwin C. Stump to My Dear Senator, February 23, March 22, 1890, George Hearst Papers, Bancroft Library, University of California at Berkeley; Swanberg, *Citizen Hearst*, p. 59; *San Francisco Examiner*, April 5, 1890, p. 1; April 6, 1890, pp. 1, 3–12; then daily to June 30, 1894.

17. For information on "The Ideal Wife" article see *San Francisco Examiner*, March 3, 1890, p. 11; March 9, 1890, p. 16; March 16, 1890, p. 12; March 23, 1890, pp. 11–12; March 30, 1890, pp. 6, 11–12; April 6, 1890, pp. 25–29. For ballot concerning federal post office see ibid., March 31, 1890, p. 3, and then almost daily through April, 1890. For "free ad service" see ibid., April 19, 1890, p. 1, and then continually, if not daily, to the end of the year. For *Webster's Unabridged Dictionary* ad see ibid., April 13–19, 1890, p. 1, as well as ads such as the one of April 18, 1890, p. 7, which ran for months. And for the purchase of a new home site see ibid., May 21, 1890, pp. 1, 6; May 22, 1890, p. 6.

18. Concerning the encyclopedia see ibid., July 2, 1890, p. 6; July 3, 1890, p. 4; July 4, 1890, p. 4; July 5, 1890, p. 10; July 6, 1890, p. 17; and daily or weekly to October 9, 1892, p. 11. For the $50,000 contest see July 25, 1890, p. 4; July 26, 1890, p. 1; July 27, 1890, pp. 1, 6, 21–28; December 9, 1890, p. 6.

19. For references to cookbook and photograph prizes see ibid., August 23, 1890, p. 7; September 25, 1890, p. 5; October 14, 1890, p. 6; October 23, 1890, pp. 6, 7. For $20 prize for guessing ads see ibid, October 2, 1890, p. 7; October 3, 1890, pp. 3, 6; October 5, 1890, p. 6. For the contest for the Most Popular Native Son see ibid., August 24, 1890, p. 11; August 26, 1890, p. 3; and then the daily tabulation until the end of the contest on September 21, 1890, p. 11.

20. Ibid., November 24, 1890, pp. 1–2; November 26, 1890, pp. 1–2; November 27, 1890, pp. 1–2; November 28, 1890, p. 1; and every day through December 25, 1890, p. 18.

21. Ibid., April 19, 1893, p. 1; April 20, 1893, p. 1; August 7, 1894, p. 1. For quote of *New York World* see ibid., December 28, 1890, p. 1.

22. Ibid., January 23, 1891, p. 1; March 1, 1891, pp. 1, 6.

23. Coblentz, ed., *Hearst*, pp. 34–35, relates a story by Michael Francis Tarpey, Democratic national committeeman from California, who was a "close friend and prospecting companion of Senator Hearst in his mining days." As the story goes, Will Hearst lamented that the "*Examiner* had been losing money, a lot of money," but that his father had refused to advance him $50,000 "to make it a paying property." The two thus contrived a plan whereby Tarpey, "in the heat of a campaign [fall, 1890]," asked George Hearst for a $100,000 donation. Then, after a positive response, Tarpey put $50,000 into the Democratic coffers and "turned over to young William for his and paper's espousal of the Democratic principles" the remaining $50,000.

24. See W. R. Hearst to Father, 1889; and Your affectionate son to Father, [December 24, 1889], WRH Papers; see also the *San Francisco Examiner*, January 23, 1891, p. 1; March 1, 1891, pp. 1, 6; March 2, 1891, p. 1; March 3, 1891, pp. 1, 6; March 4, 1891, p. 1; March 6, 1891, p. 1; Coblentz, ed., *Hearst*, pp. 26–27; Older, *Hearst*, p. 113; Creelman, "The Real Mr. Hearst," pp. 254–56; Swanberg, *Citizen Hearst*, pp. 61–62, 64; Mrs. Flint Interview, January 18, 1960.

25. Flint interviews, January 18 and February 20, 1960; Older, *Hearst*, p. 114; Swanberg, *Citizen Hearst*, pp. 62, 63–64; Rickard, *A History of American Mining*, pp. 216ff.

26. PAH to Janet [Peck], October 13, 1892, Orrin M. and Janet Peck Collection, Box 3, Huntington Library, San Marino, Calif.; Ada [Jones] to [Phebe], March 1, 1891; Jones to [Phebe], [1892], PAH Papers; H. B. Parsons to Mrs. Hearst, September 11, 1891; November 3, 1891, ibid.; Mrs. J. M. Flint interviews, January 18, February 20, 1960; Swanberg, *Citizen Hearst*, pp. 64–65; Older, *Hearst*, pp. 96–98; Winkler, *Hearst: A New Appraisal*, p. 57; Carlson and Bates, *Lord of San Simeon*, p. 59.

27. Winkler, *Hearst: A New Appraisal*, pp. 56–57; Winkler, *Hearst: An American Phenomenon*, pp. 90–91; Older, *Hearst*, pp. 106–7; Swanberg, *Citizen Hearst*, pp. 64–65; Carlson and Bates, *Lord of San Simeon*, pp. 59–60.

28. Winkler, *Hearst: An American Phenomenon*, pp. 92–93; Winkler, *Hearst:*

A New Appraisal, pp. 57–58; Older, Hearst, p. 87; Swanberg, Citizen Hearst, p. 65. See Carlson and Bates, Lord of San Simeon, p. 60, for a different interpretation of Hearst.

29. PAH to Mrs. Peck, [late 1886 or early 1887], PAH to Orrin, December 22, 1886, in Peck Papers, Box 30; Swanberg, Citizen Hearst, pp. 23–24, 64; Older, Hearst, pp. 46–47, 55–60.

30. Flint interviews, January 18 and February 20, 1960; Swanberg, Citizen Hearst, pp. 63, 67–68.

31. Flint interviews, January 18 and February 20, 1960; Swanberg, Citizen Hearst, pp. 68–69.

32. For increase in circulation during December, see San Francisco Examiner, January 1, 1894, p. 1. For the opening of the state fair see ibid., December 11, 1893, p. 3. For Mid-Winter Fair Edition see ibid., January 27, 1894, p. 3; January 4, 1894 (all 70 pp.). Concerning the balloting for county exhibits as well as announcements about gold and silver cups see ibid., January 27, 1894, p. 3; January 29, 1894, p. 3; and almost every day until July 8, 1894, p. 12. Concerning the best marksman contest see ibid., February 3, 1894, p. 10; March 26, 1894, p. 5. Concerning the Edition de Luxe see ibid., February 4, 1894, p. 10; February 6, 1894, p. 4. Concerning the Examiner party for schoolchildren at the fair see ibid., February 3, 1894, p. 9; February 7, 1894, p. 3; February 23, 1894, p. 1; February 24, 1894, p. 9; February 28, 1894, p. 6. Concerning the $148,000 contest see ibid., February 4, 1894, p. 1; February 23, 1894, p. 1, as well as every day from February 4 to March 15, 1894, p. 1. See also Swanberg, Citizen Hearst, p. 69.

33. For "Blinker" Murphy columns see editorial page of the San Francisco Examiner, March 4, 11, 18, 25, 1895. For the ongoing story of Evans and Sontag see ibid., August 6, 7, 8, 1892, p. 1, to July 29, 1893, p. 12. But see especially ibid., September 25, 1892, p. 13; September 26, 1894, pp. 1–2; September 29, 1894, p. 1; October 7, 1894, pp. 1–2; and October 9, 1894, p. 13. See also Swanberg, Citizen Hearst, p. 66; Winkler, Hearst: An American Phenomenon, p. 85; Carlson and Bates, Lord of San Simeon, p. 85.

34. San Francisco Examiner, February 27, 1890, p. 1; March 16, 1890, p. 1; April 11, 1890, p. 6; April 13, 1890, p. 13; April 14, 1890, p. 4; March 1, 1891, p. 11; June 5, 1892, p. 13; June 19, 1892, p. 13; July 17, 1892, p. 13; January 22, 1893, p. 3; July 2, 1893, p. 4; July 22, 1894, p. 16; August 5, 1894, p. 16; October 28, 1894, p. 17. For specific sketches on her see ibid., December 18, 1892, p. 13; January 1, 1893, p. 9. See also Older, Hearst, p. 100; Swanberg, Citizen Hearst, pp. 59–60.

35. For size and bulk see San Francisco Examiner, January to April, 1890, then look at ibid., September to December, 1894. For "Want Ad" comment by Hearst see ibid., April 24, 25, 1895, p. 12. The "fac-similies" and cartoons become quite evident in ibid. by the fall of 1892, but for information on Swinnerton and Davenport, see Swanberg, Citizen Hearst, p. 73, and Swinnerton

Interview, November 2, 1959. And concerning political identification see ibid., November 7, 1892, p. 8; November 8, 1892, p. 5; October to November 8, 1894, usually p. 6.

36. Kelly, *Flowing Stream*, pp. 240–41; Coblentz, ed., *Hearst*, pp. 50–51; *San Francisco Examiner*, September 25, 1892, p. 13; October 7, 1892, pp. 1–2.

37. The author found no such story in any Sunday editions of the *San Francisco Examiner* in 1894 or 1895. Swanberg, *Citizen Hearst*, pp. 69–70, cites as his source Carlson and Bates, *Lord of San Simeon*, pp. 55–56, who imply that Morphy told the story to them or that they uncovered it. But they give no extant evidence for historians.

38. Interview with John Randolph "Bunky" Hearst, Jr., by author, in the Hearst offices in New York City, August 3, 1981, first brought attention to Hearst's attitude toward personal criticism. See *San Francisco Examiner*, editorial section (usually p. 6), May, 1893, to June 30, 1895, for criticism of the Cleveland administration for its repeal of the Sherman Silver Purchase Act in 1893 and the passive acceptance of the Wilson-Gorman Tariff Act in 1894. See also Swanberg, *Citizen Hearst*, p. 72.

39. See David Lavender, *The Great Persuader* (Garden City, N.Y.: Doubleday, 1970), pp. 368–73, 427 (n. 34); Stuart Daggett, *Chapters on the History of the Southern Pacific* (New York: Augustus M. Kelley, 1966), pp. 326–28, 402–4; Oscar Lewis, *The Big Four* (New York: Alfred A. Knopf, 1951), pp. 221, 410–11; Swanberg, *Citizen Hearst*, pp. 49, 74. The *San Francisco Examiner*, July and August, 1894, is the foremost advocate of a petition drive against the Southern Pacific. See ibid., March and April, 1895, for the "People's Road."

40. See *San Francisco Examiner*, November 25, 1894, p. 17; November 29, 1894, p. 4, and daily thereafter through December 25, 1894; then January 1, 1895, p. 3; January 20, 1895, p. 17. See also Older, *Hearst*, p. 101; Carlson and Bates, *Lord of San Simeon*, p. 56; Swanberg, *Citizen Hearst*, p. 74.

41. James Melvin Lee, *A History of American Journalism* (New York: Houghton Mifflin, 1923), p. 372; Swanberg, *Citizen Hearst*, pp. 65–66; Winkler, *Hearst: A New Appraisal*, p. 59.

42. Lundberg, *Imperial Hearst*, pp. 50–51; Winkler, *Hearst: A New Appraisal*, p. 59; Older, *Hearst*, pp. 128–29; Swanberg, *Citizen Hearst*, p. 75.

43. Irvin C. Stump to Mrs. Hearst, September 18, 22, 29, 30, October 2, 8, 1895, PAH Papers; Older, *Hearst*, pp. 129–32; Winkler, *Hearst: A New Appraisal*, p. 59; Swanberg, *Citizen Hearst*, pp. 75–76.

Chapter 5

1. Lloyd Morris, *Incredible New York: High Life and Low Life of the Last Hundred Years* (New York: Random House, 1961), pp. 197–214, 234–46; Arthur Meier Schlesinger, *The Rise of the City, 1878–1898* (New York: Macmillan, 1933), pp. 78–107ff.

2. Schlesinger, *The Rise of the City*, pp. 78–84; Morris, *Incredible New York*,

pp. 198–207; Older, *Hearst*, pp. 136–37. See also Oscar Handlin, *The Uprooted* (Boston: Little, Brown, 1951), for a classic description of immigrant life in the United States; and Jacob A. Riis, *How the Other Half Lives* (New York: Dover, 1971), for a grim characterization of life in New York.

3. Morris, *Incredible New York*, pp. 197–283ff. The distinctions between New York City and San Francisco are readily apparent on the pages of the *San Francisco Examiner* from January to July, 1895, and the *New York Journal* from November, 1895, to May, 1896.

4. Older, *Hearst*, pp. 132–33; Winkler, *Hearst: An American Phenomenon*, pp. 96–98; Swanberg, *Citizen Hearst*, p. 80.

5. Older, *Hearst*, pp. 134, 137; Winkler, *Hearst: An American Phenomenon*, pp. 97–98; Abbot, *Watching the World Go By*, pp. 138–39; Swanberg, *Citizen Hearst*, p. 79.

6. Older, *Hearst*, p. 141; Winkler, *Hearst: An American Phenomenon*, pp. 101–2; Abbot, *Watching the World Go By*, pp. 134–37, 147, 151; Swanberg, *Citizen Hearst*, p. 81.

7. See the *Morning Journal*, October 1 through November 6, 1895, for ample evidence of a dying newspaper.

8. *Morning Journal*, November 7, 1895; November 8, 1895, p. 1; Winkler, *Hearst: An American Phenomenon*, p. 99.

9. Concerning the "Age and Youth Contest" see *Morning Journal*, November 9, 1895, p. 1; November 10, 1895, pp. 1, 13; and the daily thereafter to November 17, 1895, p. 32. For typical examples of Davenport's work see ibid., November 24, 1895, p. 9; November 29, 1895, p. 5; December 3, 1895, p. 1. For Winifred Black's stories see ibid., November 10, 1895, p. 20; November 17, 1895, p. 17; November 24, 1895, p. 21; December 1, 1895, p. 27.

10. See ibid., November 7, 1895, to January 31, 1896, for numerous examples of the above material.

11. Harry J. Coleman, *Give Us a Little Smile, Baby* (New York: E. P. Dutton, 1943), pp. 21–22; Abbot, *Watching the World Go By*, p. 145; Older, *Hearst*, pp. 138–39; Winkler, *Hearst: An American Phenomenon*, pp. 98, 102–3; Swanberg, *Citizen Hearst*, pp. 53, 79–80.

12. *Morning Journal*, December 13, 1895, p. 1; December 14, 1895, p. 2; January 10, 1896, p. 9; Older, *Hearst*, pp. 137, 140–41; Winkler, *Hearst: An American Phenomenon*, p. 103.

13. Winkler, *Hearst: An American Phenomenon*, pp. 99–103ff; Older, *Hearst*, pp. 141–42; W. A. Swanberg, *Pulitzer* (New York: Charles Scribner's Sons, 1967), pp. 205–6. See circulation statistics over a six-month period in *Morning Journal*, August 3, 1896, p. 1.

14. Winkler, *Hearst: An American Phenomenon*, pp. 106–7. Older, *Hearst*, pp. 142–43, relates a similar account, as does James Wyman Barrett, *Joseph Pulitzer and His World* (New York: Vanguard Press, 1941), p. 172; Swanberg, *Citizen Hearst*, pp. 81–82.

15. Winkler, *Hearst: An American Phenomenon*, p. 107; Don C. Seitz, *Joseph Pulitzer: His Life and Letters* (New York: Simon & Schuster, 1924), p. 212; Barrett, *Pulitzer*, p. 172; Swanberg, *Citizen Hearst*, p. 82.

16. Swanberg, *Pulitzer*, pp. 206–7; Older, *Hearst*, pp. 136–37; Swanberg, *Citizen Hearst*, pp. 81–82; Frank Wilson Nye, *Bill Nye: His Own Life Story* (New York: Century, 1926), p. 396.

17. Barrett, *Pulitzer*, p. 173; Swanberg, *Citizen Hearst*, p. 82; Seitz, *Pulitzer*, pp. 212–13.

18. See *Morning Journal*, February 4, 1896, p. 2, for a huge Davenport cartoon titled "He Gives It Up," which ridicules Pulitzer's price reduction. See also ibid., February 10, 1896, p. 10; April 2, 1896, p. 14; and April 5, 1896 (60 pp.) for extravaganzas. For prizes and contests see ibid., January 18, 1896, p. 5; January 30, 1896, p. 1; April 27, 1896, pp. 1, 9. For specific stories see ibid., February 4, 1896, p. 11; February 16, 1896, p. 27; April 2, 1896, p. 14; April 5, 1896, p. 29. See also Seitz, *Pulitzer*, p. 214.

19. Winkler, *Hearst: A New Appraisal*, pp. 69, 72; Swanberg, *Citizen Hearst*, pp. 82–83; Older, *Hearst*, pp. 144–45; Seitz, *Pulitzer*, pp. 212–14, 216–17.

20. Oliver Carlson, *Brisbane: A Candid Biography* (New York: Stackpole Sons, 1937), pp. 109–13; Winkler, *Hearst: A New Appraisal*, pp. 74–76; Winkler, *Hearst: An American Phenomenon*, pp. 112–17; Older, *Hearst*, pp. 145–46; Seitz, *Pulitzer*, pp. 229–31; Swanberg, *Pulitzer*, p. 241.

21. Abbot, *Watching the World Go By*, pp. 137, 140–41, 145; Swanberg, *Citizen Hearst*, pp. 89, 105; Winkler, *Hearst: A New Appraisal*, pp. 71, 84, 86–87, 88; Older, *Hearst*, pp. 147, 150–51, 154; Carlson and Bates, *Lord of San Simeon*, pp. 84, 88; *Morning Journal*, September 28, 1896, p. 1; October 11, 1896, p. 38; October 17, 1896, pp. 1, 5; October 18, 1896 (supplement, 8 pp.).

22. For sports see the *Morning Journal*, February to November, 1896, sometimes on p. 1, but always on p. 7 or 8, and usually 3 to 4 pp. on Sunday. Concerning the "Rainy-day Costume Contest" see ibid., June 30, 1896, p. 12. For "Mill of Silence" mystery see ibid., April 27, 1896, pp. 1, 9, and numerous references to June 29, 1896, p. 7. The Sunday editions in 1896 have numerous articles about attractive women. For court trials and juror selections see ibid., February through October, 1896, at times on p. 1, but often in the daily on p. 3, 9, or 12. For almost daily references to Cuba and Spain see ibid., January 5, 1896, p. 1, to June 9, 1896, pp. 1, 9. For circulation figures specifically see ibid., August 2, 1896, p. 1, and November 8, 1896, p. 1. For information concerning *Das Morgen Journal* see Swanberg, *Citizen Hearst*, p. 76; Winkler, *Hearst: A New Appraisal*, p. 62; Older, *Hearst*, p. 159. During this same time period from January to September, 1896, the *New York World*, a really excellent newspaper, was still much larger than the *Morning Journal*. See the *New York World*, April 1, 1896, p. 1, for claim of 732,379 daily circulation for March, 1896. See ibid., April 3, 1896, p. 1, for growth increase on last Sunday's paper—in 1893, the circulation was 273,010 and, in 1896, it was 567,867. The

New York World circulation did not increase much during the next four months, however. In August, 1896, the daily circulation had risen to 769,123 (a little less than 39,000 in four months). See ibid., August 2, 1896, p. 6.

23. Abbot, *Watching the World Go By*, p. 147; Winkler, *Hearst: A New Appraisal*, pp. 69–70; Flint Interview, February 20, 1960.

24. Any number of historical tomes describe this 1896 campaign. See H. Wayne Morgan, *William McKinley and His America* (Syracuse, N.Y.: Syracuse University Press, 1963), pp. 183–248; Charles S. Olcott, *The Life of William McKinley* (Boston: Houghton Mifflin, 1916), pp. 292–326; Paolo E. Coletta, *William Jennings Bryan*, Vol. I: *Political Evangelist, 1860–1908* (Lincoln: University of Nebraska Press, 1964), pp. 127–212; Louis W. Koenig, *Bryan: A Political Biography of William Jennings Bryan* (New York: G. P. Putnam's Sons, 1971), pp. 155–254.

25. Abbot, *Watching the World Go By*, pp. 156–57, 158, 159, 166–68; Winkler, *Hearst: A New Appraisal*, pp. 81–82; Older, *Hearst*, pp. 156–58; Koenig, *Bryan*, p. 204; Swanberg, *Citizen Hearst*, p. 84.

26. Abbot, *Watching the World Go By*, pp. 168–69; Older, *Hearst*, pp. 158–60; Swanberg, *Citizen Hearst*, pp. 84–85; Winkler, *Hearst: A New Appraisal*, p. 82; Robert L. Duffus, "The Tragedy of Hearst," *World's Work*, October, 1922, p. 627.

27. For Senator Richard Bland's daily articles on the campaign, see *Morning Journal*, August 4, 1896, p. 1, to August 14, 1896, p. 4. For typical samples of Henry George's reporting see ibid., September 2, 1896, p. 2, to September 30, 1896, p. 8. Concerning Julian Hawthorne see specifically ibid., August 10, 1896, p. 4; August 11, 1896, p. 1; November 2, 1896, p. 1. For article about Mrs. Bryan see ibid., August 2, 1896, p. 9. See Older, *Hearst*, pp. 160, 161; Abbot, *Watching the World Go By*, p. 169; Swanberg, *Citizen Hearst*, p. 86.

28. For the "Cross of Gold" speech see William Jennings Bryan, *The Life and Speeches of Hon. Wm. Jennings Bryan* (Baltimore: R. H. Woodward Company, 1900), pp. 247–52; Coletta, *Bryan*, I, 137–41. See also Morgan, *McKinley and His America*, pp. 231–43ff; Olcott, *McKinley*, I, 319–23; Herbert Croly, *Marcus Alonzo Hanna: His Life and Work* (New York: Macmillian, 1923), pp. 214–16; *Morning Journal*, August 15, 1896, pp. 1–8; August 27, 1896, p. 3; September 29, 1896, pp. 1, 4, 5; September 30, 1896, pp. 1, 2, 4.

29. Croly, *Hanna*, pp. 217–22; Morgan, *McKinley and His America*, pp. 224–31; Coletta, *Bryan*, pp. 192–202; Samuel Eliot Morison and Henry Steele Commager, *The Growth of the American Republic*, II (4th ed., enl. and rev.; New York: Oxford University Press, 1958), pp. 263–64.

30. For typical Hanna caricatures see *Morning Journal*, August 1, 1896, p. 1; August 3, 1896, p. 3; August 7, 1896, p. 4; September 1, 1896, p. 1; October 13, 1896, p. 3. Especially see article in ibid., November 8, 1896, p. 5, which illustrates "Mark Hanna as he is and as Davenport made him." See also Croly, *Hanna*, p. 224; Older, *Hearst*, p. 159; Winkler, *Hearst: A New Appraisal*,

pp. 84–85; Swanberg, *Citizen Hearst*, p. 86.

31. *Morning Journal*, October 13, 1896, p. 3; October 14, 1896, p. 3; October 15, 1896, pp. 1, 12; Croly, *Hanna*, pp. 224–25; Older, *Hearst*, p. 160.

32. See *Morning Journal*, August 1 to November 2, 1896, for evidence in this paragraph. Concerning the *Journal* Fund see ibid., September 6 to October 13, 1896, always on p. 6. The Fund eventually increased to $37,937.95; see ibid., October 18, 1896, p. 7.

33. For daily references to the bicycle relay race see ibid., August 24, 1896, p. 3, to September 8, 1896, p. 3, together with three final stories on September 13, 1896, p. 1, September 17, 1896, p. 1, and September 25, 1896, p. 16. Concerning the Alan Dale interview with Anna Held see ibid., September 20, 1896, p. 35. Concerning the R. Hoe & Co. color presses and the beginning of the *Evening Journal* see ibid., September 28, 1896, p. 1. And for the first Sunday supplement of comics see ibid., October 18, 1896, 8 pp.

34. Concerning the election extravaganza see ibid., November 2, 1896, p. 2; November 3, 1896, p. 1; November 4, 1896, pp. 1, 12. For circulation record see ibid., November 4, 1896, p. 1; November 5, 1896, p. 1. See also Older, *Hearst*, p. 160; Winkler, *Hearst: A New Appraisal*, p. 83; Swanberg, *Citizen Hearst*, p. 87.

35. See *Morning Journal*, November 3, 1896, p. 1, for Bryan's recognition of Hearst and the *Journal*. See also W. R. Hearst to Mrs. P. E. Hearst (telegram), November 4, 1896, WRH Papers.

Chapter 6

1. Frederick Jackson Turner, *The Significance of the Frontier in American History* (New York: Ungar Publishing, 1963); Ray Allen Billington, *The Frontier Thesis: Valid Interpretation of American History?* (New York: Holt, Rinehart and Winston, 1966); Morrison and Commager, *Growth of the American Republic*, II, 123–45ff, 322–23; Frank Freidel, *The Splendid Little War* (Boston: Little, Brown, 1958), pp. 3–6; Ernest R. May, *Imperial Democracy: The Emergence of America as a Great Power* (New York: Harcourt, Brace & World, 1961), pp. 3–13ff; Morgan, *William McKinley and His America*, p. 326.

2. Winkler, *Hearst: A New Appraisal*, pp. 97–98; Carlson and Bates, *Lord of San Simeon*, p. 92; Morgan, *William McKinley and His America*, p. 326; Swanberg, *Citizen Hearst*, p. 101; Henry F. Pringle, *Theodore Roosevelt: A Biography* (New York: Harcourt, Brace, 1931), p. 174; Swanberg, *Pulitzer*, p. 225. See also May, *Imperial Democracy*, pp. 69–70.

3. Swanberg, *Pulitzer*, pp. 225–26; Barrett, *Pulitzer*, p. 174; Seitz, *Pulitzer*, pp. 214–15, 241.

4. See *Morning Journal*, November, 1896–March, 1897, for effusive praise of McKinley and Hanna. Concerning inauguration coverage and the "New York Journal train" see ibid, March 1, 1897, p. 4; March 2, 1897, pp. 1, 2, 3; March 3, 1897, pp. 1, 2, 3, 6; March 4, 1897, pp. 1, 3; March 5, 1897, pp. 1–3;

March 6, 1897, p. 1; March 7, 1897, pp. 29, 37; Winkler, *Hearst: An American Phenomenon*, p. 131. Abbot, *Watching the World Go By*, pp. 209–10, recollects, however, that McKinley and Hanna received harsh criticism prior to inauguration day. An examination of the *Morning Journal* from November 4, 1896, to March 4, 1897, does not reveal such criticism.

5. See *Morning Journal*, December 26, 1896, p. 1; December 27, 1896, pp. 1, 2; December 28, 1896, p. 2; December 30, 1896, p. 2; December 31, 1896, p. 2; January 7, 1897, p. 5; January 27, 1897, p. 1; January 29, 1897, p. 5; January 30, 1897, pp. 4–5; February 1, 1897, p. 3; February 3, 1897, p. 3; February 10, 1897, p. 1. For the crusade for "Dollar Gas" see specifically in ibid., December 13, 1896, p. 1; January 14, 1897, p. 2; February 5, 1897, p. 1; February 6, 1897, p. 6; February 12, 1897, p. 6; February 18, 1897, p. 6; February 19, 1897, p. 1; Winkler, *Hearst: An American Phenomenon*, pp. 129–30.

6. Creelman, "The Real Mr. Hearst," p. 261. The *Evening Journal* is rife with stories concerning sports, court cases and jury trials, beautiful women and their ideas, crimes and scandals both private and public. See ibid., September 27, 1897, p. 4, for the German community endorsement. For vacations on Long Island for tenement children see ibid., June 9, 1897, p. 3; June 10, 1897, p. 6; and almost daily from June 14, 1897, p. 6, to September 2, 1897, p. 7. The total contributions amounted to $1,901, which the *Evening Journal* matched. Concerning the "Bicycle Contest" see ibid. daily from July 14, 1897, p. 3, to August 25, 1897, p. 7. For an account of the ten cyclists' trip see ibid., September 1, 1897, p. 3; September 8, 1897, p. 5; September 16, 1897, p. 7; September 25, 1897, p. 4; October 9, 1897, p. 4; October 21, 1897, p. 5.

7. See the *Evening Journal*, June 28, 1897, p. 1, through July 3, 1897, p. 1. See also Lundberg, *Imperial Hearst*, pp. 60–61; James L. Ford, *Forty-Odd Years in the Literary Shop* (New York: E. P. Dutton, 1921), p. 260; Older, *Hearst*, pp. 154–55; Swanberg, *Citizen Hearst*, pp. 105–6. Older and Swanberg, however, incorrectly state that "Murder Squad" reporter George Arnold was paid $1,000 by Hearst "on the spot." See *Evening Journal*, July 5, 1897, p. 5, for the distribution of the $1,000 reward to ten individuals who aided the investigation, with $500 going to a saloonkeeper named Martin Cowan. For further information concerning Mrs. Nack and Martin Thorn see ibid., July 9, 1897, p. 1; July 12, 1897, p. 3; July 13, 1897, p. 4; July 21, 1897, p. 4; September 2, 1897, p. 1; September 13, 1897, p. 1; October 4, 1897, p. 2; October 5, 1897, p. 7; October 12, 1897, p. 2.

8. Concerning the "New Journalism" see *Morning Journal*, December 27, 1896, p. 6; January 29, 1897, p. 6; January 30, 1897, p. 1; February 3, 1897, p. 6; February 6, 1897, p. 7; February 10, 1897, p. 6; March 15, 1897, p. 6; March 19, 1897, p. 6; April 18, 1897, p. 42; April 21, 1897, p. 6; October 5, 1897, p. 6; October 13, 1897, p. 8; and especially April 2, 1898, p. 10. Concerning fund for slain policeman's family see *Evening Journal*, October 28, 1897, p. 3. Concerning labor strike arbitration in Ohio and Massachusetts see *Morning Jour-*

nal, July 4, 1897, p. 1; July 6, 1897, p. 1; July 9, 1897, p. 1; July 10, 1897, p. 1; September 4, 1897, p. 1; September 9, 1897, p. 1; September 10, 1897, p. 8; January 23, 1898, p. 45; January 25, 1898, p. 4; January 29, 1898, p. 1. Concerning projects for urban care see typical editorials in ibid., January 4, 1897, p. 6; March 25, 1897, p. 6; May 14, 1897, p. 8; May 20, 1897, p. 4; August 2, 1897, p. 6; September 22, 1897, pp. 8, 16. For stances on city reforms see three *Journal* planks in Democratic platform in ibid., October 1, 1897, p. 5. Throughout most of 1897 see ibid. for promotion of the Greater New York City charter. After March 4, 1897, see ibid., for continual criticism of Dingley Tariff Act and trusts. See also Older, *Hearst,* pp. 167–68; Winkler, *Hearst: A New Appraisal,* pp. 88, 91; Swanberg, *Citizen Hearst,* pp. 101–5ff.

9. For reports of the Russian czar's coronation see *Morning Journal,* May 23, 1896, p. 1; May 26, 1896, pp. 1–2; May 27, 1896, pp. 1–3. For reports of the Greco-Turkish War see ibid., April 29, 1897, p. 1, to May 12, 1897, p. 3, and May 23, 1897, p. 25. For Klondike reports see ibid., August 1, 1897, p. 7, to October 4, 1897, p. 12, then again from January 25, 1898, p. 4, to February 6, 1898, pp. 17–18. For the Fitzsimmons-Corbett title fight and exclusive interviews see ibid., February 15, 1897, p. 5, to March 17, 1897, pp. 2–3. For reports on Queen Victoria's sixtieth anniversary see ibid., June 20, 1897, pp. 58–59; Swanberg, *Citizen Hearst,* p. 107; Joseph E. Wisan, *The Cuban Crisis as Reflected in the New York Press, 1895–1898* (New York: Columbia University Press, 1934), p. 25.

10. For daily criticism as well as a suit against a contractor and commission, see *Morning Journal,* September 25, 1897, p. 1, to October 7, 1897, p. 4. For conviction of policeman Hannigan see ibid., January 18, 1898, p. 7. See the poll in ibid., October 7, 1897, p. 16; October 9, 1897, p. 6; October 10, 1897, p. 5; October 12, 1897, p. 5; October 13, 1897, p. 5; October 15, 1897, p. 14; Older, *Hearst,* pp. 167–68.

11. See all *Journal* editions—morning, evening, and Sunday—from November, 1896, to April, 1898, for obvious changes in format concerning headlines and editorials. See *Sunday Journal,* March, 1897, for the beginning of impressive photo prints. For acquisition of the *Morning Advertiser* and criticism of Pulitzer see *Morning Journal,* April 2, 1897, p. 6; April 3, 1897, p. 4 (Davenport cartoon of Pulitzer); April 5, 1897, p. 6; Will to Mrs. P. A. Hearst (telegram), April 2, 1897, WRH Papers; Winkler, *Hearst: A New Appraisal,* p. 89; Carlson and Bates, *Lord of San Simeon,* pp. 86–87; Swanberg, *Pulitzer,* p. 230. For comic section information see *Sunday Journal,* October 18, 1896, and every Sunday thereafter to August, 1898; Older, *Hearst,* pp. 147–48; Winkler, *Hearst: A New Appraisal,* pp. 67, 71; Swanberg, *Citizen Hearst,* p. 81.

12. For "The American Humorist" see *Morning Journal,* beginning September 26, 1896, pp. 1–8. For "The American Woman's Home Journal" and "The American Magazine" see ibid., beginning October 17, 1896, pp. 9–16. For the new slogan "An American Paper for the American People" see ibid., beginning

January 17, 1897. For praise of flag see ibid., May 1, 1898, p. 61. See also editorials concerning the Fourth of July in ibid., June 18, 1898, p. 6; June 22, 1898, p. 6; June 24, 1898, p. 6; June 26, 1898, p. 25, as well as Swanberg, *Citizen Hearst,* p. 163. Concerning Hearst's advocacy of the "National Policy" see *Morning Journal,* May 16, 1898, p. 10, to June 20, 1898, p. 6.

13. Abbot, *Watching the World Go By,* pp. 212–14; Walter Millis, *The Martial Spirit* (Cambridge: The Riverside Press, 1931), pp. 40–46, 48; Winkler, *Hearst: An American Phenomenon,* pp. 143–44; Winkler, *Hearst: A New Appraisal,* pp. 94–96; Thomas A. Bailey, *A Diplomatic History of the American People,* 6th ed. (New York: Appleton-Century-Crofts, 1958), pp. 452–53; Swanberg, *Citizen Hearst,* pp. 107–10ff. For typical examples on the treatment of Weyler see *Morning Journal,* February 20, 1896, p. 5; February 23, 1896, p. 27; November 19, 1896, pp. 1, 6; November 30, 1896, pp. 1, 6; January 22, 1897, p. 1; January 29, 1897, pp. 1–2; January 31, 1897, pp. 2, 7; April 18, 1897, p. 59; October 10, 1897, p. 1; Charles H. Brown, *The Correspondents' War: Journalists in the Spanish-American War* (New York: Charles Scribner's Sons, 1967), pp. 78–79. See also James Creelman, *On the Great Highway: The Wanderings and Adventures of a Special Correspondent* (Boston: Lothrop, Lee & Shepard Co., 1901), pp. 158–70ff, for his negative recollections of Weyler. For studies about the Cuban Revolution and American involvement see David Trask, *War with Spain in 1898* (New York: Free Press, 1981), pp. 1–59ff; May, *Imperial Democracy,* pp. 69–132ff; Morgan, *William McKinley and His America,* pp. 326–50; and John L. Offner, *An Unwanted War: The Diplomacy of the United States and Spain Over Cuba, 1895–1898* (Chapel Hill: University of North Carolina Press, 1992).

14. Swanberg, *Pulitzer,* pp. 222–23; Millis, *The Martial Spirit,* pp. 41–42; Abbot, *Watching the World Go By,* p. 208; *New York World,* May 17, 1896, pp. 1, 2; Bailey, *A Diplomatic History of the American People,* p. 454; Swanberg, *Citizen Hearst,* p. 108.

15. Swanberg, *Pulitzer,* pp. 230–32; Abbot, *Watching the World Go By,* pp. 212–13; Swanberg, *Citizen Hearst,* pp. 108, 117; Millis, *The Martial Spirit,* pp. 43–44, 77. See also George Bronson Rea, *Facts and Fakes About Cuba* (New York: George Munro's Sons, 1897).

16. Millis, *The Martial Spirit,* pp. 41–43, 46, 48–49, 60. During 1897 the *Morning Journal* is rife with stories on Cuban atrocities. For example, for a three-week period in 1897 see specifically January 13, 1897, p. 14; January 17, 1897, p. 1; January 22, 1897, p. 1; January 31, 1897, pp. 1, 2, 7; February 2, 1897, pp. 1–2. See also Brown, *The Correspondents' War,* pp. 22–40ff, 49–50, 53, 57, 83; Rea, *Facts and Fakes About Cuba,* pp. 149–53; Swanberg, *Citizen Hearst,* pp. 109–11; John C. Hemment, *Cannon and Camera: Sea and Land Battles of the Spanish-American War in Cuba, Camp Life and the Return of the Soldiers* (Chicago: Geo. K. Hazlitt, 1898), pp. 6, 9, 11; Bailey, *A Diplomatic History of the American People,* pp. 452–55.

17. See *Morning Journal,* February 12, 1897, p. 1; February 13, 1897, p. 1;

February 14, 1897, pp. 1, 6; February 15, 1897, p. 6; Millis, *The Martial Spirit*, pp. 67–69; Brown, *The Correspondents' War*, pp. 80–82; Abbot, *Watching the World Go By*, pp. 213–14; Rea, *Facts and Fakes About Cuba*, p. 229–32; Swanberg, *Citizen Hearst*, pp. 112–13; Swanberg, *Pulitzer*, pp. 232–33.

18. For stories on Dr. Ricardo Ruiz see *Morning Journal*, February 21, 1897, pp. 1, 42; February 22, 1897, p. 1; February 25, 1897, p. 1; June 8, 1897, p. 1; Brown, *The Correspondents' War*, pp. 93–94; Wisan, *The Cuban Crisis*, pp. 224–26; Millis, *The Martial Spirit*, p. 74; Swanberg, *Citizen Hearst*, pp. 113–14; Swanberg, *Pulitzer*, pp. 233–34. For accounts of the Ruiz family see *Morning Journal*, March 8, 1897, p. 1; March 10, 1897, p. 1; March 11, 1897, p. 1; March 12, 1897, p. 1; March 13, 1897, pp. 1, 6; March 14, 1897, p. 37; March 15, 1897, p. 9; March 16, 1897, p. 5; March 22, 1897, p. 2; Brown, *The Correspondents' War*, p. 94; Swanberg, *Citizen Hearst*, pp. 113–114. Concerning American prisoners, including Ona Melton, see *Morning Journal*, April 11, 1897, p. 9; April 12, 1897, p. 1; April 15, 1897, p. 1; Brown, *The Correspondents' War*, pp. 38, 39–40, 64, 94, 107; Wisan, *The Cuban Crisis*, p. 323. For more on Weyler and his effect on Cuba see *Morning Journal*, April 25, 1897, pp. 1–2 (Remington sketches); May 24, 1897, p. 1; May 25, 1897, p. 2; May 26, 1897, p. 7; June 8–10, 1897, p. 1; Millis, *The Martial Spirit*, pp. 75–79ff; Morgan, *William McKinley and His America*, pp. 338–39, 342.

19. Morgan, *William McKinley and His America*, pp. 338–43ff; Offner, *An Unwanted War*, pp. 48–51ff; Lewis L. Gould, *The Spanish-American War and President McKinley* (Lawrence: University Press of Kansas, 1982), pp. 27–29. Concerning Evangelina Cisneros, Hearst's discovery of her, and his directives (with slight variations), see Creelman, *On The Great Highway*, pp. 179–80; Winkler, *Hearst: An American Phenomenon*, pp. 147–48; and Winkler, *Hearst: A New Appraisal*, p. 99.

20. Creelman, *On the Great Highway*, pp. 180–81; Winkler, *Hearst: An American Phenomenon*, p. 148; Abbot, *Watching the World Go By*, pp. 215–16; Older, *Hearst*, pp. 169–70; Wisan, *The Cuban Crisis*, pp. 324–25; Brown, *The Correspondents' War*, p. 95; Millis, *The Martial Spirit*, pp. 82–83; Swanberg, *Citizen Hearst*, pp. 120–21.

21. For daily coverage of Cisneros see *Morning Journal*, August 18, 1897, pp. 1, 2, 6, to September 3, 1897, pp. 5, 6. But see specifically the 70 pp. Sunday edition of ibid., August 22, 1897. See also W. R. Hearst to Mama, [August, 1897?], WRH Papers; Wisan, *The Cuban Crisis*, p. 326; Creelman, *On the Great Highway*, pp. 181–83; Brown, *The Correspondents' War*, p. 97; Abbot, *Watching The World Go By*, p. 215; Swanberg, *Citizen Hearst*, p. 122.

22. See *Morning Journal*, August 17, 1897, p. 1; August 18, 1897, pp. 2, 6; August 19, 1897, pp. 1–2, 6; August 20, 1897, p. 4; August 22, 1897, pp. 59–60; August 23, 1897, pp. 1–2, 6; August 24, 1897, pp. 2, 6; August 25, 1897, pp. 2, 6; Wisan, *The Cuban Crisis*, pp. 324–26; Brown, *The Correspondents' War*, pp. 95–96; Swanberg, *Citizen Hearst*, p. 121. See also Evangelina Betan-

court Casio y Cisneros, *The Story of Evangelina Cisneros, as Told by Herself* (New York: Continental, 1897).

23. See *Morning Journal*, August 21, 1897, p. 1; August 22, 1897, pp. 59–60; *New York World*, August 21, 1897, pp. 1, 6; Brown, *The Correspondents' War*, pp. 96–97; Wisan, *The Cuban Crisis*, pp. 326–28. See Swanberg, *Pulitzer*, pp. 236–37, for a different interpretation regarding Bryson's expulsion.

24. Abbot, *Watching the World Go By*, p. 216; Brown, *The Correspondents' War*, pp. 98–101; Carl Decker, *The Story of Evangelina Cisneros* (New York: Continental, 1897), pp. 75–105; Swanberg, *Citizen Hearst*, pp. 124–25; Older, *Hearst*, pp. 172–77.

25. Abbot, *Watching the World Go By*, pp. 215–16; Brown, *The Correspondents' War*, p. 102.

26. See *Morning Journal*, October 8, 1897, p. 1; October 9, 1897, pp. 1, 8; October 10, 1897, p. 45; October 11, 1897, pp. 1, 2, 3, 4, 6; October 12, 1897, pp. 1, 4, 6; October 13, 1897, pp. 1, 2, 3, 6; Wisan, *The Cuban Crisis*, pp. 329–30; Winkler, *Hearst: An American Phenomenon*, pp. 149–50; Swanberg, *Citizen Hearst*, pp. 126–27.

27. *Morning Journal*, October 14, 1897, p. 1; October 15, 1897, pp. 1, 2, 5, 6; October 16, 1897, pp. 1, 2; October 17, 1897, pp. 45–47; Creelman, *On the Great Highway*, pp. 185–86; Swanberg, *Citizen Hearst*, pp. 127–28; Horatio S. Rubens, *Liberty: The Story of Cuba* (New York: Brewer, Warren & Putnam, 1932), p. 240.

28. Frederick Palmer, "Hearst and Hearstism," *Collier's*, September 29, 1906, p. 16; Swanberg, *Citizen Hearst*, pp. 128–29.

29. *Morning Journal*, October 17, 1897, pp. 45–47; Rubens, *Liberty*, pp. 240–41; Swanberg, *Citizen Hearst*, p. 128; Older, *Hearst*, pp. 178–79; Winkler, *Hearst: An American Phenomenon*, p. 151; Abbot, *Watching the World Go By*, p. 216.

30. Wisan, *The Cuban Crisis*, pp. 331–32; *Morning Journal*, October 24, 1897, p. 47; Swanberg, *Citizen Hearst*, p. 129.

31. Morgan, *William McKinley and His America*, pp. 326–47ff; May, *Imperial Democracy*, pp. 134–35; Offner, *An Unwanted War*, pp. 48–50, 66–76; Gould, *The Spanish-American War and President McKinley*, p. 29; Wisan, *The Cuban Crisis*, pp. 346–58; Millis, *The Martial Spirit*, pp. 87–88. For negative reports on the Spanish government's policy see *Morning Journal*, October 28, 1897, p. 1; November 19, 1897, p. 1; November 22, 1897, p. 1; November 24, 1897, p. 1.

32. Mrs. Flint interviews, January 18, 1960, and February 7, 1960; Winkler, *Hearst: An American Phenomenon*, pp. 187–88; Swanberg, *Citizen Hearst*, pp. 104, 107, 115, 130; Abbot, *Watching the World Go By*, p. 145; Coleman, *Give Us a Little Smile, Baby*, pp. 21–22; Older, *Hearst*, pp. 181–82.

33. See daily references to the "*Journal* Campaign Fund" during December, 1897, in the *Morning Journal*. See also ibid.,December 26, 1897, p. 1; December 30, 1897, p. 1; January 1, 1898, pp. 1, 4, 5; January 2, 1898, pp. 37, 46, 60. See

Swanberg, *Citizen Hearst*, pp. 132–33, for a detailed account; the author disagrees somewhat regarding specificity.

34. *Morning Journal*, January 1, 1898, pp. 1, 4, 5; January 2, 1898, pp. 37, 46, 60; *New York Herald*, January 1, 1898, p. 1; *New York Times*, January 1, 1898, p. 1; *New York Tribune*, January 1, 1898, p. 1; Swanberg, *Citizen Hearst*, pp. 132–34.

35. Concerning labor strike arbitration see *Morning Journal*, January 2, 1898, p. 48; January 18, 1898, p. 1; January 19, 1898, p. 1; January 20, 1898, p. 2; January 22, 1898, p. 6; January 23, 1898, p. 45; January 29, 1898, p. 1. For cheap gas and antitrust legislation see ibid., January 5, 1898, p. 7; January 6, 1898, p. 1. Concerning Mrs. Nack see ibid., January 2, 1898, p. 47; January 11, 1898, pp. 4, 8; January 20, 1898, p. 14. And concerning civic improvements see ibid., January 12, 1898, p. 8; January 14, 1898, p. 14; January 15, 1898, p. 4; January 16, 1898, p. 62; January 20, 1898, p. 7; January 26, 1898, p. 2; January 29, 1898, pp. 6, 12; January 30, 1898, p. 54.

36. For typical activities by the Junta, see Wisan, *The Cuban Crisis*, pp. 60, 65, 66, 69, 70, 74, 94; Millis, *The Martial Spirit*, pp. 54, 64. For more on the "Peanut Club" see Swanberg, *Citizen Hearst*, pp. 108–11, 118, 128.

Chapter 7

1. *Morning Journal*, February 9, 1898, pp. 1–2, 8; Morgan, *William McKinley and His America*, pp. 336, 346–48; Margaret Leech, *In The Days of McKinley* (New York: Harper & Brothers, 1959), pp. 164–66; Rubens, *Liberty*, pp. 287–90; Wisan, *The Cuban Crisis*, pp. 379–81, 383; Offner, *The Unwanted War*, pp. 116–18; Brown, *The Correspondents' War*, pp. 112–13; Bailey, *A Diplomatic History of the American People*, pp. 455–56; Abbot, *Watching the World Go By*, pp. 217–18.

2. *Morning Journal*, February 10, 11, 12, 15, 1898, p. 1.

3. Morgan, *William McKinley and His America*, pp. 357–61; Trask, *The War with Spain in 1898*, pp. 28–31; Offner, *An Unwanted War*, pp. 118–22; May, *Imperial Democracy*, pp. 138–39; Millis, *The Martial Spirit*, pp. 95–104ff; Gould, *The Spanish-American War and President McKinley*, pp. 32–37; Olcott, *The Life of William McKinley*, II, 11–12.

4. Wisan, *The Cuban Crisis*, pp. 389–91; Swanberg, *Pulitzer*, pp. 247–49; James Melvin Lee, *History of American Journalism* (Boston: Houghton Mifflin, 1923), pp. 364–65; Brown, *The Correspondents' War*, pp. 122–25; Millis, *The Martial Spirit*, pp. 102–7ff, 110; Winkler, *Hearst: An American Phenomenon*, pp. 155–56; *Morning Journal*, February 16, 1898, p. 1; February 17, 1898, pp. 1–8; February 17, 1898, pp. 1–8. Both Millis, *The Martial Spirit*, pp. 110–11, and Swanberg, *Pulitzer*, p. 248, state that the *World* sold five million copies during the week after the *Maine* disaster. The *Journal* exceeded that output by at least two million. See *Morning Journal*, February 19, 1898, p. 10; February 28, 1898, p. 9.

5. Coblentz, ed., *Hearst*, p. 59; *Morning Journal*, February 17, 1898, p. 1; February 20, 1898, p. 1; February 25, 1898, pp. 1, 7; February 27, 1898, p. 57; February 28, 1898, p. 2. Concerning reports by divers see ibid., February 18, 1898, pp. 4–5; February 21, 1898, p. 1; February 22, 1898, pp. 2, 4; February 28, 1898, p. 2. See also Brown, *The Correspondents' War*, pp. 123–28ff; Millis, *The Martial Spirit*, pp. 110–11; Swanberg, *Citizen Hearst*, pp. 137–38; Wisan, *The Cuban Crisis*, p. 390; Morgan, *William McKinley and His America*, pp. 362–63.

6. *Morning Journal*, February 24, 1898, p. 1; Winkler, *Hearst: A New Appraisal*, pp. 104–5; Wisan, *The Cuban Crisis*, pp. 390–94ff. For some of their stories see ibid., February 21, 1898, p. 1; February 22, 1898, p. 2; February 25, 1898, p. 1; February 26, 1898, p. 4; February 27, 1898, p. 57; February 28, 1898, p. 2.

7. For appeal for "*Journal* Monument Fund" see *Morning Journal*, February 20, 1898, p. 3; February 21, 1898, p. 1, and then daily through April 6, 1898, p. 8; then again in August, 1898. For quotes see ibid., February–April, 1898, especially on Mondays when staffers reported "sermons from pulpit." See also May, *Imperial Diplomacy*, pp. 139–43. Concerning burial of American dead in Havana see ibid., February 19, 1898, p. 5; February 23, 1898, pp. 1, 15. For Hawthorne's series of stories, with illustrations, of Cuban death camps, see ibid., March 13, 1898, p. 41; March 14, 1898, pp. 1, 2; March 15, 1898, pp. 4–5, 6; March 16, 1898, p. 3. See also Wisan, *The Cuban Crisis*, pp. 402–3.

8. Morgan, *William McKinley and His America*, pp. 361–68; Trask, *The War with Spain in 1898*, pp. 31–36ff; Offner, *An Unwanted War*, pp. 122–26ff; Hyman G. Rickover, *How the Battleship Maine Was Destroyed* (Washington, D.C.: Department of the Navy, Naval History Division, 1976), pp. 107–30; Art Young, *Art Young: Life and Times* (New York: Sheridan House, 1939), pp. 195–96; Brown, *The Correspondents' War*, pp. 139–40; Wisan, *The Cuban Crisis*, pp. 402–23ff. For *Journal's* congressional commission see *Morning Journal*, March 2, 1898, p. 1; March 3, 1898, p. 1; March 4, 1898, p. 2; March 5, 1898, p. 2; March 6, 1898, p. 48; March 7, 1898, p. 1; March 11, 1898, p. 1; March 12, 1898, p. 1. See ibid., February 16 to April 10, 1898, for numerous references concerning unity and patriotism and preparedness. For a typical Davenport cartoon about Hanna and McKinley see ibid., April 4, 1898, p. 6.

9. Morgan, *William McKinley and His America*, pp. 361–78; May, *Imperial Diplomacy*, pp. 143–59; Trask, *The War with Spain in 1898*, pp. 31–59ff; Offner, *An Unwanted War*, pp. 123–92ff; Gould, *The Spanish–American War and President McKinley*, pp. 33–53; Freidel, *The Splendid Little War*, pp. 8, 10; Wisan, *The Cuban Crisis*, pp. 403–54ff; Millis, *The Martial Spirit*, pp. 109–45ff; Pringle, *Roosevelt*, pp. 176–80.

10. Concerning "whistle blasts for war" see *Morning Journal*, April 19, 1898, pp. 2, 3; April 20, 1898, p. 2; April 21, 1898, p. 3. For continual references to circulation gains as well as to "W. R. Hearst" see ibid., April 19 to

August 21, 1898.

11. See first 8 pp. of the *Morning Journal,* April 21 to April 30, 1898. But see specifically in ibid., April 21, 1898, p. 1; April 24, 1898, p. 45; April 25, 1898, p. 4. See also for reports on Dewey, ibid., April 26, 1898, p. 1; April 27, 1898, p. 1; April 29, 1898, p. 1; April 30, 1898, p. 1. See also Brown, *The Correspondents' War,* pp. 182–83.

12. Trask, *The War with Spain in 1898,* pp. 68–69, 95–107; Freidel, *The Splendid Little War,* pp. 13–31; Leech, *In the Days of McKinley,* pp. 158–59, 203–4; Millis, *The Martial Spirit,* pp. 185–95; Bailey, *A Diplomatic History of the American People,* p. 468; Brown, *The Correspondents' War,* pp. 190–96; Offner, *An Unwanted War,* p. 196.

13. Morris, *Incredible New York,* p. 213; Schlesinger, *The Rise of the City,* pp. 414–15, 430; Leech, *In the Days of McKinley,* pp. 208–9; Pringle, *Roosevelt,* pp. 186–89; Trask, *The War with Spain in 1898,* pp. 155–58; Freidel, *The Splendid Little War,* p. 33; Morrison and Commager, *Growth of the American Republic,* II, 330–32.

14. *Morning Journal,* May 2, 1898, pp. 1, 3–5, 10; May 3, 1898, pp. 1–3, 6, 10; May 4, 1898, pp. 1, 6, 10; May 6, 1898, pp. 2–3, 10; May 7, 1898, pp. 1, 10; May 8, 1898, pp. 38, 45–46; May 9, 1898, pp. 1, 3, 6; May 10, 1898, pp. 1, 10; May 11, 1898, p. 1; May 12, 1898, p. 2; May 18, 1898, p. 1; May 19, 1898, p. 1; May 21, 1898, p. 1; May 23, 1898, p. 1; May 25, 1898, p. 1; May 26, 1898, p. 1; May 30, 1898, p. 1; May 31, 1898, p. 1. Specifically see Brown, *The Correspondents' War,* pp. 196–201; Millis, *The Martial Spirit,* pp. 198–99.

15. Creelman, "The Real Mr. Hearst," p. 259; Creelman, *On the Great Highway,* pp. 188–91; Abbot, *Watching the World Go By,* pp. 222–23; Winkler, *Hearst: An American Phenomenon,* pp. 160–62; Brown, *The Correspondents' War,* pp. 422–23; Swanberg, *Citizen Hearst,* p. 146. For detailed information about Admiral Camara see Trask, *The War with Spain in 1898,* pp. 141–44, 272–76, 278.

16. *Morning Journal,* June 10, 1898, pp. 2, 3; Winkler, *Hearst: A New Appraisal,* pp. 107–8; Older, *Hearst,* p. 190. See also Swanberg, *Citizen Hearst,* pp. 146–47, for letters to McKinley in part or in full.

17. Abbot, *Watching the World Go By,* p. 223; *Morning Journal,* June 4, 1898, p. 6; Millis, *The Martial Spirit,* p. 163; Winkler, *Hearst: A New Appraisal,* pp. 107, 109; Winkler, *Hearst: An American Phenomenon,* p. 158.

18. Abbot, *Watching the World Go By,* pp. 140–42; *Morning Journal,* June 8, 1898, p. 1; June 10, 1898, p. 1; July 10, 1898, p. 1; *New York World,* June 9, 1898, p. 1; Swanberg, *Citizen Hearst,* pp. 148–49; Winkler, *Hearst: A New Appraisal,* pp. 107–8; Older, *Hearst,* p. 189; Swanberg, *Pulitzer,* pp. 251–52.

19. Trask, *The War with Spain in 1898,* pp. 108–38; Freidel, *The Splendid Little War,* pp. 43–58; Brown, *The Correspondents' War,* pp. 235–63ff, 290–95; Leech, *In the Days of McKinley,* pp. 218–24; Morgan, *William McKinley and His America,* p. 385.

20. Trask, *The War with Spain in 1898*, pp. 178–96, 203–8, 212–24; Pringle, *Roosevelt*, pp. 188–92; Leech, *In the Days of McKinley*, pp. 241–49; Morison and Commager, *The Growth of the American Republic*, II, 332–33.

21. Hemment, *Cannon and Camera*, pp. 62–66; Brown, *The Correspondents' War*, pp. 328–29; Coblentz, ed., *Hearst*, p. 60; Mrs. Flint Interview, February 20, 1960; Winkler, *Hearst: A New Appraisal*, p. 109; Older, *Hearst*, pp. 190–91; Millis, *The Martial Spirit*, p. 163; Leech, *In the Days of McKinley*, p. 367. See also Swanberg, *Citizen Hearst*, pp. 150–51.

22. Hemment, *Cannon and Camera*, pp. 66, 68; Coblentz, ed., *Hearst*, pp. 59–60; Brown, *The Correspondents' War*, p. 329; Winkler, *Hearst: A New Appraisal*, p. 110; Winkler, *Hearst: An American Phenomenon*, p. 158; Older, *Hearst*, p. 190; Swanberg, *Citizen Hearst*, p. 151.

23. Hemment, *Cannon and Camera*, pp. 70–83ff. See Arthur Brisbane to Mrs. Hearst, July 5, 1898, PAH Papers.

24. *Evening Journal*, June 29, 1898, p. 1; Brown, *The Correspondents' War*, pp. 330–31; Brisbane to Mrs. Hearst, July 5, 1898, PAH Papers; Winkler, *Hearst: A New Appraisal*, pp. 110–11; Swanberg, *Citizen Hearst*, pp. 153–54, 156; *New York Times*, July 1, 1898, p. 2.

25. Brown, *The Correspondents' War*, pp. 330–31; Swanberg, *Citizen Hearst*, p. 151; Trask, *The War with Spain in 1898*, p. 180; Older, *Hearst*, p. 191; Winkler, *Hearst: A New Appraisal*, p. 110.

26. Hemment, *Cannon and Camera*, pp. 80–83 (see picture opposite p. 83); *Evening Journal*, June 29, 1898, p. 1; Rubens, *Liberty*, pp. 300–01; Swanberg, *Citizen Hearst*, pp. 152–53; Winkler, *Hearst: A New Appraisal*, p. 110; Brown, *The Correspondents' War*, p. 331.

27. Hemment, *Cannon and Camera*, pp. 98, 116, 119, 130–32, 136–37, 144–50, 173; Creelman, *On the Great Highway*, pp. 194–96, 199, 211; Pringle, *Roosevelt*, pp. 184, 188, 193; Older, *Hearst*, p. 192; Swanberg, *Citizen Hearst*, pp. 152–53; Brown, *The Correspondents' War*, pp. 309–10, 313, 331; Winkler, *Hearst: An American Phenomenon*, p. 158.

28. Hemment, *Cannon and Camera*, pp. 137–49ff; Swanberg, *Citizen Hearst*, p. 155.

29. Creelman, *On the Great Highway*, pp. 194–210ff; Hemment, *Cannon and Camera*, pp. 169–71; Coblentz, ed., *Hearst*, p. 61; Brown, *The Correspondents' War*, pp. 346–47. For the Battle of El Caney see Trask, *The War with Spain in 1898*, pp. 235–38.

30. Creelman, *On the Great Highway*, pp. 211–12; Brown, *The Correspondents' War*, pp. 347–49; Hemment, *Cannon and Camera*, pp. 171–72; *Morning Journal*, July 2, 1898, pp. 1, 2, 7; July 3, 1898, pp. 33, 35–38; July 4, 1898, pp. 3–4. For Hearst's extensive report on Creelman and El Caney see ibid., July 5, 1898, p. 9.

31. Trask, *The War with Spain in 1898*, pp. 257–69; Millis, *The Martial Spirit*, pp. 293–312ff; Brown, *The Correspondents' War*, pp. 377–85; *Morning Journal*,

July 6, 1898, pp. 1–2.

32. Hemment, *Cannon and Camera*, pp. 214–25; Coblentz, ed., *Hearst*, pp. 64–67; Trask, *The War with Spain in 1898*, pp. 62, 262–66; Brown, *The Correspondents' War*, pp. 388–90; *Morning Journal*, July 20, 1898, p. 2; July 24, 1898, p. 3; Older, *Hearst*, pp. 197–99; Winkler, *Hearst: An American Phenomenon*, pp. 159–60; Millis, *The Martial Spirit*, p. 309; Swanberg, *Citizen Hearst*, pp. 157–59; Creelman, *On the Great Highway*, p. 178.

33. Trask, *The War with Spain in 1898*, pp. 111, 266, 286–319ff; Brown, *The Correspondents' War*, pp. 390, 431; *Morning Journal*, July 8, 1898, pp. 1, 2; July 11, 1898, pp. 1, 6; July 12, 1898, pp. 1, 6; July 15, 1898, p. 4; July 19, 1898, p. 1. Swanberg, *Citizen Hearst*, pp. 158–59, states that the *Sylvia* docked at Baltimore on July 18.

34. *New York World*, July 15, 1898, p. 1; *Morning Journal*, July 17, 1898, p. 40; July 19, 1898, p. 8; July 20, 1898, p. 1; Swanberg, *Citizen Hearst*, pp. 159–60; Seitz, *Pulitzer*, p. 241; Swanberg, *Pulitzer*, pp. 252–53. See Brown, *The Correspondents' War*, pp. 430–32, for a good account of this brief episode; see also Brown's footnote on p. 232 concerning the Crane authorship of the article.

35. Concerning Dewey cablegram see *Morning Journal*, July 23, 1898, p. 1. For reports on "*Journal* Monument Fund" see ibid., July 26, 1898, p. 1; July 27, 1898, p. 14; July 28, 1898, p. 4; July 29, 1898, p. 4. For Hemment's photos and numerous illustrations see ibid., July 5, 1898, to July 31, 1898. Concerning the Hearst carnival with fireworks, together with its promotion, see ibid., July 29, 1898, p. 4; August 2, 1898, p. 9; August 3, 1898, p. 4; August 5, 1898, p. 4; August 6, 1898, p. 5; August 8–10, 1898, p. 4; Swanberg, *Citizen Hearst*, pp. 163–64.

36. *Morning Journal*, July 29, 1898, p. 4; August 16, 1898, p. 1; August 17, 1898, p. 1; August 19, 1898, p. 1; August 20, 1898, pp. 1, 8; August 21, 1898, pp. 33, 40; Swanberg, *Citizen Hearst*, pp. 163, 164–66.

37. See full Sunday issue of *Morning Journal*, August 21, 1898; Swanberg, *Citizen Hearst*, p. 166.

38. Historical interpretations concerning Hearst's role in the Spanish-American War are mixed. For those attributing his actions as primary to initiating the war see Wisan, *The Cuban Crisis*, p. 458.

Chapter 8

1. Any number of American histories reinforce the author's statements concerning the domestic and foreign conditions of the United States at the end of the nineteenth century. See, for example, Schlesinger, *The Rise of the City*; Morison and Commager, *The Growth of the American Republic*, II; Bailey, *A Diplomatic History of the American People*; and May, *Imperial Democracy*.

2. See Richard L. McCormick, *From Realignment to Reform: Political Change in New York State, 1893–1910* (Ithaca, N.Y.: Cornell University Press, 1979), for numerous references to Platt and Croker.

3. See the Sunday *New York Journal*, December 31, 1899, p. 37. Hearst titled this front-page story, which he signed, "The Newspaper of the Twentieth Century." For the initial statements on journalistic power and responsibility, see a Hearst editorial on Sunday in ibid., September 25, 1898, editorial section, which he titled "The Importance of Union Among Newspapers."

4. For "The National Policy" proposals see editorials beginning in *Morning Journal*, May 16, 1898, p. 10, and then several times a week—and, often, daily—during 1898, 1899, and 1900.

5. The author came to these conclusions after taking lengthy notes on the *Morning Journal* over a five-year period. For the changes in journalism format and techniques by Hearst see ibid., November 3, 1895, to the end of 1900. See also Duffus, "The Tragedy of Hearst," pp. 624–27; Swanberg, *Citizen Hearst*, p. 59.

6. The author has again relied on his daily reading—and notetaking—of the *Morning Journal* from November 3, 1895, to December 31, 1900.

7. Millis, *The Martial Spirit*, pp. 344–50; Morgan, *William McKinley and His America*, pp. 394–95; Leech, *In the Days of McKinley*, pp. 270–76ff; Freidel, *The Splendid Little War*, pp. 295–302; May, *Imperial Democracy*, p. 250. See also the *Morning Journal*, August 2, 1898, pp. 1–2; August 5, 1898, p. 1; August 9, 1898, pp. 1–2; August 12, 1898, p. 2; August 14, 1898, p. 38; August 16, 1898, p. 16. See ibid., September 1–24, 1898, for daily coverage of the horrible conditions at army bases, especially at Camp Wikoff.

8. See Trask, *The War with Spain in 1898*, pp. 146, 336–68ff, 484–85; Millis, *The Martial Spirit*, pp. 335–39, 341–44ff, 346–53; Morgan, *William McKinley and His America*, pp. 424–29. See specifically the *Morning Journal*, September 5, 1898, p. 3 (Davenport cartoon); September 7, 1898, p. 4; September 8, 1898, p. 1; September 9, 1898, pp. 1–3; September 10, 1898, pp. 4, 6; September 15, 1898, p. 2; September 17, 1898, pp. 1, 5; September 20, 1898, p. 1; September 21, 1898, pp. 2, 8; September 22, 1898, p. 1; September 24, 1898, p. 6. See also Julian Hawthorne's daily articles on army inquiry, which he termed a "cover-up," in ibid., October 6, 1898, pp. 1, 4, to October 13, 1898, p. 4.

9. Concerning school improvements see the editorial by Hearst in the *Morning Journal*, August 11, 1898. Then see a daily campaign in ibid., September 8, 1898, p. 6; September 9, 1898, p. 7; September 11, 1898, p. 33; September 12, 1898, p. 6 (two editorials); September 14–16, 1898; and especially September 17, 1898, p. 5; September 18, 1898, p. 38; September 21, 1898, p. 4; and October 15, 1898, p. 6.

10. See the *Morning Journal*, September 14, 1898, p. 12; September 15, 1898, p. 1; September 16, 1898, p. 1; September 17, 1898, p. 3; September 18, 1898, p. 2; September 19, 1898, p. 5; September 20, 1898, p. 3; September 24, 1898, p. 14; September 25, 1898, p. 43; September 26, 1898, p. 2; September 29, 1898, p. 4; September 30, 1898, p. 3; October 1, 1898, p. 10; October 2,

1898, p. 39; October 3, 1898, p. 5; October 4, 1898, p. 3; October 7, 1898, p. 3.

11. Your affectionate and grateful son to Dear Mother, [November, 1898], WRH Papers; McCormick, *Political Change in New York State, 1893–1910*, pp. 128–31; DeAlva Stanwood Alexander, *A Political History of the State of New York, 1882–1905* (New York: Holt, Rinehart & Winston, 1923), IV, 310–15; Pringle, *Roosevelt*, pp. 201–7; Winkler, *Hearst: An American Phenomenon*, p. 163. For examples of Davenport's artistry see *Morning Journal*, September 20, 1898, p. 8; October 1, 1898, p. 6; October 2, 1898, p. 40; October 8, 1898, p. 8; October 9, 1898, p. 6; October 10, 1898, p. 6; October 11, 1898, p. 8; October 17, 1898, p. 6; October 29, 1898, p. 6; November 5, 1898, p. 6. For betting wagers see ibid., October 13, 1898, p. 1; October 18, 1898, pp. 8–9; October 28, 1898, p. 1; October 30, 1898, p. 37; October 31, 1898, p. 1. See specifically in ibid., October 15, 1898, p. 1; November 1, 1898, p. 1; November 3, 1898, p. 6; November 4, 1898, p. 1; November 7, 1898, pp. 1, 6; and November 8, 1898, p. 1.

12. Pringle, *Roosevelt*, p. 207; Alexander, *Political History of New York*, IV, 315–22; [W. R. Hearst] to Mama, [November, 1898], WRH Papers. In the *Morning Journal*, November 10, 1898, p. 6, Hearst wrote an editorial titled "The War Is the Issue," in which he stated that "the Democratic press and the Democrats in Congress urged and brought on the war, but the Democratic leaders . . . [in Congress] forced the Democratic party into an attitude of opposition to the very war they had brought on" and therefore "forced it further into an attitude" of rejecting the Jeffersonian principle of national expansion. In the above letter to "Mama," Hearst was privately castigating himself, along the same lines, for not having the foresight and drive to receive credit for his war accomplishments.

13. Your affectionate and grateful son to Dear Mother, [December, 1898], WRH Papers; *Morning Journal*, December 18, 1898, p. 59. See ibid., November–December, 1898, at the top of the front page, for references to daily circulation. Concerning Brisbane and his salary see Carlson, *Brisbane*, pp. 110–11; Older, *Hearst*, p. 202. Hearst would continue to depend on his business manager, Solomon Carvalho, to help him economize. See Will to Mother, [summer, 1899], WRH Papers.

14. For free ads see *Morning Journal*, September 14, 1898, p. 11; September 15–October 3, 1898 (almost daily), pp. 13–15; April 13, 1899, p. 13; April 19, 1899, p. 14. For prizes and gifts see ibid., January 22, 1899, p. 32; March 21, 22, 23, 24, 1899, p. 1; April 8, 10, 12, 13, 1899, p. 1; April 14, 15, 24, 1899, p. 13; April 25, 26, 1899, p. 15; May 1, 1899, p. 1; May 8, 1899, p. 13; May 9, 10, 11, 1899, p. 15; May 12, 1899, p. 15; May 13, 1899, p. 13; May 14, 1899, p. 62; May 15, 1899, p. 11; May 17, 1899, p. 1; May 19, 1899, p. 12; May 20, 1899, p. 9; May 21, 1899, p. 62. For $100 to $200 in prizes for "superfluous words" see ibid., February 9, 1899, p. 12; February 13–18, 1899, p. 1; February 19, 1899, p. 52; March 5, 1899, pp. 8, 62; March 7, 1899, pp. 7, 13; March 12, 1899, p. 58; March 19, 1899, p. 63. For $500 prize for "best story" concerning

Journal "Want" success see ibid., February 10, 1899, pp. 1, 12; February 12, 1899, p. 50; February 20, 1899, p. 4. For "Wants" growth see ibid., May 11, 1899, p. 13; see ibid. throughout 1899 and 1900 for specific claims of "Wants" increases over the previous year and in comparison to rival journals.

15. For the full extent of the Molineux "murder mystery" see *Morning Journal*, September 30, 1898, p. 1, to February 19, 1900, p. 3. For several chronologies of the Molineux case see ibid., January 8, 1899, p. 34; March 12, 1899, p. 28 (story by Winifred Black); and January 1, 1900, p. 9. For posting of a $5,000 reward see ibid., January 28, 1899, pp. 1, 6. For his last days before execution see ibid., February 17, 1900, pp. 1, 2, 6; February 18, 1900, p. 62; and February 19, 1900, p. 3. The case occupied space almost daily in ibid. from January 1, 1899, to March 12, 1899, scarcely without exception on p. 1, 2, or 3 —or in the editorials on p. 6.

16. Wayne Andrews, ed., *The Autobiography* (New York: Octagon Books, 1975), p. 126; Leech, *In the Days of McKinley*, pp. 297–300, 308–22ff; Morgan, *William McKinley and His America*, pp. 424–31; Trask, *The War with Spain in 1898*, pp. 484–85; Older, *Hearst*, pp. 214–15. See the *Morning Journal*, November 23, 1898, p. 3; November 24, 1898, p. 6; November 26, 1898, p. 1; December 23 and 24, 1898, p. 1. See almost daily in ibid., January 5, 1899, p. 1, to April 6, 1899, p. 6; and specifically ibid., January 5 and 6, 1899, p. 1; January 13, 1899, pp. 1, 8; January 14, 1899, pp. 1, 2, 6; January 17, 1899, pp. 1, 6; January 22, 1899, pp. 37–38; January 23 and 25, 1899, p. 2; January 26 and 27, 1899, pp. 1–2; January 30 and 31, 1899, pp. 1–2; February 1 and 2, 1899, p. 1; February 8, 1899, pp. 5–6; February 13, 1899, pp. 2, 6; February 20, 1899, pp. 1, 6; March 6, 1899, pp. 1–2, 6; March 9, 1899, p. 4; March 11, 1899, pp. 1, 6; March 17, 20, 24, 25, 1899, p. 1; April 3, 1899, pp. 2, 6. For comments concerning an army "whitewash" also see ibid., April 17, 1899, pp. 1–2; May 8, 1899, pp. 1, 2, 6.

17. *Morning Journal*, December 22, 1898, pp. 1, 6; December 23, 1898, p. 6; December 24, 1898, p. 1; December 25, 1898, p. 28; December 28 and 29, 1898, p. 4; December 30, 1898, p. 7; December 31, 1898, pp. 1, 6; January 1, 1899, p. 34. See ibid., almost daily, January 3 and 4, 1899, p. 4, to February 19, 1899, pp. 32, 42. For Winifred Black articles or references thereto see ibid., January 10, 1899, p. 8; January 12, 1899, p. 6; January 14, 1899, p. 4; January 22, 1899, p. 26. See also Winkler, *Hearst: A New Appraisal*, p. 117.

18. See a continuing story of Roberts (almost daily) in *Morning Journal* from October 7, 1899, p. 1, to December 20, 1899, p. 1. See also ibid., January 18, 1900, p. 1; January 21, 1900, p. 45. Note that in ibid., December 31, 1899, p. 37—eleven days after the *Journal* predicted the defeat of Roberts—Hearst wrote the all-revealing front-page editorial titled "The Newspaper of the Twentieth Century."

19. See Hearst editorials in *Morning Journal*, November 10, 1898, p. 6; November 16, 1898, p. 6; November 22, 1898, p. 6; November 28, 1898, p. 6; No-

vember 30, 1898, p. 6; December 16, 1898, p. 6. For examples of Hearst's campaign for the *Journal*'s "National Policy" see ibid., November 12, 1898, p. 1 (almost daily), to December 16, 1898, p. 6. For a typical example of "managing the news" in regard to the clergy's endorsement of American expansionism see ibid., November 25, 1898, p. 1; November 28, 1898, p. 4. For numerous references to the *Journal* as the major newspaper representing the Democratic Party's viewpoints see ibid. after the November elections in 1898 and intermittently throughout 1899 and 1900.

20. See the Sunday *Morning Journal*, February 5, 1899, p. 24, and thereafter, intermittently, in the editorial section through 1900. An excellent example of Hearst's commitment to formulating the domestic and foreign policies of the Democratic Party and, with victory at the polls, the United States is in ibid., November 8, 1900, p. 16. See also Winkler, *Hearst: A New Appraisal*, p. 117.

21. For first mention of the "currency reform" plank see the Sunday *Morning Journal*, March 19, 1899, p. 28; and March 20, 1899, p. 8. For first mention of the "no protection for oppressive trusts" plank see ibid., June 7, 1899, p. 6. See ibid., June 25, 1899, p. 24, a signed editorial by Hearst titled "Criminal Trusts and Other Trusts." See also ibid., March–June, 1899, for frequent references to trust growth. For instance, a headline in ibid., March 17, 1899, p. 3, reads, "One Day's Trusts $1526 Million"; in ibid., May 4, 1899, p. 11, "A Billion Dollars in Trusts in One Day"; in ibid., May 5, 1899, pp. 1–2, "Trusts Biggest Day. $1,289,000,000."

22. For questions concerning the integrity of Hearst's political and journalistic policies see Carlson and Bates, *Lord of San Simeon*, pp. xii–xiii. For the Hearst crusades against local trusts see Older, *Hearst*, pp. 205–10, 213–14. In the Ramapo Company negotiations concerning a water contract with New York City as well as Hearst's crusade for municipal ownership see McCormick, *Political Change in New York State, 1893–1910*, p. 177; almost daily in *Morning Journal* from September 1, 1899, pp. 1–2, to September 25, 1899, p. 1; December 12, 1899, p. 8, to December 18, 1899, p. 4; January 4, 6, and 11, 1900, p. 2; January 12, 1900, p. 8; January 23, 1900, p. 8; January 29, 1900, p. 6; February 1, 1900, pp. 8, 10. For the Gas Trust crusade see ibid., April 5, 1899, p. 10, daily to April 13, 1899, p. 5; April 17, 1899, p. 25; May 2, 1899, pp. 1, 2, 8; May 3, 1899, pp. 1–2; May 4, 1899, p. 3; May 10, 1899, p. 2. For the crusade for rapid transit see ibid., daily, from April 18, 1899, pp. 1, 8, to April 26, 1899, p. 2; May 4, 1899, pp. 3, 5; May 18, 1899, p. 3; and daily from September 4, 1899, p. 1, to September 7, 1899, p. 3. Then see ibid., January 13, 1900, p. 8; January 16 and 17, 1900, pp. 1–2, 8.

23. Concerning example of help in cold weather see *Morning Journal*, February 14, 1899, pp. 1, 2; February 15, 1899, p. 9; February 16, 1899. For preparations for one "Christmas feast" see ibid., December 14, 1899, p. 4, almost daily to December 26, 1899, p. 12. For an example of the *Journal*'s mediation attempts in a labor strike see ibid., July 17, 1899, pp. 1–2, 6, daily to July 24,

1899, p. 2. For the "Baby Clark" episode see ibid., May 25, 1899, pp. 1–2; May 27, 1899, pp. 1–2; May 28, 1899, pp. 37, 40; May 29 and 30, 1899, pp. 1–2; May 31, 1899, p. 2; June 2, 1899, pp. 1–3; June 3, 1899, pp. 1–4; June 4, 1899, pp. 41, 44; June 5, 6, and 8, 1899, p. 2; June 15, 1899, p. 1; June 16, 1899, p. 3; June 17, 1899, p. 1. Evidence of Thanksgiving dinners by the *Journal* has been referred to several times in previous chapters.

24. See *Morning Journal* almost daily from May 11, 1899, p. 1, through July 14, 1899. See specifically, however, ibid., May 12, 1899, p. 3; May 15, 17, 18, 19, 1899, p. 1; May 21, 1899, pp. 36, 42; June 19, 1899, p. 1; September 3, 1899, pp. 14–15; September 5, 1899, p. 12.

25. See ibid., September 7, 1899, p. 1; September 8, 1899, p. 4; September 9, 1899, p. 2; September 23, 1899, p. 1.

26. See ibid., September 10, 1899, p. 52; September 15, 1899, p. 6; September 15, 1899, p. 4; September 17, 1899, p. 37; September 23, 26, 28, 1899, p. 1; September 29, 1899, p. 11; September 30, 1899, p. 14.

27. See ibid., September 27, 1899, pp. 1–8; September 28, 1899, pp. 1–3, 6; September 29, 1899, pp. 1–3, 5, 6; September 30, 1899, pp. 1–6; October 1, 1899, pp. 53–61. But see ibid., September 30, 1899, p. 6, for specific quote.

28. Will to Mama, [November, 1899, in Paris]; Your affectionate son to Mama, [December, 1899], in WRH Papers; Flint interviews, January 18, February 20, 1960; Swanberg, *Citizen Hearst*, p. 179.

29. Nine letters from Hearst to Mother, December, 1899, to March, 1900; Hearst to Mrs. Hearst (telegram), March 17, 1900, WRH Papers.

30. Will to Mother, August 29, 1899, WRH Papers. See editorial pages of *Morning Journal* from November 10, 1898, through April, 1900, for continual references to the *Journal's* "National Policy" and an "American Internal Policy." Typical of Hearst's concern for building a Nicaraguan canal that was American-owned and fortified, see his four signed editorials, written while in Egypt, in ibid., March 1, 2, 3, 4, 1900, p. 8; one titled "Expansion and Imperialism," ibid., February 4, 1900, p. 26. Then, after his return from vacation, see editorial titled "Why Bryan Should Be & Will Be Nominated," in ibid., April 7, 1900, p. 8; and one concerning the direct election of senators, in ibid., April 22, 1900, p. 51.

31. James K. Jones to Bryan, April 21, 1900, Box 24, William Jennings Bryan Papers, Manuscript Division, Library of Congress, Washington, D.C. (hereafter cited as BP); *New York Tribune*, May 20, 1900, p. 5; May 31, 1900, p. 2; Winkler, *Hearst: A New Appraisal*, pp. 118–19; Older, *Hearst*, p. 217; Swanberg, *Citizen Hearst*, p. 182.

32. Willis J. Abbot to Bryan, June 4, 1900; Creelman to Bryan, June 6, 1900; Hearst to Bryan (telegrams), July 4, July 5–6, 1900, Box 24, BP; Older, *Hearst*, pp. 217–18; Winkler, *Hearst: A New Appraisal*, pp. 119–20; John J. McPhaul, *Deadlines and Monkeyshines: The Fabled World of Chicago Journalism* (Englewood Cliffs, N.J.: Prentice-Hall, 1962), p. 113. See *New York Tribune*,

July 2, 1900, p. 6, for comment on Hearst's hirings in Chicago; however, it has no mention of salaries as Swanberg, *Citizen Hearst*, p. 183, states. See also *Morning Journal*, July 1, 1900, p. 55; July 4, 1900, pp. 1, 8; July 5, 1900, pp. 1, 7; July 6, 1900, p. 7.

33. For a huge illustration as well as description of the *Journal's* new Hoe presses see Sunday *Morning Journal*, April 8, 1900, p. 53. For complete data on contest to the Democratic and Republican conventions see ibid., April 9, 1900, p. 1, daily to April 14, 1900, p. 5; also daily from April 19, 1900, p. 5, to April 29, 1900, p. 61; and daily from May 3, 1900, p. 7, to May 23, 1900, p. 7; May 27, 1900, p. 52; again daily from June 1, 1900, p. 14, to June 4, 1900, p. 7. For coverage of student delegates at the Republican National Convention see ibid., June 19, 1900, p. 5, to June 22, 1900, p. 6. For coverage of student delegates at the Democratic National Convention see ibid., June 24, 1900, p. 50; July 1, 1900, p. 25; July 2, 1900, p. 7; July 3, 1900, p. 6; July 6, 1900, p. 5; July 7, 1900, p. 2.

34. For the facsimile "Notice of Application for Injunction" by Hearst against the American Ice Company see *Morning Journal*, May 8, 1900, p. 1. Concerning testimonials praising the *Journal* and continued attacks against the Ice Trust see ibid., May 9, 10, and 11, 1900, pp. 1–2; May 12, 1900, p. 16; May 13, 1900, p. 14; May 14, 1900, p. 5. For disclosures about Mayor Van Wyck, Carroll, and other city and party officials see ibid., May 15, 1900, pp. 1–2; May 16, 1900, pp. 1–3, 8.

35. See a daily reference in ibid., May 17, 1900, pp. 1–2, to June 14, 1900, pp. 1, 8, then June 24, 1900, p. 1; June 25, 1900, p. 6; June 26, 1900, pp. 3, 6; June 29, 1900, p. 2; June 30, 1900, p. 6; July 5, 1900, p. 4. See especially in ibid., May 18, 1900, pp. 1–2, 8; May 23–26, 1900, pp. 1–2; May 27, 1900, p. 57; June 2, 1900, pp. 1–3, 8; June 3, 1900, pp. 30, 41–42; June 4, 1900, pp. 1, 3, 8; June 5, 1900, pp. 1–12. For Burton and Brooks song see ibid., June 8, 1900, p. 4. See also Older, *Hearst*, pp. 225–32; Swanberg, *Citizen Hearst*, p. 189.

36. For *Journal* polls and predictions see *Morning Journal*, July 30, 1900, p. 14; August 6, 1900, p. 12; August 13, 1900, p. 7; August 19, 1900, p. 47; August 20, 1900, p. 4; August 27, 1900, p. 6; September 3, 1900, p. 6; October 7, 1900, p. 54; October 22, 1900, p. 6; October 26, 1900, p. 1; October 29, 1900, p. 1; October 30, 1900, p. 6; November 5, 1900, p. 1. Concerning testimonials see ibid., August 20, 1900, p. 14; August 24, 1900, p. 14; September 16, 1900, p. 51; September 19, 1900, p. 6; September 30, 1900, p. 51; October 30, 1900, p. 8. For reports by campaign correspondents see ibid., August 29, 1900, p. 1; September 1, 1900, pp. 5, 14; September 4 and 6, 1900, pp. 1–2; September 7, 1900, p. 2; October 31, 1900, p. 6; November 2, 1900, p. 8; November 3, 1900, p. 12. For renditions of cartoonists Davenport and Opper see ibid., August 1–November 6, 1900 (daily). See also Leech, *In the Days of McKinley*, p. 548; Swanberg, *Citizen Hearst*, p. 185.

37. Abbot, *Watching the World Go By*, p. 238; Coletta, *Bryan*, I, 269–85ff;

Morgan, *McKinley and His America*, pp. 502–6; Leech, *In the Days of McKinley*, pp. 543–48; Pringle, *Roosevelt*, pp. 224–26.

38. For most of July and August, 1900, to September 8, 1900, Bryan and the Democratic Party almost daily occupy space of the *Morning Journal* either on p. 1 or 2—and sometimes both pages. Yet from September 9, 1900, to October 15, 1900, they receive mention on the front page in ibid., September 18 and September 27, 1900. For coverage of the Galveston disaster and Hearst's charity crusade see ibid., September 10, 1900, through September 17, 1900, pp. 1–2. Then see ibid., almost daily to October 15, 1900, pp. 1–2; October 16, 1900, pp. 3–4; October 18, 1900, p. 5. See also Ross, *Ladies of the Press*, p. 63; Older, *Hearst*, pp. 223–24; Swanberg, *Citizen Hearst*, pp. 187–88.

39. Creelman to Bryan, June 2, 1900, Box 24, BP; Coletta, *Bryan*, I, 251–52.

40. For mention of the meeting of the New York Democratic leaders see *Morning Journal*, July 30, 1900, p. 7.

41. Creelman to Bryan, June 2, 1900; Abbot to Bryan, June 4, 1900, Box 24, BP; Ihmsen to Bryan, July 24, 1900; W. S. Hutchins to Bryan, July 25, 1900, Box 25, BP; *Morning Journal*, August 5, 1900, pp. 38, 50; then almost daily in ibid., August 10, 1900, p. 4, to October 7, 1900, p. 63. See specific references in ibid., August 12, 1900, p. 30; September 2, 1900, p. 38; September 3, 1900, p. 7; September 9, 1900, pp. 50, 52; September 22, 1900, p. 8; Swanberg, *Citizen Hearst*, p. 184.

42. *Morning Journal*, September 29, 1900, p. 12; September 30, 1900, p. 59; October 1, 1900, p. 2; October 2, 1900, pp. 8, 16; October 3, 1900, p. 7. But especially see ibid., October 4, 1900, pp. 1–2, for the report of the convention by Willis Abbot, and ibid., October 5, 1900, p. 1; October 8, 1900, p. 7. See also Swanberg, *Citizen Hearst*, p. 184.

43. See *Morning Journal*, October 16, 1900, pp. 1–2; October 17, 1900, pp. 1, 3, 4; Swanberg, *Citizen Hearst*, p. 184.

44. *Morning Journal*, October 14, 1900, p. 55; October 15, 1900, p. 10; October 19, 1900, p. 7; *New York Tribune*, October 28, 1900, p. 3; Swanberg, *Citizen Hearst*, p. 185.

45. *Morning Journal*, October 19, 1900, p. 7; October 21, 1900, p. 64; October 24, 1900, p. 8; October 26, 1900, p. 3; October 28, 1900, pp. 46, 48, 50; *New York Tribune*, October 28, 1900, pp. 1, 2, 3; *New York Times*, October 28, 1900, p. 3; Swanberg, *Citizen Hearst*, pp. 185–86.

46. See Coletta, *Bryan*, I, 277–85; Koenig, *Bryan*, pp. 339–44; Morgan, *William McKinley and His America*, pp. 499–508; Leech, *In the Days of McKinley*, pp. 558–59; Morison and Commager, *The Growth of the American Republic*, II, 340–41.

Chapter 9

1. Abbot, *Watching the World Go By*, pp. 150–51; Steffens, "Hearst, The Man of Mystery," p. 15; Duffus, "The Tragedy of Hearst," p. 623; West,

"Hearst: A Psychological Note," pp. 305–6; Creelman, "The Real Mr. Hearst," pp. 263, 265; Winkler, *Hearst: An American Phenomenon,* p. 171; Winkler, *A New Appraisal,* p. 121. For an interesting assessment of Hearst entering politics see Swanberg, *Citizen Hearst,* pp. 187–91.

2. Steffens, "Hearst, The Man of Mystery," pp. 8, 10, 14–15, 17–18, 20; Creelman, "The Real Mr. Hearst," pp. 260–61; Duffus, "The Tragedy of Hearst," pp. 628, 631; West, "A Psychological Note," pp. 306, 308; Winkler, *Hearst: An American Phenomenon,* p. 174.

3. Flint interviews, January 18, February 20, 1960; Aline B. Saarinen, *The Proud Possessors: The Lives, Times, and Tastes of Some Adventurous American Art Collectors* (New York: Random House, 1958), p. 76; Winkler, *Hearst: A New Appraisal,* p. 121; Swanberg, *Citizen Hearst,* p. 191.

4. *Morning Journal,* May 20–21, 1901, pp. 1–2.

5. For daily accounts of race see ibid., May 20 to July 23, 1901. But specifically see ibid., May 20–25, 1901, pp. 1–2; May 26, 1901, p. 65; May 28, 1901, p. 1; June 1, 1901, pp. 1–2; June 4, 1901, p. 5; June 7, 1901, pp. 2, 5; June 11–12, 1901, pp. 1–2; June 16, 1901, p. 49; June 20–22, 1901, p. 5; June 27–29, 1901, p. 4; July 10–12, 1901, p. 4; July 16, 1901, p. 4; July 17, 1901, p. 1; July 18–19, 1901, p. 3; July 20, 1901, p. 2; July 21, 1901, p. 47; July 22, 1901, p. 2; July 23, 1901, p. 2. For announcement of contest and prizes see ibid., July 2, 1901, p. 3; July 5, 1901, p. 2; July 6, 1901, p. 4; July 8, 1901, p. 5; July 9, 1901, p. 2; July 14, 1901, p. 47; July 18, 1901, p. 3. John J. Hakenstrom of Chicago won the $1,000 first prize, missing the actual time by "one-fifth of a second." Mrs. Ida Asplund of New York City placed second ($300), missing by "four-fifths of a second." And James Nicholson of New York City placed third ($200), missing by "two and one-fifth seconds." See ibid., July 24, 1901, p. 5.

6. For coverage of the New York City heat wave, and especially Dorothy Dix's articles, see ibid., July 2, 1901, p. 2; July 3, 1901, pp. 1–2; July 4, 1901, p. 2. For *Journal* suit against Park Commission concerning "paid seats" see ibid., July 3–4, 1901, p. 1; July 5, 1901, p. 6; July 7, 1901, p. 35; July 8, 1901, p. 1; July 10–12, 1901, pp. 1–2; July 14, 1901, p. 40.

7. For the crusade against the 7th National Bank see ibid., June 28, 29, 1901, p. 1; June 30, 1901, p. 49; July 1, 1901, pp. 1, 4; July 2, 1901, p. 4; July 3, 1901, p. 6; July 4, 1901, p. 8; July 7, 1901, p. 48; July 9, 1901, p. 4; July 10, 1901, p. 2; July 13, 1901, pp. 1–2; July 20, 1901, p. 4; July 21, 1901, p. 44; July 24, 1901, p. 4; July 25, 1901, p. 1; July 26, 1901, p. 6; July 27, 31, August 2, 1901, p. 4; August 5, 1901, p. 5; August 9, 1901, p. 14; September 12, 1901, p. 7; September 24, 1901, p. 1. For the crusade against gambling see ibid., May 12, 1901, p. 63; May 21, 1901, p. 1; June 10, 1901, p. 10; August 2, 1901, pp. 1–2; August 3, 1901, p. 3; August 8, 1901, p. 1; August 10, 1901, pp. 1–2; August 11, 1901, pp. 35–38; August 12, 1901, pp. 1, 12; August 13–16, 21, 24, 26, 30, 31, 1901, p. 1; Morris, *Incredible New York,* pp. 220–30; Harold C. Syrett, ed., *The Gentleman and the Tiger: The Autobiography of George B. McClellan, Jr.* (New

York: J. B. Lippincott, 1956), pp. 167n, 184, 206n.

8. Leech, *In the Days of McKinley*, pp. 592–98, 600–601; Morgan, *William McKinley and His America*, pp. 519–25; Coleman, *Give Us a Little Smile, Baby*, pp. 48–49; Neale, *Bierce*, p. 93; Older, *Hearst*, pp. 237–38; Winkler, *Hearst: A New Appraisal*, pp. 123–26; Swanberg, *Citizen Hearst*, pp. 180–81, 192–94; *Morning Journal*, September 22, 1901, pp. 48–49; September 23, 1901, pp. 8–9; September 24, 1901, pp. 6, 8, 16; September 25, 1901, pp. 7–8.

9. T. T. Williams to Mrs. Phoebe Hearst, September 17, 1901, PAH Papers; Older, *Hearst*, pp. 238, 240; Winkler, *Hearst: A New Appraisal*, pp. 125–26; Coleman, *Give Us a Little Smile, Baby*, p. 49; Bleyer, *Main Currents in the History of American Journalism*, pp. 380–81.

10. John Randolph "Bunky" Hearst, Jr., in an interview by author, August 3, 1981, New York City, noted that his grandfather seemed oblivious, if not immune, to personal criticism; see also Steffens, "Hearst, The Man of Mystery," pp. 7–8. For a typical handling of the McKinley assassination and funeral see *Morning Journal*, September 7, 1901, pp. 1–9; then daily to September 14, 1901, p. 1 (and usually several more pages). For eulogy to McKinley see ibid., September 14, 1901, pp. 1, 16; September 20, 1901. See also concerning all aspects of the McKinley funeral in ibid., September 15–19, 21, 1901, p. 1. Then for the Hearst rebuttal to critics see ibid., September 22, 1901, pp. 48–49; September 23, 1901, pp. 8–9; September 24, 1901, pp. 6, 8, 16; September 25, 1901, pp. 7–8, 16; September 26, 1901, p. 16; September 30, 1901, p. 2; October 2, 1901, pp. 1, 2, 16. See also Older, *Hearst*, pp. 240–42; Winkler, *Hearst: A New Appraisal*, pp. 124–26.

11. Concerning statistics see *Morning Journal*, September 24, 1901, pp. 6, 8, 16; October 2, 1901, p. 1. See also claims on advertisements and circulation in ibid., January 2, 1902, p. 1; January 5, 1902, p. 38; January 6, 8, 1902, p. 2; January 29, 1902, p. 1; January 30, 1902, p. 3; March 30, 1902, p. 67; April 2, 1902, pp. 1–4, 10; and continually through April 21, 1902, p. 2. For change of the masthead see *New York Journal and American*, November 11, 1901, p. 1. Then see *New York American and Journal* beginning on April 1, 1902. See also Older, *Hearst*, pp. 240–42; Winkler, *Hearst: A New Appraisal*, pp. 125–26.

12. Will to Mother, [Christmas, 1901], WRH Papers; Williams to Mrs. Phoebe Hearst, September 7, 1901, PAH Papers.

13. For the "*Journal* Christmas Fund" and campaign see *New York Journal and American*, December 22, 1901, p. 46; December 23, 1901, p. 2; December 25, 1901, pp. 1–2; December 26, 1901, pp. 8–9. For the Paterson fire see ibid., February 10, 1902, pp. 1–5; February 11, 1902, pp. 1–2. For information concerning the blizzard in New York City and Hearst newspaper aid to the public see specifically in ibid., February 18, 1902, pp. 1–2; February 23, 1902, pp. 51–52; March 6, 1902, p. 5.

14. For railroad reforms see the *New York Journal and American*, January 9, 1902, p. 1; January 11, 13, 1902, p. 2; January 25, 1902, p. 1; January 29, 1902,

p. 4; February 6, 8, 1902, p. 2; April 14, 1902, p. 8. Concerning fire escape reform see *New York American and Journal*, May 8, 1902, p. 16. For demand for lower prices on meat see ibid., April 18, 1902, p. 8; April 19, 1902, pp. 1, 8; then daily from April 21, 1902, p. 8, to May 3, 1902, p. 2; then intermittently to June 5, 1902, p. 2. For plea for lower prices on coal prompted by the anthracite coal strike in Pennsylvania see ibid., May 17, 1902, pp. 1, 2, 8; May 27, 1902, p. 6; July 24, 1902, pp. 5, 8; July 28, 1902, p. 2; August 18, 1902, p. 1.

15. See ibid., February 12, 1902, p. 7; then daily to April 3, 1902, p. 2; April 8, 1902, p. 5, to April 12, 1902, p. 1; April 14, 1902, p. 2; April 16, 1902, p. 6; April 28, May 2, 12, 13, 1902, p. 9; May 14, 1902, p. 4; June 8, 1902, p. 43; June 9, 1902, p. 8; August 15, 1902, p. 9; August 18, 1902, p. 8; August 19, 1902, pp. 2–3; August 20, 1902, p. 2; August 21, 1902, p. 7; September 2, 1902, p. 1; September 3, 1902, p. 3; September 4, 1902, p. 8; Morris, *Incredible New York*, pp. 230–33.

16. Hearst to Arthur Brisbane, September 1, 1902, *New York Journal-American* morgue, Balcones Research Center, University of Texas at Austin (hereafter cited as JAM); Roy Everett Littlefield III, *William Randolph Hearst: His Role in American Progressivism* (Lanham, Md: University Press of America, 1980), pp. 87–106ff; Pringle, *Roosevelt*, pp. 265–78ff; McCormick, *Political Change In New York State, 1893–1910*, p. 157.

17. For full coverage of the anthracite coal strike see daily the *New York American and Journal*, May 8, 1902, p. 2, to October 19, 1902, p. 42. But see specifically in ibid., May 15, 1902, p. 8; May 17, 1902, pp. 1, 2, 8; May 19, 1902, pp. 1–2; May 24, 1902, p. 1; May 27, 1902, p. 6; June 5, 1902, p. 4; June 10, 11, 1902, p. 1; June 16, 19, 1902, pp. 4, 8; July 22, 24, 1902, p. 8; July 28, 1902, p. 2; August 7, 1902, pp. 1–2, 4; August 13, 14, 18, 19, 20, 1902, p. 1; August 22, 1902, p. 2; August 23, 1902, pp. 1, 2, 14; August 25, 1902, pp. 8, 9; August 26–29, 1902, pp. 1, 2, 8; September 3, 5, 1902, p. 8; September 10, 1902, pp. 1–2; September 11, 1902, pp. 1, 8; September 12, 13, 1902, p. 2; September 19, 1902, pp. 8, 9; September 21, 1902, p. 61; September 28, 1902, p. 52; September 29, 1902, pp. 1, 3; October 3, 1902, pp. 1–2, 8; October 5, 1902, pp. 41–42; October 6, 1902, pp. 1–2, 6; October 6–11, 1902, pp. 1–2, 8; October 12, 1902, pp. 39, 41, 42; October 13–15, 1902, pp. 1, 8; October 16–17, 1902, pp. 1, 2, 8. Then with name change, see *New York American*, October 20, 1902, p. 2; October 21–22, 1902, p. 8; October 23, 1902, p. 4. See specifically Hearst to Brisbane, October 1, 16, 1902, JAM; Littlefield, *Hearst: His Role in American Progressivism*, pp. 89–104; Pringle, *Roosevelt*, pp. 264–78; Older, *Hearst*, pp. 246–49; Swanberg, *Citizen Hearst*, p. 198; Richard Skolnik, "Civic Group Progressivism in New York City," *New York History* LI, no. 4 (July, 1970): 425.

18. Hearst to Brisbane, October 28, 1902, JAM; Littlefield, *Hearst: His Role in American Progressivism*, pp. 104–6.

19. Frederick Palmer, "Hearst and Hearstism," *Collier's*, October 6, 1906,

pp. 16–17; Brisbane to Hearst, October 1, 1902, JAM; Littlefield, *Hearst: His Role in American Progressivism*, pp. 115–17; Winkler, *Hearst: A New Appraisal*, pp. 126–27; Older, *Hearst*, p. 250; Winkler, *Hearst: An American Phenomenon*, pp. 174–75. For a running account of Charles Francis Murphy's battle to succeed Richard Croker as Tammany Hall chief see *New York American*, September 16, 1902, p. 1; September 17, 1902, pp. 1–2; September 18, 1902, p. 2; September 19, 1902, p. 1; September 20, 1902, p. 1; September 21, 1902, p. 61. Concerning the state convention see ibid., September 26, 1902, p. 2; September 27, 1902, p. 1; September 28, 1902, p. 51; September 30, 1902, pp. 1–2; October 2, 1902, pp. 9–10. For report of Hearst's nomination see ibid., October 3, 1902, p. 4. See also Nancy Joan Weiss, *Charles Francis Murphy, 1858–1924: Respectability and Responsibility in Tammany Politics* (Northampton, Mass.: Smith College, 1968), pp. 36–38; Gerald Kurland, *Seth Low: The Reformer in an Urban and Industrial Age* (New York: Twayne, 1971), pp. 184–85.

20. Winkler, *Hearst: An American Phenomenon*, pp. 175–78; Winkler, *Hearst: A New Appraisal*, pp. 126–29; Hearst acceptance speech, October 6, 1902, JAM; Littlefield, *Hearst: His Role in American Progressivism*, pp. 117–18; *New York Times*, October 7, 1902, p. 3; *New York American*, October 4, 1902, p. 16; October 6, 1902, pp. 5, 8; October 7, 1902, pp. 3, 6, 8.

21. Steffens, "Hearst, The Man of Mystery," p. 8; Older, *Hearst*, p. 250; Winkler, *Hearst: A New Appraisal*, pp. 126, 129; Swanberg, *Citizen Hearst*, p. 200.

22. *New York American*, October 16 and 17, 1902, pp. 1–2, 4; October 19, 1902, p. 42; October 20, 1902, pp. 9, 10; October 21, 1902, p. 2; October 22, 1902, p. 4; October 23, 1902, pp. 1–2, 4, 8; October 24, 1902, p. 4; October 25, 1902, p. 5; October 26, 1902, pp. 42, 44; October 27, 1902, pp. 8, 9–10; October 28, 1902, pp. 10–12, 14, 15; October 29, 1902, p. 9; *New York Times*, October 28, 1902, pp. 1–2; Lewis Cass Straus to Mrs. Hearst, October 28, 1902, PAH Papers; Swanberg, *Citizen Hearst*, pp. 200–2.

23. *New York American*, October 29, 1902, pp. 9–11, 16; October 30, 1902, pp. 1, 9–10, 16; October 31, 1902, pp. 2–4; November 1, 1902, pp. 5, 7; November 2, 1902, pp. 43, 57–58; November 3, 1902, pp. 1, 3; November 4, 1902, pp. 1–2, 4, 14; *New York Times*, October 30, 31, 1902, p. 2; November 3, 1902, p. 1. For excellent research on Hearst's campaign see Littlefield, *Hearst: His Role in American Progressivism*, pp. 118–20. The author disagrees only on Hearst's active participation; he did force himself to attend numerous functions. See also Swanberg, *Citizen Hearst*, pp. 202–203.

24. *New York American*, November 5, 1902, pp. 1–4; November 6, 1902, pp. 1–2, 3, 16; November 7, 1902, p. 7; November 8, 1902, p. 4; Hearst to Brisbane, November 5, 1902, JAM; Littlefield, *Hearst: His Roll in American Progressivism*, p. 120; Swanberg, *Citizen Hearst*, p. 204.

25. Note the difference of importance of the story in the following two newspapers. See *New York American*, November 5, 1902, p. 5; *New York Times*,

November 5, 1902, p. 1; November 6, 1902, pp. 1–2. See also Littlefield, Hearst: His Role in American Progressivism, pp. 121–22; Swanberg, Citizen Hearst, pp. 203–4.

26. Concerning Max Ihmsen see Littlefield, *Hearst: His Role in American Progressivism*, p. 147; Winkler, *Hearst: A New Appraisal*, p. 121; Swanberg, *Citizen Hearst*, p. 205. For specific mention of Hearst for high political office see the *New York American*, November 7, 1902, p. 7; November 8, 1902, p. 4; November 12, 1902, p. 9; November 20, 1902, p. 3; November 21, 1902, p. 5; November 30, 1902, p. 54. Concerning the Hearst suit against the coal barons see almost daily in ibid. from November 7, 1902, p. 14, to November 22, 1902, pp. 1–2; then again intermittently in ibid. during December, 1902, but especially December 21, 1902, p. 1; December 22, 1902, p. 7; December 23, 1902, p. 3; and still again almost daily in ibid. from January 7, 1903, p. 16, to January 27, 1903, pp. 1–2; and in ibid. from April 20, 1903, p. 2, to May 1, 1903, pp. 1–2, 14; and in ibid., from May 26, 1903, p. 2, to June 14, 1903, p. 53. For medical help to crippled children see ibid., November 21, 1902, p. 3; November 22, 1902, p. 11; November 23, 1902, p. 47. For Christmas charities by the Hearst papers see ibid., December 7, 1902, pp. 89–90; December 11, 1902, p. 5; December 12, 1902, pp. 5, 11; December 25 and 26, 1902, p. 3. Concerning *New York American and Journal* food and coffee wagons see ibid., December 16 and 17, 1902, p. 9; December 18, 1902, p. 2; January 10, 1903, p. 5; January 13, 1903, p. 2. For information regarding Hearst buying coal at cost see ibid., January 13, 1903, p. 16; January 14 and 15, 1903, pp. 1–2; January 16, 1903, pp. 9, 16; January 17, 1903, pp. 8, 18; January 19, 1903, p. 7; January 20, 1903, p. 10; January 22, 1903, p. 4.

27. Concerning the crusade for the "Hearst Resolution" see *New York American* beginning February 16, 1903, p. 14, and then almost daily to March 14, 1903, p. 7; then March 20, 1903, p. 2; March 26, 1903, p. 4; April 12, 1903, p. 57; and especially April 14, 1903, pp. 1–2. For examples of Hearst's full name in the headlines see ibid., January 3, 1903, p. 5; January 4, 1903, p. 40; January 14, 1903, p. 1. See Hearst editorial speeches (and regrets) in ibid., February 13, 1903, pp. 1, 4, 16; March 17, 1903, p. 16; April 21, 1903, p. 16. See also Winkler, *Hearst: An American Phenomenon*, pp. 198–99.

28. See endorsements of labor leaders and prominent citizens in the *New York American*, February 15, 1903, p. 48; February 28, 1903, p. 1; March 1, 1903, p. 48; March 10, 1903, p. 5; March 15, 1903, p. 51; March 16, 1903, p. 2; March 17, 1903, p. 2; March 22, 1903, p. 61; April 3, 1903, p. 1; April 19, 1903, p. 54; April 21, 1903, p. 1; April 24, 1903, p. 10; May 3, 1903, pp. 48, 57; May 7, 1903, p. 9; May 8, 1903, p. 16; May 15, 1903, p. 6; May 18, 1903, p. 8. For information concerning the formation of the first "Hearst Club for President" (St. Louis) see ibid., April 19, 1903, p. 47; then May 6, 1903, p. 10 (Columbia, S.C.); May 14, 1903, p. 5, and May 15, 1903, p. 6 (New York City); and May 24, 1903, p. 41 (San Francisco).

29. Flint Interview, January 18, 1960; *New York American*, April 29, 1903, p. 9; Robinson, *The Hearsts*, pp. 333–36; Coleman, *Give Me a Little Smile, Baby*, p. 60; Will to Mrs. p. A. Hearst (telegrams), April 28, May 5, 1903; Millicent to Mrs. p. A. Hearst (telegram), May 5, 1903; W. R. Hearst to Mother, May, 1903, PAH Papers; Older, *Hearst*, p. 254; Swanberg, *Citizen Hearst*, pp. 206, 208; Winkler, *Hearst: A New Appraisal*, pp. 131–32; Lundberg, *Imperial Hearst*, p. 197.

30. Older, *Hearst*, pp. 255–56; Robinson, *The Hearsts*, pp. 334–36; Princess Pignatelli Interview, November 3, 1959; Flint Interview, January 18, 1960; Swanberg, *Citizen Hearst*, p. 207; William Randolph Hearst, Jr., with Jack Casserly, *The Hearsts, Father and Son* (Niwot, Colo.: Roberts Rinehart, 1991), pp. 235–36.

31. For references to Hearst clubs and leagues see the *New York American* (intermittently), May 14, 1903, p. 5, to May 31, 1903, pp. 37, 38; June 7, 1903, p. 54, to July 14, 1903, p. 7; July 27, 1903, p. 7, to August 30, 1903, p. 42; then almost daily in ibid., September 3, 1903, p. 4, to October 3, 1903, p. 4; October 11, 1903, p. 51, to November 30, 1903, p. 10. See also Littlefield, *Hearst: His Role in American Progressivism*, p. 127; Swanberg, *Citizen Hearst*, pp. 208–9.

32. Concerning the Kishineff massacre see specifically the *New York American*, May 13 and 20, 1903, p. 1. Then see (almost daily) ibid., May 14, 1903, p. 9, to June 16, 1903, p. 2; see specifically July 7, 1903, p. 7; then see July 17, 1903, p. 1; July 18, 1903, p. 4; November 1, 1903, p. 47; December 13, 1903, p. 73.

33. Kurland, *Seth Low*, pp. 175–208ff; Harry C. Syrett, ed., *The Gentleman and the Tiger*, pp. 169–76; Winkler, *Hearst: An American Phenomenon*, p. 190; Swanberg, *Citizen Hearst*, pp. 208–9. For a full account of the "Hearst congressional delegation" see *New York American*, October 14, 15, 16, and 17, 1903, p. 4; October 18, 1903, p. 42; October 19, 20, and 21, 1903, p. 4; October 22, 1903, p. 5; October 23, 1903, p. 2; October 24, 1903, pp. 5, 9; October 25, 1903, p. 51; October 26, 1903, p. 5; October 30, 1903, p. 4; November 3, 1903, p. 4.

34. *New York American*, October 29, 1903, p. 6; November 4, 1903, pp. 3, 4, 6. Specifically see in ibid., November 5, 1903, pp. 1, 4, 5, 6; November 6, 1903, p. 8; November 7, 1903, p. 8 (full page of testimonials); November 9, 1903, p. 4 (full page of testimonials); November 10, 1903, p. 4; November 11, 1903, p. 9; November 12, 1903, p. 6; November 13, 1903, pp. 6, 7; November 14, 1903, pp. 5, 8; November 15, 1903, p. 63; November 16, 1903, p. 5; November 18, 1903, p. 7.

35. See *New York Times*, April 8, 1904, p. 9; *New York American*, November 8, 1903, p. 41; George Coleman Osborn, *John Sharp Williams: Planter-Statesman of the Deep South* (Gloucester, Mass.: Peter Smith, 1964), pp. 109, 124; Charles Willis Thompson, *Party Leaders of the Time* (New York: G. W. Dillingham, 1906), pp. 239–40; *Congressional Record*, 58th Cong., 1st sess., pp. 147, 532; Lit-

tlefield, *Hearst: His Role in American Progressivism*, p. 128; Swanberg, *Citizen Hearst*, p. 209.

36. *Congressional Record*, 58th Cong., 2d sess., pp. 146, 1495, 1543, 1692. After registering four votes in the House on February 10–11, 1904, Hearst would not record his presence until March 11, 1904. See ibid., pp. 1865, 1866, 1867, 1892, 3073. See specifically the *New York Times*, April 8, 1904, p. 9. Concerning anthracite coal companies and railroad investigations see ibid., pp. 4465, 5475; Thompson, *Party Leaders of the Time*, pp. 234–44ff; Osborn, *Williams*, pp. 124–25; Swanberg, *Citizen Hearst*, pp. 209–10. For a coverage of Hearst's fight for the eight-hour day as well as for the anthracite coal and railroad investigations see *New York American*, January 8, 1904, p. 4; February 19, 1904, p. 4; February 26, 27, 1904, p. 9; March 11, 1904, p. 4; March 13, 1904, p. 40; March 20, 1904, p. 46; March 26, 1904, p. 4; April 1, 1904, p. 2; April 6, 1904, p. 3; April 21, 1904, p. 1; April 23, 1904, pp. 1–2; April 24, 1904, p. 37; April 28, 1904, pp. 1–2. See also Littlefield, *Hearst: His Role in American Progressivism*, pp. 127–33.

37. Concerning Thanksgiving meals see the *New York American*, November 27, 1903, p. 4. For coverage of the "*American* Great Christmas Fund" see ibid., December 1, 4, 1903, p. 4; December 5, 1903, p. 8; December 6, 1903, p. 76; December 7, 1903, p. 6; December 8, 1903, p. 5; December 9, 10, 1903, p. 4; and daily from December 12, 1903, p. 12, to December 25, 1903, pp. 9–10. Concerning the basketball contest at Madison Square Garden see ibid., November 30, 1903, p. 8; December 2, 1903, p. 8; and then almost daily from December 4, 5, 1903, p. 10, to December 27, 1903, pp. 54–55; and December 28, 1903, p. 8; then January 27, 28, 1904, p. 8; January 31, 1904, p. 42. As for the "Hearst Coffee Wagons" or "*American* Coffee Wagons," see ibid., December 5, 1903, p. 7; December 24, 1903, p. 4; December 27, 1903, pp. 45, 46; December 28, 1903, p. 6; January 3, 1904, p. 45; January 4, 1904, p. 8; January 6, 1904, p. 9; January 7, 1904, pp. 2, 4. See also ibid., February 28, 1904, p. 48; March 6, 1904, p. 42.

38. See *New York American*, January 19, 1904, p. 8; February 24, 1904, p. 2; February 26, 1904, p. 8; April 5, 1904, p. 1 (full page).

39. For typical examples of Hearst testimonials see ibid., February 11, 1904, p. 10; February 27, 1904, p. 4. For quote by J. G. Johnson see ibid., January 16, 1904, p. 16; by Phelps Stokes, January 24, 1904, p. 41, and February 28, 1904, p. 42; by Bryan, February 25, 1904, p. 6; and by Tom Watson, June 19, 1904, p. 19; and C. Vann Woodward, *Tom Watson: Agrarian Rebel* (New York: Oxford University Press, 1963), pp. 355–56.

40. Concerning Hearst's acquisition of two newspapers see the *New York American*, December 13, 1903, p. 47; December 14, 1903, p. 8; February 7, 1904, p. 39; March 22, 1904, pp. 1–2. For evidences of Hearst organization (and propaganda) throughout the nation see ibid., December, 1903, through March, 1904. Winkler, *Hearst: A New Appraisal*, pp. 132–33, disputed the as-

sertion that Hearst was spending tremendous amounts of money on the campaign; he estimated the sum to be no more than $150,000. Littlefield, *Hearst: His Role in American Progressivism*, p. 153, agrees. See also the *New York Times*, March 12, 21, 1904, p. 8.

41. Brownson Cutting Papers, 1890–1910, Box 1 (1904), MSS Division, Library of Congress, Washington, D.C. Concerning the selection of St. Louis as the convention site see the *New York American*, January 12, 1904, p. 1; January 13, 1904, pp. 1–2; January 14, 1904, pp. 8, 14; January 16, 1904, p. 16; January 17, 1904, p. 42; January 18, 1904, p. 8.

42. See *The Commoner* from February 27, 1903, pp. 2, 3, through May 27, 1904, p. 3, for Bryan's constant criticism of Cleveland, Hill, the "reorganizers," and their candidate Parker. Even after eight years Bryan still remembered Hill's remark of 1896. See ibid., April 8, 1904, p. 1, in which he discusses in detail Hill's advocacy of Parker as well as the "very still" comment. See also Kent, *The Democratic Party*, pp. 362–65; Coletta, *Bryan*, I, 319–21; Glad, *The Trumpet Soundeth*, pp. 152–53; Koenig, *Bryan*, pp. 374–75; Jackson, ed., *The Encyclopedia of New York City*, pp. 1030–31.

43. See a negative interview of Hearst in the *Chicago Tribune*, January 18, 1904, which was reprinted in the *New York American*, January 19, 1904, p. 14, and January 24, 1904, p. 23. See also an article titled "William R. Hearst" from the *Cincinnati Enquirer* in ibid., January 31, 1904, p. 48. Concerning Watterson's concerns see editorial in ibid., February 26, 1904, p. 16, in regard to article in *New York Tribune*, February 21, 1904. For other anti-Hearst comments see specifically the *New York Tribune*, February 21, 1904; March 21 and 23, 1904; May 12, 1904; *New York Times*, March 12 and 18, 1904, p. 8. For evidence of typical attacks on Hearst see the *New York American*, March 6, 1904, p. 40; March 13, 1904, p. 48. For even more criticism of Hearst see Littlefield, *Hearst: His Role in American Progressivism*, pp. 148–50; Claude G. Bowers, *The Life of John Worth Kern* (Indianapolis, Ind.: The Hollenbeck Press, 1918), pp. 138–40; Swanberg, *Citizen Hearst*, pp. 213–15.

44. Typical of what was happening in every Hearst paper, see the *New York American*, February 29, 1904, pp. 4, 12; March 11, 1904, pp. 1–2; March 12, 1904, p. 6; March 13, 1904, p. 39; March 14, 1904, p. 5; March 31, 1904, pp. 1–2. For examples of many glowing reports see ibid., February 21, 1904, p. 42; March 3, 1904, p. 5; March 14, 1904, p. 4; March 23, 1904, p. 8; April 5, 1904, p. 8. See also Littlefield, *Hearst: His Role in American Progressivism*, p. 154.

45. Concerning the New York convention see *New York American*, April 16, 1904, p. 1; April 17, 1904, pp. 23, 39–40, 43; April 18, 1904, pp. 1–3; April 19, 1904, pp. 1–5. Concerning Indiana and Connecticut conventions see ibid., May 7, 1904, p. 6; May 12, 1904, p. 3; May 13, 1904, p. 4. In regard to Williams see ibid., July 9, 1904, p. 3; Osborn, *Williams*, pp. 114–15, 124; and *New York Times*, March 30, 1904, p. 1. See also Francis Butler Simkins, *Pitchfork Ben Tillman: South Carolinian* (Baton Rouge: Louisiana State University Press,

1944), pp. 390–91; Sam Hanna Acheson, *Joe Bailey: The Last Democrat* (New York: Macmillan, 1932), pp. 167–69. For Bailey's running controversy with Hearst papers see *New York Morning Journal*, November 14 and 24, 1898, p. 1; November 25, 1898, p. 6; November 28, 1898, p. 6 (editorial and Swinnerton cartoon); December 2 and 7, 1898, p. 6; December 4, 1898, p. 32; January 1, 1899, p. 1; March 4, 1899, pp. 2, 8.

46. For states pledging to Hearst see *New York American*, May 1, 1904, pp. 40–41; May 5, 1904, pp. 1, 4; May 6, 1904, p. 8; May 24, 1904, p. 2; June 7, 1904, pp. 1, 4; June 8, 1904, p. 3; June 15, 1904, p. 1. See Koenig, *Bryan*, pp. 374–77; Glad, *The Trumpet Soundeth*, pp. 152–54; Coletta, *Bryan*, I, 319–25; Kent, *The Democratic Party*, pp. 360–63; Winkler, *Hearst: A New Appraisal*, pp. 132–33; Swanberg, *Citizen Hearst*, pp. 216–17.

47. See *New York American*, July 6 and 7, 1904, p. 2; *New York Times*, July 3, 1904, p. 2; Winkler, *Hearst: A New Appraisal*, p. 135.

48. Koenig, *Bryan*, pp. 375, 386; Glad, *The Trumpet Soundeth*, pp. 152, 156; Daniel S. Lamont to Mr. President in Robert McElroy's *Grover Cleveland: The Man and the Statesman* (New York: Harper & Brothers, 1923), II, 329–30; Syrett, ed., *The Gentleman and the Tiger*, pp. 189, 211; *New York Times*, July 3, 1904, pp. 1, 2; Moses Koenigsberg, *King News: An Autobiography* (Philadelphia: F. A. Stokes, 1941), pp. 274–77. For story about Phoebe Hearst and Hill see Robinson, *The Hearsts*, pp. 255–56, 260.

49. See *New York American*, July 8, 1904, p. 2; July 9, 1904, p. 1; July 10, 1904, p. 34; Littlefield, *Hearst: His Role in American Progressivism*, pp. 156–60; Abbot, *Watching the World Go By*, pp. 250–53; Swanberg, *Citizen Hearst*, pp. 217–18; Koenig, *Bryan*, pp. 386–87.

50. Koenig, *Bryan*, pp. 387–89; Coletta, *Bryan*, I, 336–39; Josephus Daniels, *Editor in Politics* (Chapel Hill: University of North Carolina Press, 1941), pp. 186, 473–74; Abbot, *Watching the World Go By*, pp. 250–53; Kent, *The Democratic Party*, pp. 363–65. For Bryan's speech in full see *The Commoner*, July 29, 1904, pp. 1–2.

51. *Official Report of the Proceedings of the Democratic National Convention Held in St. Louis, Mo., July 6, 7, 8, and 9, 1904* (microfiche). Reported by Milton W. Blumenberg (New York: Press of the Publishers' Printing Company, [1904]), pp. 246–50; *National Party Conventions, 1831–1992* (Washington, D.C.: Congressional Quarterly, 1995), pp. 65, 208; Richard C. Bain, *Convention Decisions and Voting Records* (Washington, D.C.: Brookings Institute, 1960), p. 169; Coletta, *Bryan*, I, 339–40; Koenig, *Bryan*, p. 389; *New York American*, July 10, 1904, p. 35.

Chapter 10

1. Creelman, "The Real Mr. Hearst," pp. 249–51; Steffens, "Hearst, The Man of Mystery," pp. 3, 8; Louis Filler, *Crusaders for American Liberalism* (Yellow Springs, Ohio: Antioch Press, 1939), pp. 132–36ff; see also Chapter VIII,

pp. 136–37.

2. Creelman, "The Real Mr. Hearst," p. 267; Steffens, "Hearst, The Man of Mystery," p. 6; Mrs. Hearst Interview; Mrs. Flint Interview, January 18, 1960; Katz Interview; interview of Randolph Apperson by W. A. Swanberg, October 23, 1959, Swanberg Papers, Columbia University Library, New York. See also an interview with Hearst just after the St. Louis convention in the *New York American*, July 11, 1904, p. 5.

3. Concerning a description of Hearst's work habits see Millicent (Willson) Hearst to Mrs. p. A. Hearst, March 5, 1909, PAH Papers; Mrs. Hearst Interview; Mrs. Flint interviews, January 18 and February 20, 1960; Randolph Apperson Interview; Swanberg, *Citizen Hearst*, pp. 180, 219–20.

4. Creelman, "The Real Mr. Hearst," p. 265; Steffens, "Hearst, The Man of Mystery," pp. 4, 6, 8; Mrs. Flint Interview, January 18, 1960; Winkler, *Hearst: A New Appraisal*, p. 135. As an example of Hearst's growing disgust with the Democratic Party see Coblentz, ed., *Hearst: A Portrait in His Own Words*, p. 37.

5. For congratulatory telegram and newspaper interview see the *New York Times*, July 9, 1904, p. 3; *New York American*, July 10, 1904, pp. 33–34; July 11, 1904, p. 5; July 12, 1904, p. 2. For editorials and cartoons favoring the Democratic Party and Parker see daily in ibid., July 12, 1904, pp. 1, 2, and 12, to November 7, 1904, p. 14. See also Coblentz, ed., *Hearst: A Portrait in His Own Words*, p. 37; Winkler, *Hearst: A New Appraisal*, p. 135.

6. In regard to one aspect of Parker's thinking concerning a national campaign see editorial titled "Judge Parker and Stump Speaking" in the *New York American*, October 13, 1904, p. 16. Concerning vice-presidential nominee Henry G. Davis see ibid., July 18, 1904, p. 2; *New York Times*, July 11, 1904, p. 2; July 17, 1904, p. 5; July 18 and 19, 1904, pp. 1–2; Charles M. Pepper, *The Life and Times of Henry Gassoway Davis, 1823–1916* (New York: Century, 1920), pp. 174–80; Thomas Richard Ross, *Henry Gassaway Davis: An Old-Fashioned Biography* (Parsons, W. Va.: McClain, 1994), pp. 281–86.

7. For the bickering and divisiveness among New York Democratic leaders see the *New York Times*, July 15, 1904, p. 1; July 17, 1904, p. 1, and thereafter to the end of September; *New York American*, from July 18, 1904, p. 1, through September 30, 1904, p. 4; and the *New York Tribune* covering the same time period. Concerning D. Cady Herrick and his fight for the gubernatorial nomination see ibid., September 17, 1904, pp. 1, 4; then September 19–21, 1904, pp. 1–2; then see briefly his race for the governorship against Republican nominee Frank W. Higgins in ibid., October 2, 1904, p. 37, to almost daily coverage through October 18, 1904, pp. 1–2; and McCormick, *From Realignment to Reform*, pp. 189–91. Although the *New York American* never mentioned any communication between Parker and Hearst, the *New York Times*, July 22, 1904, p. 3, recorded that Parker invited Hearst to visit Esopus. For specific disenchantment with the Parker campaign strategy see the *New York American*, September 15, 1904, p. 1; October 4, 1904, p. 2; November 1, 1904, pp. 1–2.

For a discussion of the 1904 presidential campaign see Pringle, *Roosevelt*, pp. 354–56; Lewis L. Gould, *The Presidency of Theodore Roosevelt* (Lawrence: University Press of Kansas, 1991), pp. 139–44; and Nathan Miller, *Theodore Roosevelt: A Life* (New York: William Morrow, 1992), pp. 339–41.

8. Concerning Murphy's opposition to the Hearst renomination see the *New York Times*, August 1, 1904, p. 5; October 14, 1904, p. 7; October 23, 1904, p. 2; *New York Tribune*, December 6, 1904, p. 3; *New York American*, October 4, 1904, p. 2; Swanberg, *Citizen Hearst*, p. 222. For references to the Hearst campaign and political propaganda see the *New York American*, October 4, 1904, pp. 2, 14; October 13, 1904, p. 3; October 25, 1904, pp. 3, 9, 16; October 26, 1904, p. 2; October 27, 1904, p. 9; October 28, 1904, p. 10; October 30, 1904, pp. 39–40; October 31, 1904, p. 5; November 2, 1904, pp. 2, 4; November 4, 1904, p. 5; November 9, 1904, pp. 1–2. For betting odds on Roosevelt and Parker see almost daily in ibid, October 6, 1904, p. 2, to November 8, 1904, p. 2. Concerning claims that Hearst supported Parker, see also comment from the *Mobile (Ala.) Register* in ibid., November 20, 1904, p. 40.

9. *New York American*, November 13, 1904, p. 21. For references criticizing past leadership and recognizing Hearst as the possible leader of the Democratic Party see ibid., November 10, 1904, p. 2; November 11, 1904, p. 14; November 12, 1904, pp. 2, 14; November 13, 1904, p. 42; November 14, 1904, p. 12; November 16, 1904, p. 14; November 20, 1904, p. 40; November 27, 1904, p. 42.

10. Thompson, *Party Leaders of the Time*, pp. 233–47ff. For the introduction of the "Hearst bill" see the *Congressional Record*, 58th Cong., 2d sess., p. 3158; and for a complete rendition of the bill see the *New York American*, November 27, 1904, p. 21; January 22, 1905, p. 38. For Hearst's congressional participation as well as a record of petitions for the "Hearst bill" see the *Congressional Record*, 58th Cong., 2d sess., pp. 3, 187, 293, 395–96, 424–25, 431–32, 508–9, 618–19, 672, 729–30, 767, 998, 1754. For examples of the crusade for the "Hearst bill" see the *New York American and Journal*, November 27, 1904, p. 21; December 3, 1904, p. 16; December 6, 1904, p. 1; December 7, 1904, p. 6; December 19, 1904, p. 4; January 9, 1905, p. 5; January 10, 1905, p. 1; January 11, 1905, pp. 1–2; January 12, 1905, pp. 7, 14; January 13, 1905, p. 1; January 15, 1905, p. 40; January 17, 1905, pp. 1, 2, 16; January 18, 1905, pp. 1–2; January 20 and 21, 1905, p. 16 (Opper cartoons); January 31, 1905, pp. 3, 16; February 1, 1905, pp. 3, 4; February 3, 1905, p. 2; February 8, 1905, p. 1; February 9, 1905, pp. 1–2, 4; February 10, 1905, p. 1; February 11, 1905, p. 4. For Hearst's testimony before a congressional committee see ibid., January 19, 1905, pp. 1–3. For attacks on minority leader Williams, see ibid., February 2, 1905, pp. 4, 16; February 7, 1905, pp. 2, 16; February 8, 1905, pp. 2, 16; February 9, 1905, p. 16; February 10, 1905, p. 1; February 11, 1905, p. 4; February 12, 1905, p. 12. See also Osborn, *Williams*, pp. 123–24; Littlefield, *Hearst: His Role in American Progressivism*, pp. 128–30.

11. *Congressional Record,* 58th Cong., 3d sess., pp. 2479–2481; *New York Tribune,* February 14, 1905, p. 4; *New York American,* February 14, 1905, pp. 1–4.

12. Congressional Record, 58th Cong., 3d sess., pp. 2481–2482; *New York Tribune,* February 14, 1905, p. 4; *New York American,* February 14, 1905, pp. 1–4. For the attack on Hearst by Congressman Grove L. Johnson see *Congressional Record,* 54th Cong., 2d sess., pp. 592–93 (January 8, 1897); and Robert E. Burke, "Hiram Johnson Looks at William Randolph Hearst," a luncheon address at the Western History Association Annual Meeting, Phoenix, Arizona, October 21, 1982, in possession of author. See also Sullivan's rebuttal (and explanation) on February 14, 1905, in *Congressional Record,* 58th Cong., 3d sess., pp. 2559–2561; *New York American,* February 15, 1905, p. 4.

13. Syrett, ed., *The Gentleman and the Tiger,* pp. 10–31ff; Kurland, *Seth Low,* pp. 188–90.

14. Syrett, ed., *The Gentleman and the Tiger,* pp. 23–27, 189, 211–13.

15. Concerning stories about poison gas and the mayor see the *New York American,* November 18, 1904, p. 14; November 21, 1904, p. 12; November 23, 1904, p. 4; November 24, 1904, p. 12; November 26, 1904, pp. 7, 16; November 27, 1904, p. 41; and November 29, 1904, p. 6. See also ibid., December 1, 1904, pp. 1–2; December 2, 1904, pp. 1–2, 14; December 3, 1904, pp. 1, 4, 16. Concerning Comptroller Grout as well as testimonials for Hearst and denunciations of McClellan, see daily in ibid., from December 2, 1904, pp. 1–2, through December 17, 1904, p. 7.

16. See *New York American and Journal,* December 18, 1904, p. 38; *New York Tribune,* December 6, 1904, p. 3.

17. *New York American,* December 21, 1904, p. 14; December 22, 1904, p. 6; December 23, 1904, p. 4; Littlefield, *Hearst: His Role in American Progressivism,* p. 177 (also endnote 1); Herbert Mitgang, *The Man Who Rode the Tiger: The Life and Times of Judge Samuel Seabury* (Philadelphia: J. B. Lippincott, 1963), pp. 80–81; Walter Chambers, *Samuel Seabury: A Challenge* (New York: Century, 1932), pp. 96–98; Swanberg, *Citizen Hearst,* pp. 230–31. Concerning specific protests of labor and businessmen see the *New York American,* January 1, 1905, p. 44; January 2, 1905, p. 7; January 7, 1905, p. 4.

18. Concerning typical characterizations of McClellan see the *New York American,* January 4, 1905, pp. 1, 14; February 3, 1905, p. 4; March 14, 1905, pp. 2, 16; March 15, 1905, pp. 1, 4, 16. For stories and editorials about Murphy and Tammany see ibid., February 6, 1905, p. 5; February 17, 1905, p. 9; March 2, 1905, p. 4; March 3, 1905, pp. 4, 8; March 4, 1905, pp. 4, 16; March 5, 1905, p. 52; March 6, 1905, p. 16; March 7, 1905, p. 1; March 9, 1905, p. 14; March 21, 1905, p. 8; March 22, 1905, p. 4; March 23, 1905, p. 2; March 24, 1905, p. 24; March 28, 1905, pp. 3, 7, 16; March 31, 1905, p. 2. For photos and references to Murphy's wealth see ibid., April 4, 1905, p. 1; June 21, 1905, p. 8; June 23, 1905, p. 10. In support of this crusade, cartoons by Opper, Sullivant,

and Herriman appeared at least once daily from December, 1904, through April, 1905. See Swinnerton's "Manhattan Rhymes" in ibid., March 14, 15, 16, 18, 21, 22, 23, 31, April 1, 1905, p. 16, and April 3, 1905, p. 14.

19. For specific stories of Seabury and Hearst activities see the *New York American*, January 20, 1905, p. 1; January 31, 1905, p. 4; February 22, 1905, p. 5; March 3, 1905, p. 5; March 9, 1905, p. 2; March 31, 1905, p. 4; April 1, 1905, p. 10; April 7, 1905, p. 16; April 8, 1905, pp. 1–4; April 13, 1905, pp. 9, 16; April 14, 1905, p. 6; April 16, 1905, p. 42; April 18, 1905, p. 4; April 24, 1905, p. 4; April 30, 1905, p. 44. Concerning Judge Dunne and the Chicago campaign for municipal ownership see ibid., February 26, 1905, p. 43; April 3, 1905, p. 1; April 4, 1905, pp. 3–4; April 6, 1905, p. 9; April 7, 1905, p. 1; April 14, 1905, p. 1; April 20, 1905, p. 8. See also Mitgang, *Seabury*, pp. 80–81; Chambers, *Seabury*, pp. 97–98. Concerning trip to Europe see Will to Dear Mother, April, 1905, PAH Papers.

20. *New York Times*, September 30, 1905, p. 7; *New York American*, September 30, 1905, p. 3; Older, *Hearst*, p. 274; Swanberg, *Citizen Hearst*, p. 230; Chambers, *Seabury*, pp. 98–99. For excellent newspaper coverage of the futile attempts at "fusion" see the *New York American* and the *New York Times* for September, 1905. For listing of different political organizations eventually involved in fusion see *New York American*, October 12, 1905, p. 1.

21. Merlo J. Pusey, *Charles Evans Hughes* (New York: Macmillan, 1951), I, 141–50ff; Robert F. Wesser, *Charles Evans Hughes: Politics and Reform in New York, 1905–1910* (Ithaca, N.Y.: Cornell University Press, 1967), I, 76–77; Mitgang, *Seabury*, pp. 81–82; Chambers, *Seabury*, pp. 98–100; Swanberg, *Citizen Hearst*, pp. 232–33. For a running account of this ten-day period see the *New York American*, October 1, 1905, p. 38; then October 2, 1905, pp. 1, 2, 9, 16, to October 10, 1905, pp. 1–2, 9, 16. But see especially ibid., October 11, 1905, p. 1. For a different coverage, mainly pro-McClellan and anti-Hearst, see the *New York Times* over same period, from October 1 to October 11, 1905.

22. See the *New York American*, October 3, 4, and 5, 1905, pp. 1, 2; and especially October 11, 1905, pp. 1–2; see also the *New York Times*, October 11, 1905, p. 7, for story coverage of Hearst; and Littlefield, *Hearst: His Role in American Progressivism*, pp. 179–80.

23. Irwin Yellowitz, *Labor and the Progressive Movement in New York State, 1897–1916* (Ithaca, N.Y.: Cornell University Press, 1965), pp. 190–93. For short campaign biographies of Phelps Stokes and Ford (with accompanying pictures) see the *New York American*, October 13, 1905, pp. 4–5. For Hearst's report of campaign expenditures see the *New York Times*, November 18, 1905, p. 4. See also ibid., October 14, 1905, p. 7; October 18, 1905, pp. 5, 7. For an account of this campaign see also James Allen Myatt, "William Randolph Hearst and the Progressive Era, 1900–1912," Ph.D. diss., University of Florida, Gainesville, Fla., 1960 (Ann Arbor, Mich.: University Microfilms, 1960), pp. 64–77.

24. For daily coverage of the mayoral campaign see the *New York American* from October 5 to November 8, 1905. See also the *New York Times* during the same period for a more favorable view of McClellan. See also Winkler, *Hearst: A New Appraisal*, p. 141; Swanberg, *Citizen Hearst*, p. 235.

25. *New York American*, October 5, 1905, pp. 1–2; October 13, 1905, pp. 2–3; October 18, 1905, pp. 1–2; October 25, 1905, p. 1; *New York Times*, October 20, 1905, p. 4; October 29, 1905, pp. 3–4; October 31, 1905, p. 5; Swanberg, *Citizen Hearst*, pp. 234–36; Older, *Hearst*, pp. 276–80; Winkler, *Hearst: A New Appraisal*, pp. 138, 140–41. See also Yellowitz, *Labor and the Progressive Movement*, pp. 193–96; Littlefield, *Hearst: His Role in American Progressivism*, pp. 180–89ff.

26. *New York American*, October 5, 1905, pp. 1–2; October 13, 1905, pp. 2–3; October 18, 1905, p. 2; *New York Times*, October 20, 1905, p. 4; Winkler, *Hearst: A New Appraisal*, pp. 138, 140; Older, *Hearst*, pp. 277, 279; Swanberg, *Citizen Hearst*, p. 234.

27. Older, *Hearst*, pp. 277–78; *New York American*, October 26, 1905, p. 1; *New York Times*, October 26, 1905, p. 2.

28. *New York American*, October 28, 1905, p. 3; October 30, 1905, pp. 1–2; November 1, 1905, p. 1; November 2, 1905, pp. 2, 3, 9; November 3, 1905, pp. 3, 9; November 5, 1905, p. 35; *New York Times*, October 24, 1905, p. 4; November 1, 1905, p. 1; November 2, 1905, pp. 1–2, 6; November 4, 1905, p. 5; November 5, 1905, p. 3; Swanberg, *Citizen Hearst*, pp. 234–36; Winkler, *Hearst: A New Appraisal*, pp. 138, 141–42; Syrett, ed., *The Gentleman and the Tiger*, p. 224.

29. For rewards for election violations see the *New York American*, October 25, 1905, p. 9; October 26, 1905, p. 10; November 4, 1905, p. 3; November 7, 1905, p. 1. For an example of acquiring volunteers in the New York Vigilance Committee see ibid., October 21, 1905, p. 3. Concerning campaign promises see ibid., October 26, 1905, p. 2; October 27, 1905, pp. 1–2; November 2, 1905, pp. 1–2; November 3, 1905, p. 1; November 4, 1905, p. 2; November 7, 1905, p. 2. For example of photos see ibid., November 5, 1905, p. 47. See also the *New York Times*, October 20, 1905, p. 4; October 21, 1905, p. 4; October 22, 1905, p. 3; October 23, 1905, p. 2; October 24, 1905, p. 2; October 26, 1905, p. 2; October 27, 1905, p. 6; October 29, 1905, p. 3; November 3, 1905, p. 4; November 4, 1905, p. 5; November 5, 1905, pp. 1–2; Swanberg, *Citizen Hearst*, pp. 235–36; Older, *Hearst*, pp. 277–80ff; Yellowitz, *Labor and the Progressive Movement in New York State*, pp. 193–96; Winkler, *Hearst: A New Appraisal*, pp. 141–42.

30. *New York Times*, November 6, 1905, pp. 1–2; *New York American*, November 4, 1905, p. 9; November 5, 1905, p. 35; November 6, 1905, pp. 1–2; Older, *Hearst*, pp. 279–80; Swanberg, *Citizen Hearst*, p. 237.

31. *New York American*, November 6, 1905, pp. 1–2; *New York Times*, November 6, 1905, p. 2.

32. *New York American*, November 7, 1905, pp. 1, 10; November 8, 1905, pp. 1, 2, 3; *New York Times*, November 7, 1905, p. 4; November 8, 1905, pp. 2, 8; November 11, 1905, p. 1; Older, *Hearst*, pp. 281–82; Winkler, *Hearst: A New Appraisal*, pp. 142–43; Mitgang, *The Man Who Rode the Tiger*, pp. 84–85.

33. *New York American*, November 8, 1905, pp. 1–3, 16; November 9, 1905, p. 1; *New York Times*, November 8, 1905, p. 1; November 9, 1905, p. 4; Older, *Hearst*, p. 282; Winkler, *Hearst: A New Appraisal*, p. 143. See also Syrett, ed., *The Gentleman and the Tiger*, p. 224; Charles Edward Russell, *Bare Hands and Stone Walls* (New York: Charles Scribner's Sons, 1933), pp. 140–41. The final official election count was: McClellan, 228,397; Hearst, 224,923; Ivins, 137,193; Lee (Socialist), 11,817. See Yellowitz, *Labor and the Progressive Movement in New York State*, p. 197n.

34. *New York American*, November 10, 1905, pp. 1, 3; November 11, 1905, pp. 1–2; November 12, 1905, pp. 37–40; November 13, 1905, pp. 1–2; *New York Times*, November 8, 1905, p. 1; November 9, 1905, p. 5; November 10, 1905, p. 2; November 11, 1905, p. 1; Winkler, *Hearst: A New Appraisal*, pp. 143–44; Older, *Hearst*, pp. 282–83; Littlefield, *Hearst: His Role in American Progressivism*, pp. 188–95ff.

35. For an interesting evaluation of Hearst and the election see Nicholas Murray Butler to Theodore Roosevelt, November 6 and 9, 1905, Theodore Roosevelt Papers, Manuscript Division, Library of Congress, Washington, D.C. See also Littlefield, *Hearst: His Role in American Progressivism*, pp. 194–98; Yellowitz, *Labor and the Progressive Movement in New York State*, pp. 196–203; *New York American*, November 14, 1905, pp. 1, 4, to December 3, 1905, p. 55. See also in ibid., November 27, 1905, p. 7. See also *New York Times*, November 10, 1905, p. 2; November 21, 1905, p. 1; November 24, 1905, p. 1; November 29, 1905, p. 7; November 30, 1905, p. 3; December 1, 1905, p. 2; December 7, 1905, p. 4; December 27, 1905, p. 2; Syrett, ed., *The Gentleman and the Tiger*, pp. 227–30.

36. *Congressional Record*, 59th Cong., 1st sess., pp. 39, 55, 56, 298. For a constant drumbeat for a mayoral recount see the *New York American* from November 8, 1905, through March, 1906. For specific references in the paragraph see ibid., November 20, 1905, pp. 6, 14; December 25, 1905, p. 7; December 26, 1905, p. 8; December 28, 1905, pp. 1, 2; December 29, 1905, pp. 8, 9; February 28, 1906, pp. 1, 6; March 11, 1906, p. 39; April 17, 1906, p. 1; *New York Times*, January 11, 1906, p. 1; February 11, 1906, p. 4; February 19, 1906, p. 18; February 28, 1906, p. 1; March 1, 1906, p. 5; March 9, 1906, p. 4. For interviews see *New York American*, February 2, 1906, p. 6; March 1, 1906, pp. 1–2; March 25, 1906, p. 50; *San Francisco Examiner*, March 7, 1906, p. 11; March 26, 1906, p. 7; March 29, 1906, p. 18; June 17, 1906, p. 27; Frederick Palmer, "Hearst and Hearstism," *Collier's*, September 22, September 29, October 6, October 13, 1906; Steffens, "Hearst, The Man of Mystery." See also Yellowitz, *Labor and the Progressive Movement in New York State*, pp. 202–3; Chambers, *Seabury*,

pp. 103–5; Mitgang, *The Man Who Rode the Tiger*, p. 86; Older, *Hearst*, pp. 287–92; Winkler, *Hearst: A New Appraisal*, pp. 144–45. Concerning Phoebe Hearst's Parisian decision see Robinson, *The Hearsts*, pp. 346, 348–49.

37. *San Francisco Examiner*, April 20, 1906, pp. 1–3, 7–8; April 21, 1906, pp. 1–2; see ibid., Sunday supplement, for graphic pictures of San Francisco, May 12 to June 24, 1906; Lillian M. Wheeler to Mrs. Hearst, May 24, 1906, and Will to Mother, summer, 1906, PAH Papers; Gordon Thomas and Max Morgan Witts, *The San Francisco Earthquake* (New York: Stein and Day, 1971), pp. 51–268; Older, *Hearst*, pp. 292–95; Winkler, *Hearst: A New Appraisal*, p. 145.

38. *San Francisco Examiner*, April 21, 1906, p. 3; April 22, 1906, p. 3; April 23, 1906, p. 7; April 26, 1906, p. 3; Will to Mother, summer, 1906, and Millicent to Mrs Hearst, [May], 1906, PAH Papers; Winkler, *Hearst: A New Appraisal*, pp. 145–46; Older, *Hearst*, pp. 292–93; Thomas and Witts, *The San Francisco Earthquake*, pp. 82–83, 161–62; Walton Bean, *Boss Ruef's San Francisco* (Berkeley: University of California Press, 1952), p. 133; Swanberg, *Citizen Hearst*, pp. 240–41. For a personal account of the San Francisco disaster as well as the problems of transmitting photos to New York see Coleman, *Give Us a Little Smile, Baby*, pp. 124–31.

39. *San Francisco Examiner*, April 24, 1906, pp. 3, 5; April 25, 1906, p. 2; April 29, 1906, p. 3; May 1, 1906, pp. 3, 5; May 2, 1906, pp. 2, 3; May 4, 1906, pp. 3, 4. For lists concerning persons "found" or "missing" see daily in ibid., April 24 to May 11, 1906, usually on p. 3, 4, or 5.

40. *Congressional Record*, 59th Cong., 1st sess., pp. 6175, 6236; *San Francisco Examiner*, May 8, 1906, p. 4; Will to Mother (telegram), May 3, 1906, PAH Papers.

41. Millicent to Mrs. Hearst, [May], 1906, PAH Papers; Older, *Hearst*, pp. 294–95; Bean, *Boss Ruef's San Francisco*, p. 133; *San Francisco Examiner*, May 13, 1906, pp. 1, 3, 5; May 15, 1906, p. 2; May 17, 1906, pp. 3, 16; May 18, 1906, pp. 13, 16; May 19, 1906, p. 16; May 20, 1906, p. 1; May 24, 1906, pp. 1, 2; May 25, 1906, pp. 1–2, 15; May 26, 1906, p. 3; May 27, 1906, pp. 33–34; May 28, 1906, p. 2; May 29, 1906, p. 2; May 31, 1906, p. 5; June 8, 1906, p. 4; June 9, 1906, p. 16. Concerning Hearst's labor policy see ibid., May 20, 1906, p. 19; Winkler, *Hearst: A New Appraisal*, p. 145. For the "giants and dragons" reference see Creelman, "The Real Mr. Hearst," p. 257.

42. Bean, *Boss Ruef's San Francisco*, pp. 108–35ff; Older, *Hearst*, pp. 297–98; see also the *San Francisco Examiner*, May 15, 1906, p. 1, through July, 1906. But see charges of bribery and corruption by Schmitz, specifically in ibid., July 10, 11, 12, 13, 1906, pp. 1–2; July 14, 16, 18, 1906, p. 1. Concerning negatives on Ruef see ibid., August 1, 1906, pp. 1–2; August 2, 1906, p. 3; August 3, 1906, p. 4; August 4, 1906, p. 38; August 5, 1906, p. 1.

43. *New York American*, August 18, 1906, pp. 1, 3; August 19, 1906, pp. 38, 40; *New York Times*, August 21, 1906, p. 4; *San Francisco Examiner*, August 18,

1906, p. 1; Older, *Hearst*, p. 299.

44. Pringle, *Roosevelt*, pp. 427–29; Pusey, *Hughes*, I, 162–63; David Graham Phillips, "The Treason of the Senate," *Cosmopolitan*, March, 1906, pp. 488, 490–91; McCormick, *From Realignment To Reform*, pp. 193–210; Syrett, ed., *The Gentleman and the Tiger*, pp. 26–27, 226–34; *New York American*, December 28, 1905, p. 16 (Opper political cartoon); December 30, 1905, pp. 1, 4; December 31, 1905, pp. 38, 56.

45. For typical reports about the Gas Trust read the *New York American* from May 2, 4, 5, 1906, p. 1, to August 16, 1906, pp. 1, 4; but see specifically in ibid., May 23, 1906, pp. 1, 18; May 24, 25, 1906, pp. 1, 4, 18; June 15, 1906, pp. 1–2; June 17, 1906, p. 37; June 27, 1906, pp. 1, 18; July 15, 1906, p. 34; July 21, 1906, p. 10; July 27, 1906, pp. 2, 16; August 10, 1906, p. 4. Concerning typical stories about the railroads and rebating see ibid., July 2, 1906, p. 16; July 18, 1906, p. 11; August 4, 1906, p. 4; August 9, 1906, p. 1; August 11, 1906, p. 1; August 12, 1906, pp. 21, 33. And concerning stories of meat-packing atrocities see ibid., from May 29, 1906, to June 28, 1906, p. 13, but see especially May 30, 1906, pp. 1–2, 16; May 31, 1906, pp. 1–3; June 1, 1906, pp. 1, 4, 7; June 2, 1906, pp. 9, 15; June 3, 1906, pp. 25, 51; June 4, 1905, pp. 1, 3, 8, 9, 16; June 5, 1906, pp. 1, 4, 5, 6, 18. For attacks on Jerome see ibid., May 2, 3, 1906, p. 18; May 19, 1906, pp. 1–2; May 30, 1906, p. 5; June 2, 1906, pp. 4, 14; June 5, 1906, p. 1; June 8, 1906, pp. 1–2; June 9, 1906, p. 18; June 10, 1906, p. 37; June 13, 1906, pp. 3, 18; June 14, 1906, pp. 1, 7, 18; June 17, 1906, p. 51; June 23, 1906, p. 3; July 4, 6, 1906, p. 6; July 15, 1906, p. 46; July 28, 1906, p. 3; August 7, 1906, p. 9; August 8, 1906, p. 16; August 9, 1906, p. 8; August 11, 1906, pp. 5, 16; August 16, 1906, p. 16; August 20, 1906, p. 1; August 21, 1906, pp. 1–2, 18.

46. For coverage of the White murder and the forthcoming Thaw trial, together with every "juicy tidbit" see (almost daily) the *New York American*, June 26, 1906, pp. 1–2, to August 7, 8, 1906, p. 8. See also the *New York Times* during this same time period for ample coverage. For the exposé of the *Herald* "Personals" and "red light" trial see (almost daily) the *New York American*, June 25, 1906, p. 7, to July 22, 1906, p. 36; Winkler, *Hearst: A New Appraisal*, p. 154.

47. *New York Times*, August 21, 1906, p. 4. See specifically in ibid., November 4, 1906, Sunday Magazine section, p. 3, for an excellent article on Hearst. For further evidence of the author's conclusions see both the *Times* and the *American* from the latter part of August to November 6, 1906.

48. *New York American*, August 22, 1906, pp. 1–2; August 23, 1906, pp. 4, 18; August 24, 1906, p. 1; *New York Times*, August 22, 1906, pp. 1, 6; Older, *Hearst*, p. 300.

49. For samples of League activities during the spring and summer of 1906 see the *New York American*, May 11, 1906, pp. 1, 4, 7; May 24, 1906, pp. 1, 4; May 27, 1906, pp. 36, 46; June 3, 1906, pp. 37, 48; June 8, 1906, p. 6; June 10, 1906, pp. 38, 44, 46; June 12, 1906, pp. 4, 9; June 15, 1906, pp. 1, 7; June 22,

1906, pp. 3, 8; July 6, 1906, pp. 1, 5; July 11, 1906, pp. 9, 12; July 12, 1906, pp. 5, 11; July 14, 1906, p. 12; July 20, 1906, pp. 6, 7; July 22, 1906, pp. 36, 44; July 28, 1906, p. 6; August 1, 1906, pp. 1, 4, 16; August 3, 1906, p. 10; August 8, 1906, pp. 3, 4; August 12, 1906, pp. 37, 43. Concerning the resignation of Phelps Stokes see ibid., July 29, 1906, p. 37. In reference to the weekly rural journal see ibid., June 27, 1906, p. 13; July 2, 1906, p. 12; July 4, 1906, p. 8; July 5, 1906, p. 12; July 7, 1906, p. 6; July 11, 1906, p. 9. For the opening of the League campaign see ibid., September 4, 1906, pp. 1–2, 4; *New York Times,* September 3, 1906, p. 2; September 4, 1906, p. 5; *New York Tribune,* September 3, 1906, p. 2; September 4, 1906, pp. 2, 6. See also Littlefield, *Hearst: His Role in American Progressivism,* pp. 205–6; Chambers, *Seabury,* pp. 104–5; Mitgang, *The Man Who Rode the Tiger,* p. 86; Wesser, *Hughes,* pp. 79–81; Syrett, ed., *The Gentleman and the Tiger,* p. 286.

50. *New York American,* September 4, 1906, pp. 1–2; September 9, 1906, p. 52; September 10, 1906, pp. 2, 7; September 11, 1906, pp. 1–2, 16; September 12, 1906, pp. 1–3, 18; *New York Times,* September 8, 9, 1906, p. 5; September 10, 1905, pp. 4, 5; September 11, 1906, p. 1; September 12, 1906, pp. 1–2. See daily in ibid., August 21 to September 12, 1906, for negative comments and criticisms about Hearst and the Independence League. See also the *New York Tribune,* September 6, 8, 1906, p. 2; September 9, 10, 1906, p. 1; September 12, 1906, pp. 1–2; September 13, 1906, p. 1.

51. *New York American,* September 13, 1906, pp. 1–4, 18; *New York Times,* September 13, 1906, pp. 1–2, 6; *New York Tribune,* September 13, 1906, pp. 1, 6.

52. Yellowitz, *Labor and the Progressive Movement,* pp. 197, 202–5; Hearst to Ihmsen, September 12, 14, 1906, and Ihmsen to Hearst, September 13, 1906, in Littlefield, *Hearst: His Role in American Progressivism,* pp. 206–8; Myatt, "Hearst and the Progressive Era," pp. 81–87; Syrett, ed., *The Gentleman and the Tiger,* p. 285.

53. Yellowitz, *Labor and the Progressive Movement,* pp. 204–7; Littlefield, *Hearst: His Role in American Progressivism,* pp. 208–10; Syrett, ed., *The Gentleman and the Tiger,* pp. 285–88; *New York American,* September 13, 1906, p. 6; September 17, 1906, p. 4; September 18, 19, 1906, pp. 1–2; September 20, 21, 22, 1906, pp. 4, 5; September 23, 1906, pp. 35, 38, 40; September 24, 1906, pp. 1–4, 9, 16; September 25, 1906, pp. 1–2; September 26, 1906, pp. 1–3, 6; September 27, 1906, pp. 1–4, 6; *New York Times,* September 12, 1906, p. 8; September 13, 1906, pp. 2, 6; September 15, 1906, p. 3; September 20, 1906, pp. 1, 3; September 21, 1906, pp. 1–2, 8; September 22, 1906, p. 7; September 23, 1906, pp. 4–5, 6; September 24, 1906, pp. 1, 4; September 25, 1906, pp. 1–2, 8; September 26, 1906, pp. 1–2; September 27, 1906, pp. 1–2, 4; September 28, 1906, pp. 1–3, 8; *New York Tribune,* September 13, 1906, p. 6; September 17, 1906, p. 1; September 21, 1906, p. 1; September 23, 1906, p. 2; September 25, 1906, p. 1; September 26, 1906, pp. 1–2, 4; September 27,

1906, pp. 5, 6; September 28, 1906, pp. 2, 6; September 29, 1906, p. 1. See also Older, *Hearst*, p. 301; Winkler, *Hearst: A New Appraisal*, pp. 149–50; Swanberg, *Citizen Hearst*, p. 241; and Myatt, "Hearst and the Progressive Era," pp. 82–87ff.

54. For a short biography and picture of Chanler see the *New York American*, September 13, 1906, p. 4; see also the *New York Times*, September 13, 1906, p. 2. Concerning Hughes and the Republican strategy see Pusey, *Hughes*, I, 141–42, 158, 169–70, 172–73; Wesser, *Hughes*, pp. 40–48, 50–51, 62–64, 67–69.

55. For typical examples of cartoons, often with an accompanying editorial, see the *New York American*, October 3, 1906, p. 16; October 7, 1906, p. 51; October 14, 1906, p. 14; October 18, 1906, p. 8; October 20, 1906, p. 16; October 21, 1906, p. 51; October 24, 1906, pp. 3, 18; October 27, 1906, p. 18; November 2, 1906, p. 20; November 3, 1906, p. 9. See also speeches by Shearn and Ford in ibid., October 9, 1906, p. 4; October 13, 1906, p. 5; October 16, 1906, p. 2; October 17, 1906, p. 4; October 19, 1906, p. 4; then from October 27 to November 5, 1906. See campaign comments and speeches by Hearst in ibid., September 28 to November 7, 1906. See also Wesser, *Hughes*, pp. 86–87; Pusey, *Hughes*, I, 175–76.

56. *New York Tribune*, September 27, 1906, pp. 5, 6; October 3, 1906, p. 6; October 4, 1906, p. 1; October 6, 1906, p. 6; October 11, 1906, pp. 3, 6; October 13, 1906, p. 3; October 23, 1906, p. 6; October 26, 1906, p. 1; *New York Times*, September 28, 1906, pp. 1–2, 8; October 3, 9, 1906, p. 3; October 12, 1906, p. 2; October 17, 1906, pp. 3, 4; October 20, 1906, p. 4. Concerning the "Ananias Cup" contest see the *New York American*, October 5, 1906, p. 5, almost daily to November 5, 1906, p. 8.

57. *New York Tribune*, September 11, 1906, p. 4; October 15, 1906, p. 2; October 17, 1906, p. 1; October 31, 1906, p. 3. For similar comments about Hearst building a corporate empire see *New York Times*, October 12, 1906, p. 2; October 17, 1906, p. 4; October 18, 1906, p. 3; October 20, 1906, p. 4.

58. For a favorable, daily account of this 1906 campaign see the *New York American*, September 28, 1906, pp. 1–2, to November 6, 1906, pp. 1–4, 9, 10. Specifically see in ibid., September 28, 29, 1906, p. 1; September 30, 1906, pp. 37–38; October 6, 1906, pp. 1–2; October 10, 1906, p. 4; October 13, 1906, pp. 1, 5; October 20, 1906, p. 5; October 21, 1906, pp. 38, 39; October 22, 23, 24, 26, 1906, p. 1; October 28, 1906, pp. 31, 47. For the negative side, daily, of the Hearst campaign, see especially the *New York Tribune*, but also the *New York Times*. See also Myatt, "Hearst and the Progressive Era," pp. 84–89ff; Yellowitz, *Labor and the Progressive Movement*, pp. 207–13ff; Littlefield, *Hearst: His Role in American Progressivism*, pp. 212–21ff. For reports on Hearst's "canned speeches" see *New York Tribune*, October 28, 1906, p. 3; *New York Times*, October 28, 1906, p. 2.

59. Wesser, *Hughes*, pp. 89–96ff; Philip C. Jessup, *Elihu Root* (New York:

Dodd, Mead, 1937), II, 113–15; *New York Times*, October 9, 1906, p. 2; Myatt, "Hearst and the Progressive Era," pp. 93–96, 98–100; McCormick, *From Realignment to Reform*, pp. 223–24.

60. Jessup, *Root*, II, 114–22; Pusey, *Hughes*, I, 178–80; Wesser, *Hughes*, pp. 96–97; *New York Times*, November 2, 1906, pp. 1–3; *New York Tribune*, November 2, 1906, pp. 1–2; *New York American*, November 2, 1906, pp. 9–10; Littlefield, *Hearst: His Role in American Progressivism*, pp. 217–19.

61. *New York Tribune*, November 3, 1906, p. 1; November 6, 1906, p. 3; *New York Times*, November 3, 1906, p. 3; *New York American*, November 2, 1906, pp. 1, 2, 3, 9; November 3, 1906, pp. 1, 2, 9, 20; November 5, 1906, pp. 1–4, 20; Jessup, *Root*, II, 117, 121; Swanberg, *Citizen Hearst*, p. 252; Older, *Hearst*, pp. 308–11.

62. *New York Times*, November 4, 1906, p. 4, and especially the editorial section, p. 3; Pusey, *Hughes*, I, 180.

63. Early morning "Extra" of the *New York American*, November 7, 1906, pp. 1, 2. See Littlefield, *Hearst: His Role in American Progressivism*, pp. 220–23; McCormick, *From Realignment to Reform*, pp. 224–27.

Chapter 11

1. For magazine articles and their effects see Creelman, "The Real Mr. Hearst"; Palmer, "Hearst and Hearstism," April 7, September 29, October 6, October 13, 1906; Steffens, "Hearst, The Man of Mystery"; Older, *Hearst*, p. 302; Swanberg, *Citizen Hearst*, pp. 246–49, 251. For typical examples of Republican campaign rhetoric see *New York Tribune*, October 31, 1906, p. 6; November 2, 1906, pp. 2, 4; November 4, 1906, pp. 1, 3, 4; *New York Times*, November 1, 1906, pp. 1–3, 8; November 2, 1906, pp. 1–4, 8; November 4, 1906, p. 8. For a report on tributes to Hearst at Delmonico's as well as Hearst's speech see *New York American*, November 13, 1906, pp. 1–2, 4.

2. See the *New York American*, 1904–06, which the author outlined daily, for evidence of Hearst's and Brisbane's thinking. See also in ibid. numerous editorials (on the last page) as well as cartoons by Frederick Opper, T. S. Sullivant, and Robert Carter that reflected the sense of such editorials. See also in ibid., August 23, 1906, p. 18; September 20, 1907, p. 16; September 29, 1907, p. 2-L; October 13, 1907, p. 11-E; October 18, 1907, p. 6; November 2, 1907, p. 6. Concerning Hearst's observations about Roosevelt and the Republicans see Will to Mother, 1905, PAH Papers. See also Syrett, ed., *The Gentleman and the Tiger*, pp. 226–27, 229; Littlefield, *Hearst: His Role in American Progressivism*, p. 237.

3. See Hearst to Brisbane, December 13, [1905], and February 21, 1906, in Steffens, "Hearst, The Man of Mystery," pp. 16–18; Hearst to Brisbane, July 14, 1908, in Littlefield, *Hearst: His Role in American Progressivism*, pp. 243–44; Hearst to Charles A. Walsh, January 9, 1907, in the *New York American*, January 12, 1908, p. 2-W; ibid., September 3, 1907, p. 2; September

29, 1907, p. 2-L.

4. Will to Mother, [late fall], 1906, and Hearst to A[rthur] B[risbane], March 21, 1909, PAH Papers; *New York Times*, November 16, 1906, p. 2; November 17, 1906, p. 1; December 20, 1906, p. 1; December 22, 1906, p. 2; *New York Tribune*, November 18, 1906, p. 1; Older, *Hearst*, p. 315; Robinson, *The Hearsts*, pp. 338–39; Swanberg, *Citizen Hearst*, p. 253. Both Swanberg and Older were incorrect in stating that Hearst visited Phoebe at the Hacienda at Pleasanton, California; the *New York Times*, December 22, 1906, p. 2, states that she had just arrived in New York City from Europe on the *Kaiser Wilhelm II*.

5. For consultation concerning appointments and mayoral recount see the *New York Times*, December 22, 1906, p. 6; December 24, 1906, p. 3; December 31, 1906, p. 1; January 1, 1907, p. 3; January 2, 1907, p. 1; January 6, 1907, p. 1; January 8, 1907, p. 1; January 9, 1907, p. 2; January 10, 1907, p. 6; January 15, 1907, p. 18; *New York American*, December 31, 1906, p. 1; January 2, 1907, p. 1; January 6, 1907, p. 1; January 7, 1907, p. 14; January 8 and 9, 1907, p. 1; January 10, 1907, p. 7; January 12, 1907, p. 1; January 13, 1907, p. 29; January 15, 1907, p. 5; January 18, 1907, pp. 1, 4, 18. Hearst appeared briefly in Congress to present three bills. On February 8, 1907, he presented a bill to prevent corrupt practices in federal elections and one to require railroad companies engaged in interstate commerce to furnish cars and other transportation facilities within a reasonable time after demand. On March 1, 1907, he proposed a bill to provide for national incorporation and control of corporations engaged in interstate commerce. See *Congressional Record*, 59th Cong., 2d sess., pp. 2621, 4403; *New York American*, February 9, 1907, p. 8; February 24, 1907, p. 37; March 3, 1907, p. 40. See also Syrett, ed., *The Gentleman and the Tiger*, pp. 226–30, for McClellan's recollections concerning the mayoral recount.

6. For organizational meetings of the Independence League see *New York Times*, January 5, 1907, p. 11; *New York American*, January 3, 1907, p. 4; January 9, 1907, p. 10; February 1, 1907, p. 6. For evidence of the League's social and political agendas see *New York American*, February 24, 1907, pp. 42, 51; March 5, 1907, p. 5; April 7, 1907, p. 6-L; April 17, 1907, p. 4; April 21, 1907, p. 6-III; May 5, 1907, p. 8-I; May 12, 1907, p. 8-II; May 15, 1907, p. 12; June 23, 1907, p. 17-E; July 7, 1907, p. 8-II; July 21, 1907, p. 5-II; July 28, 1907, pp. 5, 6-II; August 18, 1907, p. 2-W; August 22, 1907, p. 12; August 23, 1907, p. 6; August 24, 1907, p. 6; August 25, 1907, p. 11-I.

7. *New York American*, March 3, 1907, p. 37; March 6, 1907, pp. 1–2; March 7, 1907, pp. 2, 11, 16; March 8, 1907, pp. 2, 7; March 9, 1907, p. 7; *New York Times*, March 6, 1907, p. 1.

8. *New York American*, March 24, 1907, pp. 20, 59; March 29, 1907, pp. 6, 7; April 1, 1907, pp. 2, 4; April 7, 1907 pp. 6-L, 11-L; April 8, 1907, pp. 8, 18; April 15, 1907, p. 7; April 17, 1907, p. 4; April 19, 1907, p. 6; May 5, 1907, pp. 8-I, 1-II; May 15, 1907, p. 12; May 18, 1907, p. 4; June 5, 1907, p. 4; June 6,

1907, p. 5; June 24, 1907, p. 18; July 2, 1907, pp. 1–2; July 3, 1907, p. 16. For the League push for a mayoral recount see ibid., throughout March, April, May, and June, 1907. But see specifically in ibid., May 11, 1907, pp. 1, 4, 6; June 5, 1907, p. 9; June 7, 1907, p. 4; June 11, 1907, p. 3; June 12, 1907, p. 6; *New York Times*, May 11, 1907, p. 2; June 5, 6, 1907, p. 1; June 7, 1907, p. 5. See full text of Hearst's speech in *New York American*, April 14, 1907, p. 4-I; *New York Times*, April 14, 1907, p. 16.

9. See letters from Will to Mother, dated 1907, PAH Papers; *New York Times*, March 2, 1907, p. 1; Mrs. Hearst Interview; interview with Martin F. Huberth by W. A. Swanberg, June 23, 1959, Swanberg Collection; Winkler, *Hearst: A New Appraisal*, p. 155; Swanberg, *Citizen Hearst*, p. 255; Robinson, *The Hearsts*, p. 352; Older, *Hearst*, pp. 317–18.

10. *New York American*, August 4, 1907, p. 11-I; August 18, 1907, p. 2-W; August 22, 1907, p. 12; August 23 and 24, 1907, p. 6; August 25, 1907, p. 11-I; September 3, 1907, pp. 1–2; *New York Times*, September 3, 1907, p. 5.

11. *New York American*, September 3, 1907, pp. 1–2; September 4, 1907, p. 4; September 15, 1907, p. 2-II; September 16, 1907, p. 10; September 18, 1907, p. 16; September 22, 1907, pp. 1, 2-F; September 24, 1907, p. 7; *New York Times*, September 3, 1907, p. 5; September 12, 1907, p. 4; September 24, 1907, p. 9; September 28, 1907, p. 2.

12. See *New York Times*, August 6, 1907, p. 1; September 24, 1907, p. 9; *New York American*, August 27, 1907, p. 1; September 19, 1907, p. 5; September 21, 1907, p. 6; September 24, 1907, p. 7; September 25, 1907, p. 4; September 27, 1907, p. 5; September 28, 1907, pp. 1, 16.

13. *New York American*, September 28, 1907, pp. 1–2; September 29, 1907, pp. 1, 2, 3-I; September 30, 1907, p. 1; *New York Times*, September 28, 1907, p. 2.

14. *New York American*, October 6, 1907, p. 9-L; October 7, 1907, p. 4; October 9, 1907, pp. 1, 4. See also in ibid., October 8, 1907, p. 4, Hearst's speech to the German-American Alliance delegates.

15. *New York Times*, October 2, 1907, p. 5; October 6, 1907, p. 2; October 8, 1907, p. 1; October 11, 1907, pp. 1, 2; October 12, 1907, pp. 2–3; *New York American*, October 1, 1907, p. 5; October 8, 1907, p. 4; October 10, 1907, p. 16; October 11, 1907, pp. 1–2, 18; October 12, 1907, pp. 6, 7.

16. See *New York Times*, October 11, 1907, p. 2; October 12, 1907, pp. 2, 3; October 13, 1907, p. 3; *New York American*, October 12, 1907, pp. 6, 7; October 13, 1907, p. 5-L; October 15, 1907, p. 6.

17. Concerning the Methodist ministers' protests see the *New York American*, October 27, 1907, p. 8-F; October 29, 1907, p. 4; November 1, 1907, p. 6; November 4, 1907, pp. 1, 2, 4. Cartoons appear daily, usually on the editorial page, but see specifically Opper's creation in ibid., October 28, 1907, p. 16. In ibid., editorials also appear on the last page; however, see specifically the ones on October 13, 1907, p. 4-L; October 29, 1907, p. 16; November 4, 1907,

p. 16. For stories about Foley see ibid., October 16, 1907, p. 6; November 2, 1907, p. 7. And for "The Foley Campaign Song" see ibid., November 2, 1907, p. 16.

18. For a record of Hearst's campaign efforts see the *New York American*, October 16, 1907, p. 6, to November 4, 1907, p. 2-W. See specific reports of speeches in ibid., October 18, 1907, pp. 6–7; October 19, 1907, p. 6; October 20, 1907, pp. 8-F, 8-L; October 22, 1907, p. 22; October 23, 1907, p. 6; October 24, 1907, p. 7; October 25, 26, 1907, p. 6; November 2, 1907, pp. 1, 6; November 3, 1907, pp. 6-L, 2-W; *New York Times*, October 18, 1907, p. 6; October 23, 1907, p. 6. See Hearst letters to New Yorkers in the *New York American*, October 14, 1907, p. 7; October 26, 1907, p. 1.

19. For negative comments about Hearst and the "fusion" campaign see the *New York Times*, October 23, 1907, pp. 6, 7; October 24, 1907, p. 8; November 1, 1907, p. 4; November 4, 1907, p. 3. See in ibid., November 2, 1907, p. 1, where Hearst announced being "out of politics" as a candidate; *New York American*, November 2, 1907, p. 1. For attempts to curb Tammany corruption in elections see ibid., October 21, 24, 1907, p. 6; October 26, 28, 1907, pp. 8, 9, 12; November 1, 1907, p. 1; November 2, 1907, p. 2; November 3, 1907, p. 2-W.

20. *New York Times*, November 6, 1907, p. 5; *New York American*, November 6, 1907, pp. 1–2; November 7, 1907, p. 4.

21. See Hearst to Ihmsen, November 17, 1907, and Hearst to Brisbane, January 10, 1908, in Littlefield, *Hearst: His Role in American Progressivism*, pp. 238–39; Older, *Hearst*, pp. 318–19; Yellowitz, *Labor and the Progressive Movement*, pp. 218–19; *New York American*, November 6, 1907, pp. 1, 4; November 8, 1907, p. 7; November 11, 1907, p. 6; November 29, 1907, p. 7; December 11, 1907, p. 16; *New York Times*, November 7, 1907, p. 2; December 11, 1907, p. 1.

22. Concerning the hiring of John Temple Graves see the *New York Times*, October 20, 1907, p. 4; *New York American*, November 3, 1907, p. 5-E. For information about the convention at Indianapolis see the *New York American*, January 12, 1908, pp. 1, 2-W; January 13, 1908, p. 5; *New York Times*, January 11, 1908, p. 16. Concerning the Lincoln day dinner see the *New York American*, January 26, 1908, p. 5-W; February 2, 1908, p. 4-S. See also Ihmsen to Hearst, November 24, 1907; January 10 and June 2, 1908; Hearst to Brisbane, January 11, 1908, in Littlefield, *Hearst: His Role in American Progressivism*, pp. 238–40, 257–58.

23. In regard to the condition of little "Weeyum" see six letters and telegrams from Hearst to Mother, dated April, 1908; Millicent to Mrs. Hearst, March 7, May 8, 1908, PAH Papers; Hearst, Jr., *The Hearsts: Father and Son*, p. 49; Winkler, *Hearst: A New Appraisal*, pp. 155–56; Older, *Hearst*, p. 316. Swamberg, *Citizen Hearst*, p. 255, implies that W. R. Hearst, Jr. was born in 1907.

24. For accounts relating to the founding of the Independence Party see the *New York American*, February 20, 1908, p. 7; February 21, 1908, p. 6; February 23, 1908, pp. 1, 2-W; February 24, 1908, pp. 1, 4.

25. See *New York American*, March 3, 1908, p. 4; March 7, 1908, pp. 1, 2, 14; March 9, 1908, p. 14; April 3, 1908, p. 6; April 13, 14, 1908, pp. 1-2; May 5, 1908, p. 6; May 6, 1908, p. 7; *New York Times*, March 7, 1908, p. 4; April 14, 1908, p. 5; April 15, 1908, p. 15; April 16, 17, 1908, p. 6; April 21, 1908, p. 3.

26. *New York American*, May 16, 1908, pp. 1-2, 7; May 17, 1908, p. 1-W; May 18, 1908, pp. 1, 14; May 19, 1908, pp. 1-2, 4, 16; May 20, 1908, pp. 1, 4, 16; May 21, 1908, pp. 1-2, 16; May 22, 1908, pp. 1, 4; May 23, 1908, pp. 1-2; May 24, 1908, p. 1-W; May 25, 1908, pp. 1, 2, 14; May 26, 1908, pp. 1-2, 4; May 27, 1908, pp. 1, 4; May 28, 1908, p. 16.

27. *New York American*, May 27, 1908, p. 6; May 28, 30, 1908, p. 1; June 9, 1908, p. 4; June 13, 1908, pp. 6-7; June 17, 19, 1908, p. 8; June 26, 1908, p. 1; June 27, 1908, pp. 1, 4. For a slightly different reporting see the *New York Times*, May 27, 1908, p. 16; May 28, 1908, pp. 4, 16; May 29, 1908, pp. 1-2; May 30, 1908, p. 3; June 2, 1908, p. 5; June 3, 1908, p. 2; June 4, 1908, p. 3; June 5, 6, 1908, p. 6; June 9, 1908, pp. 12, 16; June 27, 1908, pp. 8, 16.

28. *New York Times*, June 27, 1908, pp. 8, 16; July 1, 1908, pp. 6, 16; July 2, 1908, p. 2; *New York American*, June 30, 1908, p. 6; July 1, 1908, pp. 4, 16; July 2, 1908, pp. 1, 2. For McClellan's reminiscences concerning the disputed election see Syrett, ed., *The Gentleman and the Tiger*, pp. 227–30.

29. For multiple evidence of organization and publicity for the Independence Party see the *New York American*, February 24, 1908, pp. 1, 4, 5, 14; February 26, 28, 1908, p. 16; March 8, 1908, pp. 6-F, 2-S, 2-W; March 11, 1908, p. 5; March 15, 1908, pp. 5-F, 1-L, 2-W; March 18, 1908, pp. 4, 7; March 22, 1908, pp. 5-L, 2-W; March 24, 1908, p. 5; March 25, 1908, pp. 5, 6; March 26, 1908, p. 5; March 27, 1908, p. 6; March 28, 1908, p. 5; March 29, 1908, pp. 4-L, 10-L, 3-W; April 5, 1908, pp. 11-L, 2-W; April 7, 1908, pp. 6, 16; April 11, 1908, p. 14; April 12, 1908, pp. 1-E, 6-F, 8-L; May 1, 1908, p. 5; May 3, 1908, pp. 1-W, 2-W, 3-W; May 11, 1908, pp. 7, 14; May 12, 13, 1908, p. 6; May 16, 1908, p. 7; *New York Times*, March 15, 1908, p. 6; March 26, 1908, p. 1; April 4, 1908, p. 9; April 12, 1908, pt. 2, p. 8; April 15, 1908, p. 15; April 28, 1908, p. 16. See references to Hisgen, Graves, and Shearn in *New York American*, March 16, 1908, p. 7; March 22, 1908, p. 10-L; May 2, 1908, p. 5; May 8, 1908, p. 14; May 10, 1908, p. 1-W, Independence Party sect., p. 4; May 31, 1908, p. 3-W. For evidence that Hearst paid Independence Party bills, see New York *Times*, April 13, 1908, p. 5. See the *New York American*, May 10, 1908, p. 1-W. See also Winkler, *Hearst: A New Appraisal*, p. 158; Older, *Hearst*, pp. 321–31ff.

30. Millicent and Will to Mother, [late in May], 1908; Will to Mrs p. A. Hearst (telegrams), May 2, June 18, 1908, PAH Papers; *New York Times*, July 19, 1908, p. 2; July 26, 1908, p. 4; *New York American*, July 2, 1908, p. 6; July 5, 1908, p. 4-F; July 22, 1908, p. 6; July 26, 1908, p. 2-W; July 28, 1908, pp. 1, 3.

See especially Hearst's cablegram from Paris to Samuel Gompers in *New York American*, July 17, 1908, p. 4. See also Robinson, *The Hearsts*, p. 355.

31. See the *New York American*, July 27, 1908, pp. 1–2; July 28, 1908, pp. 1–4.

32. *New York American*, July 29, 1908, pp. 1–5; August 2, 1908, p. 2-W; Littlefield, *Hearst: His Role in American Progressivism*, pp. 238, 244–45.

33. For excellent coverage of the Republican National convention, see the *New York American*, June 7–21, 1908; and for the Democratic National Convention, July 4–13, 1908. See also Paola E. Coletta, *The Presidency of William Howard Taft* (Lawrence: University Press of Kansas, 1973), pp. 13–16ff; Judith Icke Anderson, *William Howard Taft: An Intimate History* (New York: Norton, 1981), pp. 106–14; Henry F. Pringle, *The Life and Times of William Howard Taft* (New York: Farrar & Rinehart, 1939), I, 311–57ff; Coletta, *Bryan*, I, 403–11.

34. See Samuel Gompers to Hearst, May 10, July 6, 1908; Hearst to Brisbane, July 14, September 16, 1908; Ihmsen to Hearst, September 1, 1908, in Littlefield, *Hearst: His Role in American Progressivism*, pp. 240–45, 246, 258–59. For Hearst's statement concerning fusion see the *New York American*, May 3, 1908, p. 2-W; May 10, 1908, p. 3-W; July 28, 1908, pp. 1–2; *New York Times*, May 3, 1908, pp. 1–2. See also Hearst's reply to Gompers in cablegram in the *New York American*, July 17, 1908, p. 4; July 19, 1908, p. 9-L; August 3, 1908, p. 4. See also concerning Gompers and labor in ibid, August 11, 1908, p. 4; August 13, 1908, p. 5; August 24, 27, 29, 1908, p. 4; September 10, 1908, p. 16; *New York Times*, August 4, 1908, p. 3; August 12, 1908, p. 2; Bernard Mandel, *Samuel Gompers: A Biography* (Yellow Springs, Ohio: Antioch Press, 1963), pp. 291–93.

35. For a depiction of typical Bryan cartoons with Hearst's comments see the *New York American*, August 6, 1908, p. 14. See also Carter's "Falstaff's Army" cartoons beginning in ibid., August 3, 1908, p. 4. For Bryan's evaluation of the Independence Party vote and his relationship with Hearst see *New York Times*, July 31, 1908, p. 2; Coletta, *Bryan*, I, 391, 413.

36. *New York American*, July 30, 1908, p. 1; August 1, 1908, p. 6; August 2, 1908, p. 1-W. Concerning Hearst's resignation letter see ibid., August 25, 1908, p. 4; August 30, 1908, p. 2-W.

37. *New York American*, August 30, 1908, p. 2-W; August 31, 1908, pp. 1, 4, 12; September 1, 1908, pp. 1–2; September 3, 1908, p. 4; September 4, 1908, pp. 1, 4; September 5, 1908, p. 4; September 6, 1908, pp. 1-L, 4-L; *New York Times*, September 1, 1908, p. 1. Concerning Hearst's affidavits on Bryan's declaration about "public beggars" see the *New York American*, September 8, 1908, pp. 1–2; September 9, 1908, pp. 1, 2; September 10, 1908, p. 5; September 11, 1908, p. 6; *New York Times*, September 8, 1908, p. 5. For Bryan's denial of the Hearst charges see the *New York American*, September 13, 1908, p. 1-W; *New York Times*, September 13, 1908, p. 3.

38. Ihmsen to Hearst, September 1, 1908, and Hearst to Brisbane, Sep-

tember 16, 1908, in Littlefield, *Hearst: His Role in American Progressivism*, pp. 245–46, 259; Chambers, *Seabury*, pp. 116–17; *New York American*, September 12, 1908, pp. 1, 4; September 13, 1908, p. 1-W; September 14, 1908, pp. 4, 6; September 15, 1908, p. 4; September 17, 1908, pp. 1, 2.

39. For discussion concerning the Standard Oil letters see Chambers, *Seabury*, pp. 117–18; Winkler, *Hearst: A New Appraisal*, pp. 158–59, 163; Older, *Hearst*, pp. 324–25; Swanberg, *Citizen Hearst*, pp. 260–62ff.

40. Committee on Privileges and Elections, 62d Cong., 3d sess., I, 1341–44 (better known as the Clapp Committee Report); Walters, *Foraker*, p. 281; Allan Nevins, *John D. Rockefeller: The Heroic Age of American Enterprise* (New York: Charles Scribner's Sons, 1941), II, 515, 593.

41. *New York American*, September 18, 1908, p. 6; September 19, 1908, p. 2; *New York Tribune*, September 18, 1908, p. 3; Coletta, *Bryan*, I, 419; Koenig, *Bryan*, p. 451; Nevins, *Rockefeller*, II, 593–94; Winkler, *Hearst: A New Appraisal*, pp. 160–63; Older, *Hearst*, pp. 323–24; Swanberg, *Citizen Hearst*, pp. 260–61; Littlefield, *Hearst: His Role in American Progressivism*, pp. 246–47.

42. Older, *Hearst*, pp. 325–32; *New York Times*, September 19, 1908, pp. 1, 5; *New York American*, September 19, 1908, pp. 1–2; September 20, 1908, pp. 1-L, 2-L; September 21, 1908, pp. 1, 2, 4; Acheson, *Joe Bailey: The Last Democrat*, pp. 253–55; Koenig, *Bryan*, pp. 451–52. Governor Haskell, although vehemently denying the Hearst charges, did resign as the national campaign treasurer of the Democrats. Unfortunately, Oscar Presley Fowler, *The Haskell Regime: The Intimate Life of Charles Nathaniel Haskell* (Oklahoma City: Boles, 1933), did not discuss this episode.

43. *New York American*, September 21, 1908, pp. 1–2 (Hearst Interview in Cincinnati); September 22, 1908, pp. 1, 4; September 23, 1908, pp. 4, 8; September 24, 1908, p. 4; September 25, 1908, pp. 1, 2, 6; *New York Times*, September 24, 1908, p. 4; September 25, 1908, pp. 1–2.

44. *New York American*, October 1, 2, 1908, pp. 1–2; October 3, 1908, p. 2; October 4, 1908, pp. 1-W, 2-W; October 6, 1908, pp. 5, 9; October 10, 1908, pp. 1–2; October 11, 1908, pp. 1-W, 2-W; *New York Times*, September 26, 1908, p. 3; October 1, 1908, p. 1; October 3, 1908, pp. 1, 2; October 11, 1908, p. 3; Older, *Hearst*, pp. 331–32.

45. *New York American*, October 12, 1908, p. 5; October 16, 1908, p. 4; October 18, 1908, p. 11-L; October 19, 1908, p. 4; October 23, 1908, p. 11; October 24, 1908, p. 1; *New York Times*, October 15, 1908, p. 1; October 18, 1908, p. 8; October 25, 26, 27, 1908, p. 1. See coverage of Hearst's trip to Petersburg, Indiana, in the *New York American*, October 22, 1908, p. 4.

46. *New York American*, October 27, 1908, pp. 1, 3, 6; October 28, 1908, p. 1; October 30, 1908, pp. 1–2; November 1, 1908, pp. 1-L, 2-L, 3-W; November 3, 1908, pp. 1–2; *New York Times*, October 28, 30, 1908, p. 2; November 1, 1908, p. 2.

47. *New York Times*, November 4, 1908, p. 1; November 5, 1908, p. 5; De-

cember 16, 1908, p. 6; *New York American*, November 4, 1908, pp. 1, 4, 5; Hearst to Ihmsen, November 15, 1908; Hearst to Shearn, November 17, 1908; Hearst to Brisbane, November 18, 1908, in Littlefield, *Hearst: His Role in American Progressivism*, pp. 251–55ff, 261.

48. Concerning the crusade against the Gas Trust see the *New York American*, January 5, 1909, pp. 1–2, 3, 18, then almost daily for the rest of the month. For an example of the gas "coupon" see ibid., January 8, 1909, p. 2. For the establishment of the American Gas Bureau and its effects see in ibid., January 15, 1909, p. 2; January 17, 1909, p. 1-B; February 28, 1909, p. 3-L; March 2, 1909, p. 2. For references to Hearst activities see ibid., January 15, 1909, p. 2; January 31, 1909, p. 1; February 24, 1909, p. 4; March 3, 1909, p. 11.

49. Concerning the crusade in regard to the kidnapped boy see the *New York American*, March 20, 21, 22, 23, 1909, p. 1. For typical editorials advocating local reforms see ibid., March 13 and April 9, 1909, p. 18 (municipal ownership of subways); April 16, 1909, p. 18 (parks for people); May 19, 1909, p. 18, and May 24, 1909, p. 1 (playgrounds for children); May 11, 14, 1909, p. 18 (equal pay for women teachers); July 2, 1909, p. 7, and July 8, 1909, p. 5 (summer camp for newsboys); Littlefield, *Hearst: His Role in American Progressivism*, pp. 263, 297 (n. 5). For reference to the American Information Bureau see *New York American*, May 26, 1909, p. 4; June 6, 1909, p. 7-L.

50. *New York American*, December 15, 1908, p. 1. In regard to national reforms see the following samplings of editorials and stories in ibid., February 8, 1909, p. 18; March 6, 1909, p. 18; April 9, 1909, p. 18. Concerning the crusade for women's suffrage see the three weeks in ibid. ending March 27, 1909, p. 18. Concerning a graduated income tax see ibid., July 16, 1909, p. 18, to July 29, 1909, p. 18.

51. *New York American*, April 18, 1909, pp. 6–7. See also ibid., January 1, 1909, p. 5; April 4, 1909, p. 12; June 13, 1909, p. 11-L; June 27, 1909, p. 9-L; *New York Times*, April 18, 1909, p. 20; Littlefield, *Hearst: His Role in American Progressivism*, p. 263.

52. *New York Times*, September 4, 1909, pp. 1–2; September 5, 1909, p. 2; *New York American*, September 4, 1909, p. 3; September 5, 1909, p. 1-L; September 9, 1909, p. 18; *New York Tribune*, September 7, 1909, pp. 1, 7; September 8, 1909, p. 1.

53. *New York American*, September 5, 1909, p. 1-L; September 14, 1909, p. 3; September 18, 1909, pp. 1–2; September 19, 1909, p. 2; *New York Times*, September 4, 1909, p. 1; September 5, 1909, p. 2; September 23, 1909, p. 1; September 25, 1909, p. 4; September 29, 1909, p. 7; October 2, 1909, p. 16; *New York Tribune*, September 7, 1909, p. 7; September 18, 1909, p. 1; September 20, 1909, p. 4; September 23, 1909, pp. 1–2.

54. *New York American*, September 24, 1909, p. 1; October 9, 1909, p. 1; *New York Tribune*, September 24, 1909, p. 1; September 25, 1909, p. 1; September 26, 1909, p. 8; October 9, 1909, p. 1; *New York Times*, September 24, 1909,

p. 1; September 25, 1909, p. 1; September 29, 1909, p. 7. See also Louis Heaton Pink, *Gaynor: The Tammany Mayor Who Swallowed the Tiger* (New York: International Press, 1931), p. 133; Mortimer Smith, *William Jay Gaynor: Mayor of New York* (Chicago: Henry Regnery, 1951), p. 64; Chambers, *Seabury*, p. 126. For a popular, readable account of Gaynor see Lately Thomas, *The Mayor Who Mastered New York: The Life & Opinions of William J. Gaynor* (New York: William Morrow, 1969).

55. Pink, *Gaynor*, pp. 129–31; Smith, *Gaynor*, pp. 36–60ff; Chambers, *Seabury*, p. 125; Yellowitz, *Progressivism in New York*, pp. 217–18.

56. Hearst to Brisbane, October 3, 1909, in Littlefield, *Hearst: His Role in American Progressivism*, pp. 265, 297; Pink, *Gaynor*, pp. 131–33; Smith, *Gaynor*, pp. 63–65; *New York American*, October 6, 1909, p. 2; October 7, 1909, pp. 1–2; October 8, 1909, pp. 1–2, 18; October 9, 1909, pp. 1, 18; *New York Tribune*, October 1, 1909, pp. 1, 6; October 4, 1909, p. 3; October 6, 1909, p. 2; October 7, 1909, pp. 1–2; October 8, 1909, pp. 1, 6; October 9, 1909, p. 1; *New York Times*, October 6, 1909, p. 9; October 7, 1909, p. 1. For a different interpretation on Hearst's motives see Swanberg, *Citizen Hearst*, p. 266.

57. See quote in the *New York Tribune*, October 28, 1909, p. 6. For scheduling and descriptions of Hearst meetings see the *New York American*, October 12, 1909, pp. 1, 20, then daily to November 1, 1909, pp. 1–3; October 18, 1909, pp. 1, 4, is typical. Concerning the leasing of rooms in the Hermitage Hotel see the *New York Tribune*, October 9, 1909, p. 1; October 14, 1909, p. 4; *New York American*, October 15, 1909, p. 5. For examples of political ads taken out by Hearst see the *New York Times*, October 29, 1909, p. 7; November 1, 1909, p. 7.

58. Concerning Brisbane editorials see the *New York American*, October 14, 1909, p. 18; October 18, 1909, p. 16; October 21, 22, 23, 25, 1909, p. 18. For mention of the *Times* and *World* editorials that pleaded with Hearst to enter the mayoral race see ibid., October 9, 1909, p. 18. For typical cartoons see ibid., October 12, 20, 1909, p. 2; October 21, 22, 1909, p. 18. For examples of testimonials see ibid., October 11, 1909, p. 1; October 16, 18, 25, 1909, p. 5; October 23, 1909, p. 6; October 28, 1909, p. 2; October 31, 1909, p. 1-B. For pictures of Hearst and family see ibid., October 24, 1909, p. 1–II; October 31, 1909, p. 4. John Randolph Hearst was born on September 26, 1909. See "happy birthday telegram" to John Hearst from Mama and Papa, September 26, 1910; Will to Mrs p. A. Hearst (telegram), September 22, 1909, PAH Papers. See also Littlefield, *Hearst: His Role in American Progressivism*, pp. 266–67.

59. Concerning the Independence League convention see the *New York American*, October 12, 1909, pp. 1–2, 4, 20; *New York Times*, October 12, 1909, p. 1; *New York Tribune*, October 12, 1909, pp. 1–2. For the Independence League's fight to change its name see *New York Tribune*, October 8, 9, 1909, p. 1; October 13, 1909, p. 2; October 14, 1909, p. 4; October 16, 1909, p. 4; *New*

York American, October 10, 1909, p. 2; October 15, 1909, p. 5; *New York Times*, October 13, 1909, p. 5.

60. *New York American*, October 12, 1909, p. 2; October 15, 1909, p. 5; October 16, 17, 1909, p. 4; October 18, 1909, p. 16; Pink, *Gaynor*, pp. 134–37; Smith, *Gaynor*, pp. 66–68; Swanberg, *Citizen Hearst*, p. 267.

61. *New York Tribune*, October 11, 1909, p. 2; *New York American*, October 11, 1909, p. 3; October 18, 1909, p. 6; October 19, 1909, p. 1; October 21, 1909, p. 1; October 24, 1909, p. 4; Pink, *Gaynor*, pp. 134–38; Smith, *Gaynor*, pp. 67–68, 72; Swanberg, *Citizen Hearst*, p. 267.

62. The *New York American*, *New York Times*, and *New York Tribune*, from the last week in September to November 3, 1909, clearly support the author's contentions. Concerning the fight for unionist support between Hearst and Gaynor see Yellowitz, *Labor and the Progressive Movement in New York State*, pp. 323–26.

63. For coverage of the campaign see the *New York American*, October 12, 1909, pp. 1–2, 4; October 15, 1909, p. 5; October 16, 1909, p. 4; October 19, 1909, pp. 1–2, 4; October 21, 1909, pp. 1–2; October 23, 1909, pp. 1–2; October 26, 1909, pp. 5, 6; October 28, 30, 1909, pp. 1–2; *New York Tribune*, October 12, 1909, pp. 1–2; October 19, 1909, p. 1; October 23, 1909, p. 3; October 28, 1909, p. 2; *New York Times*, October 12, 1909, p. 1; October 16, 1909, p. 3; October 21, 1909, p. 2; October 23, 1909, p. 4; October 26, 27, 28, 1909, p. 2.

64. *New York American*, October 30, 1909, p. 2; October 31, 1909, p. 1-B; November 1, 1909, pp. 1–3; *New York Tribune*, November 1, 1909, p. 3.

65. New York American, November 3, 1909, pp. 1–2, 4, 18; November 4, 1909, p. 4; *New York Tribune*, November 3, 1909, p. 1; November 4, 1909, p. 2; *New York Times*, November 3, 1909, pp. 1, 4; Littlefield, *Hearst: His Role in American Progressivism*, pp. 268–70.

66. Coblentz, ed., *Hearst*, p. 48; Silas Bent, *Newspaper Crusaders: A Neglected Story* (New York: Whittlesey House, 1939), pp. 59, 77; Bleyer, *Main Currents in the History of American Journalism*, pp. 381–88. See Rodney p. Carlisle, *Hearst and the New Deal: The Progressive as Reactionary* (New York: Garland Publishing, Inc., 1979). See also the different Hearst biographies by Winkler, Older, and Swanberg for specifics about his later life.

Index